Please Return to:
Holy Cross International Justice
Office
403 Bertrand Annex, Saint Mary's
Notre Dame IN 46556-5018

Praise for *The Great Turning*

"*The Great Turning* sets forth a compelling, devastating, and ultimately profoundly hopeful story that provides a framework for the new, unifying political conversation our nation so desperately needs. A must-read for every person of conscience."

> —Van Jones, Executive Director, The Ella Baker Center
> for Human Rights

"What a gift David Korten has given us with this prophetic book! In this well-written and thorough story of the crises of late Modernity, Korten gives us a beautifully reasoned, carefully researched look at why we absolutely have to turn away from imperial power and wealth and, instead, create an Earth Community. This is a must-read for activists, for lovers of contemporary American studies, and for Cultural Creatives."

> —Paul H. Ray, coauthor of *The Cultural Creatives*

"Employing history, psychology, economics, spirituality, and common sense, Korten not only critiques the dilemma we are in as a species, he also shows us doable and workable ways out of our morass. He has created a tour de force—a call to compassion as much as a blueprint for survival. This book is a kind of Bible to the 21st century, a revelation of where we might travel if we have the moral imagination and the courage to choose and act wisely."

> —Matthew Fox, educator and theologian, author of *Original Blessing*
> and *A New Reformation*

"If you read only one book on how to address the looming ecological and social crises facing humanity, make it this one! Korten fearlessly grapples with 'the big picture' and goes beyond merely diagnosing the problem (which he does with great precision), as he outlines a positive and realistic plan for actually creating a just and sustainable global society."

> —David Cobb, 2004 Green Party United States Presidential Candidate

"Korten has done it *again*—created a masterpiece of big thinking to help us find our way in this death-or-life historical moment. With fascinating analogies, intriguing stories, and eloquent analysis, Korten engages and emboldens us to believe that we can trust and cultivate the best in ourselves and, despite the lateness of the hour, choose life."

> —Frances Moore Lappé, author of *Hope's Edge* and *Democracy's Edge*

"In a moment when the political discourse is obsessed with immediacy, Korten calls us to pause and reflect upon what it means to be fully human. As one reads this rigorous book, one is moved by its sacredness. The spiritual reflection with deep political and economic implications demands we move with grace and dignity into the new space of equity, dignity, and, above all, abiding love. In the end, may we all be turned."

—Reverend Osagyefo Uhuru Sekou, author of *Urbansouls*

"This is the book that needed to be written. Weaving together culture patterns, politics, economics, and history, Korten demonstrates how U.S. history is NOT the democratic model that all politicians and pundits 'recall.' It is, in actuality, a legacy of imperial power and control. The time has come for a change… we need to move on and empower a different kind of story!"

—Georgia Kelly, Founder and Director, Praxis Peace Institute

"A must-read for everyone who yearns to create a positive human future. In *When Corporations Rule the World* Korten called attention to the corruption of corporate-led economic globalization and helped to launch a powerful global resistance movement. In *The Great Turning* he tells us that the scourge of economic globalization is but a contemporary manifestation of 5,000 years of rule by imperial elites. It is a wise, profound, and practical book filled with fresh insights and is destined to be even more influential than Korten's previous contributions."

—Anita Roddick, Founder, The Body Shop

"*The Great Turning* is smooth, brilliantly researched, and gripping. Korten has constructed a story of hope and insight. Alert the Democrats! Here is a blueprint for a vision they are born to promote to the world. The ending inspires poetically. Things aren't hopeless, the world is truly turning and all we need do is push ourselves along together."

—Dal LaMagna, Founder and former CEO, Tweezerman

"*The Great Turning* is a profound and inspiring masterpiece that illuminates the cultural, social, and political significance of the contrasting worldviews of the classic materialistic-mechanistic Newtonian physics and modern holistic-quantum physics. Korten eloquently points to the necessity of abandoning the dominating power-oriented plutocracy of Empire in favor of a life-enhancing, continuously diversifying, cooperatively integrated Earth."

—Professor Hans-Peter Duerr, PhD, former Director, Max-Planck-Institute for Physics, Munich; Winner, Alternative Nobel Prize, 1987

"With the majesty of a George Lucas movie, Korten's epic tale, which pits Earth Community against Empire, weaves together the great social movements of our time. It inspires us at this crucial point in history to fulfill our destiny as thinking, acting, and loving human beings."

— Judy Wicks, Proprietress, White Dog Cafe and Co-Chair, Business Alliance for Local Living Economies (BALLE)

"THIS is the book we have been waiting for! It provides the context and stories that have been missing, leaving us with piecemeal analyses and solutions. The framework of the 5,000-year history of the Empire is a powerful eye-opener about the deliberateness of enslavement and oppression."

— Jan Roberts, Director, Earth Charter USA Communities Initiatives

"This is a hugely important book, and hugely impressive! I imagine it reaching far beyond Korten's existing readership."

— Raffi Cavoukian, singer, author, ecology advocate, and Founder, Child Honoring

"David Korten is a militant for Life, Earth, and Community. This groundbreaking book provides the holistic overview of a 21st century revolution and evolution that can inspire the ordinary citizen to act and transform the activist into a long-distance runner."

— Grace Lee Boggs, coauthor of *Revolution and Evolution in the 20th Century*

"Throw away the technological fixes of Thomas Friedman and Jeffrey Sachs and enter Korten's world where communities organize to secure their rights and build a better world. I know of no writer who better embraces the wisdom of such a broad spectrum of thinkers to create new understanding, new possibilities, new inspiration, new hope."

— John Cavanagh, Director, Institute for Policy Studies; Board Chair, International Forum on Globalization

"This is indeed a spectacular book. *The Great Turning* supports our most open-hearted evolutionary process."

— Bill Kauth, Co-Founder, The ManKind Project, and author of *A Circle of Men*

"Brilliant. Challenging. Inspiring. Practical. Spiritual. Intelligent. Once again David Korten challenges us with his keen analysis and elegant wisdom—a clear call for sustainable social transformation and a timely invitation to live a different story. Korten gives us exactly what we need in order to address our current paralysis and fear. Read this book and be inspired to make a difference."

—The Very Reverend Bill Phipps, former Moderator, United Church of Canada

"Inspired by a compelling spiritual and ethical vision, *The Great Turning* argues persuasively that the 21st century presents humanity with a unique opportunity to break with its violent past and to create a just, participatory, sustainable, and peaceful future. In this major work, David Korten skillfully combines ecological, economic, social, psychological, and cultural analysis in order to issue a powerful summons to local communities and the emerging global civil society to lead the way."

—Steven C. Rockefeller, Co-Chair, Earth Charter International Steering

"David Korten has done it again!! Through careful and painstaking historical analysis, personal reflection, and myth-busting, *The Great Turning* challenges U.S. citizens to a new level of awareness of what has been and what can be. A must read!"

—Tanya Dawkins, Founder/Director, Global-Local Links Project

"David Korten's ideas are tools, like picks and shovels, that help us dig under the surface of our pessimism and fear of change. What we find is a deep core of hope for the Earth as Beloved Community and the ability to embrace the individual and collective *kuleana* (Hawaiian for 'responsibility') for our choices and their consequences."

—Puanani Burgess, Hawaiian storyteller and poet

"David Korten has presented a clear blueprint for a powerful emerging majority. This book will help to change America for the better."

—Dennis J. Kucinich, U.S. House of Representatives

"Once you dive into this book, you'll want everyone you know to read it. It is a powerful source of inspiration and guidance for those already turning to Earth Community and it can help those embedded in Empire's institutions see more clearly the choices before them."

—Alisa Gravitz, Executive Director, Co-op America

THE GREAT TURNING

The Great Turning

From Empire to Earth Community

DAVID C. KORTEN

BERRETT-KOEHLER PUBLISHERS, INC.
San Francisco
a BK Currents book

KUMARIAN
PRESS

COPUBLISHED BY

Kumarian Press, Inc.
1294 Blue Hills Avenue
Bloomfield, CT 06002-1301

Tel: (860) 243-2098
Fax: (860) 243-2867
www.kpbooks.com

Berrett-Koehler Publishers, Inc.
235 Montgomery Street, Suite 650
San Francisco, CA 94104-2916

Tel: (415) 288-0260
Fax: (415) 362-2512
www.bkconnection.com

ORDERING INFORMATION

QUANTITY SALES. Special discounts are available on quantity purchases by corporations, associations, and others. For details, contact the "Special Sales Department" at the Berrett-Koehler address above.

INDIVIDUAL SALES. Copies of this book are available through most bookstores. They can also be ordered directly from Berrett-Koehler: Tel: (800) 929-2929; Fax: (802) 864-7626; www.bkconnection.com, or from Kumarian Press at the address above.

ORDERS FOR COLLEGE TEXTBOOK/COURSE ADOPTION USE. Please contact Kumarian Press at Tel: (800) 289-2664; Fax: (860) 243-2867.

ORDERS BY U.S. TRADE BOOKSTORES AND WHOLESALERS. Please contact Publishers Group West, 1700 Fourth Street, Berkeley, CA 94710. Tel: (510) 528-1444; Fax (510) 528-3444.

Berrett-Koehler and the BK logo are registered trademarks of Berrett-Koehler Publishers, Inc.

Printed in the United States of America

This book is printed on long-lasting acid-free paper. Whenever possible, we choose paper that has been manufactured by environmentally responsible processes. These may include using trees grown in sustainable forests, incorporating recycled paper, minimizing chlorine in bleaching, or recycling the energy produced at the paper mill.

LIBRARY OF CONGRESS CATALOGING-IN-PUBLICATION DATA

Korten, David C.
The great turning: from empire to Earth community / by David C. Korten.
  p. cm.
Includes bibliographical references and index.
ISBN-10: 1-887208-07-0; ISBN-13: 978-1-887208-07-9

1. International cooperation. 2. Sustainable development. 3. Social ethics.
4. Humanistic ethics. 5. Social justice. 6. Cooperation. 7. Human ecology.
8. Economic history. I. Title.
JZ1318.K67 2005
302'.14—DC22

2005055855

FIRST EDITION

11 10 09 08 07 06   10 9 8 7 6 5 4 3 2 1

Copyediting: Karen Seriguchi. Cover and interior design and production: Valerie Brewster, Scribe Typography. Proofreading: Todd Manza, Manza Editorial and Don Roberts. Indexing: Rachel Rice, Directions Unlimited.

DEDICATED TO

My paternal grandmother, Lydia Boehl Korten,
who taught me that every person has a sacred purpose.

My parents, Ted Korten and Margaret Korten,
who made it possible to honor the call.

My brother, Robert Korten, who assumed
the family responsibilities I abandoned.

Thomas Berry, Riane Eisler, and Joanna Macy, on whose inspiration,
analysis, and language I have drawn freely in framing
the human choice at hand.

Timothy Iistowanohpataakiiwa, who initiated me into elderhood
on my sixty-fifth birthday and helped me see with greater
clarity the path of my elder years.

And George W. Bush, whose administration exposed to full view
the imperial shadow side of U.S. democracy, stripped away
the last of the illusions of my childhood innocence,
and compelled me to write this book.

Contents

Acknowledgments

The Great Turning pulls together the many strands of my journey of understanding that began more than forty-six years ago in my senior year of college. Most everyone who has since touched my life has contributed in some way to the reflections I share in the pages ahead. I mention here only those whom I have had the privilege of knowing and engaging personally during the more than three years I have devoted specifically to writing this book and who have made special contributions to my thinking.

Fran Korten, my wife and life partner, has shared in every aspect of my journey and contributed at each step in the conceptualization and writing of this book, including detailed editorial input to each chapter. Crucial framing ideas come from Janine Benyus, Thomas Berry, Marcus Borg, Riane Eisler, Matthew Fox, Mae-Wan Ho, Marjorie Kelly, Frances Moore Lappé, Joanna Macy, Nicky Perlas, Paul Ray, Elisabet Sahtouris, Vandana Shiva, Meg Wheatley, and Walter Wink. Sarah van Gelder worked with me on the original conception and outline.

I am especially grateful to Steve Piersanti, founder and publisher of Berrett-Koehler Publishers, for his exceptional support in every aspect of the creation of this book from initial conception to final production, and for his total availability. My thanks to the entire staff of Berrett-Koehler for the enthusiasm and support that have made this project possible. I am also grateful for the continuing relationship with Krishna Sondhi and the staff of Kumarian Press, with whom I have been publishing since 1983.

Danny Glover, Robert Jeffries, and Belvie Rooks raised my awareness of the centrality of race in shaping the American experience. Raffi Cavoukian drew my attention to the universal concern for children as a potential bridge across the seemingly irreconcilable political divide between conservatives and liberals. Larry Daloz, Sharon Parks, Elizabeth Pinchot, David Womeldorff, and Donna Zajonc all contributed to my understanding of the developmental stages of the human consciousness and their broad implications for actualizing the potentials of our nature.

Board and staff colleagues at *YES!* magazine have served as my primary intellectual community during the writing of this book. Those not already mentioned whose contributions merit particular note include Gar Alperovitz, Rod Arakaki, Dee Axelrod, Jill Bamburg, Richard

Conlin, Kim Corrigan, Tanya Dawkins, Carol Estes, Kevin Fong, Susan Gleason, Alisa Gravitz, Carolyn McConnell, Gifford Pinchot, Michael Ramos, Dan Spinner, and Audrey Watson.

Colleagues from two other groups, the Business Alliance for Local Living Economies (BALLE) and the International Forum on Globalization, have also provided important intellectual support. Those associated with BALLE whose contributions merit special mention include Laury Hammel, Michelle and Derek Long, Richard Perle, Don Shaffer, Michael Shuman, and Judy Wicks. Those from the IFG who bear special mention include Debi Barker, John Cavanagh, Maude Barlow, Walden Bello, Robin Broad, Tony Clarke, Edward Goldsmith, Randy Hayes, Colin Hines, Martin Khor, Andrew Kimbrell, Jerry Mander, Helena Norberg-Hodge, Sara Larrain, Simon Retallack, Mark Ritchie, Vandana Shiva, Victoria Tauli-Corpuz, and Lori Wallach.

Michelle Burkhart provided thorough and tireless assistance in the early stages of the writing as a volunteer research intern. Mark Dowie, Tom Greco, Todd Manza, Gabriela Melano, Ted Nace, and Hilary Powers all provided valuable feedback as part of the Berrett-Koehler editorial process. Doug Pibel contributed his editorial genius in a review of the completed manuscript before final submission. A combination of professional competence and collaborative working style made it a special joy to work with Karen Seriguchi as the copy editor.

Peter Bower, Susan Callan, Riane Eisler, Robert Erwin, Matthew Fox, Bill Kauth, Eric Kuhner, Don MacKenzie, Sue McGregor, Bill Phipps, Marcus Renner, Elisabet Sahtouris, Roger Simpson, Melissa Stuart, and Lama Tsomo all provided helpful feedback on early drafts. Medea Benjamin, David Cobb, John Cobb Jr., Kevin Danaher, Hans-Peter Duerr, Thom Hartmann, Bob Hasegawa, Jim Hightower, Georgia Kelly, Dal LaMagna, Dan Merkle, Anita Roddick, Juliet Schor, Tom Thresher, and Linda Wolf contributed ideas and inspiration.

Carolyn North organized an invitational seminar under the auspices of the Whidbey Institute that provided invaluable feedback on an early draft from Skye Burn, Ellen Camin, Doug Carmichael, Elizabeth Davis, Halim Dunsky, Kurt Hoelting, Stephanie Ryan, Marilyn Saunders, and Bob Stilger. Sharon Parks served as discussion leader and Larry Daloz as rapporteur.

Inspiration also came from friends and colleagues with whom I had particularly meaningful exchanges through a series of State of the Possible retreats organized by the Positive Futures Network for progressive leaders. These included Sharif Abdullah, Rebecca Adamson, Brahm Ahmadi, Nane Alejandrez, Negin Almassi, Carl Anthony, Kenny Ausubel, Rachel Bagby, John Beck, Juliette Beck, Edget Betru, Grace Boggs, Yelena Boxer, Chuck Collins, Susan Davis, John de Graaf, Drew Dellinger, Brian Derdowski, Yvonne Dion-Buffalo, Cindy Domingo, Ronnie Dugger, Mel Duncan, Sheri Dunn Berry, Mark Dworkin, Malaika Edwards, Jim Embry, Chris Gallagher, Bookda Gheisar, Tom Goldtooth, Sean Gonsalves, Sally Goodwin, Elaine Gross, Herman Gyr, Han-shan, Rosemarie Harding, Vincent Harding, Debra Harry, Paul Hawken, Pramila Jayapal, Don Hazen, Francisco Hernandez, Francisco Herrera, Cathy Hoffman, Melvin Hoover, Ellison Horne, Thomas Hurley, Timothy Iistowanoh-pataakiiwa, Verlene Jones, Don Kegley, Peter Kent, Dennis Kucinich, Wallace Ryan Kuroiwa, Meizhu Lui, Carolyn Lukensmeyer, Marc Luyckx, Melanie MacKinnon, Jeff Milchen, John Mohawk, Bill Moyer, Charlie Murphy, Eric Nelson, Nick Page, Susan Partnow, Nicole Pearson, Nick Penniman, Kelly Quirke, Jamal Rahman, Paul Ray, Joe Reilly, Anita Rios, Michele Robbins, Ocean Robbins, Jan Roberts, Vicki Robin, Shivon Robinsong, Jonathan Rowe, Peggy Saika, Osagyefo Uhuru Sekou, Priscilla Settee, Ron Sher, Nina Simons, Alice Slater, Mark Sommer, Linda Stout, Dan Swinney, Clayton Thomas-Müller, Barbara Valocore, Roberto Vargas, John Vaughn, Sara Williams, Ray Williams, Akaya Windwood, and Melissa Young.

This book was researched and written as a project of the People-Centered Development Forum (PCDForum), an informal alliance of organizations and activists dedicated to the creation of just, inclusive, and sustainable societies through voluntary citizen action. The PCDForum is a purely voluntary organization that pays no salaries. I have received no personal compensation from any source for the preparation of this book, and all royalties from book sales will go to the PCDForum to support its continuing work. The views expressed in this book are mine and do not necessarily represent those of any of the persons mentioned above or of the PCDForum or any other organization with which I am affiliated. I extend my deepest appreciation for all the many friends and colleagues who helped to make it possible and apologize to those I may have neglected to acknowledge.

David C. Korten
www.davidkorten.org
www.greatturning.org
www.developmentforum.net

We stand at a critical moment in Earth's history, a time when humanity must choose its future. As the world becomes increasingly interdependent and fragile, the future at once holds great peril and great promise. To move forward we must recognize that in the midst of a magnificent diversity of cultures and life forms we are one human family and one Earth community with a common destiny. We must join together to bring forth a sustainable global society founded on respect for nature, universal human rights, economic justice, and a culture of peace. Towards this end, it is imperative that we, the peoples of Earth, declare our responsibility to one another, to the greater community of life, and to future generations.

THE EARTH CHARTER (2000)

# The Great Turning

Future generations, if there is a livable world for them, will look back at the epochal transition we are making to a life-sustaining society. And they may well call this the time of the Great Turning.[1]

Joanna Macy

By what name will our children and our children's children call our time? Will they speak in anger and frustration of the time of the Great Unraveling, when profligate consumption led to an accelerating wave of collapsing environmental systems, violent competition for what remained of the planet's resources, a dramatic dieback of the human population, and a fragmentation of those who remained into warring fiefdoms ruled by ruthless local lords?

Or will they look back in joyful celebration on the noble time of the Great Turning, when their forebears turned crisis into op-portunity, embraced the higher-order potential of their human nature, learned to live in creative partnership with one another and the living Earth, and brought forth a new era of human possibility?

It is the premise of The Great Turning: From Empire to Earth Community *that we humans stand at a defining moment that presents us with an irrevocable choice. Our collective response will determine how our time is remembered for so long as the human species survives. In the days now at hand, we must each be clear that every individual and collective choice we make is a vote for the future we of this time will bequeath to the generations that follow.* The Great Turning *is not a prophecy; it is a possibility.*

In Search of the Possible

> Man, when he entered life, the Father gave the seeds of every
> kind and every way of life possible. Whatever seeds each man
> sows and cultivates will grow and bear him their proper fruit.
>
> *Giovanni Pico della Mirandola* (1486)

> The difference between what we do and what we are capable
> of doing would suffice to solve most of the world's problems.
>
> *Mohandas K. Gandhi*

In 1995, I observed in the prologue to *When Corporations Rule the World* that everywhere I went I found an almost universal sense among ordinary people that the institutions on which they
depended were failing them. Rising poverty and unemployment, inequality, violent crime, broken families, and environmental deteriora-
tion all contributed to a growing fear of what the future might hold.

Now it turns out that those were the good days. The financial shock
that subsequently swept through Asia, Russia, and Latin America in the
late 1990s, the bursting of the stock market bubble in the opening days
of the twenty-first century, and a continuing wave of corporate financial scandals have drawn attention to a corruption of the institutions of
the global economy well beyond what I documented in 1995.

Pundits continue to speak optimistically about economic growth,
gains in jobs, and a rising stock market, yet working families, even with
two incomes, find it increasingly difficult to make ends meet and fall
ever deeper into debt as health care and housing costs soar out of reach.
We are told that as a nation we can no longer afford basics we once took
for granted, such as living-wage jobs with benefits, a quality education
for our children, health care and safety nets for the poor, protection for
the environment, parks, public funding for the arts and public broadcasting, and pensions for the elderly. Economists tell us we are getting richer,
yet everyday experience tells a different story. Meanwhile we face global

terrorism, rapid increases in oil prices, increasingly violent weather events, a skyrocketing U.S. trade deficit, and a falling U.S. dollar.

Talk of end times is in the air. Books on biblical Armageddon and the imminent return of Christ to lift believers to heaven are selling in the tens of millions in the United States. Leading business magazines carry cover stories about the end of oil. The Pentagon has joined environmentalists in issuing warnings about the potential apocalyptic consequences of climate change.

One of the most common reactions I received from readers of *When Corporations Rule the World* was that it gave them a sense of hope. I was at first surprised, because documenting the systemic causes of increasing inequality, environmental destruction, and the disintegrating social fabric had been for me a decidedly depressing experience. Yet, reader after reader responded that, by providing an analysis that explained the cause of the difficulties they were experiencing and by demonstrating that it is possible for human societies to take another course, *When Corporations Rule the World* had given them hope that things could be different.

As the crisis has continued to intensify, I have come to see that the issues I addressed in *When Corporations Rule the World* are a contemporary manifestation of much deeper historical patterns and that changing course will require far more than holding global corporations accountable for the social and environmental consequences of their operations. This book, *The Great Turning: From Empire to Earth Community*, examines these deeper patterns. It offers no simple answers to five thousand years of human misdirection, but it does make clear that the misdirection is not inevitable and that a practical pathway to a positive human future is now within our means as a species to choose. Consequently, I expect that on balance readers will find *The Great Turning* to be an even more hopeful book than *When Corporations Rule the World*.

As I have done in my previous books, I want to introduce the issues we will be exploring together by sharing with you the outlines of the journey I have taken from the innocence of my growing up to my current understanding of the epic opportunity now before us as a species.

GROWING UP ON A SHRINKING PLANET

I am a member of a transitional generation that has experienced the profound cultural, economic, and political consequences of a communications revolution that has shrunk the planet and wiped away the barriers of geography long separating humans into islands of cultural isolation. This revolution is bringing forth a new consciousness of the reality that we humans are one people sharing one destiny on one small planet. The story of my personal awakening is far from unique among the members of my generation.

Transitional Generation

Born in 1937, I grew up white, middle class, and quintessentially conservative in a small town in the northwest corner of the United States, surrounded by an extended family of uncles, aunts, and grandparents. I rarely saw a person of a different race and never met a Muslim, Hindu, or Buddhist. I assumed, as did my family, that on completing college I would return to the town of my birth to spend my life running the family retail business. I had little interest in travel beyond visiting the nearby mountains and seashore and, until just before graduation from college, found it a bit odd that anyone blessed with U.S. citizenship would want to venture beyond our national borders. Never, even in a fleeting fantasy, did I imagine that as an adult I would reside and work for over twenty years in Africa, Latin America, and Asia.

The difference between my experience growing up and that of my daughters illustrates the dramatic shrinking of the planet and the transformation of human experience that occurred over a period of less than forty years. By the time my daughters graduated from high school, they had lived in Nicaragua, the Philippines, Indonesia, and the United States and had attended International Schools with classmates of richly varied racial, cultural, and religious backgrounds from more than sixty countries. They grew up as itinerants far removed from blood relatives other than their mother and father. During their high school years they thought nothing of traveling on their own between Indonesia and the United States with a stopover in South Korea, a country in which few people spoke English, to do some shopping. Even before graduating from high school, they had a global consciousness and skills in dealing with cultural differences wholly beyond my comprehension growing up in a day when international travel was slow, prohibitively costly, and uncommon.

Large-scale international student exchanges, voluntary service programs, and international careers in transnational governmental, nongovernmental, and business organizations now provide millions of people with sustained in-depth cross-cultural encounters. Since the early 1990s,

Internet technologies have made international communications instantaneous and nearly costless and thus open possibilities for still more varied forms of international exchange and cooperation.

By the scale of evolutionary time, this has been a virtually instantaneous break with the previous human condition. It creates new challenges even as it expands by orders of magnitude our species' possibilities. Here is the story of how I experienced this break.

From Hometown to Global Village

In 1959, as a psychology major in my senior year of college, I faced a requirement to take a colloquium taught by a professor outside my major field of study. I was attracted to an offering on modern revolutions taught by Robert North, a distinguished professor of political science. It seemed a useful opportunity to learn something about the Communist revolutions that to my conservative mind posed a threat to my American way of life. In the course of the seminar, I learned that Communist revolutions grew out of the desperation of the poor. As I absorbed the implications, I made a life-changing decision: I would devote my life to sharing the secrets of America's economic and political success so that the world's poor might become free and prosperous like Americans and thus abandon ideas of revolution.

The subsequent experience of working for some thirty years as a member of the international development establishment profoundly changed my worldview. I had gone abroad to teach. Far more consequential than what I taught was what I learned—about myself, my country, and the human tragedy of unrealized possibility. Ultimately, I realized I must return to the land of my birth to share with my people the lessons of my encounter with the world.

In 1992, Fran, my wife and life partner, and I moved to New York City. Fran continued her work as a program officer at the Ford Foundation's headquarters, and I began the research that led to publication in 1995 of *When Corporations Rule the World*.[2]

To this day, I retain my conservative suspicion of big government. I am now, however, equally suspicious of big business and big finance. I remain critical of the shortcomings of unions and public welfare programs, but have a far greater appreciation of their positive and essential role in protecting the rights and well-being of otherwise defenseless working people in the hard-knocks world of big business and global finance.

Although my love for my own country and its possibilities remains firm, I no longer view the United States through the eyes of innocence. I have seen firsthand the devastating negative impact that the economic and military policies of the U.S. government have had on democracy, economic justice, and environmental sustainability, both at home and abroad. That experience has also brought me to an understanding that the leadership to create a world that works for all can and must come from the bottom up through the creative work and political activism of ordinary people who know from their own experience the consequences of these policies.

Therefore, in most respects, I continue to align with what I grew up believing to be conservative values. Yet I find I have nothing in common with extremists of the far right who advance an agenda of class warfare, fiscal irresponsibility, government intrusions on personal liberty, and reckless international military adventurism as conservative causes.

THE TRAGEDY OF UNREALIZED POTENTIAL

Much of my professional life has been devoted to an inquiry into the tragedy of unrealized human potential. In setting after setting, I experienced a persistent tendency in formal organizations—whether business or government—to centralize control in the interest of order and predictability. It is so pervasive that most of us take it for granted as inevitable.

The costs in lost opportunity came into focus for me when Fran and I became involved in the early 1970s in an effort to improve the management of clinic-based family-planning programs in Central America. Procedures and organizational structures were dictated by foreign advisers employed by aid agencies or by professionals at national headquarters—none of whom had contact with the women the program was intended to serve. The result was abysmally poor program performance as measured by the number of women served, staff morale, and client satisfaction.

By contrast, the best performing clinic we identified had a courageous and innovative nurse who ignored the formal procedures and focused on organizing the services to be convenient for clients and responsive to their needs. The staff and the program flourished.[3] Unfortunately, such cases were actively discouraged by program officials.

Fran and I subsequently observed the same devastating consequences of rigid central control play out in programs throughout South and Southeast Asia in health care, agricultural extension, irrigation, forestry, land reform, education, and community development. Programs intended to serve the poor consumed substantial human and material resources to no useful end. Even more alarming was the frequent disruption of the ability of villagers and their communities to control and manage their own resources to meet their needs.

For example, small family farmers throughout Asia have for many centuries joined together to build and manage their own irrigation systems, some of which are marvels of engineering ingenuity and operating efficiency. Yet when government programs inventoried irrigation capacity, they counted only irrigation systems built by the government. They then proceeded to replace the village-built and village-managed systems with more costly, less-efficient centrally managed systems. Commonly the new systems were financed by multimillion-dollar loans from the World Bank and the Asian Development Bank, which the children of the farmers would one day be taxed to repay.

In an effort to demonstrate the possibilities of an approach that strengthened local control, Fran and I became involved in a ten-year intervention to transform the Philippine National Irrigation Administration (NIA) from a top-down engineering bureaucracy to a service organization responsive to the technical and organizational needs of community irrigation associations. The process involved transforming the structures, procedures, purpose, staffing, and capabilities of the NIA in order to shift its focus from implementing agency procedures to working with farmers as partners in solving problems. The results unleashed the creative potential of both farmers and agency staff, improved irrigation performance, increased staff morale, strengthened local control and democracy, and resulted in a more efficient use of public resources. The intervention strategy became a model for subsequent Ford Foundation initiatives throughout the world.[4]

During the fifteen years we lived in Asia, Fran and I saw the same lesson repeated time after time. When power resides with people and communities, life and innovation flourish. When power is centralized in distant government agencies or corporations, the life is sucked out of the community, and services are organized to serve the needs and convenience of the providers. Those who make the decisions prosper, and the local people bear the consequences. We began to see what we witnessed as part of a recurring pattern. We also saw that whether power and authority are centralized or decentralized is a question of choice.

The centralization of authority was rarely the consequence of malicious intent. More often people were simply trying to do their jobs, unaware of the consequences of their actions. If things were going badly, the problem was assumed to be local, likely a failure to follow prescribed procedures. Training and tighter controls to assure compliance were the standard solutions—thus affirming the expertise and authority of the central power holders and the incapacity of those at the bottom.

I later came to see how this pattern plays out at all system levels. I saw that the system of foreign aid itself shifts control to global bureaucracies headquartered half a world away from the needs of the people they presume to serve, that institutions of the global economy shift the power of decision from people and communities to corporations and financiers who have no knowledge of the social and environmental consequences of their decisions. Eventually I saw the pattern playing out everywhere on the planet at every level of organization.

In the late 1980s, with the help of astute colleagues from a number of Asian nongovernmental organizations (NGOs), I began to see the bigger picture of the ways in which official aid agencies actively, if unintentionally, undermine local control and capacity. Even most NGO leaders, however, were not attuned to these larger issues.

In 1990, then living in Manila, I joined with a few close Filipino colleagues to found the People-Centered Development Forum to serve as a mutual support network for a scattered, often beleaguered band of activists engaged in raising public awareness of the destructive consequences of official aid policies. The further we took our analysis, the more evident it became that, far from being the global benefactor I had once assumed it to be, the United States was the major impetus behind what I had come to recognize as a deeply destructive and antidemocratic development model.

A conversation with a colleague from India, Smitu Kothari, brought it together. He politely suggested that I would best serve the cause of improving conditions for the poor of Asia by returning to the United States and devoting myself to educating my own people about the consequences for the world of the misguided policies of our government. On reflection and consultation with other Asian colleagues, I realized he was right. It was another major turning point in my life.

RESISTING CORPORATE-LED ECONOMIC GLOBALIZATION

When Fran and I moved to New York City in 1992, I turned my attention to sharing the lessons of my experience with my fellow Americans. By this time, I was becoming increasingly aware of the extent to which otherwise perverse economic policies were serving corporate interests. Living in an apartment just off Union Square between Madison Avenue and Wall Street proved to be an ideal location for focusing my attention on the corporate connection. It was there I wrote *When Corporations Rule the World*.

In 1994, I accepted an invitation to participate in an international gathering of activists concerned with issues of global trade and investment. We subsequently formed ourselves into the International Forum on Globalization (IFG), an alliance dedicated to raising global awareness that "trade" agreements promoted by global corporations had less to do with freeing trade than with freeing corporations from public accountability. These agreements systematically stripped away the ability of communities, and even nations, to determine their own economic and social priorities and left those decisions to global financiers, corporate CEOs, and trade lawyers.

When Corporations Rule the World appeared in October 1995 at an auspicious moment. There was a growing sense in the United States that things were not right with the world. Stories were fresh in the public mind of corporate CEOs taking home multimillion-dollar bonuses for laying off thousands of workers and outsourcing their jobs to sweatshops in Mexico, Indonesia, and other low-wage countries. *When Corporations Rule the World* connected the dots and provided the analysis for which many people were looking. Suddenly I found myself a figure in an emergent global resistance movement.

The fifty thousand people who took to the streets of Seattle in November 1999 to protest the World Trade Organization and disrupt its secret negotiating processes gave the movement public prominence and sent out a message that ordinary citizens are not so powerless in the face of the corporate juggernaut as they might seem. From that point forward, most every time the corporate elites and their legal minions met to circumvent democracy through international trade agreements, they were confronted by massive street protests. The often violent response of police battalions awakened many minds to the historical reality that, the rhetoric of democracy notwithstanding, when the rights of property conflict with the rights of people, the police powers of government usually align with the rights of property.

My belief in the power of an awakened human consciousness comes from my participation in building a global resistance movement, one that—in the space of little more than ten years—grew from fleeting exchanges among a few dedicated but marginal activists to a movement able to challenge some of the world's most powerful institutions. This experience is a major source of my hope for the human future and my belief that change, if it comes, will emerge through the leadership of millions of people creating a new cultural and institutional reality from the bottom up.

FOR EVERY NO THERE MUST BE A YES

I had realized even in the early 1980s that critiques of conventional growth-driven development models of the previous decade had influenced the rhetoric of development, but not the practice. Practitioners almost inevitably fell back on the frame of a discredited theory because they had no other theory to guide them.

In its simplest terms, the theory underlying corporate-led economic globalization posits that human progress is best advanced by deregulating markets and eliminating economic borders to let unrestrained market forces determine economic priorities, allocate resources, and drive economic growth. It sounds like decentralization, but the reality is quite different. A market without rules and borders increases the freedom of the biggest and most economically powerful players to become even bigger and more powerful at the expense of the freedom and right to self-determination of people and communities. Corporations and financial markets make the decisions and reap the profits. Communities are left to deal with mounting human and environmental costs.

These costs have awakened millions of people to the reality that the health of a community depends in substantial measure on its ability to set its own economic priorities and control its own economic resources. Strong communities and material sufficiency are the true foundation of economic prosperity and security and an essential source of meaning. Street protests are one response to this awakening. Calls for reform of corporate legal structures are another. Less visible, but even more important, is a spreading commitment to rebuild local economies and communities from the bottom up.

Such bottom-up efforts can seem like futile efforts to stem the tide
—until one begins to recognize that they are springing up at every hand
and in every sphere of life, including the cultural and political, demonstrating by results that a different world is possible. To make these
demonstrations more visible is to speed the awakening of a new consciousness of the possible and thus encourage yet more local initiatives.

With this in mind, Sarah van Gelder and I joined with other colleagues in 1996 to found the Positive Futures Network (PFN), which
publishes *YES! A Journal of Positive Futures*, to tell the stories of creative
social entrepreneurs in an effort to speed the awakening of such a consciousness, help people engage, and facilitate the formation of new
alliances. I have since served as board chair. Sarah formed the organization, took on the role of executive editor, and later invited Fran to become executive director and publisher. In 1998, we moved from New
York City to Bainbridge Island, on Washington State's Puget Sound,
where the PFN offices are located.

YES! has become a valued resource for those engaged in the work
of birthing the era of Earth Community and is a go-to place for readers
of *The Great Turning* who want to keep up with new developments and
find new allies and ways to engage. Find it on the Web at http://www
.yesmagazine.org/.

Local Living Economies

Even before completing *When Corporations Rule the World*, I was aware
that simply constraining corporate excess was not an adequate solution
to the issues I had identified. Protests could slow the damage, but real
change would depend on the articulation of a compelling alternative to
the existing profit-driven, corporate-planned, and corporate-managed
global economy. It seemed that healthy living systems might offer helpful
insights. Yet conventional biology, which seeks to explain life in terms of
material mechanisms and assumes that a competition for survival by the
most fit is the key to evolutionary progress, offered little of evident use.

Then I met two extraordinary women—microbiologist Mae-Wan Ho
and evolution biologist Elisabet Sahtouris. Both were taking the study of
life to a profound level that reveals life to be a fundamentally cooperative, locally rooted, self-organizing enterprise in which each individual
organism is continuously balancing individual and group interests.[5]
Here was the natural model for which I had been searching. Life has

learned over billions of years the advantages of cooperative, locally rooted self-organization. Perhaps humans might be capable of doing the same.

Such insights are a key to recognizing that there is a democratic, market-based, community-serving alternative to the unappealing choice between a socialist economy centrally owned and administered by government and a capitalist economy centrally owned and administered by an elite class of wealthy financiers and corporate CEOS. The key distinction between a capitalist economy and the market alternative is that a proper market economy operates with rules, borders, and equitable local ownership under the public oversight of democratically accountable governments. I spelled it out in *The Post-Corporate World: Life after Capitalism*, released in March 1999.

That same year, I joined a drafting committee of the International Forum on Globalization charged with producing the consensus report *Alternatives to Economic Globalization*, edited by John Cavanagh and Jerry Mander. First published in 2002 and reissued in an updated and expanded edition in 2004, this report sets forth a comprehensive institutional and policy framework for a democratic, market-based global economic system based on local ownership and control.

Change through Emergence

I still struggled, however, with how best to advance the transition from a corporate-led global economy to a planetary system of community-led local living economies. At the beginning of 2001 I attended an invitational consultation at the Esalen Institute at which Sahtouris and Janine Benyus, a biological scientist and a leading proponent of biomimicry, made presentations. Both noted that the processes of natural succession by which forest ecosystems evolve offer a potential model for economic transformation. The earliest, colonizing, stage of forest-system development is dominated by fast-growing, aggressively competitive, and transient species that are eventually displaced by the emergence of the more patient, cooperative, settled, energy-efficient species that define the mature phase.

This model pointed to a strategy of change through emergence and displacement. These living system concepts defined the underlying strategic premise of the Business Alliance for Local Living Economies (BALLE), which was cofounded that same year by Laury Hammel and Judy Wicks, two visionary entrepreneurs with a passionate commitment to the idea that the proper defining purpose of business is to serve life and community.

Soon, local economy initiatives across the United States and Canada were signing on as BALLE chapters. (For more information, see http://www.livingeconomies.org/.) These chapters are devoted to growing and linking local independent businesses, nonprofit organizations, and local governments in mature, locally rooted, life-serving economies with the potential to displace the rootless, opportunistic, money-driven, and ultimately suicidal corporate global economy. The experience of watching the mobilizing power of this idea catch hold is yet another source of my hope for the human future.

Gifford and Libba Pinchot, noted management gurus and founding board members of the Positive Futures Network, launched the Bainbridge Graduate Institute (BGI) simultaneously with the formation of BALLE. BGI offers a pioneering MBA program devoted to preparing business leaders with the sensibility and skills to manage truly life-serving businesses. Its larger mission is to transform business education. It draws the most creative faculty members from existing schools to start afresh and design a new MBA curriculum for developing managers for businesses that seek to advance positive social and environmental outcomes as a core business purpose. (For more information, see http://www.bgiedu.org/.) I joined the board of BGI in 2005, the year *BusinessWeek* reported on a steep decline in applications to conventional business schools and the year student applications to BGI tripled.

GETTING TO THE GREAT TURNING

Transforming the institutions of the economy is critically important to the human future. I was learning, however, that the need for transformation also extends to culture and politics. In this regard, I was also witness to a global dialogue from which an extraordinary consensus was emerging about the world that growing numbers of people were committing themselves to create.

Awakening Consensus

In the late 1980s and early '90s I regularly participated in international conferences of NGOs. Many of these gatherings, particularly those organized by NGOs from Southern nations, issued declarations calling for a radical realignment of development practices to give priority to securing the rights of people and communities to the lands, forests, and fisheries on which they depend for their survival. These declarations rarely asked for anything from governments or foreign donors other than that they respect and secure the rights of ordinary people to the means of creating their own livelihood.

These citizen conferences prepared the way for the International NGO Forum that met in parallel with the official UN Conference on Environment and Development (UNCED) held in Rio de Janeiro in 1992. The NGO forum brought together some eighteen thousand private citizens representing virtually all the world's nationalities, races, religions, and social classes to engage in drafting citizen "treaties" spelling out shared values and common goals.

I had the privilege of participating in the NGO forum in Rio and in drafting its final declaration. It was one of the formative experiences of my life, as it burned into my consciousness the reality that for all their profound diversity, the people who came together for the forum shared similar values and a similar vision of the just, sustainable, inclusive, and democratic world they were committed to creating.

The consensus building was carried forward subsequently under the auspices of a private international commission that organized consultations involving thousands of individuals and hundreds of organizations from all regions of the world. That process produced a document called the Earth Charter. Often referred to as a people's Declaration of Interdependence, the Earth Charter elaborates four overarching principles of Earth Community: (1) respect and care for the community of life; (2) ecological integrity; (3) social and economic justice; and (4) democracy, nonviolence, and peace.[6] It is also a declaration of universal responsibility to and for one another and the living Earth. I had the privilege of being a keynote speaker at the U.S. launch of the Earth Charter on September 29, 2001.

Through these experiences, I have grown in my understanding of the processes by which the world's people are awakening to the reality that we are one people with one destiny on a small planet and that we can and must accept adult responsibility to and for one another and the web of life that sustains us all.

Naming the Time, Changing the Story

From 1999 to 2004, the Positive Futures Network convened a series of invitational retreats that engaged some two hundred social-change leaders from diverse social-movement constituencies in deep dialogue to identify common goals, build relationships of mutual trust, connect with the sacred nature of our work, and facilitate the formation of new alliances. We called the retreats "The State of the Possible."[7]

Buddhist scholar and teacher Joanna Macy was among the participants, and we found that her term "The Great Turning" captured well our sense of the time in which we live as a transition between eras. Herman Gyr, who was one of our facilitators, captured our sense of the dying of the old and the birthing of the new in an iconic image of two interconnected swirls, one turning inward as it exhausts itself, and the other reaching outward as it grows in energy and potential. Macy speaks of the Great Turning as a spiritual revolution grounded in an awakening consciousness of our spiritual connection to one another and the living body of Earth.

Filipino civil society leader and strategist Nicanor Perlas, who also participated in the retreats, helped us to understand a simple truth: the advantage of civil society in advancing the transition lies in the moral power of authentic cultural values. Perlas helped me recognize that the power of the institutions of economic and political domination depends on their ability to perpetuate a falsified and inauthentic cultural trance based on beliefs and values at odds with reality. Break the trance, replace the values of an inauthentic culture with the values of an authentic culture grounded in a love of life rather than a love of money, and people will realign their life energy and bring forth the life-serving institutions of a new era. The key is to change the stories by which we define ourselves. It is easier said than done, but I have found it to be a powerful strategic insight.

Confronting Our Imperial Legacy

In July 2002, Fran and I hosted our friend and colleague Vandana Shiva, the globally renowned Indian scientist, writer, farmer leader, and global peace and justice activist, as our guest on Bainbridge Island. It was the summer following the September 11, 2001, terrorist attack on the United States.

Within days of the attack, the U.S. government declared perpetual war against terrorism, began rolling back civil liberties, and branded dissent as support for terrorists. Leaders of many other governments, glad for an excuse to limit dissent and buttress their own power, followed the U.S. example. Around the world, voices of resistance against corporate globalization were briefly stunned into silence.

By the time of Shiva's visit, the U.S. administration had launched an invasion of Afghanistan and was talking of possible preemptive military action against Iraq, North Korea, Iran, Syria, and Libya. Influential policy analysts were debating the merits of an American Empire, and documents were circulating in which key administration officials openly advocated imposing a Pax Americana on the world by the unilateral application of U.S. military power in the manner of the ancient Roman Empire.

During our conversations, Shiva noted that the mobilization of global civil society to thwart the misuse of trade agreements to circumvent democracy was based on the by then widely accepted critique of corporate globalization to which we had each contributed. Civil society, however, had no generally accepted framework for addressing the larger and even graver threat to liberty and democracy of forthright military domination. Shiva and I invited Perlas to join us in preparing a discussion paper on "Global Civil Society: The Path Ahead."[8]

This collaboration brought into focus the relevance of the work of another colleague, cultural historian Riane Eisler. In her classic work *The Chalice and the Blade*, Eisler placed the conflict between dominator and partnership models of organization in deep historical context and brought to bear the lens of gender analysis to illuminate the deeper roots of our contemporary political struggles for justice, peace, and environmental stewardship. By her reckoning, the repression of creative potential I had been witnessing for more than thirty years has been playing out for some five thousand years at every level of human organization, from relations among states to relations among family members. She traced the tragedy to the subordination of the feminine to the masculine and of the organizing principle of partnership to the organizing principle of domination. Once we made this connection to Eisler's work we could see that we were dealing with issues that have far deeper historical roots than we had previously considered. This insight led to the book now in your hands.

My intention in writing *The Great Turning: From Empire to Earth Community* is to provide a historically grounded frame for understanding the possibilities of the unique time in which we live and thereby enable us to envision the path to a new era. Failing such understanding, we will continue to squander valuable time and resources on futile efforts to preserve or mend the cultures and institutions of a system that cannot be fixed and must be replaced.

Note that throughout *The Great Turning* I use the term *Empire* with a capital *E* as a label for the hierarchical ordering of human relationships based on the principle of domination. The mentality of Empire embraces material excess for the ruling classes, honors the dominator power of death and violence, denies the feminine principle, and suppresses realization of the potentials of human maturity.

Similarly, I use the term *Earth Community* as a label for the egalitarian democratic ordering of relationships based on the principle of partnership. The mentality of Earth Community embraces material sufficiency for everyone, honors the generative power of life and love, seeks a balance of feminine and masculine principles, and nurtures a realization of the mature potential of our human nature.

I urge you to read actively and critically, testing my observations and conclusions against your own knowledge and experience. I hope you will also participate in expanding the circle of dialogue by discussing the underlying issues with friends and colleagues. You might open such dialogue by recommending to those you want to engage that they read *The Great Turning*. Perhaps you might organize a discussion group. You will find supporting tools and discussion guides at http://www.greatturning .org/. To redirect humanity's course, break the silence, end the isolation, and change the story.

Please bear in mind that it is impossible for me to engage individually with each reader of this book who might wish to dialogue with me directly. Much as I might wish the contrary, I am unable to respond to personal inquiries.

SYNOPSIS OF THE ARGUMENT

The human species is entering a period of dramatic and potentially devastating change as the result of forces of our own creation that are now largely beyond our control. It is within our means, however, to shape a positive outcome if we choose to embrace the resulting crisis as an opportunity to lift ourselves to a new level of species maturity and potential.

The outcome will depend in large measure on the prevailing stories that shape our understanding of the traumatic time at hand—its causes and its possibilities. Perhaps the most difficult and yet essential aspect of this work is to change our stories.

If we succeed, future generations may look back on this as a time of profound transition and speak of it as the time of the Great Turning. If we fail, our time may instead be known simply as the tragic time of the Great Unraveling.

Histories written by the victors of Empire's endless wars, intrigues, and deceits have greatly exaggerated Empire's accomplishments while neglecting the costs and lost opportunities. Current attempts by the world's imperial elites to salvage the power and privilege of Empire are accelerating the collapse of critical social and environmental systems and threatening the survival of human civilization, if not the human species.

We now have the means to end the five-thousand-year era of Empire that has reproduced hierarchies of domination at all levels of human organization. A global cultural and spiritual awakening is building momentum toward the birthing of a new era of Earth Community based on a radically democratic partnership model of organizing human relationships. This awakening gives us cause for hope.

There are those who say that the violence and greed of Empire are defining characteristics of our human nature, that ruthless competition for power and material goods is inescapable. They say our impulses must be disciplined either by central authority or by market competition, both of which create hierarchies of power that consign the majority of humans to lives of desperation and suppress the creative potential of the species.

The truth is at once more complex and more hopeful. Our human nature actually embodies many possibilities, ranging from violence and greed to love and service. Contemporary human societies fail to manifest the higher-order potentials of love and service, not because of an inherent flaw in our human nature, but because the dominator relations of Empire actively suppress the development and expression of this potential. As a species, we now face both the imperative and the opportunity to say no to Empire, grow up, and accept the responsibilities of mature adulthood.

Our failing environmental and social systems create the imperative. The global revolution in transportation and communications is creating the opportunity. Leadership in actualizing the possibilities is coming from people everywhere who are making the choice to walk away from Empire's false promises and engage the work of turning our cultures, economies, and politics from dominator to partnership relations.

THE CULTURAL TURNING. The Great Turning begins with a cultural and spiritual awakening. Economic and political turning can only follow a turning in cultural values from money and material excess to life and spiritual fulfillment, from relationships of domination to relationships of partnership, from a belief in our limitations to a belief in our possibilities, and from fearing our differences to rejoicing in our diversity.

THE ECONOMIC TURNING. The values shift of the cultural turning calls us to turn from measuring well-being by the size of our yachts and bank accounts to measuring well-being by the health of our families, communities, and natural environment. It leads us from economic policies that raise those at the top to policies that raise those at the bottom, from economic plutocracy to economic democracy, from hoarding to sharing, and from the rights of ownership to the responsibilities of stewardship.

THE POLITICAL TURNING. The economic turning creates the necessary conditions for a turn from a democracy of money to a democracy of people, from passive to active citizenship, from competition for individual advantage to cooperation for mutual advantage, from retributive justice to restorative justice, and from social order by coercion to social order by mutual responsibility and accountability.

Some critics will surely complain that "Korten wants to change everything." They miss the point. Everything is going to change. The question is whether we let the changes play out in increasingly destructive ways or embrace the deepening crisis as our time of opportunity. Now as never before we must unleash the creative potential of the species and direct it to democratizing our cultures and institutions and bringing ourselves into balance with one another and Earth. It is the greatest creative challenge the species has ever faced. Success would seem a futile dream, except that all around the planet momentum is already building.

THE BOOK

Although the issues addressed in *The Great Turning* are global and universal, I have chosen to focus my analysis on the United States. It is the nation among all others that is most challenged by the imperatives of the Great Turning. Few other nations are so accustomed to living beyond their own means, so imbued with a sense of special virtue and entitlement, or so burdened by a political leadership as out of touch with global reality and as incapable of accepting responsibility for the consequences of its actions. Because of its global presence, whether the United States responds to the imperatives with the logic of Empire or the logic of Earth Community is likely to have far-reaching consequences for all nations. Furthermore, the United States is the nation of my birth, the nation I know best and love most, and the nation for whose role in the world I feel most responsible.

The Great Turning is presented in five parts. Part I, "Choosing Our Future," explores the choice at hand and the nature and implications of the distinctive imperatives and opportunities now before us.

Part II, "Sorrows of Empire," reviews the conditions that led humans in an earlier time to turn away from a reverence for life and the regenerative power of the feminine to pursue the path of violence and domination. A synopsis of the imperial experience illustrates the self-replicating social dynamics of Empire, charts the transition from the institutions of monarchy to the institutions of the global economy as the favored instruments of imperial rule, and reveals the costs of Empire's often overly idealized accomplishments. It also draws lessons from the early Athenian experiment in popular democracy and the insights of the great Athenian philosophers.

Part III, "America, the Unfinished Project," turns to the United States and the history of the challenge now before us as a nation. In an effort to dispel the myths underlying a dangerous complacency about our institutions and global intentions, it takes a sober look at the reality that we have never been the democracy we imagine ourselves to be and we have always had imperial ambitions. It concludes with a look at the actions of a particularly corrupt and incompetent administration as a national wake-up call to confront the reality of our history and engage a popular mobilization to build the democratic society of our founding ideal.

Part IV, "The Great Turning," outlines the scope of the work of the Great Turning by contrasting the stories and deep assumptions underlying the values and relationships of Empire and Earth Community that legitimate a hierarchy of domination and wealth concentration on the one hand, and networks of partnership, sharing, and mutual learning on the other. It draws on the deeper insights of both science and religion to make the case that learning and partnership are integral not only to life, but as well to the whole of Creation.

Part V, "Birthing Earth Community," outlines a strategic framework for bringing forth a new era of Earth Community. It describes how self-organizing processes of citizen action, based on grassroots leadership, can advance an agenda of cultural, economic, and political democratization that roots power in people and liberates the creative potential of the species. It further makes the case that the foundation of a majoritarian political consensus based on family and community values and a concern for children is already in place.

PART I

Choosing Our Future

The capacity to anticipate and choose our future is a defining characteristic of the human species. The recent global spread of communications technologies has combined with a confrontation with planetary limits to present us with a unique opportunity, and the necessity, to use that capacity with conscious collective intent.

The defining choice is between two contrasting models for organizing human affairs. Give them the generic names Empire and Earth Community. Empire, which features organization by domination and which has been a defining feature of the most powerful and influential human societies for some five thousand years, appropriates much of the productive surplus of society to maintain a system of dominator power and elite competition. Racism, sexism, and classism are endemic features of Empire. Earth Community, which features organization by partnership, unleashes the human potential for creative cooperation and allocates the productive surplus of society to the work of growing the generative potential of the whole.

The defenders of Empire teach that we humans are by nature limited to a self-centered and ultimately self-destructive narcissism. Their favored organizing model suppresses development of the higher orders of human consciousness and thereby creates a self-fulfilling prophecy. The organizing model of Earth Community, by contrast, nurtures expression of the higher-order human capacities for responsible service that Empire denies. A convergence of imperative and opportunity unique to the present moment in the human experience sets the stage for an intentional collective choice to put the way of Empire behind us as we live into being a new era of Earth Community.

CHAPTER 1

The Choice

> Energy always flows either toward hope, community, love,
> generosity, mutual recognition, and spiritual aliveness or it
> flows toward despair, cynicism, fear that there is not enough,
> paranoia about the intentions of others, and a desire to
> control.[1]
>
> *Michael Lerner*

> All societies are patterned on either a dominator model—in
> which human hierarchies are ultimately backed up by force
> or the threat of force—or a partnership model, with varia-
> tions in between.[2]
>
> *Riane Eisler*

In the early 1970s, while teaching at the Central American Management Institute in Nicaragua, I made several visits to a cattle ranch in Costa Rica I'll call Hacienda Santa Teresa. The simple but compelling story of this ranch captures for me the essence of the tragedy of unrealized human possibility that plays out at all levels of society, from relationships among nations, to relationships within nations, between races and genders, within families, and among individuals. The names are fictional. The story is true.[3]

HACIENDA SANTA TERESA

When Juan Ricardo took charge of the Hacienda Santa Teresa as manager in 1970, its lands, roads, fences, and buildings were in poor repair; many of its cattle were in poor health from a lack of necessary mineral supplements and vaccinations. Most of the *sabaneros*, the workers who looked after the cattle, were single men who lived in a dilapidated, unpainted one-room bunkhouse, where they slept on wooden planks. The *peones*, who did the manual labor, shared a similar but separate facility in which they simply slept on the floor for lack even of wooden planks. Each received a small wage plus a ration of rice, beans, lard, coffee, and occasionally corn flour for tortillas. These conditions were standard for the region.

Sabaneros in those parts were often related to one another and formed tight-knit groups. For the most part they were cleaner and more concerned with the appearance of their quarters than the peones, but were still lax in their personal hygiene and generally in poor health. They had a reputation for honesty, did their jobs well, and commanded a certain grudging respect from the ranchers, who depended on them to care for the cattle on distant pastures.

Like most others in the region, the sabaneros at Hacienda Santa Teresa were responsible for providing their own equipment, which was often in poor repair. Their bridles had no bits, their ropes were old, and they lacked basic rain gear even though heavy rainstorms were common. The ranch provided their horses, which received minimal care. The sabaneros did not know how to trim their horses' hooves properly and took no care to remove ticks from the animals' hides.

The peones built fences, repaired roads, cleared land, and constructed corrals and buildings—tasks for which some of them had considerable skill. They were, however, considered incorrigible thieves who needed strict supervision. They were expected to respond to any order with subservience and respect. Because labor-code provisions only took effect after three months of employment, many ranchers made a point of never keeping a *peón* that long. The sabaneros were disdainful of the peones, whom they considered dirty, unprincipled, irresponsible, and ignorant, and felt they were entitled to give the peones arbitrary orders.

Ricardo observed that many of the peones, who were paid hourly wages, were hardworking and, by working voluntary overtime, sometimes earned more than the salaried sabaneros. However, the peones lived in complete filth and took no initiative even in matters directly affecting their own comfort and well-being. At the end of the workday, they dropped their tools where they stood and returned to the bunkhouse unless otherwise instructed. The next morning they lined up awaiting orders. If a peón saw a cow walking through a hole in a fence, he would stand and watch unless ordered to retrieve it. Petty theft was a continuing annoyance.

Ricardo concluded that both the ranch and its staff had unrealized possibilities. He set out to test his theory that by treating his workers like responsible adults they would respond accordingly. One of his first steps was to improve their health by providing each with a raincoat and a mattress and adding eggs, meat, vegetables, and cheese to their diet. He then raised the wages of the sabaneros by 25 to 30 percent, raised the starting wage of the peones by 20 percent, and implemented a policy of deducting the cost of lost tools.

He appointed the informal leader of the sabaneros as head sabanero and gave him an additional raise and a wristwatch. However, instead of assigning each sabanero ten to fifteen horses, as was standard in the area, he cut them back to three, bought them new saddles, and taught them to de-tick their horses and trim the hooves. The initial blow to the sabaneros' status from the reduction in their number of horses soon gave way to a sense of pride in having the best horses in the region.

Ricardo took a similar approach with the peones. Instead of simply issuing orders to the peones when they gathered for work in the morning, Ricardo started asking them to suggest what work most needed doing —for example, cleaning a field or digging post holes. At first, they were confused. One quit, complaining he was being asked to make too many decisions. Others, once they got used to speaking up, became contentious, insisting they should finish one job before doing another that Ricardo considered more urgent. Ricardo recognized this as a normal and necessary part of the process.

At the time of my final visit to the ranch, two years after Ricardo's arrival, the ranch and its workers were advancing toward an extraordinary transformation. The sabaneros were regularly treating the cattle for parasites, vaccinating them, providing them with salt licks, doing pregnancy tests, and managing breeding.

Ricardo had assigned individual sabaneros and peones responsibility for managing remote sections of the ranch. For the sabaneros this meant tending to the cattle. For the peones it meant maintaining the fences and pastures. For the married workers among them, Ricardo was also building individual cement blockhouses in which a worker would live with his family on his assigned section of the ranch. Ricardo had upgraded other peones to positions as tractor drivers and carpenters. One was responsible for heavy-equipment maintenance.

During the two-year period the herd had increased from seven hundred to thirteen hundred with no increase in the size of the staff. The calving rate had increased from 33 percent to 62 percent, and Ricardo hoped to get it up to 85 percent by the end of the next year.

DEMONSTRATING POSSIBILITIES

By replacing relationships based on domination and disdain with relationships based on partnership and mutual respect, Ricardo awakened
otherwise suppressed potentials in both his workers and the natural
productive systems of the ranch, enhancing the life of the whole and all
its members—including the horses and cattle.

Long conditioned to subservience and degrading living arrangements, the sabaneros and peones needed time to respond. For some,
accepting their own potential for skilled and responsible self-direction
was more than they could handle and they took their leave. Others,
however, found the courage to embrace the opportunity that Ricardo
presented to them.

I find an important lesson in this story for those inclined to describe
human nature in terms of some basic characteristic of individualism,
selfishness, or greed. Anyone who observed these men at the time of
Ricardo's arrival might have concluded, with justification, that it was
their nature to be lazy and incapable of responsible self-direction. Anyone who saw them three years later would likely conclude it was their
nature to be hardworking and self-managing. Both conclusions, however, describe only possibilities. Neither describes the workers' nature,
which embodied a remarkable capacity to adapt to their circumstances.

Such stories of microexperiments are almost a cliché in the field of
organizational development. Skilled and thoughtful managers have
achieved such results endless times in countless settings. Negotiate the
turning from the organizing principles of Empire to the organizing principles of Earth Community, and long-suppressed creative energies flow
forth to actualize extraordinary potential. The results of such microexperiments, however, are rarely sustained. The reason is a lesson in the
implications of a world organized by the dominator principles of Empire.

Consider a larger truth not addressed in the story of the Hacienda
Santa Teresa as presented above. The real power resided not with the
sabaneros and peones, nor even with Ricardo, but with the owners of
the ranch.

These were three wealthy playboys who lived in the United States and
used the ranch as a tax write-off. The grandly elegant ranch house served
as a secluded trysting place for liaisons with the U.S. girlfriends they from
time to time brought down in their private airplane on tax-deductible

vacations. Ricardo was also a U.S. citizen of European extraction. He took great pride in his work and in particular his role in the transformation of the hacienda's workforce, but he was not an owner and would one day return to the United States. The positive innovations he introduced notwithstanding, the legal relationships of a dominator society remained in place.

For instance, Ricardo retained the power to fire any of the workers at any time with minimal recourse. Similarly, the owners had the power to fire Ricardo at will and reestablish the old way of working. Furthermore, the profits from what Ricardo and the ranch hands accomplished went to those absentee owners, who had had no part in transforming the ranch into a profitable enterprise and for whom even the profits were an incidental windfall.

For these reasons, although the case powerfully demonstrates a range of human possibility, the organizational context in which it occurred also exemplifies the injustices of an imperial global order. We can imagine, however, the possibilities if one day those whose labor made the ranch productive were to become its worker-owners and thus truly the masters of their own fate.

For me, the Hacienda Santa Teresa story has come to serve as a metaphor of the human condition in a world divided between those who rule and those who live in dependence, exclusion, and marginalization. When juxtaposed with the missed possibility of how things can work, the human condition as we know it is a tragic, self-inflicted crime against ourselves.

I also see in this story an important lesson in practical politics. Creating societies that support all their individual members in realizing their full humanity is neither a distinctively liberal nor a distinctively conservative cause.

Ricardo's approach honors both liberal and conservative values. He increased individual initiative and accomplishment at the same time he increased the sense of community and mutual responsibility. He increased the productivity of the ranch and at the same time made it far more equitable, democratic, and alive. His innovations increased freedom, discipline, individual responsibility for the self, and collective responsibility for the overall performance of the ranch.

There was greater competition to excel but also more genuine cooperation. Ricardo pursued neither ideology nor personal power, but rather a mature vision of human possibility and the benefits of a healthy living community of people, plants, and animals. In so doing, he affirmed and expressed his own humanity.

THE DEFINING CHOICE

Within the limits of its ownership structure, the Hacienda Santa Teresa case illustrates two primary models of organizing human relationships. The first approach features the classic model of a dominance hierarchy, in which direction flows from top to bottom. The second, quite different approach emphasizes teamwork and self-direction. Cultural historian Riane Eisler calls these, respectively, the *dominator* and *partnership* models.[4] One both denies and represses the human potential for creative self-direction, cooperation, and voluntary service to the well-being of the whole. The other nurtures and rejoices in it. Each creates its own self-fulfilling prophecy. The differences in outcome can be breathtaking, as the Hacienda Santa Teresa case illustrates.

Throughout this book, I use *Empire* and *Earth Community* as generic labels for these two contrasting models for organizing human relationships. Each model is supported by its own cultural values, institutional forms, and supporting narratives. Since pure cases of either model are rare in the complex world of human affairs, think of them as competing tendencies. Table 1.1 summarizes their defining characteristics. By recognizing their contrasting natures and consequences, we can be more conscious of which we serve in each cultural, economic, and political choice we make.

I have chosen to use the term *Earth Community* rather than simply *Community* throughout *The Great Turning* to underscore the integral

TABLE 1.1: The choice

Empire	Earth Community
Life is hostile and competitive	Life is supportive and cooperative
Humans are flawed and dangerous	Humans have many possibilities
Order by dominator hierarchy	Order through partnership
Compete or die	Cooperate and live
Love power	Love life
Defend the rights of the self	Defend the rights of all
Masculine dominant	Gender balanced

relationship so important to the human future between human communities and the natural communities that sustain them. The term *Earth Community* comes from the Earth Charter, a "Declaration of Interdependence and Universal Responsibility" created through a multiyear collaborative process involving hundreds of organizations and thousands of individuals of diverse religious faiths, cultures, races, languages, and nationalities.[5]

Competing Narratives

Empire and Earth Community flow from sharply contrasting worldviews.[6] The narrative of Empire, which emphasizes the demonstrated human capacity for hatred, exclusion, competition, domination, and violence in the pursuit of domination, assumes humans are incapable of responsible self-direction and that social order must be imposed by coercive means. The narrative of Earth Community, which emphasizes the demonstrated human capacity for caring, compassion, cooperation, partnership, and community in the service of life, assumes a capacity for responsible self-direction and self-organization and thereby the possibility of creating radically democratic organizations and societies. These narratives represent two sides of a psychic tension that resides within each of us. One focuses on that which divides us and leads to fear and often violent competition. The other focuses on that which unites us and leads to trust and cooperation.

These competing tendencies are expressed in the tension between the feminine predisposition to bond for mutual protection in the face of danger and the masculine predisposition to fight or take flight. Yet while one tendency or the other may be more fully expressed in a given individual or society, both reside in each of us—male or female—which helps to account for the wide variety of the human experience. Healthy social function depends on maintaining a balance between these tendencies. Empire's five thousand years of male domination demonstrate the tragic consequences of imbalance.

The competing narratives are also reflected in the range of qualities attributed to God in different cultures. At one extreme is the wrathful God of Empire who demands exclusive loyalty, favors one people over another, lives apart from his creation, rules through anointed earthly representatives, and extracts a terrible vengeance on his enemies and the unbelievers. At the other extreme is the universal loving God/dess of

Earth Community, the intrinsic, omnipresent living Spirit beyond gender that manifests itself in every aspect of Creation.

Love and fear are both integral to our human nature and necessary for our full development. Love is a binding spiritual force that opens our minds and hearts to life's creative possibilities. Fear alerts us to real dangers and focuses our attention to ensure that we do not neglect our own survival needs. However, when fear awakens our defenses, it also evokes our capacity for violence, including violence against those we love. How we resolve the tension between love and fear has major consequences for the course of our lives—and our politics. The deep democracy of egalitarian civic engagement that is integral to Earth Community necessarily depends on a mature sense of mutual trust, responsibility, and caring.

Relationships of Empire

Empire, which gives expression to the authoritarian impulse, features a drive for *dominator* power, to use Eisler's term: the power to take, control, and destroy by coercive means. It organizes every relationship at every level of society according to a hierarchy of power, control, status, and privilege. The ever present focus is on attaining more power by co-opting and monopolizing the power of the many below, often at great cost to the whole.[7] Males have been socialized to specialize in the cultivation of dominator power.

The cultural and institutional systems of Empire support a monopolization of resources by the ruling elites, whose lives become consumed in competing with one another for the top positions in the dominance hierarchy. Because power struggles are continuous and often treacherous, relationships commonly feature a substantial element of distrust, fear, and duplicity. Fear is Empire's friend, as it creates a psychological need for certainty, control, and structured relationships that motivates acquiescence by those below.

Empire routinely extends rights and freedoms to those at the top of the hierarchy that it denies those on the bottom. By the logic of Empire's narrative, the smartest, toughest players have the right and the duty to seize and hold power by whatever means are available to impose peace and order on an unruly world in the interest of all—a service for which they believe themselves to be rightfully rewarded with even greater power and wealth. The legitimating culture extols the virtues of the powerful winners, attributes the condition of the hapless losers to incompetence or a lack of character, and communicates a message that the only alternative to the power elite's domination is chaos—along with a scornful insinuation that trust, compassion, and cooperation are for fools and cowards.

Social Pathology

Empire's hierarchy of dominance creates an illusion of order and security. In fact it is a social pathology that feeds a violent and self-destructive competition, suppresses creative potential, and promotes a grossly inefficient use of resources. Feeding on its own illusions, Empire becomes a kind of collective addiction—a psychological dependence on domination, violence, and material excess. The afflicted embrace it as a crutch because it satisfies their need for a sense of power and security—albeit in a tragically self-destructive way.

Empire places nations and individuals alike in a situation akin to that of the hapless gladiator in the pit of the Roman Colosseum: fight for a chance at living another day or accept immediate death. Kill or be killed. Be a winner or be a loser. Rule or be ruled. Empire has its own golden rule: "He who has the gold rules." So "Go for the gold," and be sure you get more of it than your neighbor.

Once the basic winner-take-all dynamic is in place, it creates what political analyst Jonathan Schell calls an "adapt or die" system—more accurately a "compete or die" system—from which it becomes extremely difficult for either individuals or societies to break free, as thousands of years of human history demonstrate. Commit to the winner-take-all competition and submit to its draconian rules, or suffer the loser's fate of oppression and exclusion.[8] The high stakes create a powerful incentive to win by any means and exert a strong downward pressure on ethical standards, a pattern endlessly repeated at all levels of imperial societies. Once the cultural and institutional dynamics of Empire are in place, the generative choice of Earth Community is off the table.

The dynamics and consequences of Empire are documented in detail by Andrew Schmookler in his social science classic *The Parable of the Tribes*.[9] In the parable, a number of peaceful tribes live together harmoniously for many generations, until one day a tribe with an aggressive warrior culture appears, begins to overrun the peaceful tribes, and forces them to embrace the ways of the violent tribe, run away, or be decimated.

The pathology of Empire spreads from one society to another through this dynamic. The culture and institutions of the infected society undergo a gradual transformation from supporting and rewarding relations based on partnership to supporting those based on domination.

Rulers are reduced to a choice: conquer and absorb the territory of their neighbors, or risk being conquered and absorbed by them. The greater the wealth and power of a ruler, the more covetous his foreign and domestic enemies, the larger the armies required to secure the realm, and the greater the need for subject lands and people to meet the insatiable patronage demands of the retainer classes on whom the ruler's wealth and power rest. The work of growing the potential of the whole to the mutual benefit of all is subordinated to the work of maintaining the system of domination. The cost to society in lost lives, resources, and opportunity is beyond calculation, even comprehension.

It is for good reason that history provides few examples of wise and benevolent kings. Only the most ruthlessly ambitious are capable of the violence and treachery required to reach the highest levels of power in an imperial system. Those of sound mind and mature ethical sensibility are prone to withdraw voluntarily, and those of less mature sensibilities are likely to eliminate those of more mature sensibility who attempt to stay the course without sacrificing their principles. It is not simply that absolute power corrupts. More to the point, it is the corrupt who are the most highly motivated to seek absolute power.

Empire offers a Faustian bargain even for the winners. Wealth and power come at the expense of the qualities that make both winners and losers fully human. Empire is a psychological, as well as a social, affliction that is at once both cause and consequence of our collective failure to actualize the potential of our humanity. This failure presents a crucial barrier to making a collective human transition from the dominator relationships of Empire to the deeply democratic partnership relationships of Earth Community, because the successful negotiation of the transition will require the creative contribution of every person.

Relationships of Earth Community

Earth Community, which gives expression to the democratic impulse, features a drive for what Eisler calls *partnership* power, the power to create, share, and nurture. It organizes through consensual decision making, mutual accountability, and individual responsibility. Its focus is on cultivating mutual trust, caring, competence, and an equitable distribution of power and resources. This is more fulfilling, more efficient, and ultimately more human. In addition, it allows for a massive reallocation of the available human surplus away from maintaining hierarchies of domination to the work of improving the lives of all.

Because females have been socialized to specialize in the cultivation of partnership relations, recognizing the possibilities of Earth Community often comes more easily to them than to males. Indeed, much of the pathology of Empire has arisen from suppression of the feminine. Part of the transformation of social relationships at Hacienda Santa Teresa involved a shift from all-male bunkhouses to family living units, which brought wives and children into the social mix of the ranch. The current global turn to more balanced gender relationships is a significant source of hope for the future of the species.

The golden rule of Earth Community is "Do unto your neighbor as you would have your neighbor do unto you as you work together to create a better life for all." Service, compassion, and cooperation are valued as essential social goods and considered a measure of healthy maturity. If each individual has the opportunity to experience the intrinsic rewards that come from responsible service and shares in the benefits of the growing generative power of the whole, then trust, compassion, and cooperation become self-reinforcing. Conflict can be embraced as an opportunity for creative learning. It becomes natural to expand the circle of cooperation in anticipation of the increasing opportunities for mutual gain that expanded cooperation makes possible.

In Earth Community, violence and competition for dominator power are considered irrational, because they destroy the cooperative nurturing relationships essential to the welfare of the individual and society. It becomes self-evident that such behaviors are morally wrong because they are destructive of life. Through their daily experience, people learn that meaning and purpose are found in equitably sharing power and resources to explore life's creative possibilities in ways that secure the well-being of all.

The *cultural* principles of Earth Community affirm the spiritual unity and interconnectedness of Creation. They favor respect for all beings, nonviolence, service to community, and the stewardship of common resources for the benefit of generations to come. The *economic* principles of Earth Community affirm the basic right of every person to a means of livelihood and the responsibility of each person to live in a balanced relationship with their place on Earth without expropriating the resources of others. They favor local control, self-reliance, and mutually beneficial trade and sharing. The *political* principles of Earth Community affirm the inherent worth and potential of all individuals and their right to a voice in the decisions that shape their lives, thereby favoring inclusive citizen engagement, cooperative problem solving, and restorative justice.

THE LAST FREEDOM

Like every other species, we humans must contend with the inherited physical limitations of our genetic coding. However, the limits of human possibility are more psychological and cultural than genetic and are largely self-imposed—a consequence of individual and collective fears that blind us to our own and to life's creative possibilities.

One of the most powerful commentaries on human choice in the face of seemingly impossible odds comes from the report of the distinguished European psychiatrist Viktor Frankl on his years in the German death camps at Auschwitz and Dachau.[10] For the prisoners, life in these camps was a nightmare of deprivation and dehumanization, with the constant threat of instant, arbitrary, and meaningless death. One might think of these camps as a brutal study in the variety of human responses to the most extreme of Empire's dehumanizing dynamic. The range of responses by both prisoners and guards to circumstances none of them had chosen left a deep impression on Frankl. In Frankl's words, some behaved like saints, others like swine.

> There were always choices to make. Every day, every hour, offered the opportunity to make a decision, a decision which determined whether you would or would not submit to those powers which threatened to rob you of your very self, your inner freedom; which determined whether or not you would become the plaything of circumstance, renouncing freedom and dignity to become molded into the form of the typical inmate....
>
> Man does not simply exist but always decides what his existence will be, what he will become in the next moment.[11]

By Frankl's account, some prisoners enthusiastically curried favor with the guards by informing on their fellow prisoners or serving as overseer, cook, storekeeper, or camp policeman—positions from which they might participate in the arbitrary treatment and humiliation of their fellow prisoners. Others, who remained steadfast in their dignity and humanity, "walked through the huts comforting others, giving away their last piece of bread. They may have been few in number, but they offer sufficient proof that everything can be taken from a man but one thing: the last of the human freedoms—to choose one's attitude in any given set of circumstances, to choose one's own way."[12]

Much the same range of possibility was observed among the guards. Some were sadists in the purest clinical sense, finding special pleasure in inflicting physical and psychological pain. Known to both officers and prisoners, they were the ones assigned to conduct interrogations and administer punishment. Others, despite the brutal environment of the camp, refused to take part in the sadistic measures. Some extended acts of genuine compassion to the prisoners. The SS commander of one camp secretly paid considerable sums out of his own pocket to purchase medicines for his prisoners from a nearby town.

Although our circumstances may limit our individual choices, human circumstances are often collective human constructs and thereby subject to collective choice. The excuse that "it's just human nature" carries no more moral weight than the young child's claim that "everybody does it." It is our nature to be creatures of choice. We humans are ultimately the architects of our own nature.

Empire and *Earth Community* are generic names for two models of organizing human relationships at all levels of society, from relationships among nations to relations among family and work-group members. Empire orders relationships into dominator hierarchies that monopolize power in the hands of elites to expropriate the life energy, and thereby suppress the creative potential, of the rest. Earth Community orders relationships by partnership networks that distribute power equitably to nurture the well-being and creative potential of each individual and the whole of the community. Each model is within our means, and ultimately it is ours to choose between them.

Cynics argue that the idea of human societies organized on the principle of partnership is idealistic nonsense beyond our capacity, because we humans are by nature violent, individualistic, and incapable of cooperating for a higher good. Failing to recognize that our nature embodies many possibilities, the cynics look only at the readily observable lower-order possibilities of our nature and neglect the higher-order possibilities. It is ours to actualize these higher-order possibilities. First, however, we must acknowledge their existence.

CHAPTER 2

The Possibility

> A human being is a part of the whole called by us Universe, a part limited in time and space. He experiences himself, his thoughts and feelings as something separated from the rest, a kind of optical delusion of his consciousness. This delusion is a kind of prison for us, restricting us to our personal desires and to affection for a few persons nearest to us. Our task must be to free ourselves from this prison by widening our circle of compassion to embrace all living creatures and the whole of nature in its beauty.
>
> *Albert Einstein*

According to conventional wisdom, hierarchies of dominance are required to bring order to human societies because we humans are by nature an inherently unruly and self-centered species prone to violence and lawlessness. We therefore require the discipline of a ruling class and the competition of an unregulated market to impose order. By telling only part of the story, this conventional wisdom becomes a self-fulfilling prophecy, defining our beliefs about human possibility, the preferred architecture of our institutions, and the appropriate parameters of our political conversation.

Chapter 1 framed two narratives—one a dominator narrative of Empire, the other a partnership narrative of Earth Community. These stem from sharply contrasting assumptions about the human condition and our human nature. Although they appear to be in opposition, in truth they define possibilities. The dominator narrative defines the limited possibilities of the immature consciousness. The partnership narrative defines the far larger possibilities of the mature consciousness. Neither defines our destiny.

We are blocked from realizing our positive potential, not by our nature, but rather by the social dynamics of Empire. We now have the opportunity to liberate ourselves from its deadly addictions. The story of the journey of the individual human consciousness from newborn to elder is a tale rich with insight into the nature of and pathway to the realization of more mature human societies.

AWAKENING CONSCIOUSNESS

The first experience of individual human consciousness begins in the mother's womb, where we float effortlessly in undifferentiated oneness with the warm and comforting fluids of the amniotic sac. The well-rehearsed processes of the body's physical development take place at the cellular level far beyond the ability of our budding consciousness to monitor or influence. Our conscious mind experiences no demands, bears no responsibilities. There is no beginning, no ending. There is no "I" and no "not I." Just to be is sufficient.

Suddenly an involuntary traumatic passage unceremoniously thrusts us into a world of unfamiliar and generally discomforting sensations. Our first reaction is typically one of outrage—an elemental expression of grief at what has been lost. We now face the challenge of adapting to our new circumstance, ordering sounds into rhythms, sights into images, and learning to distinguish between them. We experience the blanket as scratchy and irritating or smooth and pleasant, but with no awareness that these sensations come from an external object. The feel of a soggy diaper evokes discomfort unassociated with any cause or object. Suckling on the mother's breast brings comfort, but with no sense of separation between breast and lip.

Our next important challenge is learning to differentiate the "I" from the "not I"—the first step in learning to relate to our world, and most importantly to other persons. Throughout our lives we will depend on our relations with other humans not only to meet our physical needs and secure ourselves from physical threat but also to obtain support in developing the cognitive, moral, and emotional capacities of our consciousness. Learning to relate to other humans is thus foundational both to ensuring our survival and to actualizing the possibilities of our humanity.

Below I set out a five-stage map of the developmental pathway from the least mature to the most mature orders of human consciousness. I draw from the work of many prominent students of human development, including Larry Daloz, Erik Erikson, Carol Gilligan, Stanley Greenspan, Robert Kegan, Lawrence Kohlberg, Abraham Maslow,

Rollo May, Sharon Parks, Jean Piaget, and Carl Rogers. The map provides a framework for understanding the central place of a politics of consciousness in the work of the Great Turning.[1]

First Order: Magical Consciousness

The Magical Consciousness of a young child of two to six years of age experiences the world as fluid and subject to the whims of magical beings both benevolent and malevolent. It has only a rudimentary ability to recognize causal relationships; the lines between fantasy and reality are blurred. These are the years of Santa Claus, the Tooth Fairy, and the Easter Bunny. The classic fairy tales of magical worlds populated by friendly and sinister spirits give expression to the rich fantasy life of these early years.

Because the Magical Consciousness is unable to distinguish between the enduring self and the emotional impulse of the moment, behavior is impulsive, immediate, and emotion driven. Limited in its ability to recognize the connection between the actions of the self and future consequences, the Magical Consciousness depends on external figures to make things magically right, experiences betrayal when trusted protectors fail to do so, and is unable to recognize the consequences of its own actions or accept responsibility for them.

Second Order: Imperial Consciousness

The transition from Magical to Imperial Consciousness normally occurs somewhere around the age of six or seven, when the child develops a greater capacity to distinguish between real and imagined events and discovers that many relationships are predictable and that actions have consequences. The discovery of order, regularity, and stability in the world is a significant advance that opens possibilities for controlling what once seemed a fluid and unpredictable reality.

The primary learning agenda at this stage is to develop an understanding of relationships and consequences and to explore one's ability to influence the world through one's actions. The residual of the Magical Consciousness is manifest in Imperial Consciousness through identification with superheroes, through which it plays out fantasies of possessing superhuman powers. As with the Magical Consciousness, the perspective of the Imperial Consciousness is primarily, if not exclusively, self-referential, even narcissistic.

During the transition to Imperial Consciousness, children learn that other people have other points of view and that getting what they want for themselves generally requires some form of reciprocity. To the understanding of the Imperial Consciousness this means an elemental "You scratch my back and I'll scratch yours" market exchange. The idea of justice is generally limited to a primitive and personally enforced "an eye for an eye and a tooth for a tooth" retributive justice. The ability to consciously constrain an emotional impulse—for example, anger—rather than to act it out physically, remains limited.

The Imperial Consciousness is able to acknowledge another person's point of view for purposes of calculating how best to get what one wants, but with little concept of loyalty, gratitude, and justice. Kegan cites the example of an adolescent offender who was asked by a judge, "How can you steal from people who trusted you so?" The youth replied in all sincerity, "But Your Honor, it's very hard to steal money from people if they don't trust you."[2]

Most children of the age of Imperial Consciousness can recite the Golden Rule without hesitation—"Do unto others as you would have them do unto you"—but find it difficult to experience the self in the feeling place of the other. When asked, "What should you do if someone walks up and hits you?" a characteristic answer, at least for boys, is "Hit 'em back. Do unto others like they do unto you."[3]

The Imperial Consciousness recognizes that conforming to the expectations of authority figures generally results in rewards. Good behavior is motivated more by a desire to please others in order to improve one's position, or to avoid being caught, than by a selfless concern for others' needs or an internalized ethical code. The Imperial Consciousness justifies bad behavior with the excuse "I didn't intend to hurt anyone" or "Everyone else is doing it."

Third Order: Socialized Consciousness

The transition from Imperial Consciousness to Socialized Consciousness normally begins around eleven or twelve. Coinciding with the onset of teenage rebellion against parental authority, it marks the transition to the internalization of the cultural norms of a larger reference group. It brings a growing emotional intelligence and a recognition of the extent to which personal security depends on the mutual loyalty of the members of one's group in a sometimes hostile world. The Socialized Consciousness defines itself by its relationships with others whose acceptance becomes a primary criterion for assessing self-worth.

The Socialized Consciousness brings an ability to see one's self through the eyes of another. In contrast to the Imperial Consciousness, which is able to take the view of others only to manipulate them in the service of one's own purposes, the Socialized Consciousness is capable of empathy, the ability to feel and care sufficiently about what another person is experiencing emotionally to subordinate one's own needs and desires to theirs. It also brings a recognition of group interests that transcend immediate self-interests.

The Socialized Consciousness brings a growing appreciation of the need for rules, laws, and properly constituted political and religious authority to maintain essential social and institutional order, and it internalizes a play-by-the-rules, law-and-order morality. In the eye of the Socialized Consciousness, fairness means a society that rewards those who work hard, leaves slackers to suffer their fate, and demands of wrongdoers that they pay their debt to society through fines, imprisonment, or execution. Not yet grasping the reality that complex system relationships might prevent whole classes of people from finding and holding jobs or staying on the right side of the law, the Socialized Consciousness views the concept of restorative justice as an invitation to break the rules with impunity.

The Socialized Consciousness constructs its identity through its primary reference groups, as defined by gender, age, race, ethnicity, religion, nationality, class, political party, occupation, employer, and perhaps a favored sports team. It is commonly militantly protective of its own group and prone to take any criticism of it as a serious affront. It internalizes and adheres to the culturally defined moral codes of the groups with which it identifies in an effort to avoid a sense of guilt or shame, but lacks the ability to subject those codes to critical examination. Because it is highly responsive to prevailing cultural norms and expectations, the Socialized Consciousness might also be called the Acculturated Consciousness. It is the consciousness of the Good Citizens, who have a "Small World" view of reality defined by their immediate reference group, play by the existing rules, and expect a decent life in return for themselves, their families, and their communities. They represent the swing vote that tips the balance toward either Empire or Earth Community, depending on the cultural frame.

Highly adaptive to the dominant cultural and institutional context, the Socialized Consciousness is the foundation of conventional good citizenship. On the downside, it is also susceptible to manipulation by advertisers, propagandists, and political demagogues, and it is prone to demand rights for the members of its own identity group that it is willing to deny others.

Fourth Order: Cultural Consciousness

Adulthood commonly brings encounters with people who have cultural perspectives and beliefs different from those of one's own identity groups. The initial reaction to such encounters is commonly a chauvinistic sense of cultural superiority and possibly an embrace of cultural absolutism: "The way of my people is the only right way."

If the Socialized Consciousness is sufficiently secure in its identity, however, it may come to recognize that culture is itself a social construct, that each culture has its own logic, that different cultural "truths" lead to different outcomes for individuals and society, and that cultural norms and expectations are subject to choice. This represents a profound step in the development of a true moral consciousness based on examined moral principles, and the beginnings of a capacity for cultural innovation.

The Cultural Consciousness recognizes the need for legal sanctions to secure the order and security of society from the predation of sociopaths who lack the moral maturity to avoid doing harm to others. Whereas the Imperial Consciousness is primarily concerned that the law protect and advance its own security and interests, the Cultural Consciousness is concerned with equal justice for all people, not just for oneself and those of one's own kind, and it works to repeal or revise unjust laws.

A Cultural Consciousness is rarely achieved before age thirty, and the majority of those who live in modern imperial societies never achieve it, partly because most corporations, political parties, churches, labor unions, and even educational institutions actively discourage it. Each of these institutions has its defining belief system to which it demands loyalty. Those who raise significant challenges are likely to be subjected to a loss of standing, if not outright rejection. But because those who achieve a Cultural Consciousness have the capacity to question the dysfunctional cultural premises of Empire, they are the essential engines of the cultural renewal and maturation that the Socialized Consciousness is inclined to suppress as threatening to the established social and moral order. Persons who have achieved a Cultural Consciousness have an "Inclusive World" view that sees the possibility of creating inclusive, life-affirming societies that work for all. As elaborated in chapter 4, such persons recognize culture as a social construct subject to change by conscious choice. Thus, we may call them Cultural Creatives, to use the terminology of Paul Ray and Sherry Anderson.[4]

Fifth Order: Spiritual Consciousness

The Spiritual Consciousness, the highest expression of what it means to be human, manifests the awakening to Creation as a complex, multidimensional, interconnected, continuously unfolding whole. It involves coming full circle back to the original sense of oneness of the womb experience, but with a richly nuanced appreciation for the complexity and grandeur of the whole of Creation as manifest in each person, animal, plant, and rock. The womb experience is wholly passive. Persons who have attained a Spiritual Consciousness have an evolving "Integral World" view and find meaning in serving as active partners or co-creators in Creation's evolutionary quest to actualize its possibilities. Call them Spiritual Creatives.

Spiritual Consciousness is the consciousness of the elder statesperson, teacher, tribal leader, or religious sage that supports an examined morality grounded in the universal principles of justice, love, and compassion common to the teachings of the most revered religious prophets. It approaches conflict, contradiction, and paradox not as problems to overcome, but as opportunities for deeper learning.

Like each of the previous transitions to a higher order of consciousness, the transition from Cultural Consciousness to Spiritual Consciousness is acquired by relating to diverse people and situations in search of an ever deeper understanding of life's possibilities. Each such encounter opens a window to a piece of reality previously hidden from the conscious mind. Eventually, what once appeared to be disconnected fragments of experience link together to awaken a profound sense of the spiritual unity of Creation.

Far from marking the end of the developmental process, the step to Spiritual Consciousness opens the way to new learning opportunities. As observed by psychologists John and Linda Friel, "The depth and breadth of an aged person's connectedness with creation is wondrous to behold, and it can only emerge if he is gradually willing to let go of his narcissism in stages all the way along life's path."[5]

The Socialized Consciousness is prone to characterize persons who have achieved a Spiritual Consciousness as lone contemplators disaffiliated from society, because they disavow special loyalty to any group or identity. That, however, is a misinterpretation. The Spiritual Consciousness simply transcends the exclusiveness of conventional group loyalties to embrace an identity that is inclusive of the whole and all its many elements. Thus, it extends outward to encompass a larger whole: the sense of duty and loyalty once reserved for members of one's immediate family, ethnic group, nationality, or religion now extends to the whole. To the Spiritual Consciousness, the satisfaction of living in creative service to the whole is its own reward.

Able to take a holistic view of social relationships, the Spiritual Consciousness rejects retributive justice as neither just nor pragmatic, because it leads to an endless cycle of revenge that fails to advance the well-being of either the individual or the society. The Spiritual Consciousness is focused instead on restorative justice that, to the extent possible, makes the victim whole and rehabilitates the wrongdoer while deterring both past and potential future wrongdoers from committing harmful acts. The Imperial or Socialized Consciousness sees this as coddling, or even siding with, the wrongdoer, as it lacks an inclusive systems perspective that allows it to think and act in terms of a larger concept: the well-being of the whole.

The Spiritual Consciousness joins the Cultural Consciousness in seeking to change unjust laws. It recognizes, however, that at times it must engage in acts of principled nonviolent civil disobedience both to avoid being complicit in the injustice and to call the injustice to public attention. It undertakes such acts with awareness of the potential legal consequences.

PSYCHOLOGY OF EMPIRE

In the work of the Great Turning, we face a paradox. One of the highest priorities of a mature society devoted to the partnership principles of Earth Community is to support every individual in negotiating the pathway to a fully mature consciousness. Creating a mature society, however, requires leadership by people of a mature consciousness.

This creates a difficulty. Cultures and institutions afflicted with the addictions of Empire throw up active barriers to the acquisition of a mature consciousness and favor leaders who act from an Imperial Consciousness. The Imperial Consciousness is a normal and essential stage in the developmental processes of children. In adults, however, it is sociopathic.

Adulthood and Magical Consciousness

In adults, Magical Consciousness is expressed in a fuzzy grasp of elemental causal relationships, fantasies of possessing supernatural powers, and faith in magical protectors to set things right. The adult operating from a Magical Consciousness lives in an "Other World" in denial of its responsibilities in this world. Primary examples are those economists who fantasize a world in which markets magically turn greed into a public good and those religious believers who point the finger of responsibility for earthly ills to a distant God and thus absolve themselves of responsibility for their complicit actions. In adults, the Magical Consciousness is most likely to be experienced as a subtext of the Imperial Consciousness.

Adulthood and Imperial Consciousness

The self-referential morality of the Imperial Consciousness can be quite jarring when encountered in an adult. Kegan offers the example of Roxanne, an inmate in a women's correctional institution who had a history of picking pockets, stealing welfare checks, and using other people's credit cards. When interviewed, she expressed the view that stealing was wrong except when necessary to meet her needs. When asked whether it would be fair for another person with similar needs to steal her checks, she replied that it would not be fair because she herself needed the money.[6] Members of the ruling class who think nothing of demanding millions in government subsidies, but excoriate the poor who accept government help exhibit this same self-referential double standard on a grand scale.

When an Imperial Consciousness manifests in adults, the self-referential morality leads to a division of the world into friends and enemies: "Those who are not for me are against me." Definitions of good and evil are similarly self-referential. Good is what serves my interests, and evil is what conflicts with my interests. The Imperial Consciousness has a "My World" view of most everything, assessing each situation with an eye to potential gains and losses for the self. These are the Power Seekers, who play up to those more powerful and exploit those less powerful—in colloquial language, they "kiss up and kick down."

Adult expressions of the Magical and Imperial orders of consciousness are generally far more complex than their childhood expressions. Although adults operating from these lower orders of consciousness may be incapable of ethical behavior based on empathic understanding, they may possess a highly developed intellect capable of formulating and executing complex political strategies. They are often accomplished liars skilled in crafting moral arguments attuned to the emotional and moral sensibilities of the persons whose loyalties they seek to manipulate. Unable to distinguish self-interest from collective interest, admit error, accept responsibility for the consequences of their actions, or feel guilt or remorse for harms caused, these individuals may be incapable of acknowledging even to themselves that they are engaged in deception. Truth becomes what they want it to be. Believing their own lies, they are able to lie with great sincerity.

Combine a highly developed cognitive intellect with a morally and emotionally challenged Imperial Consciousness, and the result is likely to be a skillful practitioner of the Machiavellian art of political manipulation. Such individuals may possess highly advanced abilities to plan, make deals, manipulate others, and strategize to achieve their goals, and to use dominator power to personal advantage. Furthermore, they may be highly skilled in developing elaborate arguments to justify self-interested acts as acts of self-sacrifice in the interest of a larger good, and will respond with self-righteous indignation to any suggestion that such claims are less than sincere.

Such persons are easily identified by their inability to acknowledge their mistakes, by their claims to righteous exemption from rules that apply to lesser mortals, and by their habitual scapegoating—projecting their own moral flaws onto perceived evil enemies to justify acting out their fear and anger as a righteous mission. The emotional drive for retribution may be so strong that questions of actual guilt or innocence are dismissed as irrelevant.

Shortly after the September 11, 2001, terrorist attack I happened to be seated on an airplane next to a senior executive of a major U.S. corporation. The United States had just launched the invasion of Afghanistan, and I shared with him my reservations about the war and its cost in innocent Afghan lives. He responded that in his opinion, since "they" had killed five thousand of our people (an early estimate later revised downward to three thousand) we, the United States, would not be even until we killed at least five thousand of their people.

I countered that most of the people we were killing in Afghanistan were innocent of any involvement in the attack. He replied that this was irrelevant, as the people killed in the attack on the World Trade Center were also innocents. I was stunned. This was an educated man in his fifties or sixties who held a position of considerable power and responsibility and yet lacked the moral maturity to recognize that retribution against innocents was as immoral as the original act of the terrorists and would lead to a pointless escalation of violence. It brought me face-to-face with a reality I had long denied.

In my earlier writing and speaking, I had held to the argument that the failures of our ruling institutions were the result of bad systems, not bad people. Yet a wave of exposés in 2002 and 2003 of pervasive corruption at the highest levels of corporate and governmental power suggested that many of our most powerful institutions are in the hands of ethically challenged human beings.

Moral Autism

For all the efforts of the corporate media to portray the scandals as the work of a few bad apples, it became clear that the corruption was on a grand scale and carried out by profoundly ethically challenged individuals. The responsible individuals did not necessarily intend to harm others. Rather, they appear to have been acting from the purely self-referential perspective common to young children. Catholic theologian Daniel Maguire refers to this pattern as *moral autism*.[7]

Like the young delinquent mentioned earlier, the adult operating from an Imperial Consciousness may have the social intelligence to recognize that it is easiest to steal from those who trust you, but lack the moral capacity to recognize that to do so constitutes a wrong in itself and destroys the fabric of trust essential to healthy social relationships. When such adults appear among the lower socioeconomic classes, the ruling establishment commonly identifies them as sociopaths and confines them to a prison or mental institution. By contrast, when they appear among the higher socioeconomic classes, the ruling establishment is prone to judge them especially suited for positions of leadership in the political and corporate institutions of imperial power. Persons of an Imperial Consciousness are also likely to be most highly motivated to endure the ruthless competition to achieve such positions of power. Products of the dominator cultures and institutions of Empire, the developmentally challenged become its servants.

PSYCHOLOGY OF EARTH COMMUNITY

In contrast to Imperial Consciousness, Cultural Consciousness and Spiritual Consciousness embody the human capacities for creative self-direction and choice within a framework of responsibility to and for the whole. These capacities are the foundation of positive cultural innovation, democracy, and the higher possibilities of our human nature. Potentially within the reach of each human, they are most likely to be achieved if intentionally cultivated by the individual and supported by the community. Chapter 4 points to evidence that the number of people operating from these higher orders of consciousness is growing rapidly in response to an intensification of cross-cultural communication, the great social movements of the twentieth century, and a growing awareness of the realities of an interdependent world.

Those who lead an examined life grounded in a mature worldview understand complexity, identify with the well-being of the whole, have no interest in acquiring arbitrary power, and are unlikely to succumb to the manipulations of advertisers, propagandists, and demagogues. They encompass the whole within a greatly enlarged circle of individual identity and see opportunities for the peaceful resolution of conflict and advancement of the common good that are invisible to those of a Magical or Imperial Consciousness. At their best, they are the visionaries and wisdom keepers of Earth Community and mature democratic citizenship.

Persons acting from the different orders of consciousness understand the nature and meaning of democracy quite differently. The Imperial Consciousness views democratic participation as a contest for power to advance one's personal interests and even as an opportunity to impose one's own values and preferences on others. The Socialized Consciousness is likely to approach democratic participation rather like voting in a popularity contest or rooting for the home team at a sporting event. Neither provides a sound basis for mature self-governance. By contrast, the Cultural or Spiritual Consciousness approaches the practice of democracy as a process of collective problem solving aimed at enhancing the well-being and potential of all. These two orders of consciousness may be referred to jointly as the *democratic orders of consciousness.*

CULTURAL POLITICS

The simple model of the five orders of consciousness defines a range of possibilities that provide a framework for understanding the cultural politics of the Great Turning. Magical and Imperial Consciousness support the dominator cultures of Empire. Cultural and Spiritual Consciousness support the partnership cultures of Earth Community. Whichever prevails as the primary culture of the global society will determine what the future developmental direction of the human species will be and thereby whether future generations will look back on our time as the Great Unraveling or the Great Turning.

Competing for the Swing Vote

Socialized Consciousness, which is the consciousness of most American adults, adapts to the values and social roles of the prevailing culture. It represents the swing voters, and it is pivotal to the cultural politics of the Great Turning because it can adapt to either the dominator culture of Empire or the partnership culture of Earth Community. (See figure 2.1.)

To the extent that the culture of Empire prevails, the Socialized Consciousness will lean politically in favor of the agenda of Empire. To the extent that the culture of Earth Community prevails, it will lean politically in favor of the agenda of Earth Community. In the contest for the loyalty of the swing voters, each side has its natural advantage.

Empire's Advantage

Empire's well-established cultural and institutional hegemony gives it a decided advantage. Empire also enjoys another important advantage: anyone who has reached the level of the Socialized Consciousness has experienced the world through the lens of the Imperial Consciousness and thus is familiar with its organizing principles. By contrast, only those who have moved beyond the Socialized Consciousness to a Cultural or Spiritual Consciousness can understand fully the deeply democratic possibilities of Earth Community. Empire also enjoys an advantage in

Fifth Order: Spiritual Consciousness
Spiritual Creatives live in a complex, evolving **Integral World,** which they engage as evolutionary co-creators.

Fourth Order: Cultural Consciousness
Cultural Creatives live in an **Inclusive World** and see the possibility of creating inclusive, life-affirming societies that work for all.

Third Order: Socialized Consicousness
Good Citizens live in a **Small World,** play by the rules of their identity group, expect a fair reward, and comprise the swing voters.

Second Order: Imperial Consciousness
Power Seekers live in **My World,** play up to the powerful, and exploit the oppressed.

First Order: Magical Consciousness
Fantasizers live in an **Other World** and place their faith in magical protectors.

Culture of Earth Community

Culture of Empire

Figure 2.1: Culture and consciousness.

the inclination of adults of an Imperial Consciousness to be attracted to the competitive struggle for positions of institutional power from which they can dominate others—thus reproducing the dynamics of Empire.

Finally, the uncertainties of our time, including job insecurity, severe weather events, and terrorist threats, favor Empire. Fear causes a regression to a more primitive consciousness and increases susceptibility to manipulation by advertisers and demagogues who seem instinctively to speak to our fears and insecurities. "Buy my product and it will bring you beauty and love." "Elect me and I will make you prosperous and protect you from evil enemies." "Believe in my God and he will grant you salvation for your sins and eternal bliss in the afterlife." "Trust in the magic of the unregulated market to convert your unrestrained greed and self-indulgence into a better life for all." Each of these refrains plays to the fears and fantasies familiar to the frightened child that resides in each of us.

The culture and institutions of Empire feed on, and reward, psychological immaturity and dysfunction and reproduce it from generation to generation. In so doing they stifle healthy human development and the creative capacity required to adapt to rapidly changing circumstances. This has been a chronic condition of the dominant human societies for five thousand years and now threatens the very survival of the species. Taking the step to maturity requires that we accept individual and collective responsibility for the shadow side of our human nature and set about to create a mutual support system, rather like a global Alcoholics Anonymous meeting that provides the emotional support required to move beyond our psychological dependence on domination and violence.

Earth Community's Advantage

Although Empire would seem to have an insurmountable advantage, four circumstances give the ultimate advantage to the possibilities of Earth Community. First, the drive to realize the fullness of our humanity is inherent in our nature. Second, a substantial majority of people have achieved a Socialized Consciousness or beyond and are therefore capable of understanding the concept of a public good that transcends narrowly defined individual interests and requires cooperation to achieve. Third, as elaborated in chapter 3, we face ecological and social imperatives distinctive to this moment in the human experience to embrace the higher potentials of our nature. Fourth, as elaborated in chapter 4, breakthroughs in global communication and in our understanding of the interdependent nature of our relationship to one another and the planet are supporting the awakening of the higher orders of consciousness at an unprecedented rate. Although persons of a mature consciousness are generally averse to the competitive struggle for dominator power, they are strongly attracted to leadership roles in social movements engaged in challenging Empire's dominion.

Perhaps the best indicator that the values of Earth Community ultimately hold the edge is the behavior of contemporary demagogues. Those who seek to align the electorate behind imperial agendas favoring elite power and privilege find they must resort to stealth tactics that hide their true aims and values. To gain political support they must profess a commitment to advancing the Earth Community values of care for children, family, community, justice, democracy, and environmental stewardship. Like the young man who observed that it is easiest to steal from people who trust you, they prey on the trust that people are naturally inclined to place in their leaders. Such deceptions may work for a time, but eventually trust persistently betrayed becomes trust denied.

Contrary to those who maintain that we humans are destined to lives of violence and greed, our nature embodies a wide range of potential. The possible levels of achievement range from the criminal sociopath who is unable to consider any need or interest other than his own to the profound social and spiritual sensibility and vision of a Jesus, Gandhi, Buddha, or Martin Luther King Jr.

At birth, we humans do not have the physical capabilities normal for an adult. Nor do we have the consciousness of an adult. The journey by which the human individual acquires the higher-order moral and emotional maturity required for responsible adult function is one of life's most extraordinary adventures. As we saw in the case of the Hacienda Santa Teresa, success depends in substantial measure on a supportive setting and the guidance of mentors who themselves possess a mature consciousness.

Five orders of human consciousness define the path to emotional and moral maturity. The lower orders of Magical and Imperial Consciousness produce a culture of Empire. The higher orders of Cultural and Spiritual Consciousness produce a culture of Earth Community. The Socialized Consciousness, from which the majority of people operate, is capable of adapting to the values and expectations of either Empire or Earth Community, depending on which culture prevails. Dramatic changes in the human context since the mid-twentieth century have created the imperative and the possibility for the human species to make a conscious collective choice for a culture of Earth Community.

CHAPTER 3

The Imperative

Since Auschwitz we know what man is capable of. And since Hiroshima we know what is at stake.[1]

Viktor E. Frankl

This troubled planet is a place of the most violent contrasts. Those that receive the rewards are totally separated from those who shoulder the burdens. It is not a wise leadership.[2]

Spock, "The Cloud Minders," Star Trek

The "Cloud Minders" episode of the original science fiction television series *Star Trek* takes place on the planet Ardana. The planet's rulers live in peaceful splendor in the beautiful city of Stratos suspended on a platform high in space. Far removed from the planet's desolate surface, they are also far removed from the misery and violence endured by the Troglytes, who toil under slavelike conditions in the planet's mines below to earn the interplanetary exchange credits used to import the luxuries that the Stratos rulers enjoy. The rulers consider their privilege to be wholly fitting given their perception that it is their superior intelligence, cultural refinement, and moral sensibility that set them apart from the Troglytes below.

This transparent political allegory speaks to the stark division between the elite rulers of planet Earth who live in gated mansions, work in tall office towers, and fly by private jet to meetings and luxury vacation homes and those whose toil makes their luxuries possible. To legitimate the injustice of the imperial system, the Stratos dwellers of our planet Earth construct stories that praise their personal virtues and glorify the greatness of their rule and of the institutions that place them beyond accountability to ordinary mortals. It is virtually impossible for rulers to rule wisely when they are so far removed from the reality of the lives of those who shoulder the burdens of their decisions.

The consequences can be deadly, especially when the isolation of the rulers prevents them from recognizing and responding to rapid and dramatic changes that create an imperative for adaptation to new human realities. That is our present human circumstance. Our profligate consumption is destroying the living systems of the planet on which our lives depend. Modern weaponry has turned war into an instrument of self-destruction.

Far removed from the realities of the rapidly changing human context, conditioned by the beliefs of imperial culture, and constrained by the imperatives of imperial institutions, those who rule from the clouds attribute the growing threat to life, civilization, and the existing institutions of social order to external enemies and to those who question established authority. In deep denial of the truth that the root source of the problem traces to the institutions of Empire that secure their privilege, they respond as imperial rulers have for five thousand years: by seeking to secure and expand their own power they thereby hasten the impending collapse.

The imperatives of this distinctive moment in the human experience have been long in coming. The earliest humans, *Homo habilis*, appeared on the planet some 2.6 million years ago. Living as one with the animals of plain and forest, this physically unimpressive species exhibited little of the capacity for choice and self-reflection that would manifest in future generations. Our early ancestors learned to cultivate and use their capacities in a slow but steadily accelerating progression that set us ever further apart from the other species with which we share the planet.

During the twentieth century, the speed at which we humans acquired new technological powers to reshape our relationship to one another and the planet accelerated to a blur, arguably exceeding the sum of the technological advances of the previous twenty-six thousand centuries. Within the space of the last hundred years alone, we have reached out to the planets, looked back through time to the origins of the universe, and delved into the deepest mysteries of subatomic particles and genetic codes to acquire seemingly godlike powers of destruction and creation. We have not, however, used these powers wisely—in large measure because those to whom we yield the power to lead continue to live and rule from the clouds.

This chapter deals with the imperative born of massive institutional failure. The following chapter will address the opportunity.

A PLANET UNDER CRIPPLING STRESS

Somewhere around 1980, we humans crossed an evolutionary threshold: the burden we place on the life support systems of the planet passed beyond the sustainable limit. The figures are sobering. Just since 1950, in barely more than fifty years, the global human population more than doubled from 2.6 billion persons in 1950 to 6.4 billion in 2005. The value of the global economic output increased from $6.7 trillion in 1950 to $48 trillion in 2002, as measured in constant U.S. dollars.[3] The number of motor vehicles is ten times what it was in 1950.[4] Fossil fuel use is five times what it was, and global use of freshwater has tripled.[5] Spending on advertising aimed primarily at getting the 1.7 billion people—27 percent of humanity—who currently enjoy material affluence to consume even more goods and services was nearly ten times greater in 2002 than in 1950.[6]

By 2002, humans were consuming food, materials, and energy at a rate of about 1.2 Earth-equivalent planets.[7] The difference between human consumption and the regenerative capacity of Earth is made up by depleting the natural capital of the planet—both nonrenewable capital, like minerals and fossil fuels, and renewable capital like forests, fisheries, soil, water, and climatic systems. The consequence is to extract a temporary and unsustainable subsidy from Earth to support current consumption at the expense of our children and their children for generations to come.

The World Wildlife Fund regularly publishes a Living Planet Index that tracks the health of the world's forest, freshwater, ocean, and coastal ecosystems over time. This index declined by 37 percent over the thirty-year period from 1970 to 2000. The index is unlikely to reach zero—a dead planet—because the planet will surely rid itself of the offending species long before this occurs.[8]

About 420 million people now live in countries that depend on imported food because they lack sufficient farmland per capita to feed their people. By 2025, this number could exceed 1 billion as population grows and the amount and quality of cropland decline. More than a half billion people now live in regions prone to chronic drought. This number is expected to grow to as high as 3.4 billion by 2025.[9]

A combination of ecosystem disruption, malnutrition, a lack of access to clean water, and the rapid movement of people and goods across ecological boundaries has spread devastating new diseases such as HIV/AIDS with unprecedented speed. Diseases like malaria and tuberculosis, once thought to be all but eradicated, are reasserting themselves in more virulent forms. Climatic disruptions and the imminent end to the ready availability of cheaply extracted oil that has made many of our contemporary human excesses possible will accelerate the crisis and constrain our human capacity to address it.

Climate Disruption

The scientific consensus that climate change is real and is in substantial measure caused by human activity grows each year as the evidence becomes ever more compelling. The average global surface temperature increased by 0.6 degrees centigrade over the twentieth century, with accelerating increases projected for the twenty-first century.[10] The warming is greatest in the Northern Hemisphere, particularly in the Arctic region, where the polar ice cap has thinned by 46 percent over twenty years and may begin melting entirely in the summer months as early as 2020. The ocean thermals in the Atlantic that drive the Gulf Stream that warms Europe have substantially weakened, creating concern that it may slow or stop entirely—with devastating consequences for European nations and particularly European agriculture.[11]

Even small increases in temperature can have major climatic effects, as demonstrated by a steady increase over the past five decades in severe weather events such as major hurricanes, floods, and droughts. Globally there were only thirteen severe events in the 1950s. By comparison, seventy-two such events occurred during the first nine years of the 1990s. The cost of the damage caused has risen from roughly US$3 billion annually in the 1950s to $40 billion annually in the 1990s.[12] Hurricanes Katrina and Rita, which ravaged the Gulf Coast of the United States and Mexico in 2005, are only a foretaste of what is to come.

Agricultural disruption and major population displacements are now imminent because of climatic change and a resulting rise in the sea level. A study commissioned by the U.S. Pentagon warns that global warming during the twenty-first century could "result in a significant drop in the human carrying capacity of Earth's environment... [and] potentially de-stabilize the geo-political environment, leading to skirmishes, battles, and even war due to resource constraints.... Disruption and conflict will be endemic features of life."[13]

The End of Oil

A sharp rise in oil prices in 2004 and 2005, coupled with revelations that Shell and other oil companies were systematically overestimating their proven petroleum reserves, spurred a lively discussion of when global oil production will peak and begin an inexorable decline in the face of growing demand and rising extraction costs. Referred to as "peak oil," this event is predicted to send energy prices skyrocketing and result in massive economic dislocation as the cheap oil subsidy that fueled much of the economic expansion of the past hundred years is withdrawn.

According to *Fortune*, the most optimistic estimates from credible sources place peak oil as much as thirty-five years in the future. Other credible experts suggest that 2005 may have been the fateful year. Meanwhile China has gone from having virtually no private automobiles in 1980 to having a projected 24 million in 2005, with anticipated exponential growth for the foreseeable future.[14] In 2004, China surpassed Japan as the world's second-largest consumer of oil.[15] The United States, of course, is the number one oil consumer. As *Fortune* correctly notes, it really does not matter whether peak oil has already occurred or will not be encountered for another thirty-five years.[16] Reconfiguring the world's economy to move beyond dependence on petroleum and reverse the buildup of greenhouse gases must be an essential and immediate priority.

If we humans do not choose to act on our own, Earth is poised to make the choice for us by forcing the mother of all market corrections. It will be a traumatic lesson in the market principle that subsidies cause markets to misallocate resources, the systems principle that infinite growth cannot be sustained in a finite system, and the cybernetic principle that failure to take timely action to restore system equilibrium results in overshoot and collapse.[17] In everyday language, we humans have used cheap oil subsidies to create economies and lifestyles that depend on the unsustainable consumption of Earth's resources, our consumption already exceeds sustainable limits by a substantial margin, and if we do not take immediate corrective action, economic collapse is imminent.

By the calculations of the Living Planet Index, we humans have been in ecological overshoot since roughly 1970. In fact, the process began nearly a hundred years earlier, when the modern transformation of human economies to petroleum dependence began in earnest. The intervening years have been devoted to building an infrastructure dependent on cheap oil while at the same time accelerating the depletion of Earth's accessible petroleum reserves and the release of carbon dioxide and other greenhouse gases into the atmosphere.

The twentieth century has been Empire's most profligate period of excess. We are poised to pay a terrible price. Slowly awakening from the stupor of petroleum intoxication, the raging headache of humanity's hangover is starting to set in. We humans must now deal not only with the five-thousand-year legacy of Empire but also with the consequences of imperial excess that cheap oil made possible. The longer we delay abandoning the way of Empire for the way of Earth Community, the more devastating the collapse will be and the greater the price we all will pay.

REALITY ATTACK

The twentieth century was the century of oil. Cheap to extract and available in seemingly inexhaustible supply, we treated petroleum and natural gas as free resources and priced them primarily by the costs of extraction, processing, and delivery. We shrugged off the environmental costs of releasing CO_2 and other greenhouse gases into the atmosphere and ignored the fact that within the scale of human time oil and gas are finite and nonrenewable resources.

The forms of economic development that followed World War II, from the Green Revolution to export-oriented industrial policies, suburbanization, and automobile-dependent transportation systems, in many respects constituted a drive to convert the world to dependence on petroleum and natural gas. By 2001 world oil consumption was 7.5 times as great as its 1950 level. Consumption of natural gas, nearly 24 percent of current world energy use, increased to 12.9 times its 1950 level.[18]

Earth creates the real wealth on which human life and well-being depend. We humans convert it to our use and consume it. During the twentieth century, we humans perfected powerful technologies to accelerate the rate of conversion by several orders of magnitude. We thought we had mastered the secrets to creating wealth without limit. In truth, we were not accelerating the creation of wealth so much as we were accelerating its consumption by drawing down the natural wealth and living capital of the planet. We similarly failed to recognize that the profligate lifestyles of the world's consumer class that we had taken to be a measure of our economic and technological genius were unsustainable and more accurately represented a measure of our capacity for shortsighted self-delusion. We are now on the threshold of a serious reality attack.

Journalist James Howard Kunstler spells out the details in *The Long Emergency*.[19] Virtually every feature of modern life now turns on the availability of cheap oil, including automobiles, computers, synthetic fibers, plastics, construction and manufacturing processes, central heating and air conditioning, air travel, industrial agriculture, international trade, suburban living, and modern warfare. Without oil, much of the capital infrastructure underlying modern life becomes an unusable asset, including the infrastructure of suburbia, the global trading system, and the industrial food production, processing, and distribution system.[20]

Dislocations caused by climate change and the disruptions from terrorist attacks by desperate people will greatly exacerbate the consequences of withdrawal of the oil subsidy. Economic incentives will shift dramatically in favor of downscaling and localization, shifting the focus from mobility to making a life in the place where one is. Business models based on twelve-thousand-mile supply lines will become increasingly expensive, giving the advantage to a more energy-efficient, smaller-scale local production of food and basic necessities.[21] The advantage will go to compact, self-reliant communities that bring people close to their places of work, commerce, and recreation; rely on wind, solar, and mini-hydro as their primary energy sources; and devote arable lands to growing food and fiber using low-input farming methods.

By any measure it will not be an easy transition. The adjustment can play out in the mode of Empire, as a violent, self-destructive, last-man-standing competition for individual advantage. Or it can play out in the mode of Earth Community, as a cooperative effort to rebuild community; to learn the arts of sufficiency, sharing, and peaceful conflict resolution; and to marshal our human creativity to grow the generative potential of the whole. The process depends on whether we find the courage and vision to embrace the transition as a moment of opportunity.

Too far removed from reality to recognize the stresses eroding the foundations of the societies they rule, the Cloud Minders of planet Earth have responded in classic imperial mode. They have sought to deflect attention away from tensions created by real security threats by declaring war on real or imagined enemies—apparently unmindful that changing human circumstances have made war itself a futile and irrational act of self-destruction.

WARS OF SELF-DESTRUCTION

The military battles of the Roman Empire were fought with swords, spears, and arrows. Our wars are fought with bombers, tanks, missiles, cluster bombs, land mines, nuclear bombs, high explosives, lasers, computers, and munitions tipped with depleted uranium. The increased killing efficiency of the individual warrior made the twentieth century the bloodiest in human history. As the killing efficiency of modern weapons continues to increase, they produce ever more devastating consequences not only for those they target, but as well for those who deploy them.

Weapons of Self-Destruction

The World Health Organization estimates that 72 million people died during the twentieth century from war and another 52 million from genocide. Other estimates place the combined total as high as 203 million.[22] For every person killed another three were wounded—which in many instances means they were maimed for life.[23] Millions more escaped serious physical injury but suffered permanent mental disabilities. Whole cities were reduced to rubble, economies were disrupted, priceless cultural artifacts were destroyed, millions were rendered homeless, and the wealth of Earth was consumed to destroy life rather than to nurture it. Worst of all, some modern weapons go on killing long after hostilities have ceased and render uninhabitable vast areas of a crowded world.

A buried mine can remain active for more than fifty years. The United Nations estimated in 1996 that more than 110 million active mines lie in wait for hapless victims in seventy countries, and that they kill or maim twenty-four thousand people every year—mostly civilians and often children.[24] Depleted uranium, which is used to increase the power of advanced munitions to penetrate armor, vaporizes into a fine powder on impact to slowly kill and maim both friend and foe, deform the children they sire and bear, and render vast land areas permanently unfit for habitation.[25] A 1996 United Nations resolution classified depleted-uranium ammunition as an illegal weapon of mass destruction. The United States and other nations continue to use it in large quantities.

Of the 696,778 U.S. personnel who served in the Persian Gulf during the 1991 Iraq war, only 760 were killed or wounded in action or as a result of accidents. By May 2002, the U.S. Veterans Administration had classified 168,011 persons who served in the Gulf during 1991 as "disabled veterans" due to combat-related injuries or illnesses and reported that another 8,306 had died from service-related causes. This brought the total casualty rate from the first Gulf War to a staggering 25.4 percent—and the numbers continue to grow. Former army colonel Doug

Rokke, who was in charge of the military's environmental cleanup following that war, attributes the majority of these casualties to exposure to depleted uranium, as do other experts. Pentagon spokespersons deny the charge. Whatever the actual cause, the cost to U.S. military personnel was horrific, to say nothing of the cost to Iraqi civilians who live in the contaminated area.[26]

The harm to the victors is not solely physical. When a nation sends its children off to war, it first sends them to boot camp not only to learn the arts of death but also to break down their natural moral resistance to killing other humans. Those who survive the horrors of the battlefield return to their families and communities trained and practiced in settling disputes by violent means and with minds filled with images of death. A study of soldiers returning from combat in the second Gulf War estimated that one in six suffered from major depression, generalized anxiety, or posttraumatic stress disorder.[27] Big weapons in a small world have made the act of war a strategy of mass self-destruction.

Nuclear Bombs versus Box Cutters

The most powerful military forces are unable to prevail over small but committed terrorist networks and popular resistance movements in an age of easy access to high explosives, automatic firearms, shoulder-fired rockets, nuclear materials, deadly biological agents, cell phones, instant messaging, and the Internet. Such weapons give resistance movements the means to make sustained occupation by the military forces of a foreign nation virtually impossible and place the invading army's homeland at significant risk. Call the armed resisters terrorists, guerrillas, freedom fighters, or minutemen, the mechanized military machinery of Empire is useless against a determined population adept in the ways of terrorism and guerrilla warfare. France faced this reality in Algeria and Vietnam. The Soviet Union faced it in Afghanistan, and Russia faced it subsequently in Chechnya.

The United States has the capability to liquidate whole nations, but its terrifying firepower is of little use in ferreting out clandestine international terrorist networks, gaining the willing submission of the peoples of occupied nations, or securing civilian populations against attacks by committed terrorists. Economic historian Immanuel Wallerstein points out that the U.S. military fought three serious wars between 1945 and 2002: Korea, Vietnam, and the first Gulf War. It fought to a draw in

Korea and the Gulf and was defeated in Vietnam. None of the three opponents was close to being a credible world-class military power.[28] Failing to learn the evident lessons of this experience, the United States was in
2005 bogged down in enormously costly, unwinnable wars in Afghanistan and Iraq.

Conventional armies are organized, trained, and equipped to control
territory. Since terrorist networks are everywhere and nowhere, the
control of territory is not at issue. Responding to terrorist attacks with
conventional military force can take a devastating toll in lives and property, but as a response to terrorism, it is actively counterproductive. The
only way to defeat terrorism is to eliminate the conditions that motivate it.

The contemporary reality of warfare presents a strange paradox. Although modern technology has given the world's ruling elites the power
to make the planet unlivable, it has also stripped them of their capacity
to impose their will on subject people by armed force.

Clueless rulers order searches for weapons of mass destruction
(WMD) in Iraq and elsewhere, while ignoring the WMDs in our own
midst. Jet airliners, chemical plants, oil refineries, nuclear facilities, power
grids, gas pipelines, and municipal water systems are easily turned into
instruments of death and disruption by a committed terrorist of modest means, as the September 11, 2001, attack on the United States so
graphically demonstrated. Metaphorically speaking, in a contest between nuclear weapons and box cutters, the box cutters hold the strategic
advantage.

As argued by geopolitical analyst Jonathan Schell, we now live in an
unconquerable world.[29] Unless we learn to live in peace by eliminating
the causes of violence, we will live in perpetual fear and insecurity.
Rather than address the root causes of the violence, however, the rulers
of planet Earth respond by augmenting their security forces and attempting to lift their city in the clouds to a higher orbit further removed
from the spreading devastation on the planet's surface.

GOING TO A HIGHER ORBIT

Had the benefits of the sixfold increase in global economic output
achieved since 1950 been equitably shared among the world's people,
poverty would now be history, democracy would be secure, and war

would be but a distant memory. Driven by the imperatives of dominator power, however, the institutions of Empire allocated more than 80 percent of the benefit of this extraordinary growth to the most fortunate 20 percent of the world's people.

Growing Gap

In the 1990s, per capita income fell in fifty-four of the world's poorest countries; already high poverty rates increased in thirty-seven of the sixty-seven reporting countries. More than 1.2 billion people now struggle to survive on less than $1 a day. Some 2.8 billion, nearly half the world's population, survive on less than $2 per day.[30]

At the other end of the scale, the number of billionaires worldwide swelled from 274 in 1991 to 691 in 2005, with a combined net worth of $2.2 trillion.[31] It is estimated that 1.7 billion people—27 percent of humanity—currently enjoy the material affluence of the consumer society.[32] The demands of the existing consumer class continue to surge as its tastes turn to ever larger cars and homes. It would take at least an additional three to four planets to support the excluded populations of the world at the level of consumption now prevailing in Europe. The United Nations projects that the world population will continue to grow from the current 6.4 billion to 8.9 billion in 2050,[33] requiring the resources of yet another one to two planets to support everyone at the current European standard. The human species is quite literally consuming the future of its children, consigning billions of people to lives of desperation, and calling the survival of our species into question.

It is a grim calculus. The response of the orbiting Stratos dwellers is to further shift the tax burden from the investor class to the working class, increase downward pressure on wages, ease restraints on financial speculation and the extraction of monopoly profits, and free corporations from bearing the social and environmental costs of their actions. Those who object are condemned as advocates of class warfare and instructed to focus on bringing the bottom up by giving greater freedom to the top to create new wealth, rather than on bringing the top down.

The persistent claim of the ruling Cloud Minders that raising the top will ultimately bring up the bottom by expanding the total pool of wealth is a cruel deception. Justice and sustainability are impossible in an inherently unjust and unsustainable system.

Grand Illusion

The key to the deception is money. To understand how it works, it is necessary to be clear on the distinction between real wealth and financial wealth.

Real wealth consists of those things that have actual utilitarian or artistic value: food, land, energy, knowledge, technology, forests, beauty, and much else. The natural systems of the planet are the foundation of all real wealth, for we depend on them for our very lives. Without these natural systems, none of the other forms of wealth, including human labor and technology, can exist.

Money by contrast has no intrinsic utilitarian or artistic value. It is only a number on a piece of paper or an electronic trace in a computer file. It is an accounting chit that has value only because by social convention people are willing to accept it in exchange for things of real value. Money, however, bestows enormous power and advantage on those with the power to create and allocate it in societies in which access to most everything of real value requires money.

The Cloud Minders have enjoyed rapid growth in their financial assets throughout the period of deepening environmental decline, thus bestowing on them claims against a growing portion of the real wealth of planet and society, and creating an illusion that we are all growing richer, when the opposite is true. Take just one key indicator: the combined market capitalization—financial asset value—of the shares traded in the world's major share markets grew from $0.8 trillion in 1977 to $22.6 trillion in 2003.[34] This represents an enormous increase in the buying power of the ruling class relative to the rest of the society. It creates an illusion that economic policies are increasing the real wealth of society, when in fact they are depleting it.

Bear in mind that in the United States less than 50 percent of households own shares of stock in any form. The wealthiest 1 percent of households own 42.1 percent of the value of all stock shares, more than the total for the entire bottom 95 percent of households.[35] Although specific figures are not available, it is a safe estimate that far less than 1 percent of households globally have consequential stock holdings.

Unfortunately, most people miss the true implications of this inequality because we are in the habit of thinking of money as wealth. Indeed, although the distinction between money and real wealth is essential to understanding the allocation of power in society, the language of finance provides no easy way of expressing it. The terms *capital, assets, resources, wealth,* refer equally to financial wealth and real wealth.

If people understood the difference, they would know that when a financial pundit joyfully announces that a rising stock market is "creating wealth," this means the richest households are increasing their claims over what remains of the real wealth of the rest of us. We might then feel less inclined to share in the pundit's exuberance.

Living High on Borrowed Money

Entranced by the bubble economy of the 1990s, delusional pundits of the Cloud Minder class declared an end to the laws of economic gravity. By their reckoning, the business cycle had become a relic of the ancient past, U.S. trade and financial imbalances with the rest of the world no longer mattered, and environmental limits had been transcended. Realists who expressed concern about a financial bubble were dismissed as know-nothing pessimists, out of touch with the miracles wrought by the new information economy. The real value added, so the delusional argued, was in finance, marketing, entertainment, information technology, and intellectual property rights. They concluded that the most profitable economic strategy was to import finished products produced by cheap nonunion labor in the poorest countries rather than to import raw materials for domestic fabrication by workers who expect a family wage.

The U.S. trade deficit, which in 2004 was an annual $665 billion and growing, was covered by borrowing from foreigners at the rate of $2.6 billion every business day.[36] This accelerated a precipitous decline in the U.S. dollar, starting at the beginning of 2002. By the end of 2004, the dollar had lost roughly a third of its value.[37] In his 2002 European bestseller *After the Empire,* French demographer Emmanuel Todd characterizes the United States as "a sort of black hole—absorbing merchandise and capital but incapable of furnishing the same goods in return."[38]

As the wave of corporate scandals in the opening years of the twenty-first century revealed, the supposed U.S. economic miracle of the 1990s was mostly a stock bubble built on accounting fraud and unfounded expectations. The growing U.S. trade deficit demonstrated that an open trading system managed by corporations to maximize short-term profits results in dangerously unstable imbalances in the global system. Far from being concerned, however, the Cloud Minders stepped up their efforts to restore the bubble and accelerate the export of jobs and the related manufacturing capacities. Soon they were also exporting technological capacities, including those in advanced research and development—fueling a continuing precipitous increase in the U.S. trade deficit and international debt as we become ever more dependent on foreign factories, workers, and technology.

In the mid-1990s, the United States still produced 90 percent of what it consumed. By the end of 2004 it produced only 75 percent,[39] and the decline was accelerating.[40] U.S. exports of computer hardware fell from $45 billion in 2000 to $28 billion in 2004. U.S. companies were investing very little in new capacity domestically and the ranks of U.S. engineers were thinning.[41] Young Americans planning their careers were quick to get the message. Reversing a previous growth trend, applications to U.S. computer science and software engineering bachelor's degree programs fell by as much as 30 percent in two years. India and China now lead the United States in computer science graduates.[42]

U.S. export surpluses are now mostly in commodities, such as oil seeds, grains, iron, wood pulp, scrap paper, and raw animal hides. The top U.S. import from China is computer components. China's top import from the United States is soybeans.[43] The U.S. trade profile is increasingly that of a third-world country that exports commodities and imports finished goods.[44]

In the economic vision of the myopic U.S. Cloud Minders, the proper U.S. role in the global economy is to specialize in consuming the products and technologies produced by sweatshop labor in other countries and paid for with borrowed money, thereby keeping U.S. profits and unemployment high and wages low, while passing the bill to future generations. To paraphrase the late economist Kenneth Boulding, anyone who thinks this a winning long-term economic strategy is either a lunatic or a neoliberal economist.

The Perfect Economic Storm

The gathering clouds of a perfect economic storm have the potential to severely disrupt the corporate global economy and force a restructuring in favor of local production and self-reliance. Four conditions combine to produce an unprecedented threat to the status quo.

1. The imminent encounter with the point at which oil production peaks and goes into inexorable decline will eliminate the energy

subsidies on which much of the capital infrastructure of the corporate global economy depends.

2. Severe weather events and climatic changes associated with global warming will disrupt food production and global supply chains.

3. A collapse in the international exchange value of the U.S. dollar will force the United States to restructure its economy to live within its means; those countries that have built economies geared to exporting to U.S. markets will need to redirect their attention to producing for their own domestic markets.

4. The changing terms of warfare will bring an end to the ability of militarily powerful nations to seize with impunity the resources of weaker nations.

These conditions will shift the economic incentives from favoring global supply lines to favoring local production and self-reliance. The adjustments will be made all the more difficult by a growing scarcity of freshwater, declining forests and fisheries, the paving over of arable land, soil loss, and declining soil fertility, all combined with continued population growth. The transition will be particularly difficult for nations like the United States that have become accustomed to living far beyond their own means and to depending on foreign labor, resources, and credit.

How we humans choose to respond to these changing circumstances will determine whether the situation degenerates into persistent wars for the last of Earth's bounty or brings forth a new era of cooperation based on an ethic of equitable sharing to meet the needs of all. When economic collapse hit the people of Argentina at the end of 2001, they rallied as a community to make the latter choice. It is an inspiring story well told in the video documentaries *Argentina: Hope in Hard Times* and *The Take*.[45]

History suggests that the ruling Cloud Minders are too captive to the addictions of Empire to respond in any way other than their characteristic pattern of competing for control of the last remains of the planet's resources. Their delusions are well summed up in the 2005 book by Peter Humber, of the Manhattan Institute, and Mark Mills, of Digital Power Capital, titled *The Bottomless Well: The Twilight of Fuel, the Virtue of Waste, and Why We Will Never Run Out of Energy*. In an ode to the Magical Consciousness, they conclude, "The more energy we seize and use, the more adept we become at finding and seizing more."

Leadership to create a world that works for all is more likely to come from those who live in the real world and consequently are intimately acquainted with the injustice, violence, and environmental failure that Empire has wrought.

THE GREAT WORK

Attempting to preserve imperial privilege is not a rational choice. We can choose by default to let the collapse follow its natural course of a massive dieback in the human population and a descent into a fragmented world of local imperial fiefdoms reminiscent of the aftermath of the Roman Empire. Alternatively, we can acknowledge the irreversible changes in human circumstance that create an imperative to join together as one people on one planet to bring forth a new era of Earth Community based on the strong and caring families and communities that are the true foundation of prosperity, security, and meaning.

Theologian Thomas Berry calls this affirmative choice the Great Work. It requires a commitment to

- bring our collective material consumption into balance with Earth to allow the healing and regeneration of the biosphere. This requires that we

- realign our economic priorities from making money for rich people to assuring that all persons have access to an adequate and meaningful means of making a living for themselves and their families. Because equity becomes an essential condition of a healthy, sustainable society in a full world, we must

- democratize human institutions, including our economic institutions, to root power in people and community and replace a dominant culture of greed, competition, materialism, and the love of money with cultures grounded in life-affirming values of cooperation, caring, spirit, and the love of life. Because recognition of the essential spiritual unity of the whole of Creation is an essential foundation of the deep respect for the rights and needs of all living beings on which fulfillment of this agenda depends, it is necessary that we individually and collectively

- awaken to the integral relationship between the material and spiritual aspects of our being to become fully human.

The technological revolution of the twentieth century fundamentally altered the relationship of humans to the planet and to one another, created an unsustainable economic dependence on depleting the finite resources and regenerative capacities of the planet, and placed the human species at increasing risk of destruction by its own hand. Yet the circumstances of the lives of Empire's privileged rulers so isolate them from the negative consequences of this change in the human condition that they are unable even to comprehend the import of what is happening, let alone come forward with appropriate leadership.

Hope for the human future lies in the fact that Empire has created the conditions for the emergence from the bottom up of a new leadership of the whole. The same technological revolution that brings the imperative for change is also facilitating a global cultural and spiritual awakening to the interdependence of life, the unrealized possibilities of our human nature, and the opportunity before us to bring forth a cultural, economic, and political transformation as a conscious collective choice. It is the work of Ricardo and the Hacienda Santa Teresa on a planetary scale. Millions of people the world over are already engaging in it.

Some would call it a reawakening to the spiritual wisdom of our ancient past. Others might liken it to the sense of awe at the wonder and beauty of life that commonly follows a near-death experience. However we choose to characterize it, this awakening is opening the way for an evolutionary leap to a new level of human social, intellectual, and spiritual possibility. We now turn to the evidence that a unique and epic opportunity is presently at hand.

CHAPTER 4

The Opportunity

> The light-skinned race will be given a choice between two
> roads. If they choose the right road, the seventh fire will light
> the eighth and final (eternal) fire of peace, love, and brother-
> hood. If they make the wrong choice, the destruction they
> brought with them will come back to them, causing much
> suffering, death and destruction.[1]
>
> *Seven Fires Prophecy of the Ojibwe people*

> We are now experiencing a moment of significance far be-
> yond what any of us can imagine.... The distorted dream of
> an industrial technological paradise is being replaced by the
> more viable dream of a mutually enhancing human presence
> within an ever-renewing organic-based Earth community.[2]
>
> *Thomas Berry*

Perhaps nature's most powerful metaphor for
the Great Turning is the story of the metamorphosis of the monarch
caterpillar to the monarch butterfly, popularized by evolution biologist
Elisabet Sahtouris. The caterpillar is a voracious consumer that devotes
its life to gorging itself on nature's bounty. When it has had its fill, it fas-
tens itself to a convenient twig and encloses itself in a chrysalis. Once
snug inside, it undergoes a crisis as the structures of its cellular tissue
begin to dissolve into an organic soup.

Yet guided by some deep inner wisdom, a number of *organizer cells*
begin to rush around gathering other cells to form *imaginal buds*, initially independent multicellular structures that begin to give form to
the organs of a new creature.[3] Correctly perceiving a threat to the old
order, but misdiagnosing the source, the caterpillar's still intact immune
system attributes the threat to the imaginal buds and attacks them as
alien intruders.

The imaginal buds prevail by linking up with one another in a cooperative effort that brings forth a new being of great beauty, wondrous possibilities, and little identifiable resemblance to its progenitor. In its rebirth,
the monarch butterfly lives lightly on Earth, serves the regeneration of

life as a pollinator, and migrates thousands of miles to experience life's possibilities in ways the earthbound caterpillar could not imagine.

As the familiar cultural and institutional guideposts of Empire disintegrate around us, we humans stand on the threshold of a rebirth no less dramatic than that of the monarch caterpillar. The caterpillar's transformation is physical; the human transformation is institutional and cultural. Whereas the caterpillar faces a preordained outcome experienced by countless generations before it, we humans are path-breaking pioneers in uncharted territory. The rebirth is no wishful fantasy. It is already under way, motivated by a convergence of the imperatives described in the previous chapter and a spreading cultural and spiritual awakening of the higher orders of human consciousness.

The conditions of the human rebirth are likely to be traumatic and filled with a sense of loss, particularly for those of us who have enjoyed the indulgences of Empire's excess. Our pain, however, pales by comparison with the needless, unconscionable suffering endured for five millennia by those whose humanity and right to life Empire has cruelly denied. If we the privileged embrace the moment, rather than fight it, we can turn the tragedy into an opportunity to claim our humanity and the true prosperity, security, and meaning of community.

The cultural and spiritual awakening underlying the prospective human metamorphosis is driven by two encounters: one with the cultural diversity of humanity and the other with the limits of the planet's ecosystem. A rapid increase in the frequency and depth of cross-cultural exchange is awakening the species to culture as a human construct subject to intentional choice. The spreading failure of natural systems is creating an awareness of the interconnectedness of all life.

These encounters are bringing forth the higher and more democratic orders of human consciousness, expanding our sense of human possibility, and supporting the formation of powerful global social movements dedicated to birthing a new era of Earth Community. To understand the nature and significance of this awakening, we must first understand the nature and function of culture.

CULTURAL CONSCIOUSNESS

One of the brain's most important functions is to translate vast quantities of sensory data into information meaningful to the organism's survival, for example, alerting the organism to the presence of food, danger, or a prospective sexual partner. The human brain must sort and translate the data of our senses not only into information useful to our survival, but as well into the complex abstractions of ideas, values, and spiritual understanding essential to our creativity, social coherence, and sense of meaning.

In translating sensory data into meaningful information the brain necessarily sorts out the relevant from the irrelevant to draw the attention of the conscious mind to the data the brain's filtering mechanisms deem most important. Thus, information presented to the conscious mind is determined partly by the raw sensory data and partly by the brain's filtering mechanisms, which in turn are shaped by a combination of genetics, individual learning, and group culture.

Culture is the system of customary beliefs, values, perceptions, and social relations that encodes the *shared* learning of a particular human group essential to its orderly social function. The greater the individual and cultural learning components of the brain's interpretive mechanism, as contrasted to the genetic component, the greater the capacity of the species to adapt rapidly to new circumstances.

In the case of humans, the individual and cultural learning components are substantial, which gives us an unequaled capacity to adapt and innovate through individual and shared learning. The greater our conscious awareness of culture as a social construct subject to critical examination and intentional choice and the greater our capacity to communicate with one another, the greater our capacity to choose our future.

Social Construction

Culture shapes our perceptions mostly at the unconscious level. It rarely occurs to us to ask whether the reality we perceive through the lens of the culture within which we grow up is the "true" reality. As evolution biologist Elisabet Sahtouris observes,

> Until the last half century before the new millennium, it did not occur to people that they could have anything to do with creating their worldview. All through history, people thought the way they saw the world was the way the world really *was* —in other words, they saw *their* worldview as the *true* worldview and all others as mistaken and therefore false.[4]

In our first encounters with people from different cultures, we are likely to experience them as weird, difficult to understand, and possibly dangerous. Through extended intercultural experience, however, we come to see the deeper truth of culture as an organizing construct that defines a shared worldview essential to social coherence. Coming to understand the nature of culture is the essence of the critical transition from Socialized Consciousness to Cultural Consciousness described in chapter 2.

The spreading awakening of Cultural Consciousness is of particular importance to us in this time of rapid change in the human circumstance. It is essential to our ability to live on a small planet in peaceful and mutually beneficial relationship with peoples of cultures different from our own; to identify and change those aspects of human culture that are actively self-destructive; and to consciously bring forth a new culture of Earth Community.

For five thousand years, successful imperial rulers have intuitively recognized that their power rests on their ability to fabricate a falsified culture that evokes fear, alienation, learned helplessness, and the dependence of the individual on the imperial power of a great ruler. The falsified culture induces a kind of cultural trance in which we are conditioned to deny the inherent human capacity for responsible self-direction, sharing, and cooperation that is an essential foundation of democratic self-rule. The trance creates an emotional bond with the leader, alienates us from one another and the living Earth, erodes relations of mutual self-help, and reduces us to a state of resigned dependence much like the one Ricardo encountered among the sabaneros and peones of the Hacienda Santa Teresa when he first took over its management.

Cultural Awakening

In the United States, an important step in the awakening to the role of culture as a social construct came with the civil rights movement in the 1950s and '60s. Participation in that movement awakened many people to the truth that relations between races are defined by cultural codes that have little to do with reality. Once people learned to recognize the difference between reality and an unexamined belief system in reference to race relations, it became easier to see similar distortions in the cultural codes that define the relations between men and women, people and the environment, heterosexuals and homosexuals, and people and corporations.[5] The civil rights movement thus prepared the way for the social movements that followed.

Globally, a rapid increase in international travel, exchange, and communication has exposed millions of people to sometimes unsettling but usually enriching encounters with cultures not their own. That experience has opened many to viewing their own culture and the larger world in a new light. The experience of cultural awakening has become a contagious, liberating process of global scale that involves hundreds of millions of people and transcends the barriers of race, class, and religion.

Each of the world's many cultures captures some elements of a deeper truth, yet represents only one of many possible ways of interpreting the data generated by the human senses. Sustained cross-cultural experience can break the cultural trance and awaken a new consciousness of and appreciation for the varieties of the human experience and potential of the species. My life story, as outlined in the prologue, of moving from the cultural island of my childhood to the life of an itinerant global citizen offers an example of how the communications revolution of the last half of the twentieth century created conditions conducive to an accelerated liberation of the human consciousness.

An awakened Cultural Consciousness is relatively immune to the distorted cultural conditioning promoted by the corporate media, advertising, and political demagogues. Racism, sexism, homophobia, and consumerism are more easily seen for what they are—a justification for domination, exploitation, and violence against life—and a barrier to realizing the possibilities of Earth Community. An implicit underlying cultural premise of all the great progressive movements of our time is that a partnership world is possible.

SPIRITUAL CONSCIOUSNESS

The same shrinking of geographic space that is accelerating the awakening of Cultural Consciousness is also accelerating the step to Spiritual Consciousness. Those who travel the world to engage in the life of the peoples and places they visit experience both the vitality of the world's cultural diversity and the beauty of the planetary web of life. The iconic image of planet Earth taken from space gives visual expression to the profound reality that the world's people are one people sharing a common destiny on a solitary living spaceship alone in the vast darkness of space.

From a recognition of the interconnectedness of life it is only a short step to an encounter with the yet deeper truth that all life flows forth from the same spiritual source and that Empire's war against life is a war against ourselves. This awakening of a spiritual consciousness has profound practical implications, as it is the foundation of the cultural turning:

- From a belief that Earth belongs to humans and is ours to consume as suits our fancy to an understanding that Earth is our sacred home and that it is our responsibility to be respectful partners.

- From a belief that we humans are by nature incapable of responsible self-governance to an understanding that our nature embodies many possibilities, including the potential for responsible self-governance and democratic citizenship.

- From a belief that those who differ from us pose a threat to our security and way of life to an understanding that all persons are born of the same sacred sprit with an equal right to respect and the pursuit of happiness and that cultural and racial diversity is a source of learning and creative potential.

- From a self-justifying belief that those who align with us are the champions of good and those who oppose us are evil enemies to an understanding that we are all both victims and perpetrators of the violence inherent in the structures of Empire.

A GLOBAL PHENOMENON

Evidence of a spreading awakening of Cultural and Spiritual Consciousness comes from a variety of sources, including the work of values researcher Paul Ray and feminist author Sherry Anderson. They report data from U.S. values surveys showing that a growing segment of the U.S. adult population is embracing a new culture that values social inclusion, environmental stewardship, and spiritual practice. They call the holders of the new culture *Cultural Creatives* and estimate that in the late 1990s there were 50 million Cultural Creatives in the United States, roughly 26 percent of adult Americans—compared with less than 5 percent in the early 1960s. They further estimate there are another 80 to 90 million Cultural Creatives in the European Union.[6] Essentially those whom Ray and Anderson are calling Cultural Creatives are people who from their survey responses appear to have attained a Cultural Consciousness; many have achieved a Spiritual Consciousness.

In subsequent chapters, I will from time to time use the term *Cultural Creatives* to refer to people who have achieved a Cultural Consciousness.

International polling data suggest that hundreds of millions more Cultural Creatives are spread throughout the world. A 1993 Gallup International "Health of the Planet Survey" covering twenty-four nations found a substantial concern for the environment among people of both industrial and developing nations, with majorities agreeing that protecting the environment is more important than economic growth.[7]

The World Values Survey, which gathered longitudinal data from forty-three countries from 1970 to 1994, found that residents of countries that achieve significant economic security show a strong inclination to challenge traditional sources of authority, including government, science, and organized religion, in favor of greater freedom of self-expression and personally examined values. The World Values Survey data reveal a growing acceptance of equal rights for women, a greater interest in the quality of life relative to pursuit of material gain, and an increasing sense of the importance of family life to individual and community well-being. Although the survey reports that church attendance is generally falling, it found an increase in the percentage of people who report that they often think about the purpose and meaning of life.[8] These findings are all consistent with a spreading awakening of Cultural and Spiritual Consciousness.

Ray and Anderson estimate that roughly half of all Cultural Creatives combine a deep commitment to social and environmental values with some form of spiritual practice—embracing an integral spirituality that connects them with the whole of Creation in both its inner and outer manifestations. By the framework of chapter 2 these are the Spiritual Creatives, who have achieved a Spiritual Consciousness. Ray and Anderson call them *Core Cultural Creatives*. Affirming the importance of a spiritual awakening to the Great Turning, they conclude from their research that virtually all the leaders of progressive social movements in the United States are Core Cultural Creatives. My own experience with many hundreds of movement leaders suggests that this assessment is largely valid both domestically and internationally.

According to Ray and Anderson, Cultural Creatives come from all races, religions, classes, and political parties. The only clear demographic predictor is gender. Sixty percent of all Cultural Creatives are women. Sixty-seven percent of Spiritual Creatives are women.

Spiritual Creatives are not only leading the growing resistance against the global violence and economic injustice of Empire. They are also leading the proactive work of growing the imaginal buds of Earth Community. Leadership in the pro-democracy, peace, environmental, human and civil rights, economic justice, gender equality, holistic health, gay rights, organic agriculture, and voluntary simplicity movements comes from within the Spiritual Creative ranks. Together they are creating a new politics of partnership centered on a spiritually grounded affirmation of peace, justice, democracy, and life. Although many of these leaders have no formal religious affiliation and few speak openly of their spiritual orientation, a substantial proportion are deeply spiritual and approach their work as a form of spiritual practice.

INSTITUTIONAL AND TECHNOLOGICAL MEANS

At the same time as the species is experiencing the cultural and spiritual awakening necessary to the cultural turning, it is acquiring the institutional and technological means to translate that advance into the economic and political turnings that the cultural turning makes possible. To appreciate the epic nature of these developments, we must place them in historical perspective.

International Institutions

The very first international organization aimed at advancing cooperation among nations, the International Telegraph Union, was established only in 1865. The Universal Postal Union followed it in 1874. It seems noteworthy that both these pioneering institutions dealt with expanding the capacities for international communication.

Shortly thereafter, the International Peace Conference held in The Hague in 1899 made an initial effort to abolish the use of war as an instrument of national policy. It adopted the Convention for the Pacific Settlement of International Disputes, which established the Permanent Court of Arbitration to provide a means for peacefully settling international disputes. The Treaty of Versailles of 1919 created the International Labor Organization and the short-lived League of Nations.

It was only in 1945, just sixty years ago as of this writing, that the United Nations was founded as the first international organization to bring together all the world's nations to sit in permanent assembly to address the range of global human needs. Of even more recent origin is the electronic communications capability that has virtually eliminated the geographic barriers to human communication for a substantial portion of the population and is moving the species toward a capacity to make informed collective choices.

Communications Technology

Much of Empire's power has come from the ability of ruling elites to control the flow and content of the information by which subject peoples define themselves and their circumstances. Until quite recent times, ordinary people had virtually no means of communicating with one another other than through the unassisted spoken word. It was rare for people to have contact with anyone beyond their immediate village.

Modern humans, *Homo sapiens*, have been around for about two hundred thousand years. Public mail service became accessible to ordinary people only about two hundred years ago. Telephones did not come into general use until the mid-1900s, and the cost of a long distance call made it a luxury item until the 1980s. The first commercial airline service across the Atlantic was established in the 1930s. The explosive growth in international travel began only with the first transatlantic commercial jet service in 1958. It was not until the 1990s that the capability for interactive, instantaneous, multiparty global conversations became available via satellite-linked Internet, teleconferencing, and video-conferencing technologies. Development of the World Wide Web began in 1990. The first Web browser for popular use, Mosaic, was released in March 1993.

Although a serious digital divide remains, these technologies are connecting the world's people into an interactive communications web. Millions are now using them to create a dynamic, self-directing social organism that transcends the boundaries of race, class, religion, and nationality to function as a shared conscience of the species. The computer communications revolution has happened within the space of little more than ten years. It is so new that even most of its participants are scarcely aware of the profound significance of the transformation in which they are participating.

The computer communications revolution is transforming the very nature of news and opinion media through an unprecedented process of democratization. Public interest groups are rightly concerned that a handful of publicly traded corporations have monopolized conventional print, radio, and television media outlets to serve purely commercial interests. The revolution in computer communications technology, however, is producing an end run around corporate efforts to monopolize and centralize access to the public mind. Every person in the world with a computer and an Internet connection has access to virtually all of the world's consequential print, audio, and video news sources and the capability to create an electronic newsletter or radio or television station of their own free from any licensing requirements or monopoly controls. Bloggers (short for *Web loggers*) are regularly scooping the professional newscasts on major stories, and many are posting audio versions of their news and opinion pieces for instant download to portable playback devices.

The expansion of Internet access is creating the possibility of a democratic media network in which every voice has its potential outlet and people have near infinite variety in their choice of sources for news and opinion—blurring the distinction between mass and individual communication. Through a process of self-organization, a system is evolving in which stories and opinion pieces enter the communications web from millions of independent sources to be sorted and aggregated by Web sites that serve as trusted portals for specific constituencies. This radical democratization of media makes it increasingly difficult for any individual or group to monopolize the venues of cultural regeneration in order to control a society through the falsification of culture.

Quality and reliability will be continuing issues resolved through the same dynamics of user feedback and evaluation now used to assess the integrity and reliability of individual commercial Web vendors. With a virtually unlimited number of broadcast and publication channels, media monopolization and the suppression of news or opinion are becoming impossible.

FROM CONSCIOUSNESS TO ACTION

The conditions are now in place for the species to take an essential step beyond the self-limiting cultural beliefs and stories that divide us to an appreciation of the deeper values and spiritual origins of life that unite us.

You're Not Crazy – You're Human

Educator Parker Palmer has outlined the process by which the individual experience of awakening to a Cultural Consciousness translates into individual commitment and ultimately into an irresistible force for transformation.[9] It begins when an individual functioning at the level of the Socialized Consciousness awakens from the trance induced by the prevailing culture. This awakening commonly leads to a deep disconnect between the realities of family, work, and community life grounded in the previously unexamined values and the examined, authentic values of a maturing consciousness. This disconnect confronts the individual with the often painful choice between conformity and authenticity.

Palmer notes that those who make the choice to align their lives with their authentic values experience a sense of isolation from family members, friends, and associates whose views are defined by the codes of the old culture. The individuals undergoing this transition may at times feel like creatures from outer space in the midst of a family gathering or class reunion. With time, however, they find others, even among their immediate family, friends, and associates, who are feeling a similar sense of tension and isolation and join with them to create what Palmer calls a community of congruence. It may begin with only two or three others with whom they share an occasional conversation or meal. Together they help one another discover that the craziness is not in themselves, but in what many institutions decree as "normal."

Once the nucleus of such a community forms, it attracts others and may become regularized in the form of a book club, study group, spiritual retreat, conversation café, or quilting party, where people who share the struggle of reconciling their lives with an awakened consciousness gather for mutual support. In the civil rights movement, these communities of congruence commonly formed within African American churches.

Such communities are forming by the millions all around the world. To draw on the butterfly metaphor, we might think of them as the imaginal buds of the new culture. With time, individual communities of congruence reach out to form alliances with others to create larger cultural spaces, such as a farmers' market or food co-op; these create the imaginal buds of a new economy and allow participants to live more authentic and fulfilling lives. Gradually they build the power to transform or displace the institutions of the dominant culture.

Such communities and alliances formed in significant numbers during the latter half of the twentieth century to bring forth great social movements for national independence, human and civil rights, women's rights, peace, environmental protection, and economic justice. During a period of only fifty years these movements dismantled the prevailing system of European colonial empires, codified human rights in international law, rewrote the legal codes of nations, and redefined the prevailing cultural codes regarding relationships among men and women, races, nations, and species. These alliances are now linking into the most powerful and truly global social movement in the whole of the human experience.

Birthing Global Civil Society

The alliance-building processes that gave birth to this global meta-movement became visible only in 1992 in Rio de Janeiro during the UN Conference on Environment and Development (UNCED), at which the world's heads of state gathered for an Earth Summit. The conference proved to be a landmark event in the human experience.

Its significance came not from the accomplishments of the official meetings. Their effectiveness was limited by the organized intervention of global corporations working under the banner of the Business Council on Sustainable Development and the International Chamber of Commerce to make certain the official meetings did not produce conclusions contrary to corporate interests. On the other side of town, however, a gathering of eighteen thousand private citizens of every race, religion, social class, and nationality was making history as participants drafted informal citizen treaties setting forth agendas for cooperative voluntary action.

I had the privilege of being a participant in the citizen forum. It was a life-transforming experience. It was here that many thousands of leaders of what would only later come to be known as global civil society discovered that underlying our differences there is a common dream of a world that works for the whole of life. We committed ourselves to bring it into being.

The citizen deliberations, which called for a sweeping transformation of human cultures and institutions, demonstrated that the peoples of the world share a common vision of the world in which they want to live. Key elements of the consensus were summarized in the People's

Earth Declaration: A Proactive Agenda for the Future. It ends with the following commitment:

> We, the people of the world, will mobilize the forces of transnational civil society behind a widely shared agenda that bonds our many social movements in pursuit of just, sustainable, and participatory human societies. In so doing, we are forging our own instruments and processes for re-defining the nature and meaning of human progress and for transforming those institutions that no longer respond to our needs. We welcome to our cause all people who share our commitment to peaceful and democratic change in the inter-est of our living planet and the human societies it sustains.[10]

From this modest beginning, global civil society has grown significantly in strength and sophistication to become an increasingly influential moral force for global transformation.

The process of documenting an emerging global consensus contin-ued after the Earth Summit with the drafting of the Earth Charter. Of-ten referred to as a Declaration of Interdependence, the Earth Charter reflects a global consensus reached through a decade-long worldwide cross-cultural conversation about common goals and shared values that began in Rio de Janeiro in 1992. Drafting it involved thousands of indi-viduals and hundreds of organizations from all regions of the world in an open and participatory consultation process.[11]

As a charter of people, rather than governments, it has no legal force. Rather than present a list of prescriptions or demands, it outlines the values of the emergent era, articulating an integral vision of a world dedicated to respect and caring for all life, deep democracy, human rights, economic justice, and peace. It affirms that once "basic needs have been met, human development is primarily about being more, not having more." The charter recognizes that far from being at odds, indi-vidual liberty, strong communities, and respect for Earth are inseparable one from the other. Its moral principles align with the wisdom under-lying the teachings of all the world's great religions.

The Second Superpower

Global civil society first established its identity as a significant political force in 1999, when fifty thousand demonstrators from around the world gathered in Seattle and staged a massive protest that successfully disrupted the Third Ministerial Conference of the World Trade Organization. The demonstration brought an end to the myth of the invincibility of the forces of corporate rule. From that time forward, whenever the corporate elites gathered in major closed-door conferences to advance the interests of corporate Empire, massive international protests, some involving hundreds of thousands of persons, presented them with a powerful message: *The people of the world are watching and will no longer acquiesce in silence to your assault on democracy, justice, and the planet.*

In 2001, global civil society began organizing its own massive forums under the banner of the World Social Forum and the theme "Another World Is Possible." The 2001 forum drew 20,000 participants to Porto Alegre, Brazil. By the third year, it drew upwards of 100,000 people. The fourth World Social Forum, held in Mumbai, India, drew 80,000 people from 132 countries, with especially strong representation and leadership from India's Dalit community—once known as the "Untouchables." In its fifth year, 2005, the forum returned to Porto Alegre and drew 150,000 participants.

The World Social Forum process has inspired the creation of regional and national social forums around the world. The call went forth from the November 2002 European Social Forum and then the January 2003 World Social Forum, which brought more than ten million people to the streets of the world's cities, towns, and villages on February 15, 2003, to demonstrate for peace in the face of the buildup to the U.S. invasion of Iraq.[12] Commenting on the demonstrations and their impact, the *New York Times* observed that "there may still be two superpowers on the planet: the United States and world public opinion."[13]

It is a perceptive observation. This, however, is a superpower struggle like no other in human history. Rather than a classic contest for dominion between states, it is a struggle between two globalizations grounded in sharply contrasting visions of human possibility—one imperial and the other democratic. It pits an alliance of state and corporate power devoted to a vision of global Empire against an alliance of people power devoted to a vision of Earth Community. Empire holds the edge in institutional power; Earth Community holds the edge in the moral power of the authentic cultural values of a mature consciousness.

Rather than mobilize around an ideology or charismatic leader, the people-power alliance of global civil society has mobilized around an emergent values consensus. Far from being leaderless, however, it is a leader-full movement self-organized by hundreds of thousands of leaders linked in a seamless web of electronic communication. It manifests the qualities of an emergent social organism with a capacity for democratic self-governance grounded in authentic life-affirming human values transcending race, gender, nationality, ethnicity, and religion wholly new to the human experience. Its rapidly expanding capacity for mutual learning, consensus convergence, and global coherence hints at the human possibilities that lie ahead.

Less dramatic, and therefore less visible, are the millions of participants who are forming local alliances devoted to rebuilding community institutions and democratic participation from the bottom up. This, however, is the most important work of all—the work of living the cultures and institutions of the new era into being.

The institutions of imperial power have responded to this challenge in the manner of the disintegrating caterpillar's immune system: with a well-organized effort to reassert their dominion even as global civil society grows stronger. Whether the organized violence of Empire will be succeeded by the peace and justice of a new era of Earth Community or by the chaotic violence of social breakdown and warring feudal fiefdoms remains to be determined. Either way, the established pattern of global imperial power has reached its limit and cannot endure. An exhausted planet and politically conscious peoples will no longer support it.

A new human era is in gestation. The choices we humans make over the next few decades will determine whether the birthing is successful. To paraphrase civil rights activist Miles Horton, "We make our road by walking."

Modern humans have been around for some two hundred thousand years. It is only during the most recent five thousand years that a drive for dominator power brought forth the era of Empire and its reckless squandering of lives, resources, and human possibility to support the privilege and extravagance of the few.[14]

Humans have always suffered hardship and deprivation from acts of nature over which they have no control. Slavery and poverty are not, however, acts of nature. They are social constructs that create an intentional and pervasive condition of exclusion. No ruling class in five thousand years has delivered on a promise to eliminate either poverty or slavery and its equivalents, because to do so would mean the elimination of elite privilege. There is no elite class without a servant class. The maintenance of a dominator system depends on violence or the threat of violence to maintain the extreme class division.

Now, through a global awakening of Cultural and Spiritual Consciousness, ordinary people are coming forward by the millions to say five thousand years is enough. Empire's power brokers will not readily relinquish their power. An understanding of Empire's deep roots and the lessons of its history illuminates the nature and magnitude of the challenge at hand as we set about putting Empire's addictions behind us.

PART II

Sorrows of Empire

Every empire we know of in human history has succumbed to this idolatry of power.[1]

Cornel West

By the accounts of Empire's historians, civilization, history, and human progress began with the consolidation of dominator power in the first great Empires. Much is made of the glorious accomplishments and heroic battles of the rise and fall of subsequent imperial civilizations. Rather less is said about the brutalization of the slaves who built the great monuments, the racism, the suppression of women, the conversion of free farmers into serfs or landless laborers, the carnage of the battles, and the hopes and lives destroyed by wave after wave of invasion, pillage, and gratuitous devastation of the vanquished. These are among the sorrows of Empire.

Many of the proudest and most enduring of human intellectual and cultural achievements came before Empire, when societies were more egalitarian and women had important leadership roles; during brief respites from the despotic violence and oppression that defined the imperial era; or during the most recent two hundred years of democratic reform. The deeper human truth is that Empire marked a destructive and self-limiting detour from the path to realizing the possibilities of our human nature.

To liberate ourselves from Empire's self-limiting patterns of domination we must understand their dynamics, acknowledge their destructive consequences, and embrace the truth of the human possibilities that Empire has long denied. We must also recognize the limitations of the contemporary human experiment in democracy and the process by which the institutions of imperial states have morphed into the institutions of imperial corporations to present a more benign appearance while leaving the underlying structures of domination in place.

A brief historical survey is in order to remind ourselves of how brutally destructive Empire has been for all but the favored elites who rule from their perches high in the clouds and to deepen our understanding of the nature, dilemmas, and possibilities of the mature democracies of Earth Community. This review is also a useful reminder of how difficult it is to break free from Empire once its play-or-die dynamic is established.

CHAPTER 5

When God Was a Woman

> Neolithic art, and even more so the more developed Minoan art, seems to express a view in which the primary function of the mysterious powers governing the universe is not to exact obedience, punish, and destroy but rather to give.[1]
>
> *Riane Eisler*

Early human learning centered on three challenges: developing the art of complex speech to facilitate communication, discovering technologies to extend the capabilities of the human mind and body, and mastering the arts of living in ever larger units of social organization to accommodate population growth. Early humans learned to use fire, domesticate plants and animals, and construct houses of wood, stone, skins, and sun-dried mud. They created complex languages and social codes. They undertook continental and transcontinental migrations to populate the planet, adapting to vastly different physical topographies and climates as they went. Along the way, they negotiated the transition from roaming as bands of gatherer-hunters[2] to living as settled agriculturalists in villages, towns, and cities, and they established the intellectual, technological, and social foundation on which human civilization rests to this day. At each step they moved ever further away from life as one with the beasts of jungle, plain, and forest on the path to becoming distinctively human.

We now take these accomplishments so much for granted as to ignore the extraordinary learning and sharing they involved. We further ignore or deny the archaeological evidence that this all occurred during the period prior to the era of Empire, in the days of goddesses and high priestesses that most historians give short shrift.

A WELL-KEPT SECRET

As cultural historian Riane Eisler observes, "One of the best-kept historical secrets is that practically all the material and social technologies fundamental to civilization were developed before the imposition of a dominator society."[3] The domestication of plants and animals, food production and storage, building construction, and clothing production all were discoveries and inventions of what she characterizes as the great partnership societies in which women often had lead roles in developing and applying the underlying technologies.[4] These societies developed the institutions of law, government, and religion that are the foundations of complex social organization and cultivated the arts of dance, pottery, basket making, textile weaving, leather crafting, metallurgy, ritual drama, architecture, town planning, boat building, highway construction, and oral literature.

It is also noteworthy that when historians do mention the accomplishments of the early humans, they rarely mention the relatively egalitarian nature of their social structures and until very recently were prone to use a language that might lead the reader to believe that the early societies comprised only men. For example, a respected college history text published in 1958 offers this observation on pre-Empire humans:

> Whereas all of the men who had lived heretofore were mere food-gatherers, Neolithic man was a *food-producer*. Tilling the soil and keeping flocks and herds provided him with much more dependable food resources and at times yielded him a surplus.[5]

Such a statement would presumably be unthinkable in a contemporary history text, not only because of the sexist language, but as well because it overlooks gender as a critical dimension of the human experience and the seminal contributions of women to many of the most important early human advances. Recognizing the distinctive role of women in the initial humanization of the species, we can more easily understand the enormous cost to our humanity of five thousand years of imperial repression of women, the importance of gender balance, and the essential role of women leaders in birthing Earth Community.

Credit for exposing the consequences of the male chauvinist view of history rightly goes primarily to women like Eisler who have examined the archaeological evidence through the lens of gender to provide a fuller understanding of human experience and possibility. Eisler presented the result of her inquiry in 1987 in the pathbreaking feminist classic, *The Chalice and the Blade*, which juxtaposes the chalice as the symbol of the power commonly associated with the feminine to give and nurture life—the ultimate creative power—against the blade as the symbol of the power commonly associated with the masculine to dominate and extinguish life—the ultimate destructive power.

There were, of course, no written languages during this early period. Therefore, we know its people only by what remains of their physical artifacts, the stories and legends eventually recorded by early scribes, and practices of isolated Stone Age cultures that have survived as a living record. We can only infer from the available fragments of data what went on in the minds of these early people, their values, their spiritual beliefs, and the variety of their ways of living. There is, however, compelling evidence to suggest that during the crucial pre-Empire days humans lived in relatively egalitarian social units, worshipped the regenerative powers of the Goddess, and depended on women for leadership in many aspects of family and community life.

Given the ambiguity of the data and the variety of human experience, it is inevitable that modern interpretations of preliterate life differ significantly, and all interpretations are subject to challenge. My intention in this chapter is not to document or resolve the contrasting interpretations, but simply to place the current five-thousand-year era of Empire in the larger context of the long trajectory of human development.

IN THE BEGINNING

The available fossil evidence suggests that the earliest humanlike species appeared in Africa some four to five million years ago and that the earliest modern humans, *Homo sapiens*, emerged on that continent somewhere between one hundred thousand and two hundred thousand years ago and migrated outward to populate the planet.[6]

The broad outlines of the lives of these early peoples are reasonably clear. Until about 11,000 BCE, when the Ice Age ended, most humans were organized into bands of five to eighty male and female adults and their dependent children. They were food gatherers, rather than producers, and lived by scavenging for wild berries and roots, hunting wild animals, and fishing the streams. The women replenished the tribe by bearing the children, nursing the infants, and gathering food; the men were generally larger and stronger than the women and thus more naturally suited to roles as hunters and warriors. Members of the band shared the available food and the benefits of community life.[7]

Because the gatherer-hunter lifestyle supports only low population densities, in most settings some bands had to migrate periodically as the population increased, in search of berries, roots, wild grains, and game, perhaps following the seasonal movements of the animals they hunted for flesh and skins.

Some took advantage of new opportunities as glaciers receded and water levels rose to create new habitats that brought forth an abundance of fish, shellfish, and waterfowl. Warming temperatures encouraged the growth of a lush variety of fruits and other edible vegetation available for the picking. As the communities grew, they learned to augment nature's largesse through active participation in its regenerative processes by collecting and planting the seeds of edible plants. The establishment of permanent settlements also facilitated processes of wealth accumulation that were impossible for itinerant gatherer-hunters.

Others who had lived by following animal migrations reduced the uncertainty of the hunt by learning to domesticate animals into managed herds. These people became nomadic pastoralists who guided their flocks and herds of goats, sheep, cattle, and horses across the landscape in search of green pastures. Moving regularly with their animals, the nomadic pastoralists could accumulate only the surplus they could transport. Thus, they commonly measured wealth primarily by the size of their herds.

GODDESS CIVILIZATIONS

Beginning about 7000 BCE, centers of settled agriculture began to appear in favored regions of Eurasia, sub-Saharan Africa, and the Americas. Many of the more important were located in the Near and Middle East in what are now the territories of Turkey, Greece, Iraq, Iran, and Syria; throughout the Mediterranean region; and as far north as England. The ancient Aegean civilization centered in Crete and the lesser islands of the Aegean Sea between the present states of Greece and Turkey was one of the earliest and most enduring.[8]

Settled Agriculture

Settled agriculture no doubt grew out of the astonishing accumulation of botanical knowledge that modern ethnobiologists find to be characteristic of gatherer-hunter peoples — representing the shared learning of many individuals over generations spanning many thousands of years.

Drawing on this knowledge, some among those responsible for gathering experimented with selecting and cultivating the seeds of particularly useful crop species. As the gathering was predominantly the women's responsibility, it is likely that women led the early development of the arts of cultivation.

Because settled agriculture allowed for higher population densities, it accelerated technological innovation and created a requirement for more complex forms of organization as the first sizable towns appeared. Because it generated surpluses, it created the possibility for a few to expropriate the surplus for their exclusive personal use.[9]

As best we can determine, early humans were relatively undifferentiated by occupation, status, or power. The fortunes of the individual rose and fell with the fortunes of the band or tribe. Generative power, as manifested in the power to reproduce, to heal, to gather food, and to win the favor of the animal spirit for a successful hunt, was at the center of community life. Symbols and rituals that acknowledged and honored the power of Creation in its feminine form were among the earliest expressions of a distinctively human consciousness.

One of the few specialized roles in the pre-agricultural societies was that of the shaman, either woman or man, who demonstrated the power to heal through communication with the spirit world. This was perhaps the earliest occupational specialization. These times were scarcely free from violence and competition, yet a cultural commitment to the collective potency of band and tribe generally prevailed. The generative power of the Spirit was the foundation of social organization; the cooperative quest for generative power generally prevailed as organizing principle.

Temples of the Goddess

As humans formed themselves into larger social units, the functions of the lone shaman became the functions of an organized body of priestesses and priests, and the temple emerged as one of the first centers of institutional power responsible for administering affairs affecting the whole of the community. The many functions of the temple ranged from allocating land to mediating disputes and divining the most auspicious time for planting.

Eisler points to the general absence of heavy fortifications and thrusting weapons in the archaeological record of the large pre-Empire agriculture-based Neolithic civilizations as evidence that their people were peaceful and relatively egalitarian. There was little sign of damage through warfare. Burial practices and the generally uniform size and design of houses further suggested generally egalitarian societies with little of the differentiation by class, race, and gender that is characteristic of the societies that followed. The varied artworks of these Neolithic civilizations support a similar conclusion. There are no scenes of battles, images of noble warriors and wrathful gods, nor depictions of conquerors dragging captives in chains.

There is, by contrast, an abundance of female figures and symbols of nature associated with the worship of the Goddess. A central religious image of these early times appears to be a woman giving birth, creating and nurturing life in the manner of Earth. According to Eisler, "those places where the first great breakthroughs in material and social technology were made had one feature in common: the worship of the Goddess." Similar Goddess symbolism is found in each of the three main centers where agriculture was first developed: Asia Minor and southeastern Europe, Thailand, and Middle America.[10]

In *When God Was a Woman,* artist and art historian Merlin Stone identifies accounts of sun goddesses in the lands of Canaan, Anatolia, Arabia, and Australia and among Eskimos, Japanese, and the Kasis of India. There are accounts from Sumer, Babylon, Egypt, Africa, Australia, and China of female deities who brought forth not only the first people but also the entire Earth and the heavens above.[11] Eisler, Stone, and others conclude that the cosmology of the earliest religions of both the gatherer-hunter and agricultural societies centered on a Great Mother deity as the source of life and protection from nature's threatening forces.

For a period of as much as six thousand years, prior to the emergence of Empire, the emphasis in the Goddess societies was on the development and application of technologies that nurture life.[12] Humans were expected to enter into partnership with the productive processes of nature, an activity for which women—the life givers of the human species—were presumed to have special affinity.[13]

Eisler argues that evidence the early Goddess-worshipping societies were matrilineal, tracing descent through the woman, does not necessarily mean they were matriarchal in the sense of treating men as subservient. She explains:

For here both men and women were the children of the

Goddess, as they were the children of the women who headed the families and clans. And while this certainly gave women a great deal of power, analogizing from our present-day mother-child relationship, it seems to have been a power that was more equated with responsibility and love than with oppression, privilege, and fear.[14]

Others, including some feminist historians, have challenged Eisler's conclusions as too sweeping in suggesting that the Goddess-worshipping societies were all peaceful and egalitarian. Merlin Stone maintains that at least some of the Goddess societies were not only matrilineal, but as well matriarchal and reduced men to an inferior and dependent position. She points to evidence that through their control of the temple the priestesses controlled inheritance, "the urban activities of the craftsmen, the traders and the rural employment of farmers, shepherds, poultry keepers, fishermen and fruit gardeners,"[15] and the buying, selling, and renting of land.[16]

Stone cites evidence that in some societies, women arranged to take multiple lovers of their choice, often in the context of temple rituals, thereby securing their own sexual freedom, obscuring the paternity of their children, and thus creating a situation in which the line of succession could be traced only through the woman.[17] Later stories from the lands of Libya, Anatolia, Bulgaria, Greece, Armenia, and Russia also describe the Goddess as a courageous warrior and leader of armies.[18]

Millennia after the shift from partnership to domination, Diodorus Siculus (Diodorus of Sicily) wrote of his travels to northern Africa and the Near East forty-nine years before the birth of Jesus. Among his accounts are reports of women in Ethiopia who carried arms and practiced a form of communal marriage in which children were raised so communally that even the women themselves often became confused as to who was the birth mother of a particular child. He reported on warrior women in Libya who formed armies and invaded neighboring countries.[19]

Our concern here is not with whether women-led societies are always more peaceful and egalitarian than male-led societies, but merely to note the evidence of the rich variety of the early human experience, which included peaceful, egalitarian, highly accomplished societies of substantial size in which women had strong leadership roles.

TURNING TO EMPIRE: A GENDER PERSPECTIVE

According to Eisler, divergent paths taken by the nomadic pastoralists and the settled agriculturalists played out in divergent worldviews and social structures. The settled agricultural societies organized around the generative partnership power we think of as feminine, worshipped female goddesses of life, honored female as well as male leaders, and directed their creative energies to the discovery and development of technologies that sustain and enhance life. Some historians believe that the story found in the biblical account of the Garden of Eden, where woman and man lived an idyllic life, is based on a collective memory of these distant times.[20]

By contrast, the nomadic pastoralist tribes tended toward venerating the power dominator societies associated with the masculine. Their path led them to worship violent male gods, honor the warrior, treat women as male property, and devote substantial creative energy to producing ever more effective weapons. As Eisler observes, they sought to improve their condition "not by developing technologies of production, but through ever more effective technologies of destruction." This gave them an advantage in subsequent combat with the more prosperous agriculturalists, whose lands and labor they eventually appropriated through conquest.[21]

Rejecting the Feminine

Ultimately, the early Goddess-worshipping agricultural civilizations fell to invasions by the God-worshipping nomadic pastoralist tribes that began in earnest around 4300 BCE and continued in a succession of waves through 2800 BCE. As the invaders penetrated the first great agricultural civilizations that inhabited the lakeshores and riverbanks of the fertile heartlands, they killed the men, enslaved the women, and replaced their relatively equitable, life-centered, and partnership-oriented religions, cultures, and institutions with wrathful male gods, warrior cultures, institutions of domination, and technologies of destruction. Earth Goddess gave way to the sky God.

Thus began what Eisler calls "a bloody five-thousand-year dominator detour." As the pre-Empire societies honored the power to give life, so later societies honored the power to take life. Kings and emperors bolstered their demands for obedience with claims of personal divinity or divine appointment.[22] Angry male gods representing dominator power displaced the female and male gods representing generative power. Priestesses were gradually stripped of power and replaced by priests. Wives became the chattel of their husbands. The poor became the servants of the rich. The regenerative power of the Spirit gave way to the dominator power of the sword. Humans came to mistake dominance for potency, domination displaced partnership as the organizing principle of society, and the era of Empire was born.

According to Eisler, the invasions typically brought periods of cultural regression and stagnation. Towns and villages disintegrated. The magnificent painted pottery, shrines, frescoes, and sculptures of the Goddess civilizations fell into neglect or were destroyed. The primary use of metals for ornamentation and tools gave way to a primary use of metals for weapons.[23] Artifacts from this period depicted heavily armed male warrior gods. Graves from the subjugation period might contain an exceptionally tall or large-boned male skeleton and a variety of weapons along with the skeletons of sacrificed women who were the wives, concubines, or slaves of the man who died. As social structures became more authoritarian and hierarchical, it appears that those most likely to rise to the pinnacles of power were the physically strongest and presumably the most ruthless and brutal. Women were reduced culturally and institutionally to "male-controlled technologies of production and reproduction."[24]

With time, the conquered societies entered into a new period of material production and accumulation, but with a striking change in the pattern of distribution. Previously priority had gone to public works and an improved standard of living for all. Now the men at the top appropriated the bulk of the wealth and power. Their subjects had little choice but to make do with the leftovers. Those who achieved their positions of power by destroying and appropriating the wealth of conquered peoples continued their established pattern of appropriation, distributing the spoils among those who faithfully served them—a pattern that remains familiar to this day.[25]

Domesticating People

As the capacity to produce a surplus increased, rulers learned that, much as the pastoralists had learned to domesticate animals, so too they could domesticate other humans. Rather than kill their captives, they consigned them to forced labor tending the flocks and fields, freeing themselves for less arduous endeavors. Thus, the institution of slavery was born as a new tool of production that also served to humiliate and punish vanquished foreign enemies. As urban markets for agricultural products grew and became more profitable, the demand for slaves and serfs grew accordingly.

As rulers came to recognize the benefits of slavery, they began stripping citizenship from criminals in their own cultural group and condemned them to slavery rather than death or imprisonment as the preferred punishment for their crimes. The institution of debt generated its own crop of slaves. The last resort of the desperately poor was to borrow against a pledge of their labor or the labor of their children. A debtor who defaulted became a slave. Some were so desperate in their impoverishment that they "voluntarily" chose slavery over starvation, much as the desperately poor now "voluntarily" present themselves to companies offering sweatshop work under slavelike conditions or sign up for military service. The demand for slaves made trafficking in slaves acquired through kidnapping and piracy one of the earliest and most profitable forms of commerce.[26]

TURNING TO EMPIRE: A SCALE PERSPECTIVE

In contrast to Eisler's analysis, Jared Diamond, in *Guns, Germs, and Steel*, deals with the transition to Empire as purely a response to the practical need to organize large numbers of unrelated people into peaceful and coherent social units.

Small Is Equitable

In the early gatherer-hunter days, the survival of the band typically required that all able-bodied members contribute to gathering food, which largely precluded class-based social stratification. Land and other resources were shared in common. Similarly, in the early permanent agricultural settlements, which involved tribal units of several hundred people, it was necessary for every able-bodied person to share in the physical labor of tilling and harvesting the fields and—when necessary—in the defense of the village. Crafts like weaving baskets and cloth, pottery, carpentry, and simple metalworking were a routine part of life in most every household. The sharing of assets and labor combined with a lack of surplus beyond immediate daily needs left little opportunity for any individual to become disproportionately wealthy.

The social unit of the tribal village was still small enough that most people knew each other by name and relationship, which eased the task of mediating relationships without formal systems of laws and enforcement. Governance mechanisms were characteristically both informal and highly egalitarian, with major decisions normally reached in meetings of all adult members, conducted without an evident leader, in which all information was public and freely shared. There were no specialized occupational functions, everyone shared in the labor, and there were no slaves or specialized menial roles. Visitors to contemporary tribal assemblies are commonly impressed by this practice of the purest form of democracy.

Beyond Kinship

Trust and group identity have long been important issues for humans for the very reason that our nature embodies a broad range of possibility, from deadly violence to self-sacrificial love. When contiguous concentrations of population became too large for all members to be related by blood or marriage or to know each other by name, the problem arose of how to assess the intentions of strangers and minimize the potential for violence.

The solution, according to Diamond, was to establish the formal hereditary office of the chief. The chief was a permanent centralized authority who made all the significant decisions, held a monopoly on the right to use force, controlled important information regarding relationships with neighbors and the promises of the gods regarding future harvests, wore distinctive identifying regalia, and expected obsequious respect from those of lower rank.

The chief was in turn supported by one or two levels of bureaucracy composed of generalist retainers, who carried out functions such as extracting tribute, managing irrigation, and organizing labor for public works projects—and received a portion of the tribute in return for their services. Commonly, the office of the chief either combined the offices of political and religious leader or provided support for priests who affirmed the divine nature of the chief's appointment to legitimate the extraction of tribute. Specialized priests received a share of the tribute in return for this service.

Perils of Coercive Power

The solution of a powerful ruler to maintain order set in play a dilemma that has confounded the human species since the size of the human population exceeded the limits of organization based on kinship. To fulfill his function the ruler must have the right and the means to impose his will and to extract tribute by coercive force. This requires a retinue of loyal warriors and tax collectors. He must also invest in legitimating symbols of authority and in culture workers who keep the populace enthralled with stories of his divine powers and righteousness. Those who perform these functions must be supported out of the surpluses produced by farmers, artisans, traders, and others engaged in actual productive work.

Rulers had to be skilled in the political arts of maintaining the loyalty of retainers, the acquiescence of the ruled, and a monopoly on coercive power, while fending off internal competitors for the throne and the armies of neighboring states. The larger the state, the greater the cost of maintaining necessary public functions, including security, and the greater the need for extraction to support these functions—which in turn depended on the exercise of coercive power. Yet the greater the coercive power of the ruler and his retainers, the greater the temptation to abuse this power for personal gain.

As Diamond points out, the distinction between statesmanship and kleptocracy is largely a matter of how the surplus, extracted as taxes or tribute, is divided between serving public purposes and supporting the self-indulgence of the ruling elite. The right to use coercive power to maintain order and extract a surplus creates an almost irresistible temptation to abuse.

SMALL AND BALANCED

Diamond and Eisler both offer important insight into the cultural and institutional realities of the human experience. Diamond brings a scale perspective, Eisler a gender perspective. Neither is complete in itself. The scale perspective directs attention to the complexity of the organizational challenge created by increasing population density in an interdependent world, quite apart from gender considerations. The gender perspective points to the profound truth that addressing the organizational challenge in ways consistent with the needs of life and the potentials of the species requires balancing the masculine and feminine principles.

Security in the Service of Life

The society that honors only the masculine principle traps itself in a destructive cycle of predatory competition and violence. The society that honors only the feminine principle invites predation by societies organized exclusively on the masculine principle. A viable society must have the capacity to defend its integrity against predators of both domestic and foreign origin.

Societies that successfully balance the feminine and masculine principles to the end of nurturing life will be more prosperous and more productive of technological advances suited to improving human well-being than societies that suppress the feminine principle and give priority to the destruction and domination of life. To bring the feminine and masculine principles into balance is a defining challenge of the cultural turning.

Spiritual Identity

The gender perspective also offers important insights into human spiritual expression and highlights the centrality of spirit and gender to our identity and sense of meaning, our contemporary politics, and the choices we now confront as a species. We humans are born with a capacity distinctive among Earth's species to reflect on our own mortality, ponder the meaning of Creation, and ask "Why?" By our answers, we define ourselves, our possibilities, and our place in the cosmos.

In our efforts to comprehend and communicate about the incomprehensible, we necessarily resort to familiar metaphors to describe that which is beyond description. Whatever our choice of metaphor, the image of the sacred evoked can never reveal more than a small fragment of the infinite. The choice of metaphor speaks volumes, however, about our political orientation and spiritual maturity.

When women held significant power, they chose female deities represented by life-giving and nurturing images associated with the feminine. When men subordinated women, they also subordinated the life-nurturing female deities to violent male deities. A rendering of the divine as exclusively masculine or feminine diminishes the reality of the Spirit, which transcends gender.

Matriarchy and patriarchy are both within the range of human possibility; neither one is the natural condition of human society. The challenge for the future, as Eisler suggests, is to move ahead to a society of gender equality beyond matriarchy, patriarchy, monarchy, and their other dominator equivalents. This understanding is foundational to our effort to become whole human beings and to create whole and balanced human societies reflective of the possibilities of an integral Spiritual Consciousness.

HIS-STORY

We humans live by the stories that define our origins and our nature. History as written by male historians has been quite literally his-story —the heroic story of male warriors, male kings, male presidents, male religious leaders, male philosophers, and male artists. From time to time his-story may include mention of a queen, an empress, a Joan of Arc, a female writer, poet, or artist presented as aberrant deviations from the normal course of events. Raised on his-stories, we grow up taking for granted that it is the natural place of men to rule and women to submit.

Similarly, most of his-story consists of stories of one imperial ruler conquering another or one elite faction prevailing over another in a competition for power. We come to understand that competition, greed, and violence are simply the natural order and that, no matter how destructive they may be, they are the necessary drivers of technological and social progress. The "masculine" power to dominate and destroy is good and just; the feminine power to create life is dangerous and deceitful, a pathway to sin and self-destruction. To worship a male god is "pious." To worship a female god is "pagan."

Contemporary feminist scholars challenge us with some audacious questions. Why should the power to take life rank above the power to create it? Why do we assume that the worship of a male god is more advanced than the worship of a female god?

Much of what we have come to take for granted about ourselves is choice, not destiny. Whether or not the gendered perspective of Eisler and others is correct in every detail or was true of all early societies is less relevant than the deeper understanding that the gendered analysis gives us of the variety and possibility of the human experience.

The gendered perspective invites us to open our minds to the possibility that greater participation of women in leadership positions is not only just but may also be essential to the process of freeing ourselves as a species from the grim self-limiting organizational calculus of Empire. In any event, opening our minds to the truth that the era of Empire is no more than a five-thousand-year blip in the four- to five-million-year arc of human learning about ourselves and our possibilities is an essential first step in the great work of our time.

The early human experience offers a powerful reminder that we humans are a complex species with an extraordinary range of possibilities. One of history's best-kept secrets is the evidence that the most significant advances on the path to the actualization of our distinctive humanity came during a period when human relationships with one another and Earth were in relative balance and people worshipped the nurturant power of the Goddess. The turn to Empire was in part a practical response to the need to bring order to relationships among strangers in the face of population growth. This is the perspective of scale. The turn to Empire was, at a deeper level, a consequence of the suppression of the generative power of the feminine by the dominator power of the masculine. This is the perspective of gender.

The scale perspective and the gender perspective each point to important lessons for our time. The scale perspective points to the truth that equity and consensual decision making come most naturally in self-reliant communities of place in which people have enduring personal relationships of mutual trust and caring, and in which they control the resource base on which their livelihoods depend. The misguided turn to the dominator relations of Empire as a solution to demands for order in the face of population growth undermined the relationships of trust and caring essential to the realization of the fullness of our humanity and transferred resource control to an elite ruling class.

The gender perspective points to the truth that the healthful and dynamic functioning of human society depends on balancing the generative and nurturant power associated with the feminine and the more as-sertive dominance power associated with the masculine. The era of Em-pire not only upset this balance but actively deprecated and denied the feminine, resulting in a violent human assault against life itself.

Empire is a social pathology of some five thousand years in the mak-ing. To replace the life-destroying cultures and institutions of Empire with the life-serving cultures and institutions of Earth Community, we must recognize the enduring presence of Empire beneath the veneer of contemporary democratic institutions, the costs of Empire, and the dy-namics of domination by which Empire creates a self-fulfilling prophecy of diminished human possibility. We must know our history.

CHAPTER 6

Ancient Empire

> Spiritual leaders throughout the world knew that this time
> was coming—a time when all things feminine would be
> exploited, smashed, and destroyed, including all Mother Earth–
> based cultures, feminine-based spirituality, and women.... It
> is said that only when humans are open enough in the heart
> will there be the deep reconnection that allows a true sharing
> of the sacred and secret teachings.[1]
>
> *Ilarion Merculief*

The widely accepted myth that imperial hegemony
brings peace, stability, and well-run public services is pretty much just
that—a myth. It *has* happened: Rome had a succession of five relatively
wise and benevolent emperors over a period of eighty-four years, but
examples in history are so rare as to be considered mainly curious aber-
rations. Wise benevolence is rarely a quality of those who achieve and
hold positions of absolute power. Empire creates its own violence in the
suppression of dissent, its internal intrigues for power, and its incessant
wars to extend its dominion.

Even as Empire invented the technologies to construct great works,
it also invented the technologies to destroy them more quickly and
completely. Even more troublesome is Empire's propensity to impose a
cultural context that suppresses the development to maturity of the human consciousness.

The enduring positive contributions to human betterment of five
thousand years of Empire pale in significance against the contributions
of pre-imperial societies and the technological advances brought forth
as the democratic reforms of the twentieth century unleashed the creative potential of a substantial portion of the human population. In
short, the benefits of Empire have been as overstated as its costs have
been understated. Beneath Empire's carefully constructed myth of
beneficent progress lies a dark truth of five thousand years of diminished human progress.

Asia, Africa, and South and Central America all had their ancient empires. Each fell into ruin, leaving little trace. The focus of my concern is on the ancient empires of the Middle East and Mediterranean and the modern empires of western Europe and North America to which they gave way, for these are the empires that have shaped the modern human experience and brought the species to the brink of self-destruction.

The brief historical review that follows draws mostly from standard history texts and reference sources to highlight the realities of Empire that are commonly overshadowed by history's untiring accounts of glorious battles, great kings, brave warriors, and imperial accomplishment.[2] It reviews the rise and fall of the first of the great ancient city-state empires in Mesopotamia and Egypt, as they offer iconic examples of the structure and dynamics of imperial culture, economies, and political institutions. It also briefly visits the rise and fall of the Roman Empire, which elitists of our time look to as a model for the United States. Finally, it turns to the subsequent descent into the feudalism and religious conflict of Europe's Middle Ages, which our own future may repeat if we leave the choices at hand to those who look to the Roman Empire as their model of governance.

MESOPOTAMIA

In mid-fortieth century BCE the peoples of the Tigris and Euphrates river valleys were organized into twelve walled city-states, each surrounded by the villages to which it offered protection and from which it extracted the food surpluses essential to its sustenance. Each city worshipped its own deity, whose temple was the city's central structure.

Historians believe that initially the citizens of each of the twelve cities shared power more or less equitably and that women may have had the key roles in the affairs of the temples, which were centers of administrative and economic as well as religious power. To survive during hard times, free farmers placed themselves in debt to the temple, leading to a gradual transfer of land to the temples and ultimately the city-states. Over time, the temples came to own vast tracts of the best agricultural land and played a major role in both local and foreign trade—an early manifestation of the principle that in hard times the moneylenders win.

The region had fertile soil, and its rivers provided an abundant and reliable water supply. A lack of rainfall during the main growing season, however, made large-scale irrigation a necessity, which led to a further centralization of administration. A lack of basic natural resources, including stone, minerals, and even trees, made long-distance trade a necessity and created the need for an organized military to secure trade routes that linked rival cities competing for distant resources. The need to maintain both irrigation and an organized military created the need to increase tax collections from free farmers and local artisans while exposing them to competition from subsidized imports. These dynamics contributed to a gradual consolidation of power under powerful kings and a displacement of the feminine by the masculine.

Commerce and administration required written records, leading to the invention of cuneiform writing and the first schools—located in the temple precincts—in which prospective scribes were taught to read and write. This served both to centralize power and to give special advantage to those trained in this powerful technology.

A gradual evolution in religious beliefs regarding the nature and power of the gods mirrored changes in the defining relationships of the society itself. In the earlier period, when people lived in a more intimate relationship with nature, they worshipped goddesses that represented the natural forces of sun, rain, wind, and fertility. Ishtar, the goddess of nature, the elements, and sexual love, was chief among them. With the advance of urban civilization and the rule of male kings, male gods with more human qualities—including the capacity to do both good and evil—gained prominence. As earthly kings became more powerful, Mesopotamia's gods took on political characteristics, and notions of an omnipotent god who ruled over all others came to the fore.[3]

As they consolidated their power, the kings of the rival city-states began to compete for dominance. The region was unified under a single king around 2800 BCE, but the competition for power continued, leaving the region divided and vulnerable to external conquerors. Over the centuries, succeeding imperial dynasties rose and fell. Some were the creations of foreign invaders and others of local revolts. The greatest of the rulers of this period set new standards for both grandeur and ruthless brutality as successive waves of invasion, revolt, and conquest built great cities, destroyed them, and rebuilt them again at an enormous cost in lives and resources.

The Assyrians, who had settled in the northernmost portion of Mesopotamia, consolidated their rule over the region in 1225 BCE with the defeat of Babylon. To prevent the emergence of a prosperous and educated class that might challenge the arbitrary power of the king, the Assyrians mandated that only foreigners could engage in commercial activity. They also imposed the complete subjugation of women. Wives were decreed the property of their husbands. Men were allowed to take several wives and given the sole power of divorce. Married women were permitted to appear in public only with their faces veiled.[4] The suppression of the feminine was complete. We know little of the life of slaves in this period except that they existed, had no rights whatsoever, and were subject to cruel mutilation as punishment for minor offenses.[5]

The mythos of imperial splendor and accomplishment has a factual foundation. The Assyrians are properly celebrated for their exceptional engineering, artistic, intellectual, and botanical capacities and achieved grand works that are impressive even by contemporary standards. During the reign of Sennacherib (705–681 BCE) they built the city of Nineveh on the banks of the upper Tigris. Its great wall had a circumference of seven and a half miles and enclosed magnificent temples and a royal palace of seventy-one chambers. The area outside the wall featured orchards with rare trees and zoos with exotic animals brought from far lands. A great aqueduct brought fresh mountain water to the city from a distance of fifty miles. The city's library was a repository of all the region's learning and literature.

The legendary grandeur of these early imperial city-states was of brief duration and came at the price of an equally legendary brutality. What Empire built, Empire also destroyed. When in 689 BCE Sennacherib suppressed a revolt in rival Babylon, another city of fabled splendor, he boasted, "I made Babylon's destruction more complete than that by a flood."[6]

The frightful brutality of Assyria's military campaigns was intended to instill abject terror in the hearts of its enemies, an early version of the military tactic of "shock and awe" implemented with bombs and rockets by the U.S. military in its 2003 invasion of these same ancient lands. By their own surviving records, the Assyrians skinned their enemies alive; impaled them on stakes; cut off ears, noses, and sex organs; and exhibited mutilated victims in cities that had not yet surrendered. The Assyrians accomplished their goal of instilling terror, but at the price of instilling an unrelenting hatred that led to a sustained and ultimately successful resistance.[7] The mutilation of the innocents caused by modern weaponry is no less brutal and, as the aftermath of the U.S. shock and awe assault on Baghdad demonstrates, provokes the same response. How slow we are to learn!

For reasons of prestige, Sennacherib's son rebuilt Babylon soon after his father had destroyed it. By 651 BCE Babylon had again become a center of revolt. Sennacherib's grandson forced its surrender in 648 BCE, again destroying the city and slaughtering its citizens. In an echo of his grandfather, the grandson boasted that he cut their corpses into small pieces and fed them to dogs, pigs, and vultures. Again, terror fed hatred and resistance.[8]

Hated by all around them, the brutal Assyrian military rule lasted less than a century. The people of southern Mesopotamia formed an alliance with an Indo-European tribe that held power in Iran. In 612 BCE, the alliance captured and laid waste to Nineveh and slaughtered its inhabitants, ending the Assyrian Empire and giving rise to a new Babylonian Empire. This pattern of successive waves of creation and destruction of human and natural potential would define the era of Empire for thousands of years to come.

The positive accomplishments of Mesopotamian civilization included the construction of major irrigation works, the invention of the earliest forms of writing, wheeled transport, and the calendar. In later periods, the region made major contributions to mathematics and astronomy—plotting and predicting the movement of the stars and the planets.

However, the early imperial civilizations of the Fertile Crescent and the eastern Mediterranean failed to maintain their early advantage because, in the words of Jared Diamond, "they committed ecological suicide by destroying their own resource base" as they cleared their forests for timber and agriculture. A combination of overgrazing and loss of forest cover led to soil erosion and the silting up of river valleys. Dependence on irrigation to bring parched lands into production created a buildup of salts in the soil. Once its soil could no longer sustain large population concentrations, the region fell into a decline from which it has never recovered.[9] It was an early local version of the ecological suicide the human species is now committing on a global scale for the same reason: failure to consider the long-term consequences of short-term gains.

The dominator power of Empire breeds a hubris of invincibility that carries the seeds of self-destruction. It invites corruption, the rebellion of subjugated peoples, and environmental devastation. We can only speculate on what the people of the early Mesopotamian civilization

might have accomplished if they had avoided falling under the sway of
Empire, acted as stewards of Earth, renounced violence against one another, and focused their considerable intellectual, architectural, and creative energies on building on, rather than periodically obliterating, the
accomplishments of their neighbors and forebears. If we fail to negotiate the transition to Earth Community in our time, future generations
of humans may ponder the question of why we too were so blind.

EGYPT

Prior to the imperial rule of the pharaohs, the goddess Isis, giver and
protector of life, ruled supreme in the Nile Valley. Somewhere around
3000 BCE, Menes united the people of the valley and established his
capital at Memphis, near modern Cairo. Some historians believe that
the development of the writing system known as hieroglyphics made
this unification possible and that the need for a free flow of commerce
up and down the Nile made it essential.

For a period of some nine hundred years, Egypt lived in peace and
prosperity under a unified state based more on cooperative need than
on exploitation. For a time Isis continued to rule, women enjoyed high
legal status and social freedom, property passed through the female
line, and abundant fertile land isolated between two deserts insulated
the state from competition with its neighbors. During the course of a
succession of pharaohs, however, Osiris, the husband of the goddess
Isis, rose to prominence along with Re, the great sun god. Eventually,
the Egyptians came to believe that Re gave immortality to the state and
that the pharaoh was his living representative.

The deification of the pharaoh and a growing concern for the afterlife accompanied an increasing narcissism among Egypt's rulers and the
dedication of a growing share of available wealth to constructing pretentious monuments of self-glorification, such as the Great Pyramids,
to facilitate the comfortable passage of deceased rulers into the afterlife.
The unified state was unable to survive a series of crop failures due to
climatic disaster and, beginning about 2200 BCE, Egypt fell into a
period of banditry, chaotic competition between rival local nobles, and
invasions by desert tribes.

There followed a relatively more democratic period of two hundred
years (1990–1786 BCE), commonly referred to as Egypt's golden age,

during which order was restored by an alliance of farmers, merchants, officials, and artisans. The alliance kept the nobles in check, supported public works like irrigation and drainage that benefited the entire population, and ushered in a period of comparative social justice, intellectual achievement, and prosperity. Some scholars refer to it as history's first democratic kingdom.[10]

An invasion by the Hyksos of western Asia provoked a two-hundred-year rebellion that gave rise to a strong national unity, the creation of a strong military force, and the installation of a new series of powerful pharaohs. By the time the Hyksos rulers were overthrown, however, the Egyptian culture of pacifism and isolation had been displaced by the Hyksos culture of aggressive imperialism and military expansion. Egypt reached out to establish its rule over a domain that came to extend from the Euphrates to the southern reaches of the Nile.

With a diversion of manpower to military operations on the front lines, there was a significant increase in the demand for slaves to provide labor for the domestic economy, creating ever deeper social divisions and a corruption of the ruling classes. This was the setting in which the Egyptians enslaved the Hebrews who lived in their midst. Think of it as an early version of the use of outsourcing and immigrant labor to depress domestic wages and force the working classes to an acceptance of military service as their major alternative to destitution.

Eventually the territory of the Egyptian Empire expanded beyond the ability of its rulers to manage. Constant revolts at the periphery, an inflow of wealth from conquered peoples, and a system of authority based solely on military power fueled corruption, weakened the national fiber, and left Egypt vulnerable to foreign invasion and rule. The Libyans invaded around 950 BCE, then the Nubians from the south, followed by the Assyrians, later by the Persians (525 BCE), and then the Greeks and Romans.

The corruption of the state that accompanied Egypt's imperial expansion following its golden age carried over to the corruption of a priesthood increasingly consumed by its own greed. The ethical foundation of Egypt's religion gave way to the commercialization of redemption in the afterlife, as magic charms sold by the religious establishment came to replace good deeds as the best guarantee of entrance into the kingdom of Re.[11]

Centuries later, the sale of indulgences by a corrupt Roman Church to ensure passage to heaven would provoke the rebellion of a dissident priest named Martin Luther. Still later, Calvinists would carry to North America a belief that only faith and tithing, not works, assured passage to the heavenly kingdom.

The Egyptian Empire exemplifies Empire's pattern of expropriating and squandering its resources and life energy to construct monuments to the vanity of brutal rulers, support wars of conquest, and support the luxurious lifestyles of vain and corrupt political and religious elites. The cultures and institutions of life and partnership gave way to the cultures and institutions of domination and death. The specifics differed, but once established these patterns remained strikingly consistent among the empires that followed.

After Mesopotamia and Egypt, the next of history's great empires was initiated by Cyrus the Great of Persia (Iran), who came to power in 559 BCE and by the time of his death had conquered and consolidated into his empire much of the territory that is now Iran, Afghanistan, Pakistan, Iraq, Syria, Lebanon, Israel, and Turkey. In 529 BCE, his son Cambyses conquered all of Egypt and brought it under Persian rule.

Philip of Macedonia assumed the throne of a Greek-speaking territory north of Greece in 359 BCE and quickly built a professional army that conquered and consolidated its rule over the whole of Greece. When Philip was murdered, rule passed to his twenty-year-old son, Alexander, who put to death all potential rivals for the throne and went on to conquer and claim for Greece all the lands of the former Persian Empire.

Inspired by Alexander, an Indian adventurer named Chandragupta Maurya established the first Indian Empire in the late fourth century BCE, building a military force of 600,000 infantry, 30,000 cavalry, 9,000 elephants, and an army of spies supported by a land tax equal to one-fourth to one-half of the crops produced in the areas he controlled.[12] An earlier urban civilization grounded in warfare and imperial rule had emerged in China in the second millennium BCE. There is also evidence of imperial civilizations in parts of Africa (first millennium CE) and in the Americas (first to second millennium CE), although the archaeological evidence relating to their social structures remains sketchy.

ROME

For the advocates of Empire, the Roman Empire is the defining symbol of the glorious benefits and accomplishments of imperial rule. For

advocates of Earth Community, it is a defining symbol of Empire's oppressive, destructive, life-denying corruption.[13] When contemporary
U.S. elitists evoke admiring references to Roman rule, it is instructive to
have clearly in mind the reality behind the myth.

The Republic

Founded in 753 BCE, Rome was ruled initially by kings whose primary
responsibility was to maintain order and military efficiency at a time
when the various city-states of the Italian peninsula were engaged in
nearly constant warfare against one another. The early Romans were a
proud and aggressive people, and their rapidly growing population created a hunger for land. Operating on a concept much like that underlying the Italian fascism of World War II, the state was paramount, and
the duty of the individual was to serve it.

Around 500 BCE, the Roman Senate, a deliberative body of little
power comprising representatives of the aristocracy, asserted itself to
found the Roman Republic. The Senate claimed for itself control over
public funds and the power to elect consuls, whose powers were much
the same as those of the former kings but whom the Senate could depose.

The primary responsibility of a consul was to lead Rome's armies in
wars against neighboring cities. The Senate's concern was to curb the
most extreme abuses of arbitrary power, not to democratize power or
secure the liberty of the individual.

The patricians ruled. The plebeians, small farmers, tradesmen, and
even some wealthy families of recent foreign origin had no defined rights.
Plebeians were required to serve in the military but excluded from
holding office. In the absence of written laws, the patricians were free in
judicial proceedings to interpret the rules to their own benefit.

Continuous war fed an increasingly martial spirit as Rome's victories
expanded the territory under its control. By 265 BCE, Rome had established its dominion over the entire Italian peninsula and turned its
attention to contesting the control of Sicily by Carthage, a great maritime empire on the North African coast built on trade and the exploitation of North Africa's resources. In 146 BCE, Rome launched an assault
on Carthage. Following their victory, Roman soldiers went house to
house slaughtering Carthaginian citizens, laid waste to this once magnificent city, sold fifty-five thousand survivors into slavery, and plowed
salt into the soil to render it infertile and incapable of supporting

human habitation. From there Rome went on to establish its dominion over all the lands surrounding the Mediterranean Sea, including most of Europe and the Middle East.[14]

In the days of the early Republic, most Romans were farmers; few engaged in trade or crafts. Conscripted to fight unending wars, many farmers were unable to tend their fields, fell into debt, and lost their farmland to creditors who consolidated it into large estates worked by slaves acquired through conquest. Creditors also had the right to sell the hapless debtors into slavery as a means of recovering their funds—an especially odious form of war profiteering at the expense of the conscripted that brings to mind contemporary reports of creditors foreclosing on the assets of U.S. soldiers unable to pay their debts while fighting in Iraq.

By 150 BCE, slaves filled the republic's countryside, and its cities teemed with unemployed farmers dependent on state welfare and struggling to get by as best they could. At the end of the second century BCE, Italy's slave population numbered about a million, "making Rome one of the most slave-based economies known to history."[15] The resulting social pressures played out in the Senate's demand for further conquests to acquire new land on which to settle Roman citizens who had been displaced from lands and employment by creditors and slaves.

In Rome, an increasing flow of wealth and slaves from conquered territories undermined traditional authority and discipline among members of the aristocracy. Privileged and pampered, Rome's ruling elite embraced extravagantly self-indulgent and wildly hedonistic lifestyles and devoted their civic energies to avoiding taxes and assuring the exemption of their children from military service.

Intrigue in the struggle for power within the ranks of the nobles was commonplace and included assassinations, the wholesale slaughter of political opponents, and even battles between the armies of competing Roman generals. Major slave revolts at times threatened the security of the state. Six thousand captives from one slave revolt that lasted two years and overran much of southern Italy were left crucified along a 150-mile stretch of road from Capua to Rome. Thousands of spectators gathered in the Colosseum and other amphitheaters to be entertained by the human slaughter of gladiatorial contests and human sacrifice to wild animals. Over time, what had once been a republic of farmers became a complex and differentiated society racked by intrigue, brutality, and rebellion and deeply divided between the rich, who became fewer and wealthier, and the destitute poor, who became more numerous and desperate.

Myth of the Roman Peace

The Roman Empire is often celebrated for what is referred to as the Pax Romana, or the Roman peace—a period of more than two hundred years extending from the beginning of the rule of Augustus Caesar (27 BCE to 14 CE) to the death of Emperor Marcus Aurelius in 180. The British would later claim the Pax Romana as a model for their own empire, as would the neoconservative militarists who have held key foreign- and military-policy positions during the U.S. administration of George W. Bush and who openly advocated the imposition on the world of a Pax Americana. There was no naval battle during these two hundred years in the portion of the world ruled by Rome, but otherwise the Pax Romana was scarcely peaceful.

Augustus Caesar began his rule by sending out unsuccessful military expeditions to conquer Ethiopia and Arabia. He was more successful in conquering the territories of what are now Switzerland, Austria, Bulgaria, and Germany to the Elbe.[16] Tiberius (14–37) ended his reign in a paranoid fit of random and ferocious torture and executions, including those of his own generals and members of the Senate. Gaius Caesar Augustus Germanicus (37–41), known more infamously as Caligula, was legendary for his cruelty, extravagance, debauchery, and despotism, and is generally considered to have been clinically insane. He executed his own military commanders and closest supporters and confiscated the estates of nobles to support his lavish lifestyle.

Emperor Claudius (41–54), who was the target of numerous rebellions and assassination attempts, added Britain to the Empire by invasion in 43, conquered additional territories in North Africa and Asia Minor, and for a time expelled Jews from Rome. Nero (54–68) was infamous for his personal debauchery, extravagance, persecution of Christians, and the execution of his mother and first wife. Similar patterns prevailed through the reigns of Vespasian (69–79), Titus (79–81), and Domitian (81–96).[17] All of this and more occurred during the much celebrated Pax Romana. Overall, it is a curious idea of peace.

Only during the latter part of the Pax Romana, during the rule of what historians refer to as the "Five Good Emperors" (96 to 180), might the Roman Empire be considered by any reasonable standard a model of peace and good governance. Nerva (96–98), the first among the five, recognized the limitations of his own son and introduced the practice by which he and his successors chose and adopted a young man designated to be the successor emperor, rather than trust to the luck of heredity. Thus it was that through five administrations each emperor took it upon himself to select and groom as his successor one of the empire's most worthy and talented men.

Nerva was followed by Trajan (98–117), Hadrian (117–38), Antoninus Pius (138–61), and Marcus Aurelius (161–80). Compared to those who went before them they were paragons of wisdom, virtue, sanity, and humble benevolence, responsible for many positive accomplishments in administration, infrastructure, justice, and the well-being of the poor. They also treated the Senate with a degree of respect. Each one, however, ruled as dictator. Rebellions, conquests, palace intrigues, and executions continued, but with diminished frequency and less gratuitous brutality. Expansion of the empire slowed, and greater attention was paid to good governance and the maintenance of relatively stable boundaries.

The line of appointed succession worked reasonably well until Marcus Aurelius failed to recognize that his natural son Commodus (180–92) was a vicious incompetent and named him successor. Commodus proved a throwback to Nero and Caligula, and his brutal rule, which ended when he was strangled in a palace coup, marked the beginning of the decline of the Roman Empire. Hunger and disease became endemic. By 284, the empire was on the brink of ruin.[18]

For all its violence and excess, the Roman Empire did make positive contributions to human progress. To administer its vast territories, it developed modern systems of codified law and rule-based administrative systems. It pioneered high-speed transportation in service to commerce, agriculture, and military movement that served as models for those who followed. It also made important contributions to city planning and infrastructure—particularly with regard to plumbing, sewage disposal, dams, and aqueducts that set new standards for public sanitation.

Those who put forward the Roman Empire as a model for world peace and governance, however, are on weak ground. Its accomplishments came at a cost in lives, liberty, and corruption that is arguably unsurpassed in the human experience. Its more positive accomplishments were largely confined to the good luck of an eighty-four-year reign by five strong emperors of sound mind who offered a brief respite from hundreds of years of rule by the brutal and the deranged.

Historic Irony

One of history's most ironic twists occurred during the period of Rome's decline when Emperor Constantine (312–37) became a Christian, gave Christianity his official support, and built Christian churches throughout the empire. The empire whose soldiers had crucified a Hebrew prophet named Jesus as an enemy of the state thus embraced him as its own.

During his life, Jesus had renounced violence, preached unconditional love, sided with the poor and oppressed, and taught his followers to live by values antithetical to the way of Empire. By advocating a life of active nonparticipation in Empire's corruption of the soul, he presented a practical moral challenge to Empire's established secular and religious order.

Following his execution by order of Pontius Pilate, the Roman governor of the province of Judea, Jesus's disciples carried forward his message, and with time the numbers of Jesus's followers grew, although prior to Constantine's conversion they were never sufficiently numerous to present a serious threat to Roman authority. Subsequently, a corrupt Church of Rome would replace the corrupt institutions of Rome's secular empire as the primary institutional force for European unification.

When Constantine embraced Jesus as his own, he redefined the meaning of Jesus's life and teaching to claim for himself and the empire the moral authority of the prophet of justice, peace, and love. In the words of Christian writer Walter Wink:

> Once Christianity became the religion of the empire… its success was linked to the success of the empire, and *preservation of the empire became the decisive criterion for ethical behavior.*… The church no longer saw the demonic as lodged in the empire, but in the empire's enemies. Atonement became a highly individual transaction between the believer and God; society was assumed to be Christian, so the idea that the work of Christ entails the radical critique of society was largely abandoned.[19] (italics in the original)

To this day Christianity remains divided between those who embrace Jesus's teachings of love and forgiveness as the foundation of Christian morality and those who invoke the name of Jesus in the pursuit of righteous vengeance, imperial conquest, and authoritarian rule.

FEUDAL FIEFDOMS

By 700, the unified Roman Empire that had once encircled the Mediterranean Sea had been replaced by competing Byzantine, Islamic, and western Christian empires. Thus began what historians refer to as the Middle Ages, the period of European history between the Roman Empire and the rise of the modern European nation-state during which no individual ruler or nation was able to establish dominion over the whole.

Europe's early Middle Ages (600–1050), sometimes referred to as the Dark Ages, were days of classic feudalism. Power was fragmented among competing fiefdoms. The roads, water-supply systems, and other public infrastructure created by the Roman Empire, as well as its cultural life, went into decline. The Church of Rome, with its vast bureaucracy and influence over spiritual life, acted in shifting political alliances with secular rulers to provide the only unifying force among those European countries previously united under Rome's secular rule.

Life during this period was harsh. Starvation and disease were commonplace. Intellectual and artistic achievements were undistinguished. There were repeated invasions by Vikings, Hungarians, and Muslims. By contrast, the period of Roman secular rule had been a time of comparative stability, security, and prosperity.

In the High Middle Ages (1050–1300) the harshness of life gradually eased. Improved agricultural methods and the use of water and animal power allowed for the support of a growing population, transformed Europe from a primarily agricultural to an increasingly urban civilization, and substantially improved living standards for the nobles. National monarchies began to assert their authority over competing fiefdoms, although they often found that the loyalty of their subjects to the authority of the Crown was subordinated to their loyalty to the authority of the Roman Church.

Corruption remained rampant within both the religious and political establishments as each vied for imperial power. This was the period of the largely disastrous Crusades, carried forth as uncoordinated initiatives by various princes and independent brigands in response to the call of the pope. Lacking either a secure political base or coherent leadership, the Crusades were largely a form of violent adventurism with no capacity to capture and incorporate new territory into an imperial structure.

The late Middle Ages (1300–1500) were a time of famine due to exhausted farmlands and bad weather, the pestilence of the Black Death, and protracted warfare among competing kings, princes, and petty nobles in search of dominion, independence, and personal enrichment from the spoils of war. Death rates soared and fortunes were in constant flux. This period, however, also marked the beginning of the European Renaissance, which brought a flourishing of art, culture, and philosophy beginning in Italy that with time launched a growing challenge to authority, whether secular or ecclesiastic, as a source of absolute truth.

On October 31, 1517, the act of a dissident Catholic priest sparked a rebellion against the religious monopoly of the Roman Christian Church, launched the Protestant Reformation, and added a new element of division and instability to European politics. Martin Luther posted his Ninety-five Theses on the door of the Castle Church in Wittenberg, Germany, in protest against a corrupt Roman Catholic Church that he charged had lost its moral authority and become a self-indulgent imperial power in its own right. He professed that the ultimate spiritual authority is the authority of conscience, not the authority of the church. The hundred years from 1560 to 1660 featured periodic outbreaks of religious slaughter of Protestants by Catholics and of Catholics by Protestants, often encouraged or aided by rulers whose political interests aligned with one side or the other. It was a time of destructive wars, rapacious tax collectors, and looting soldiers.[20]

Gradually the western European nations would resolve the chaos of competition and intrigue among feudal lords and feuding religious functionaries by consolidating the powers of monarchy in the institutions of the modern nation-state, which for most people offered a welcome relief from the turmoil of feudalism.

Those who lived in the Middle Ages might have looked back with justification on the comparative order and amenities of the Roman Empire, especially during the brief reign of the Five Good Emperors, as a better time than their own. Those who eulogize the Roman Empire in the age of the democratic ideal, however, should recall the violence, injustice, and debauchery that were hallmarks of Roman rule. Mesopotamia, Egypt, and Rome were three of history's most celebrated empires. Each had its moments of greatness, but at an enormous cost in lives, natural wealth, and human possibility, as vain and violent rulers played out the drama of Empire's inexorable play-or-die, rule-or-be-ruled, kill-or-be-killed logic.

Social pathology became the norm as the god of death displaced the goddess of life and the power of the sword ruled over the power of the chalice. The creative energy of the species was redirected from building the generative power of the whole to advancing the technological instruments of war and the social instruments of domination. Empire built great civilizations, but then swept them away in successive waves of violence and destruction as jealous winners sought to erase the memory of those they vanquished.

The sacred became the servant of the profane. Fertile lands were converted to desert by intention or rapacious neglect. Rule by terror fueled resentments that assured repeating cycles of violent retribution. War, trade, and debt served as weapons of the few to expropriate the means of livelihood of the many and reduce them to slavery or serfdom. The resulting power imbalances fueled the delusional hubris and debaucheries of psychopathic rulers who fancied themselves possessed of divine privilege and otherworldly power. Attention turned from realizing the possibilities of life in this world to securing a privileged place in the afterlife.

The ruling elites maintained cultural control through the institutions of religion, economic control through the institutions of trade and credit, and political control through the institutions of rule making and organized military force. Although elite factions might engage in ruthless competition with one another, they generally aligned in common cause to secure the continuity of the institutions of their collective privilege, often using intermarriage as a mechanism of alliance building.

If many of the patterns associated with ancient kings, pharaohs, and emperors seem strangely familiar to our own time of the democratic ideal, even though democracy has ended monarchy in its historic form, it is because the dominator cultures and institutions of Empire simply morphed into new forms in the face of the democratic challenge. To free ourselves from Empire's deadly grip we must understand not only its historical roots, but as well its contemporary expression. So let us now take a brief look at the formation of the colonial empires of the modern European nation-states and their transmogrification into the institutions of the global corporate empires of the late twentieth century as the ruling class negotiated an end run around the modern democratic challenge to its power and privilege.

CHAPTER 7

Modern Empire

No man can serve two masters: for either he will hate the one,
and love the other; or else he will hold to the one, and despise
the other. Ye cannot serve God and mammon.

Matthew 6:24

As we look deeper for the soul of capitalism, we find that, in
the terms of ordinary human existence, American capitalism
doesn't appear to have one. In the economic sphere, efficiency
trumps community. Maximizing returns comes before family
or personal loyalty. What seems priceless in one realm may be
wasted freely or even destroyed by the other.[1]

William Greider

By the reckoning of Western historians, the modern
era began in 1500. The turmoil of endless and pointless wars in which
rival noble factions fought one another to exhaustion for largely personal ends had created a readiness to welcome a restoration of rule by
monarchs with the power to impose order.

Prior to 1500, empires had been based primarily on the expansion of
borders through military conquest to incorporate new territory under
the central military and administrative control of a city-state ruled by
a king or emperor. Center and periphery were territorially contiguous,
and the boundaries between them often lacked significant definition.
Land and trade were the foundations of wealth, and the institutions of
monarchy generally controlled and profited from the power to tax and
allocate the rights to both. Independent commercial enterprises were
individually far too small to challenge the power of the sovereign king.

The imperial model of the modern era replaced city-states with
nation-states defined by clearly delineated territorial borders under a
well-defined central administration. Rather than exhaust themselves in
military campaigns against one another to redefine the territorial division of Europe, the European kings of the modern era satisfied their
ambitions for imperial expansion by projecting their power outward

over long sea routes from their relatively secure and stable domestic borders on the European continent and establishing dominion over the lands, peoples, and resources of distant colonies. By the logic of Empire, they were enormously successful. Although persons of European descent were only a tiny percentage of the world's people, by 1878 they ruled 67 percent of the planet's land surface.[2]

The transition from city-states to nation-states brought a growing challenge to the institutions of monarchy. Growing demands for the accountability of the institutions of the state gradually stripped monarchy of its absolute power. Monarchy died. Empire, however, retained its dominion in a new form.

CRIME LORDS AND SYNDICATES

National military forces and colonial administrations remained important to the new model of Empire, but for the most part the European kings of the modern era projected their power by granting commissions to favored adventurers, brigands, and corporations who worked for their own account in return for a share of the spoils. Thus began the transition from rule by imperial monarchs to rule by imperial corporations. Herein lies the story of how money came to rule the world.

Adventurers

Most of us know the period of Europe's drive for colonial expansion primarily by the names of the great adventurers commissioned and financed by their sovereigns to carry out great voyages of discovery, plunder, and slaughter. In search of a westward sea route to the riches of Asia, Christopher Columbus (1451–1506) landed on the island of Hispaniola (present-day Haiti and the Dominican Republic) in the West Indies in 1492 and claimed it for Spain. Hernando De Soto (1496–1542) made his initial mark trading slaves in Central America and later allied with Francisco Pizarro to take control of the Inca Empire based in Peru in 1532, the same year the Portuguese established their first settlement in Brazil. De Soto returned to Spain one of the wealthiest men of his time, although his share in the plunder was only half that of Pizarro.[3] By 1521, Hernán Cortés had claimed the Mexican Empire of Montezuma for Spain.

Spain ultimately extracted so much gold from South and Central America that it ruined its own economy and fueled inflation throughout

Europe. With so much gold available to purchase goods produced by others, Spain's own productive capacity atrophied as it became dependent on importing goods from abroad. The result was a domestic economic decline from which it never recovered. It was a pattern disturbingly similar to that of the current import-dependent U.S. economy—with the primary difference that U.S. imports are financed not by stolen gold, but by foreign borrowing.

Although licensed by the Crown, these celebrated adventurers operated with the independence and lack of scruples of crime lords, competing or cooperating with one another as circumstances dictated for personal gain and glory. Their mission was to extract the physical wealth of foreign lands and peoples by whatever means—including the execution of rulers and the slaughter and enslavement of Native peoples—and to share a portion of the spoils with their sovereign. Securing lands for settlement would become important later but had no place in these early ventures.

Supported by improvements in the tools of navigation, Portugal and Spain initially led the way. By the mid-1500s, Spain had established control over nearly all of Central and South America. Highly profitable for Portugal and Spain, these conquests came at an unconscionable cost to the peoples of the colonized territories. The profits from Spain's conquests in the Americas inspired the imperial exertions of the English, Dutch, and French, who were soon dividing Africa, Asia, and North America into colonies from which to extract plunder and trading profits for the benefit of the mother state.

Privateers

The competition for foreign spoils among the European powers led to the elevation of the ancient practice of privateering—essentially legalized piracy—to a major instrument of state policy and a favored investment for both sovereigns and wealthy merchants. Why endure the arduous exertions of expropriating the wealth of foreign lands through conquest and trade when it was much easier to attack and plunder the ships carrying the spoils on their way back to European ports?

Monarchs often found it advantageous to grant a license to privately owned, financed, and captained armed vessels to engage in this profitable enterprise. These privateers offered important advantages to cash-strapped rulers. They provided revenue with no cash outlay, and official responsibility could be disavowed more easily than if the warships of the Crown had pillaged the victim vessels. Crew, captain, private investors, and the commissioning king divided the revenues from the booty while the king's license lent a patina of legality to the acts of plunder and granted the ships safe harbor. A new era was in gestation.

The English, Dutch, and French all had their commissioned privateers licensed to pillage the ships, lands, and treasure of their primary colonial competitors, especially Spain. English privateers first sought their fortunes in the New World during the reign of Elizabeth I (1558–1603) by plundering Spanish shipping in the Caribbean. Elizabeth, who was preoccupied with conquering Ireland, largely left the English privateers to their own devices without support or supervision.[4]

Famous English privateers included Sir John Hawkins (1532–95), Sir Francis Drake (1540–96), and Sir Henry Morgan (1635–88).[5] It was not only an honored vocation, as their titles suggest; it was also a lucrative one. British economist John Maynard Keynes referred to Drake's profits from his three major privateering expeditions as "the fountain and origin of British foreign investment." Tax records for 1790 indicate that four of Boston's top five taxpayers that year obtained their income in part from investments in privateering—including John Hancock, famed for his outsize signature on the Declaration of Independence.[6]

Some privateers operated powerful naval forces. In 1670, Morgan launched an assault on Panama City with thirty-six ships and nearly two thousand buccaneers, defeating a large Spanish force and looting the city as it burned to the ground.[7]

In 1856 the major European powers, with the exception of Spain, signed the Declaration of Paris, declaring privateering illegal. The United States, which relied heavily on privateers as its primary source of naval power and a major source of commercial profits in its early years, declined to join the agreement on the argument that it lacked an adequate navy to protect itself in time of war. The United States, which to this day regularly declines to honor treaties aimed at securing the international rule of law, did not stop commissioning privateers until the end of the nineteenth century.[8]

Chartered Corporations

Over time, the ruling monarchs turned from swashbuckling adventurers and chartered pirates to chartered corporations as their favored instruments of colonial expansion, administration, and pillage. It is instructive to note that in England this transition was motivated in part by its incipient step to democracy.

By the beginning of the seventeenth century the English parliament, one of the first modern efforts to limit the arbitrary power of the king, had gained the authority to supervise the Crown's collection and expenditure of domestic tax revenues. Chafing under this restriction, sovereigns such as Elizabeth, James I, and Charles I found that by issuing corporate charters that bestowed monopoly rights and other privileges on favored investors, they could establish an orderly and permanent source of income through fees and taxes that circumvented parliamentary oversight. They also commonly owned personal shares in the companies to which they granted such privileges.[9]

In addition, chartered corporations sometimes assumed direct responsibility for expenses that otherwise would have fallen on the state, including the costs of maintaining embassies, forts, and other naval, military, and trade facilities. English corporations were at times even given jurisdiction over Englishmen residing in a given territory.[10]

Several of the earliest colonial settlements in what later became the United States were established by corporations chartered by the British Crown; they were largely populated with bonded laborers—many of them involuntarily transported from England—to work corporate properties. The importation of slaves from Africa followed.

The British East India Company (chartered in 1600) was the primary instrument of Britain's colonization of India, a country the company ruled until 1784 much as if it were a private estate. The company continued to administer India under British supervision until 1858, when the British government assumed direct control.[11]

In the early 1800s, the British East India Company established a thriving business exporting tea from China and paying for its purchases with illegal opium. China responded to the resulting social and economic disruption by confiscating the opium warehoused in Canton by the British merchants. This precipitated the Opium War of 1839 to 1842 —which Britain won.

As tribute, the victorious British pressed a settlement on China that required the payment of a large indemnity to Britain, granted Britain free access to five Chinese ports for trade, and secured the right of British citizens accused of crimes in China to be tried by British courts.[12] This settlement was a precursor to the modern "free trade" agreements imposed by strong nations on weak nations to secure the rights of global corporations to act in disregard of local interests.

The Dutch East India Company (chartered 1602) established its sovereignty over what is now Indonesia and reduced the local people to poverty by displacing them from their lands to grow spices for sale in Europe, a forerunner of the practices of contemporary global corporations that displace local farmers in order to consolidate their lands into foreign-controlled estates producing goods for export. The French Company of the East Indies (1664) controlled commerce with French territories in India, eastern Africa, the East Indies, and other islands and territories of the Indian Ocean.

The Hudson Bay Company, which was founded in 1670 to establish British control over the fur trade in the Hudson Bay watershed of North America, was an important player in the British colonization of what is now Canada. Armed skirmishes with the rival North West Company were common until the British government forced their merger in 1821 into a single company with a monopoly over the fur trade in much of North America, including the Northwest Territories. The British South Sea Company, which was chartered primarily to sell African slaves to Spanish colonies in America, became the centerpiece of the "South Sea Bubble," one of history's most famous financial scams.[13]

The new corporate form, the joint stock company created to fulfill the above functions, combined two ideas from the Middle Ages: the sale of shares in public markets and the protection of owners from personal liability for the corporation's obligations. These two features made it possible to amass virtually unlimited financial capital within a single firm, assured the continuity of the firm beyond the death of its founders, and absolved owners of personal liability for the firm's losses or misdeeds beyond the amount of their holdings in the company.

Furthermore, separating owners from day-to-day management allowed for a unified central direction that was difficult or impossible with management control divided among a number of owner partners. The new enterprise form made it possible to amass financial power, in perpetuity and virtually without limit, under a central authority on behalf of the financial interests of owners who bore no liability for the consequences of its actions and with rare exception took no part in management.

It is no exaggeration to characterize these forebears of contemporary publicly traded limited-liability corporations as, in effect, legally sanctioned and protected crime syndicates with private armies and navies backed by a mandate from their home governments to extort tribute, expropriate land and other wealth, monopolize markets, trade slaves, deal drugs, and profit from financial scams. One of the defining institutions of the modern era, publicly traded limited-liability corporations of gigantic scale now operate with substantial immunity from legal liability and accountability even in the countries that issue their charters.

Institutional Sociopaths

The publicly traded limited-liability corporation is an artificial entity legally accountable to the owners whose financial interests the corporation's managers and workers are hired to serve to the disregard of public interests or their own values. Since the owners of publicly traded corporations rarely have personal knowledge of the corporations they own or involvement in their operations, there is no effective mechanism for them to express their values through their ownership participation even if they wish to do so. Shareholders committed to socially responsible investment who attempt to express their views on values issues at formal shareholder meetings are routinely ignored, even when they represent major blocks of stock.

Professors of law and businesses commonly teach their students that bringing ethical considerations into corporate decision making is unethical, as it may compromise the bottom line and unjustly deprive shareholders of their rightful return. It is a rather perverse moral logic given that, as Marjorie Kelly points out in *The Divine Right of Capital*, shareholders contribute less than any other corporate stakeholder to the success of the enterprise.[14]

Although the principle that the legal and ethical obligation of management is to place financial returns to shareholders above all other interests is not spelled out in any legislation, it has become deeply embedded in the U.S. legal culture and case law and has spread to other national jurisdictions. It is a pure case of judge-made law based on the arguments of corporate-interest lawyers.

Consequently, under current U.S. law, the publicly traded limited-liability corporation is prohibited from exercising the ethical sensibility and moral responsibility normally expected of a natural-born, emotionally mature human adult. If it were a real person rather than an artificial legal construction, we would diagnose it as sociopathic. Unless constrained by rules set and enforced by a public body functioning as a kind of parent surrogate, the publicly traded corporation operates in an ethical vacuum.[15]

Corporations spend billions of dollars on lawyers, lobbyists, and PR flacks whose job is to gain corporate freedom from such rules by manipulating the political process. Corporate CEOs have suggested, only partly in jest, that in their ideal world their corporate headquarters would be located on a private island outside the jurisdiction of any government and their plants would be on barges that could be moved on a moment's notice to wherever labor is cheapest, public subsidies and tax breaks most generous, and regulations most lax.

DEMOCRATIC CHALLENGE

Absolutism, the belief in the absolute right of kings, had been put to rest in England by 1689. The monarchy remained, however, and the nobles and other men of property who had secured the power of the vote for themselves showed no enthusiasm for broadening the democratic franchise at home or ending colonial rule abroad. Absolutist monarchy remained strong in much of the rest of Europe, particularly France, for another hundred years. However, the erosion of monarchy had begun.

End of Monarchy

As the American Revolution of 1776 challenged the concept of foreign rule, so the French Revolution of 1789 was a direct challenge to the institution of monarchy. It began as a revolt of the French middle class against the power of the nobles and the clergy. A growing peasant rebellion in the provinces panicked the nobles and clergy sufficiently to persuade them to join with relatively conservative members of the merchant middle class—the bourgeoisie, in the terminology of the day—to draft a Declaration of Rights and a new constitution that stripped the nobles and clergy of their special power and privilege. The loss by Spain and Portugal of control over their Latin American colonies followed in the early 1800s during the Napoleonic Wars, when those colonies followed the example of the United States and established themselves as independent states ruled by descendants of their European occupiers.

The fears of other European monarchs that the French Revolution might inspire others to rebel proved well founded. Europe experienced a wave of democratic revolutions. The Spaniards revolted against Joseph Bonaparte in 1808. Insurrections followed in Greece, Italy, Spain, France, Belgium, and Poland between 1820 and 1831, and in 1848 in France, Austria and Hungary, Germany, and Italy. A flourishing of democracy in the twentieth century was accompanied by extraordinary technological and economic advances that brought to roughly 20 percent of the world's population a level of material comforts that would have been the envy of nobles in generations past.

End of Colonialism

The aftermath of World War II brought another wave of dramatic advances in the democratization of human cultures and institutions as the spirit of freedom swept the world. In India, a modest and diminutive man named Gandhi rallied a nation behind an independence movement that countered British military power with the moral power of principled nonviolence in the cause of a universal right to self-governance.

The inspiration of Gandhi's victory energized oppressed people the world over to join a struggle for human liberation from European imperial domination. Independence movements throughout Europe's colonial territories built an unstoppable momentum with the support of human-rights movements organized in solidarity by citizens of the colonial powers themselves.

The institution of the corporation remained alive and well throughout this period of democratic reforms, but emerged from World War II constrained by government oversight, the countervailing power of strong labor unions, and a social contract that supported an equitable sharing of wealth and power and cooperative working relations among government, labor, and business. Various social movements successfully lobbied for strong consumer, worker, and environmental protections. It appeared for a time that the corporate beast had been tamed to the service of the public interest.

By the end of the second millennium, the institutions of political democracy had replaced the institutions of monarchy in most of the world, and classic colonialism had come to a much deserved end. The Soviet Empire had disintegrated, and China, although far from democratic, had opened its economy to market forces. Pundits declared the universal triumph of democracy and the free market.

The democracy, however, was more a democracy of money than of people, and the markets were only truly free for corporations and big investors. In its actual expression, market freedom means that corporations are free to do whatever they like. People are free to buy or do without whatever products or jobs corporations choose to offer them on terms of the corporation's choosing.

IMPERIAL COUNTERATTACK

The extreme and growing inequality that has turned out to be a hallmark of the corporate global economy did not happen by accident. It results from the work of skilled planners who designed the institutional framework for a post–World War II global economy with the intention to secure U.S. global economic and political dominance based on well-proven principles of imperial rule.

Grand Plan

Britain entered World War II as the world's dominant colonial power and intended to maintain that position at the war's conclusion. Secret British planning documents from 1945 and beyond outline plans to strengthen British access to raw materials in Africa and to develop the Middle East, in the words of Ernest Bevin, Britain's postwar foreign secretary, as "a prosperous producing area to assist the British economy and replace India as an important market for British goods." To this end Britain would use development assistance to influence other countries' internal decisions to protect and advance British economic and political interests.[16]

The United States, for whom World War II was an opportunity to pull itself out of an economic depression and strengthen its industrial base while the European economies were being devastated by the conflict, had a similar, but larger and bolder, vision by which it, not Britain, would dominate the postwar global economy. The U.S. intention was to use to its own advantage a principle the British had demonstrated prior to the war: an open global economic system works to the benefit of the strongest player.

The plan, which is discussed in more detail in chapter 11, "Empire's Victory," centered on opening national economies to unfettered access by U.S. corporations and financial institutions, which at that point were unquestionably the most powerful on the planet. A set of three international institutions formed at U.S. initiative and known collectively as the Bretton Woods institutions—the World Bank, the International Monetary Fund, and the General Agreement on Tariffs and Trade (later replaced by the World Trade Organization)—would be key players in implementing the U.S. strategy.

Easy Credit

The Bretton Woods institutions played their roles well. As country after country emerged from colonialism, the World Bank encouraged them to spur the growth of their economies by accepting foreign loans to finance the purchase of goods and services from the industrialized nations. Soon the new nations found themselves in a condition of debt bondage to the very countries from which they had presumably gained their independence.[17]

Corrupt rulers for whom the loans were a win-win proposition eagerly joined in the scam. They gained political capital from projects paid for with borrowed money, and they profited directly from bribes related to the deal making. Generous grace periods granted on interest and the repayment of principal assured that the burden of repayment would fall on their unfortunate successors.

Former colonies borrowed not only to finance development projects but also to get the foreign exchange to import luxury goods for their ruling elites and arms to repress dissent. Later they used new loans to finance the debt-service payments that eventually came due on previous loans. This pyramiding of the debt burden accelerated dramatically in the late 1970s due to significant increases in energy costs.

Adjusting the Poor

By 1982, it was evident that many low-income countries would never be able to repay their accumulated foreign debts. Fear that default could bring a collapse of the global financial system spread panic in the ranks of global financiers. The International Monetary Fund (IMF) and the World Bank stepped in as debt collectors to impose a package of standardized economic "reforms" known as structural adjustment.

The IMF and World Bank are both headquartered in Washington, D.C., and operate under the influence and close oversight of the U.S.

Treasury Department, which has traditionally served as the U.S. government representative of Wall Street banks and investment houses. It was therefore no surprise that the policy prescriptions demanded as conditions for new credit served the interests of global finance at the further expense of the people in whose name corrupt leaders had incurred the debt. The standard "structural adjustment" agreement called for

- rolling back regulations that benefited workers and protected public health, safety, and the environment but increased business costs;
- eliminating restrictions on foreign imports, foreign ownership, cross-border financial flows, the export of natural resources, and the activities of foreign banks and financial houses so that global corporations could move goods and money across their borders at will;
- privatizing public assets and services, including communications, power, and water, by offering them for sale to private investors at bargain prices;
- slashing public expenditures for health and education to free funds for the repayment of foreign loans; and
- providing special tax breaks and subsidies to foreign investors.

These measures attracted foreign investment and increased exports to generate foreign exchange to repay outstanding debts to foreign creditors —starting with the IMF and World Bank. They also gave foreign corporations and financiers unrestricted access to national economies to extract the maximum amount of wealth with the minimum investment of time and money.

Deeper in Debt

Faithful implementation of the mandated policies made a government eligible for yet more loans. Foreign indebtedness thus continued to grow in tandem with growing foreign control of national economies—playing out much the same scenario by which the moneylenders of ancient time consolidated their control over the lands of once independent farmers and reduced free farmers to serfdom. The new colonialism had a friendlier face than the old, but the consequences in terms of foreign control and expropriation were much the same.

In the 1990s, the corporate plutocrats turned to international trade agreements as their favored instrument for rewriting national laws to implement their corporate-friendly agenda of deregulation, open borders, and privatization. A single international trade agreement could at a stroke effectively overturn hundreds of laws inconvenient to foreign corporate interests in each of the signatory countries with virtually no public debate. It was far more efficient than overturning the democratic process one country at a time, and it worked for rich and poor countries alike.

Each new agreement further constrained the ability of governments to hold global corporations accountable for the consequences of their actions, thus advancing the transition from elite rule by unaccountable monarchs to elite rule by unaccountable corporations and financial markets.[18] It was an undeclared class war of the owners and managers of big capital against democracy and those who actually produce wealth, and it continues today without respite. The weapon of choice is a money system that silently and invisibly transfers an ever growing portion of the world's real wealth to the control of a small ruling class.

MONEY RULES

In modern societies in which access to most everything essential to survival depends on money, money has become the ticket to life itself. Through a kind of psychological transference, the instinctual human love of life becomes a love of money. Money becomes an object of worship. This gives almost total power to those who have the means to create and allocate money, silently and invisibly ruling from their temples in the sky those who must serve them in return for the money on which their very lives depend. The rule of money works all the better for corporate plutocrats because most people are wholly unaware of the ways in which the organizing principles of Empire have become embedded in the money system.

The Ultimate Con

Recall the observation in chapter 3 that money is simply an accounting chit created out of nothing, without substance or intrinsic value, which has value only because we believe it does and therefore willingly accept it in exchange for things of real value. In modern financial systems, banks create money when they issue a loan. The bank opens an account in the name of the borrower and enters a number representing the amount of the loan in the account. The bank in essence rents to the borrower money it has created from nothing at whatever interest rate the market will bear. It may also acquire a mortgage on the home, farm, or other real property of the borrower. If the borrower cannot make the payments, the bank gets the real property.

This is the relatively straightforward and widely understood part of the modern money con. The more complex part relates to the ability of laxly regulated corporations, banks, and financial markets to facilitate the artificial inflation of the market value of financial assets—including stocks, land, and housing—through accounting fraud, lending pyramids, financial bubbles, and other forms of financial speculation and manipulation.

These financial games contribute nothing of value to the larger society. They do, however, significantly increase the buying power of the ruling elites and their claims on the real wealth of society relative to the claims of those persons who contribute to the creation of that wealth by producing real goods and providing real services. They are the most successful of financial cons because the mechanisms are invisible and the marks—the objects of the con—rarely realize they have been conned. Even if they were to recognize they have been conned, there is nothing they can do about it because the con is both legal and culturally accepted.[19]

Money from Money

Through the mechanisms of the financial system, the control of real assets inexorably moves over time from those who create real wealth by doing real work to an owning class that lives on the returns on money. In the wake of banking deregulation, nonbanking corporations in the United States have been establishing their own banks to attract government-insured deposits that allow them to lend money to themselves at substantially lower rates than they could get from nonproprietary banks. They recycle the borrowed money into deposits in their own banks to create new reserves from which to make yet more loans to themselves and others.[20] It is a kind of a government-guaranteed financial pyramid scheme that generates handsome profits on minimal initial investment, another bit of a smoke-and-mirrors, self-dealing gaming of the money system.

The ideal of finance capitalism is to make money solely by collecting monopoly rents or through speculation on financial bubbles and debt pyramids without the inconvenience of producing anything of actual value in the process—an ideal exemplified by Enron until its collapse in disgrace in the hallmark financial scandal of the twenty-first century.

Pervasive Bias

The money system's bias in favor of the owning class is so pervasive and widely accepted as the natural order as to go largely unnoticed. For example, by the logic of the prevailing money culture, every public and private economic choice is properly vetted on the basis of which of the available options will produce the highest returns on money, which generally works out to mean to people with money.

Another source of bias comes from central bankers, whose publicly acknowledged function is to manage the financial markets of supposedly "free market" economies to maintain a downward pressure on the price of labor. If full employment shows signs of putting upward pressure on wages, the central bankers raise interest rates to slow the economy to reduce inflationary pressures. The unmentioned consequence is to assure that benefits from gains in worker productivity go to profits and the owners of capital rather than to workers.

The gradual transition from monarchy to political democracy during the last half of the second millennium stimulated a corresponding transition from imperial rule by the power of the sword to imperial rule by the power of money. The new rulers donned business suits rather than imperial robes and embraced more subtle tactics as they deftly circumvented the democratic challenge to their power and privilege.

The transition began with the rise of the European nation-states in the aftermath of the Middle Ages. Of a mind to expand their imperial dominion while minimizing the prospect of direct military confrontation with their powerful neighbors, they projected their expansionist ambitions outward to the far reaches of the planet to triumph over weaker states. Rather than turn to loyal generals as their agents of imperial conquest, they issued commissions to swashbuckling adventurers, licensed pirates, and chartered corporations that functioned as officially sanctioned criminal syndicates working for their own account under an imperial franchise. British kings issued corporate charters primarily as a means to create income streams not subject to democratic oversight by the nobles of the early British parliament. Contemporary publicly traded corporations carry forward the mantle of the Crown corporations of an earlier day. The largest now wield more economic and political power than most contemporary nation-states and continue to serve as institutional vehicles by which the propertied class circumvents the institutions of democratic accountability.

The money system, however, is an even more powerful and successful weapon than the corporation in the war of the ruling class against the middle- and lower-income working classes. By controlling the creation and allocation of money, the ruling class maintains near total control over the lives of ordinary people and the resources of the planet.

Empire, in the guise of democracy, remains alive and well. True democracy remains an essential but elusive ideal. As we need to confront the reality of the imperial legacy, so too we must confront the limitations of the democratic experiment. To that end let us now turn to an earlier effort to break free from the play-or-die logic of Empire.

CHAPTER 8

Athenian Experiment

> To save the democracy we thought we had, we must take it to where it's never been.[1]
>
> *Frances Moore Lappé*

Between the time of the Mesopotamian and Egyptian empires and the time of the American Revolution, the era of Empire was punctuated by two celebrated human encounters with egalitarian greatness. The first was Egypt's golden age (1990–1786 BCE). The second, and better known, was centered in ancient Athens, a Greek city-state known for the graceful beauty of its art and architecture, its belief in the nobility of human achievement, and its devotion to human freedom. Our word *democracy* comes from the Greek word *dēmokratiā*: literally, "people power." The two preceding chapters sought insight into the challenges of the Great Turning from the experience of five thousand years of Empire; this chapter seeks insights from the Athenian experiment in popular democracy and the reflections of its three most fabled philosophers.

As the violence and domination of Empire manifest the lower orders of human possibility, so the mutual caring and partnership of the mature democracy of Earth Community manifest the higher orders of human possibility. The realization of the potential of a democratic society goes hand in hand with the realization of the potential of each citizen. Together the practical politics of the Athenian experience and the philosophical reflections of Socrates, Plato, and Aristotle illuminate the importance and implications of this relationship and thereby provide a framework for a deeper understanding of the work of bringing the still limited democracy of our own time to full fruition.

ATHENIAN DEMOCRACY

Perhaps the proximity of Athens to the island of Crete, the center of the Aegean society—believed to be the last, most peaceful, and most equitable of the Goddess societies—had something to do with igniting the Greek imagination to the possibilities of an egalitarian form of government. Remnants of the Aegean civilization survived until the eleventh century BCE and retained a presence in the temples of the Greek city-states in which priestesses continued to play a central role. It is also noteworthy that Athens had never been the subject of armed invasion and no military caste had ever imposed its rule.

Athens was ruled as a monarchy until roughly 750 BCE, when the nobles began to wrest power from the king to establish a hereditary aristocracy that lasted until around 600 BCE. Rich mineral deposits and splendid harbors made trade a foundation of economic life and of a vibrant urban culture. The Athenian merchant fleet plied the Mediterranean under the power of sails and galleys of up to two hundred slave rowers, buying cheap in one place and selling dear in another.[2] Rural aristocrats who had the resources to sustain them through the five years required to bring grape and olive cultures into profitable production prospered in the rocky Athenian countryside and expanded their land holdings by buying up the lands of failed grain farmers.

Less fortunate farmers who could only afford to plant grains faced the changing fortunes of the harvest and competition from cheap imports from regions better suited to grain production. Forced to borrow against their land at exorbitant interest rates to survive the bad years, they were being driven from their land in large numbers. Sharecroppers who worked land owned by others for a one-sixth share of what they produced survived the bad years by borrowing against their future labor and that of their families. The almost inevitable default on their loans resulted in their sale into slavery. The resulting social tensions created a growing political crisis.

Rise and Fall

Political tensions came to a head in 594 BCE, with threats of revolution in the air. The urban middle class sided with the peasants in a demand for political liberalization and a radical redistribution of wealth. To forestall a potentially violent revolution, all parties agreed to appoint Solon, a respected Athenian statesman, member of the Council of Areopagus, poet, and tradesman, as a magistrate with absolute power to carry out reforms.

Solon canceled outstanding debts, freed all debtors from bondage, made it illegal to enslave debtors, limited the amount of land any individual could own, provided loans on favorable terms to small farmers to assist their conversion to grape and olive production, and expanded the political franchise to all but women, residents born to foreign parents, and slaves. No one was wholly satisfied. The aristocracy resented its loss of privileges. The middle and lower classes felt the aristocracy retained too much power.

Athenian political democracy gained little real traction until Cleisthenes, a liberal-minded aristocrat, enlisted the support of the masses to gain the office of chief archon, or highest magistrate (525–524 BCE). He is known as the father of Athenian democracy for granting full rights of citizenship to all free men who resided in the territory of Athens at that time and establishing the Council of Five Hundred as the chief organ of government. The council, whose members were selected by lot from male candidates over thirty years of age submitted by the townships, had supreme authority over executive and administrative functions and the power to prepare and submit legislative proposals to the assembly.

All citizens, thirty thousand adult males at that time, were entitled to participate in the assembly, with six thousand required for a quorum.[3] The assembly had the power to debate and pass or reject proposals from the council. It also had the power to declare war, appropriate money, and audit the accounts of retiring magistrates.

The highest point of Athenian democracy was reached during the thirty-year tenure (461–429 BCE) of Pericles as chief strategus, or president, of the Board of Generals, a body comparable to the British cabinet, whose members were chosen by the assembly for one-year terms with unlimited eligibility for reelection. During this period the assembly acquired the authority to initiate legislation without the prior recommendation of the Council of Five Hundred.[4]

At this point Athenian democracy came as close to the practice of direct democracy—securing the right of every citizen (although a small percentage of the population) to direct participation in the political process—as has been achieved by any state before or since. Yet it fell far short of realizing the democratic ideal of universal suffrage, as the rights of citizenship were denied to women, slaves, and those born to foreign parents.[5] Indeed, by some accounts the treatment of women, and even more so of slaves, was as bad as that found in the most brutal of ancient civilizations.[6]

There were other problems, as illustrated by the trial of Socrates, who was condemned to death by the council for nonconformity. Ultimately,

Athenian democracy became the victim of its own imperialist ambitions. Reaching out to dominate its neighbors through military force, Athens provoked a war with Sparta in 431 BCE that ended in defeat for Athens in 404 BCE. The war was accompanied by corruption, treason, and growing brutality. Defeat dealt a serious blow to trade and democracy. Culturally, Athens remained strong for a time, and the democrats regained their hold until Athens was defeated by Philip of Macedonia at the battle of Chaeronea in 338 BCE.

Lessons

Perhaps the most sobering, but essential, lesson of the Athenian experiment in democracy is its uniqueness, limited scale, and relatively short tenure. By the most generous definition, Athenian democracy, with all its serious flaws, lasted only 250 years, from the appointment of Solon and the start of the process of democratic reforms in 594 BCE to Athens's ultimate defeat and subjugation by Philip of Macedonia. At its peak, the population of the peninsula of Attica, which defined the boundaries of Athens as a city-state, was about 315,000 persons. Of those, 43,000 were enfranchised citizens and 155,000 were slaves.[7]

Consider the stunning implications. With the possible exception of Egypt's golden age, Western historians take no note of any comparable group of people enjoying equivalent political rights and freedom during the nearly three-thousand-year period between the fall of the early Aegean Goddess civilization and the birth of the United States in 1776. Other examples are found primarily among relatively small tribes of indigenous peoples.

Freedom and democracy are not divine gifts. They are earned and maintained by a vigilant, mindful, and mature citizenry through sustained struggle, and once lost they are not easily regained. Imperial ambition is their almost certain undoing. These are sobering lessons for our own time.

Solon's choice to respond to the stress of growing economic injustice with internal economic and political reforms that lessened the divide was a distinctive feature of the Athenian experience. It stood in stark contrast to the more common imperial response of leaving a growing economic divide unchecked while seeking to relieve the tension by acquiring new lands for resettlement through the military conquest and enslavement of foreign populations. The conventional response affirms the culture and institutions of Empire. Solon's choice, although only partial, created the necessary economic foundation for Athenian democracy.

Unfortunately, the challenge Athens presented to the classic imperial cultures and institutions of Empire was as temporary as it was partial. Only slaves sold into bondage for payment of their debts gained their freedom under Solon, and slavery remained an important institution. Women never gained political franchise, and Athens on occasion succumbed to the temptations of wars of conquest. In the end the partial nature of the economic reforms and the failure to develop a mature, inclusive democratic culture dedicated to securing the same rights for all people left in place the seeds of the undoing of the Athenian experiment in popular democracy.

A society divided between the enfranchised and the disenfranchised must create a moral justification for denying the humanity and right of participation of the disenfranchised by exaggerating the virtues of the former and the vices of the latter. The racism, sexism, and classism that inevitably follow bar the development of a mature democratic culture that recognizes the natural rights of every person by the fact of their birth. So long as the culture defines some people as inherently less worthy than others, the only question becomes how the division of society between the free and the slave will be decided; the underlying cultural and institutional foundations of Empire remain in place.

The Athenian experience points to the difference between the more mature and less mature democratic forms. The less mature democracy centers on securing the individual rights of members of particular favored categories of persons in relation to the institutions of the state. A more mature democracy seeks to secure the rights, affirm the responsibilities, and support the full human development of all persons through their full and active engagement in civic life to create what three celebrated Athenian philosophers referred to as the "good society."

POLITICAL PHILOSOPHY

The most celebrated of Athenian philosophers—Socrates, Plato, and Aristotle, the fabled three—were men of exceptional intellectual power and curiosity. Their inquiries into the nature of the good society remind us of the deeper purpose of democratic governance and the barriers that make the attainment of this purpose so challenging.

The Good Society

The fabled three believed that truth is real, is discoverable through disciplined intellectual inquiry, and is the proper basis for a good society. Underlying all their work was a belief in the goodness of Creation and in the human capacity to reach beyond competitive power and greed in the quest for a good society.

Much like most contemporary democracies, the Athenian democracy of their day was primarily concerned with protecting the rights of the individual. The fabled three began from a different starting point. Their goal was a virtuous politics and a good society, which by their definition is a society that nurtures the full development of the qualities that make us distinctively human. This distinction embodies an insight at the core of contemporary studies of human maturity, that is, that the concept of individual rights and responsibilities has a very different meaning to those who function at the self-centered lower orders of human consciousness than it does to those who have achieved the inclusive perspective of the higher orders of consciousness. Socrates, Plato, and Aristotle believed that the good society needs the kind of leadership that comes only with the wisdom and discipline of a mature consciousness. They were thus less concerned with securing individual rights than with solving the puzzle of how a society might best identify and appoint wise leaders of a mature moral consciousness who would guide the society to achievement of its higher-order possibilities.

Socrates (470–399 BCE) laid the foundation with his belief in the ability of man to discover enduring principles of right and justice as a guide to virtuous living independent of selfish desire. He equated true happiness with goodness and taught that the highest obligation of the statesman is to tend to the spiritual health and development of the souls of the nation's citizens. The idea that those who understand the nature of true happiness recognize that the pursuit of unlimited wealth and power leads ultimately to misery and the loss of one's humanity was a foundation of his political philosophy. Presumably, Thomas Jefferson had Socrates' definition of happiness in mind when he proclaimed in the U.S. Declaration of Independence that the pursuit of happiness is an inalienable right.

Socrates was an outspoken critic of Athenian democracy because he believed it wrong to put decisions of governance in the hands of men who lack true insight and to treat the views of all citizens as equal on matters of morality and justice. He thus articulated one of democracy's basic dilemmas: all persons may be created equal in the eyes of God, but many fail to achieve the mature understanding and capacity for moral judgment essential to the practice of a mature citizenship that looks beyond individual advantage to the well-being of the whole.

The Republic

Plato (428–348 BCE), Socrates' most distinguished student, taught that the ethical foundation for human affairs is to be found in an ordered universe that is both spiritual and purposeful. In his search for an ideal state free from the turbulence of self-seeking political competition between individuals and classes, Plato proposed a plan in *Republic* for a society divided into three classes: the working class, the soldier class, and a ruling class that would be specially prepared to rule by rigorous intellectual training. An educational screening system would sort out the candidates by aptitude and moral character to assure that the men who ruled would be those best suited to serving the interests of all.

Plato favored what he called a true aristocracy, or rule of the best. He distinguished true aristocracy from both oligarchy, which he defined as domination by merchant princes, and democracy, which he dismissed as subjecting the state to the irresponsible will of the masses. In short, he accepted the dominator hierarchy of Empire as organizing principle, but sought reforms that would reduce many of the more destructive aspects of political competition by assigning the positions of power to people of an advanced moral sensibility.

Although Solon, Cleisthenes, and the eighty-four-year rule of the Five Good Emperors of ancient Rome approximated Plato's ideal republic, throughout five thousand years of history the imperial norm has more often resulted in rule by brutal and arrogant psychopaths than by wise and selfless sages. The logic of rule by wise saints is difficult to question, but it creates a problem: Who will judge the qualifications of the available candidates, and who will guarantee the integrity and wisdom of the judges?

RESOLVING THE LEADERSHIP DILEMMA

Athens dealt with the leadership dilemma by limiting the vote to those deemed worthy—which turned out to be those who were sufficiently organized to demand representation. This solution had a deeply pernicious consequence.

As noted earlier, a society divided between the enfranchised and the disenfranchised must create a moral justification for the domination of one group by another. This invites abuse of power expressed through racism, sexism, and classism, thus undermining the ethic of equal rights. Yet an ethic of equal rights is the essential foundation of democracy and of a society dedicated to supporting all individuals in the realization of true happiness through the full development and expression of their talents. To deny to whole classes of people that which is the sacred obligation of the society to nurture is both illogical and immoral.

Civil Society

Aristotle (384–322 BCE), who was in turn Plato's most distinguished student, shared with Socrates and Plato the belief that ethics is not a matter of adherence to moral absolutes. Rather, ethical behavior follows from a mature and considered choice for the true happiness achieved through a virtuous life of intellectual contemplation and a balanced disposition free from the extremes of excess and moral deficiency. Aristotle taught that a proper moral education seeks not to inculcate specific rules of behavior, but rather to help the student recognize the reasons for virtue and to experience the pleasure inherent in virtuous action.

Aristotle believed that, although each individual is born with a capacity both for virtue and intellectual contemplation and also for savage lust, brutality, and gluttony, the former capacity is what makes us distinctively human and is the capacity we properly strive to cultivate. He believed that ethics and politics are inseparable one from the other, because the highest development of the individual, which he took to be the measure of the moral standard of a society, is inseparable from the problems of political association.

Aristotle conceived of the state as a community of politically engaged citizens who share a common set of norms and values cultivated through a rigorous process of education devoted to developing a highly refined capacity for reason. He called such a state a "political society," the Greek term later translated into Latin as *societas civilis*, or civil society. According to political theorists Jean Cohen and Andrew Arato, Aristotle's ideal was a state whose citizens were sufficiently united by their goals and lifestyles to be able to function as a "single homogeneous, organized solidary body of citizens capable of totally unified action."[8]

Collective Wisdom

In his struggle with the problem of how the good society might best select wise leaders, Aristotle arrived at the pragmatic conclusion that the government best suited to supporting man in the development of his highest nature will be controlled by a strong, numerous, and educated middle class in a state unburdened by extremes of wealth and poverty. He reasoned that, although the individual members of a polity may not be the best of men, they are more likely as a collective to arrive at a reasoned judgment in their choice of leader than are the members of a smaller group, even though those who make up the smaller group may be individually wiser. Aristotle thus arrived at a democratic solution to the leadership dilemma based not on a theory of individual rights but rather on a theory of collective wisdom.

Aristotle is also among those great political philosophers, including notably Thomas Jefferson, who recognized that the institution of private property is an essential foundation of a strong and democratic middle-class society. He also recognized, as did Jefferson, the essential need for governmental intervention to prevent a concentration of ownership by any individual beyond that required to support modest comfort, as well as the need for government to assist the poor in becoming property owners by helping them buy land for small farms or otherwise become established in self-owned trades or professions. Aristotle considered such measures integral to each citizen's prosperity and self-respect, which are in turn a foundation of responsible political participation. His wise counsel, with some glaring exceptions, is of considerable relevance to the present human circumstance.

For Men like Me

For all of his wisdom and the importance of his contributions to political theory, however, Aristotle's vision included a crucial flaw: a defense of slavery and the male domination of women.

> For that some should rule and others be ruled is a thing not
> only necessary, but expedient; from the hour of their birth
> some are marked out for subjection, others for rule.... Again,

the male is by nature superior, and the female inferior; and the one rules, and the other is ruled; this principle, of necessity, extends to all mankind.... It is clear, then, that some men are by nature free, and others slave, and that for this latter slavery is both expedient and right.[9]

In effect, Aristotle's vision of the good society was built in part on a self-serving elitist fantasy in which women and a permanent slave class toil to support a philosopher class of male citizens in the good life of refined leisure and reflective contemplation. He shared with Socrates and Plato this hypocritical chauvinism that ultimately was the seed of the undoing of Athenian democracy—and the inevitable undoing of any democracy that persists in similar contradictions.

Another crucial flaw in Aristotle's vision that has no place in the good society is his ideal of the civil society as "homogeneous." Diversity is essential to a society's vitality, as it is to the vitality of all living systems.

Enduring Principles

Setting aside for the moment the flaws of their elitist chauvinism, the great Athenian philosophers defined a number of enduring and ennobling principles of considerable relevance to our own time.

- Humans have a capacity for both good and evil, and nurturing the former is an essential task of the good society.
- The state is a unifying force essential to civilized life, because of the need to nurture our positive nature and to restrain our destructive impulses. The priority is to nurture the positive.
- Wise rulers who understand the nature of the good society and the proper role of the state in supporting its realization are required to guide the state in its responsibilities.
- Economic democracy based on a just distribution of ownership rights is an essential foundation of political democracy.
- The most promising solution to the challenge of assuring that those elevated to positions of power meet a minimal standard of maturity and wisdom is to vest the power to choose in a materially comfortable, strong, and well-educated middle class and to make the development and maintenance of what is essentially a classless society a priority of the state.

On reflection, it seems almost axiomatic that if a society is to be ruled by the good and the wise, the state must give priority to supporting a cultural and institutional context that nurtures the goodness and wisdom of its citizens. Think of it as the experience of Ricardo and the Hacienda Santa Teresa writ large.

This of course poses a classic conundrum: if the wise state is a product of a wise citizenry, and a wise citizenry is the product of a wise state, which comes first? Perhaps what comes first is neither the wise state nor the wise citizenry, but rather a vision of the benefit and possibility of an inclusive and egalitarian world ruled by wise and mature citizens who share power and rotate leadership roles to create a dynamic, democratic leadership of the whole. The vision then becomes a template for what the people of an organized civil society join in living into being.

Democracy and political maturity must evolve in tandem through the engagement of all in the responsibilities of citizenship. Proper schooling and a strong civic culture are important, but in the end democratic citizenship is a practice, and the experience of doing it is our best teacher.

The political philosophers Cohen and Arato observe that for democracy to work, all citizens—not just the elites—must be supported in developing through practice a political consciousness and a sensibility that embraces the needs and well-being of the whole.

> For it is through political experience that one develops a conception of civic virtue, learns to tolerate diversity, to temper fundamentalism and egoism, and to become able and willing to compromise. Hence the insistence that without public spaces for the active participation of the citizenry in ruling and being ruled, without a decisive narrowing of the gap between rulers and ruled, to the point of its abolition, polities are democratic in name only.[10]

The contemporary phenomenon of global civil society may be an early manifestation of the human capacity to actualize on a global scale Aristotle's ideal of a society able to achieve coherence primarily through nonhierarchical self-organization. In sharp contrast to the self-limiting social homogeneity of the Aristotelian ideal, however, global civil society is inclusive of a diversity of races, religions, classes, languages, genders, and nationalities that Aristotle could scarcely have imagined.

Global civil society manifests a leadership of the whole around a unifying vision of a possible world grounded in universal human values of justice, sustainability, and compassion.

THE ENLIGHTENMENT

The Enlightenment, the next period of significant inquiry into the nature and potential of humankind and the democratic state, followed the death of Aristotle by some two thousand years. Presenting a powerful challenge to the absolutism of the institutions of both state and church, the Enlightenment began in England about 1680, spread rapidly to most of the countries of northern Europe, and established its center in France. John Locke (1632–1704) and Jean-Jacques Rousseau (1712–78) were two of the Enlightenment's most influential political philosophers.

Locke articulated the ideals of liberalism, which gave primacy to protecting the natural property rights of the individual (which he defined broadly to include life, liberty, and estate) as absolute and inalienable. He reasoned that to secure the orderly protection of their property rights, individuals ultimately agree among themselves to establish a government to which they surrender certain powers. Because a government properly exercises only the authority expressly granted to it by the people, the people may overthrow it if it exceeds or abuses that authority. Focused on property rights as the foundation of liberty and dismissive of the idea that it is the purpose of government to serve some larger good, the propertied classes embraced Locke's concept of liberty and the responsibilities of government with particular enthusiasm as it lent a patina of democratic legitimacy to their privilege.[11]

Much like Locke, Rousseau grounded his political theory in a concept of popular sovereignty and a "social contract" by which the people create a civil society with morally binding laws and duties through their mutual agreement. Rousseau reckoned that binding laws require both a legislative body to make the laws and an executive body to see to their enforcement. The power to make and enforce laws necessarily passes, respectively, to the legislative and executive bodies created by the social contract and thereby to those individuals the people commission to fill those offices and to act in the name of the popular will. The people are thereby morally bound to abide by the law as established and enforced by the chosen officeholders until the people choose to replace them or change the form of government—rights that remain irrevocably with the people. Rousseau's conception was more inclusive and revolutionary than Locke's and presented a great challenge to elite privilege.

More than two millennia passed between the end of the democratic experiment of ancient Athens in 338 BCE and the next democratic experiment in Western culture that began with the Declaration of Independence of the United States of America in 1776. This long gap is a sobering reminder of the challenge facing those committed to carrying the democratic experiment forward to a new level of maturity.

Athens's turn to democracy began with a wise strongman leader who responded to the social tension of growing inequality with domestic economic reforms that strengthened economic justice rather than with efforts to defuse the tension through foreign conquest. Although only partial, these economic reforms were a sufficient step in the direction of economic democratization to provide an underpinning for the political reforms that followed.

Unfortunately, Athenian democracy never matured. Even at its height it was concerned primarily with securing the individual rights of a privileged minority. The majority—women, slaves, and persons born to foreign parents—were excluded in a denial of democracy's essential principle that every person acquires certain inalienable rights by the fact of his or her birth.

The great Athenian political philosophers—Socrates, Plato, and Aristotle—began not with a concern for individual rights, but rather with a definition of the nature of the good society as one that nurtures the full development of the higher qualities of the mind of each person through a combination of education, disciplined reflection, and civic engagement. Such a society requires a wise and mature leadership, thus raising the question: who will decide who is sufficiently wise and mature to lead?

Aristotle, who believed the choice of leadership is best left to the collective wisdom of the largest possible group of well-educated, involved citizens, articulated a concept of a leadership of the whole grounded in active civic engagement in all spheres of community life. This vision— minus Aristotle's blatant sexism, racism, and classism—is the vision of a mature democratic ideal. The distinction between democracy in its more and less mature forms is important to our understanding of the challenges now facing the nation that embarked on the first, yet partial, democratic experiment of the modern age.

The ideas of the Enlightenment philosophers reignited democratic passions and made major contributions to shaping the political institutions of modern democracy. In contrast to the Athenian political philosophers, however, Locke and Rousseau were primarily concerned with limiting the role of government to maintaining order and protecting individual rights. They took a less expansive view on questions relating to human perfectibility, the good society, civic participation, and the role of the state in supporting each individual in achieving the qualities of wisdom and moral judgment that are foundations of the more robust and mature democracy of Earth Community. The modern democratic experiment has suffered accordingly.

PART III

America, the Unfinished Project

Of all the nations of the world, few confront a greater challenge in facing up to the imperatives of the Great Turning than the United States of America. Few nations have been accustomed for so long to living so far beyond their means. Few labor under the burden of greater inequality or a greater gap between their idealized self-image and their troubled historical reality. We can achieve the mature democracy that is a defining condition of Earth Community only by acknowledging that, like the democracy of ancient Athens, ours is a partial and immature democracy.

We think of ourselves as a nation of problem solvers. To solve a problem, however, we must first acknowledge it. To this end, the following chapters take an unflinching look at the realities and implications of our national imperial legacy, the imperfections of our democracy, our reckless relationship with the natural environment, and the real and inspiring struggles for justice of people of color, women, and working people, to whom justice has long been denied.

Democracy is neither a gift nor a license; it is a possibility realized through practice grounded in a deep commitment to truth and an acceptance of the responsibility to seek justice for all.

CHAPTER 9

Inauspicious Beginning

> We hold these truths to be self-evident, that all men are created equal, that they are endowed by their Creator with certain unalienable Rights, that among these are Life, Liberty and the pursuit of Happiness. — That to secure these rights, Governments are instituted among Men, deriving their just powers from the consent of the governed, — That whenever any Form of Government becomes destructive of these ends, it is the Right of the People to alter or to abolish it, and to institute new Government, laying its foundation on such Principles, and organizing its powers in such form, as to them shall seem most likely to effect their Safety and Happiness.
>
> *The Declaration of Independence, July 4, 1776*

> We the People of the United States, in Order to form a more perfect Union, establish Justice, insure domestic Tranquility, provide for the common defense, promote the general Welfare, and secure the Blessings of Liberty to ourselves and our Posterity, do ordain and establish this Constitution for the United States of America.
>
> *Preamble to the Constitution of the United States, March 1789*

The history of the United States of America underscores the harsh reality that a declaration of liberty and a new constitution promising tranquility, liberty, and prosperity for all do not suddenly wipe away the cultural and institutional legacy of five thousand years of Empire. In the case of the United States, this legacy includes extremes of plutocracy, theocracy, genocide, slavery, racism, and sexism. This truth is crucial to understanding current U.S. politics and the challenge the Great Turning presents to the nation that has long prided itself on being the world's beacon of liberty.

We easily forget just how inauspicious the prospects for the foundation of a democratic nation were on July 4, 1776, when the representatives of thirteen English colonies in North America issued their declaration of independence from the most powerful nation of their day. Those of sober mind might well have concluded the rebels had taken leave of their senses. General Washington's ragtag part-time army of volunteers stood against a much larger British force of disciplined professional soldiers. British loyalists controlled most of the institutions of government, and as much as a third of the population was composed of royalists who remained loyal to the English king and the institutions of hereditary rule. As to the prospects for securing the rights of all men even if they were able to out-last the British army, the social condition of the colonies could hardly have been further from Aristotle's ideal of a "single homogeneous, or-ganized solidary body of citizens capable of totally unified action."

In the first centuries following Europe's discovery of the New World, Europe's ruling class had approached it as an alien land of interest only for what it might yield in slaves, gold, and other forms of natural wealth to support their power and comfort. Kings looked to it as a source of tax revenue, and investors as a source of profit. Later kings would come to see it as a dumping ground for their human refuse to reduce crime and ease revolutionary pressures for the redistribution of wealth and power at home.

At the time of the American Revolution, the ranks of the colonists who aligned with the revolutionary cause included pretentious slave-owning aristocrats, abolitionists, impoverished backwoods farmers, re-bellious militiamen, privateers, smugglers, swindlers, former slaves and bonded laborers, profiteering merchants, Enlightenment thinkers, and religious theocrats of a mind to flog, imprison, or hang all who did not share their particular faith. Most of those involved had little if any ed-ucation, knew only conditions of extreme servitude and hardship, and felt no sense of national identity until well after the Revolutionary War was under way. The motives of those who joined the rebellion were as diverse as their circumstances.

Furthermore, the assertion in the Declaration of Independence, in-spired by the Enlightenment philosophers and drafted in a moment of revolutionary fervor, that all men are created equal and that govern-ments derive their just powers from the consent of the governed, defied the evidence of five thousand years of history. It also defied the reality of the genocide, slavery, profiteering, and religious bigotry that were defining features of the North American colonial experience. The idea of creating a democratic nation with equal rights for all had no place in the thoughts of the economic plutocrats and religious theocrats who founded the early settlements. Recognition of these early circumstances is essential to any understanding of how far we have come as a nation and how much we have left to do to realize the ideals of the Declaration of Independence.

PLUTOCRACY

Foreshadowing the corporate rule of our own day, the colonial settlements were created more as economic than political jurisdictions — essentially company estates established by corporate charters issued by the Crown to be managed for the profit of their owners. Beginning in 1584, with the permission of Elizabeth I, Walter Raleigh made several unsuccessful attempts to establish the first English colony in America as a private investment on Roanoke Island off the North Carolina coast.[1] Private entrepreneurs and joint stock companies established a dozen permanent English colonies on other sites along the coast of America during the reigns of James I (1603–25) and Charles I (1625–49).

The technology of the time limited communication to letters or word of mouth via small sailing ships, which meant that administration and finance were necessarily in the hands of the individuals who held the charters, with virtually no governmental oversight. A few impoverished settlements struggling for subsistence survival were of little interest to a home government happy to leave their management as semifeudal principalities to their owners. Within the limits of their circumstances, the early settlements generally replicated Europe's well-defined social stratification. Over time, most settlements developed governing bodies composed of their wealthiest white male property owners.

In the early years, the isolation of the colonies from one another was even greater than their isolation from England. The settlers in the colonies did not begin to think of themselves as belonging to a land with its own distinctive character, destiny, and interests until the eighteenth century.

THEOCRACY

As was characteristic of the countries from which they came, secular and religious authority were closely linked, as evident in the early legal codes of the individual colonies. The official charter that established the first colony in Virginia in 1609 stated that one purpose of the colony was to convert the "people in those Parts unto the true Worship of God and Christian Religion," as practiced by the Anglican Church of England. Anglicanism was also the officially mandated state religion in Maryland and the Carolinas.

The theocratic nature of colonial governance is revealed in the types of crimes assigned the death penalty in *The General Laws and Liberties of New Hampshire*, published in 1680: these included worshipping any God but the Lord God, taking the name of God in vain, witchcraft, sexual intercourse with an animal, sodomy, and cursing or rebelling against one's parents. Doing unnecessary work or travel on the Lord's day was punishable by fine and whipping. *The Laws and Liberties of Massachusetts* (1647), the *Capitall Lawes of Connecticut* (1642), and the *Articles, Laws, and Orders, Divine, Politic, and Martial for the Colony in Virginia* (1610–11) had similar provisions. In Virginia the death penalty applied as well for false witness and for thrice failing to properly observe the Sabbath.[2]

Because the southern colonies worshipped the Anglican God and the northern colonies worshipped the Calvinist God, the religious practice legally required in one colony on pain of death was a heresy punishable by death in another. This not only restricted freedom to practice one's chosen faith but also hampered relationships among the colonies. The Puritan Calvinists were particularly clear in their theocratic designs.

A Special Righteousness

The Puritans, dissenters from the Anglican faith, came to North America in search of the freedom to establish a theocracy based on the teachings of John Calvin, which meant using the authority of government to deny others the same religious freedom they had come to American to gain for themselves.[3] Church membership was voluntary, but everyone, whether a member or not, was bound by law to attend Sabbath worship and contribute to the support of the clergy.[4]

John Winthrop, a pious, tough-minded Puritan lawyer and landed gentleman, sailed from England in 1630 to serve as the first governor of the newly chartered Massachusetts Bay Company. On that voyage, Winthrop declared to his fellow passengers that it was their mission to fulfill a biblical prophecy to create the New Jerusalem, the millennial kingdom, the righteous city on a hill of God's chosen people.[5] Puritans settled Massachusetts, Connecticut, and New Hampshire. When they arrived, they established Congregational churches throughout these northern colonies, made Calvinism their officially mandated faith, and banned the practice of any other.[6]

The influential Puritan preacher John Cotton preached without equivocation that theocratic rule, not democracy, was the will of God.

> Democracy I do not conceyve that ever God did ordeyne as a fitt government eyther for church or commonwealth. If the people be governors, who shall be governed? As for monarchy, and aristocracy, they are both of them clearly approoved, and directed in scripture, yet so as referreth the soveraigntie to himselfe, and setteth up Theocracy in both, as the best forme of government in the commonwealth, as well as in the church.[7]

The Calvinists defined religious liberty as freedom from the heresies of Anglicanism, Catholicism, and all other deviant faiths. The only religious freedom they granted dissenters from Calvinism was the liberty to choose between silence, voluntary exile, banishment, or execution should they insist on returning.

Mary Dyer was an outspoken Quaker preacher who was twice forced into exile from Massachusetts with the warning that if she returned a third time she would be executed. She returned and became one of four Quakers hanged by Massachusetts between 1659 and 1661 for refusing to stop preaching their faith.[8]

The early New England colonies were divided into parishes, each of which had one church that served as the center of civic life and administration. All competing religious influences were suppressed, and no outside preacher could cross the border into the parish without permission. The early town meetings for which New England has been noted were essentially meetings of the congregation in the parish church.

Although each considered the other to be heretics, Calvinists and Anglicans shared a belief that the moral order of society depended on religious uniformity and a single religiously defined moral standard enforced by the civil administration. Both reckoned that religious freedom was both wrongheaded and a threat to the public order. Eighty-five percent of the nearly half million early settlers lived in colonies in which either the Church of England or the Congregational Church had officially sanctioned religious monopolies. Both groups took a dim view of the Quakers who settled in Pennsylvania and other central states, for whom religious pluralism was a basic tenet of their faith.

This is the historical background of the provision for a strict separation of church and state in the U.S. Constitution. The purpose is to preclude use of the secular power of the state to enforce the beliefs of a particular faith. It would otherwise have been impossible to establish the Union.

God Loves Plutocrats

It is with good reason that German sociologist and economist Max Weber, in *The Protestant Ethic and the Spirit of Capitalism*, noted a natural affinity between Calvinism and capitalism. Rarely has any religious doctrine aligned more perfectly with the cause of plutocracy, capitalism, and Empire. It not only served to lend moral legitimacy to the concentration of financial wealth and the subservience of lesser mortals to men of wealth and power, it as well lent capitalism a motive force.

The teachings of Calvinism emphasize the depravity of the human condition and maintain that, because of his sinful nature, man can have no role in his own salvation, which is granted to God's chosen purely as a miracle of divine grace. Embracing a belief in predestination, Calvinism teaches that God settled the question of individual salvation or damnation at the beginning of time. Consequently, the individual is powerless to influence his circumstances in the afterlife through good works in this. Nor can he know until death his true condition.

According to Calvinism, a predisposition to righteous behavior is evidence that one may be among the chosen. Hard work, righteous living, and material prosperity provide no guarantee that one is saved, but they are taken to be favorable signs. Wealth and power are the surest signs that one is among the saved, because it is self-evident that those who are blessed with wealth and power are among God's chosen since he has clearly favored them. Deference is therefore their natural due.

By contrast, poverty, drunkenness, a propensity to question authority, and other vices are signs that one is out of favor with God and was probably condemned to hell from the beginning of time. By this line of reasoning, the poor are not victims of a failed economic system; they are the damned, the instruments of the devil, and no fate is too harsh for them.

Calvinist belief in human depravity affirms the underlying dehumanizing premise of neoliberal economics that humans are by nature capable only of selfish acts. This belief, combined with the belief in the superior righteousness of those blessed with wealth and power, provides a foundation for an easy alliance between contemporary religious theocrats and contemporary corporate plutocrats. The theocrats affirm the moral righteousness of the plutocrats, and the plutocrats provide media and funding support for politicians committed to the theocrats' restrictive social agenda.

GENOCIDE

When Christopher Columbus landed on a Caribbean island to "discover" America in 1492, a generous Native people greeted him warmly with food, water, and other gifts. It was their first encounter with Empire. Columbus wrote in his log:

> They... brought us parrots and balls of cotton and spears and many other things, which they exchanged for the glass beads and hawks' bells. They willingly traded everything they owned.... They were well-built, with good bodies and handsome features.... They do not bear arms, and do not know them, for I showed them a sword, they took it by the edge and cut themselves out of ignorance. They have no iron. Their spears are made of cane.... They would make fine servants.... With fifty men we could subjugate them all and make them do whatever we want.... They are so naïve and so free with their possessions that no one who has not witnessed them would believe it. When you ask for something they have, they never say no. To the contrary, they offer to share with anyone.... As soon as I arrived in the Indies, on the first Island which I found, I took some of the natives by force in order that they might learn and might give me information of whatever there is in these parts.[9]

Similar reports of the generosity and egalitarianism of the Natives of North America from early European visitors and settlers were commonplace.[10] Columbus responded by taking what gold he could find, killing those Natives who displeased him, and abducting others as specimens of the slaves he later promised to deliver to the Spanish crown in return for further support.

It is instructive in light of the discussion of pre-Empire civilizations in chapter 5 that in this initial encounter between the "civilized" men of Europe and the "savages" of the pre-imperial tribes of the New World, the latter thought first of sharing their abundance. The former thought only of subjugating and enslaving the innocents and confiscating their gold by force of arms.

According to the historian Howard Zinn, Columbus arrived in a world that in places "was as densely populated as Europe itself, where the culture was complex, where human relations were more egalitarian than in Europe, and where the relations among men, women, children, and nature were more beautifully worked out than perhaps any place in the world."[11] In many tribes, the systems of governance were more democratic than any encountered in the five-thousand-year experience of the empires that historians equate with civilization. There is evidence that America's founders drew on the lessons of the Native experience in the design of the new nation's democratic institutions.[12]

Columbus was unimpressed. Dismissing the Natives as primitive and savage, he set the pattern for the genocide that was to decimate Native populations throughout the New World. As Zinn notes, "What Columbus did to the Arawaks of the Bahamas, Cortés did to the Aztecs of Mexico, Pizarro to the Incas of Peru, and the English settlers of Virginia and Massachusetts to the Powhatans and the Pequots."[13] The genocide continued throughout the period of westward expansion of what later became the United States.

Historians estimate that at the time Columbus arrived in 1492 some 250,000 indigenous people were living in Hispaniola, a population reduced to only about 400 persons in 1538. During the first hundred years of Spanish rule, the far larger population of Mexico was reduced by some 70 percent.[14] The Native population living north of what became Mexico was ultimately reduced from as many as ten million to one million through disease, physical violence, and despair[15] as waves of invading European immigrants cleared the land of the Native inhabitants with the same lack of moral reservation they brought to clearing the land of trees.

SLAVERY

I use the term *slavery* here in a broad sense to include all members of the working class who shared the condition that they were not at liberty to negotiate the terms of their labor or to leave their master. These included legally defined slaves, bonded workers, and wives considered the property of their husbands.

A 1708 census in South Carolina "counted 3,900 free whites, 4,100 African slaves, 1,400 Indian slaves, and 120 indentured whites."[16] In 1770, 20 percent of the population of the colonies lived in slavery. At the time the Declaration of Independence was issued, 75 percent of the people who lived in the territories of Pennsylvania, Maryland, and Virginia were or had been slaves or indentured servants.[17]

Involuntary Conscripts

Slavery in its many forms was foundational to the colonial economies, which the ruling elites sought to staff with the cheapest and most subservient labor available. The current press to outsource U.S. jobs to the lowest-wage countries and to recruit undocumented workers for those jobs that cannot be outsourced builds on this well-established historical precedent.

Investors who sought to profit from the new land's physical wealth through trade, resource extraction, and agriculture required cheap labor to fulfill their dreams. Getting settlers to come voluntarily to North America was difficult. Passage from Europe in small wooden sailing vessels was long, dangerous, and for most involved unspeakable crowding, filth, and starvation. Many perished along the way. The harsh conditions did not end with arrival in the new land, even for free whites. The ground was fertile, but new settlers had to construct their own shelter and clear and plant the land with the crudest of tools in unfamiliar climates. Many perished within their first year of arrival.

Supplying investors with slaves from Africa and bonded laborers from Europe to satisfy the demand for cheap labor became a major business in its own right for enterprising merchants who arranged for the collection, shipping, and sale of the unfortunates they acquired from both Europe and Africa. Rulers saw the forced emigration of prisoners as a way to reduce the expense of maintaining them in prisons. Responding to the market demand, gangs of thugs roamed the back streets and slums of London to kidnap the destitute and sell them into bondage with the tacit blessing of officials who considered the clearing of their neighborhoods of paupers, orphans, and other undesirables as something of a public service.

The economies of the coastal settlements evolved according to differences in soil and climate. The fertile soil, favorable growing seasons, and level topography of the South were suited to vast plantations worked by slaves to produce tobacco and cotton for export. The stony soil, harsh climates, and narrow coastal plains of the North led to smaller farms and more varied crops that required the skill and determination of experienced free farmers. Looking for more agreeable occupations than farming under such harsh conditions, the privileged classes of the North turned to industry and the sea. Shipbuilding, whaling, fishing, trading, slaving, and privateering became the favored occupations.

Desperate 'Volunteers'

Some whites came voluntarily from Europe to join the ranks of bonded laborers, but only as a desperate last resort. Land in Europe was scarce and its ownership concentrated. Surplus labor kept wages low and unemployment high. Tales of America's vast fertile lands and great wealth free for the taking stirred the imagination of Europeans of all classes, but especially the poor and starving whose homelands afforded them neither land nor employment.

Those unable to pay for passage agreed to commit themselves to a period of indentured service to whoever was willing on their arrival to pay their debt to the ship captain who had provided passage. Many a young woman came voluntarily to become the wife of whatever man paid the captain's fee. Once married, a woman and all she owned, acquired, or produced became the property of her husband. Runaway wives were treated much the same as runaway slaves.[18] The status of an indentured servant differed from that of an outright slave mainly in having a promised date of release.

The Race Card

Widespread hardship and servitude created significant social tension and led to periodic rebellions against the ruling elites of the day. The most famous of these was Bacon's Rebellion of 1676, which resulted in the near total destruction of Jamestown, Virginia, and rallied a broad alliance of white and black free farmers, black and Indian slaves, white indentured servants, and members of the free white working class eager to take their revenge against Jamestown's arrogant and brutal propertied ruling class. Even the Virginia governor, who was forced to flee as Jamestown burned, acknowledged that the majority of Virginia's populace supported the rebellion. British troops eventually restored order, but the rebellion left a deep impression on the ruling elites throughout the colonies.[19]

Specifically, the experience awakened the propertied classes to the importance of keeping the working classes divided against one another along the lines of race, gender, and trade. Their chosen strategy centered on shifting the focus from class to race by codifying the institution of black slavery into the laws of many of the colonies and denying blacks what few rights and freedoms they had previously enjoyed—thus placing them permanently on the bottom rung of the social ladder. The Calvinists, for example, supported this injustice by declaring that blacks had no soul; thus, not being truly human, they had no claim to human rights—the same argument made down through the ages to justify the enslavement of women.

This gave poor whites a floor of failure below which they could not fall and a human target against which to direct the frustrations of their station, encouraging them to define their identity by their whiteness rather than by their class. It proved to be one of history's most odious and successful bits of social engineering. At the same time, members of the elite class proceeded to secure their own claim to preeminent status by cultivating the social and intellectual graces of their sons, providing them personal slaves and tutors, and sending them to England for finishing at elite colleges.[20]

The conditions of race-based slavery became especially harsh. Virginia and other British colonies gave slaves no rights even to such basics as personal security, marriage, or even parenthood of their own children. It was not considered a felony for a Virginia master to kill his slave. After 1721 it was, however, a crime for him to set a slave free except under rare circumstances.[21] Individual and collective rebellion by slaves was commonplace, and fear of the simmering volcano of the anger of black slaves left whites desperate to maintain control through a reign of terror that included torture, mutilation, and lynching.

By the time the new nation was founded, a clear geographic division of functions had been established. The South owned and managed slaves to work its vast plantations; the North procured the slaves from Africa and transported them in merchant ships for sale to the Southern plantation owners.

The realities of life in the English colonies on the Atlantic coast of what was to become the United States of America were not auspicious for the founding of a new nation based on the premise that all men are created equal with an inalienable right to life, liberty, and the pursuit of happiness. The early settlements were operated as privately owned company estates ruled by their overseers. Parishes were ruled as theocracies by preachers who believed democracy to be contrary to the will of God. The colonial economies depended on slaves and bonded labor, and the family structure placed women in a condition of indentured servitude. The lands the colonies occupied were acquired by genocide, and their social structures embodied deep racial and class divisions.

This history exposes the deep cultural and institutional roots of the challenges we citizens of the United States now face in birthing the mature democracy of Earth Community. Before turning to these challenges as they are playing out in our own time, however, there is much else to be learned from our history—including the story of how a group of patriots awakened to possibilities long denied, mobilized to walk away from their king, and thereby created a new political reality.

CHAPTER 10

People Power Rebellion

> Britain was forced not to give, grant, concede, or release our
> independence, but to acknowledge it, in terms as clear as our
> language afforded, and under seal and under oath.[1]
>
> *John Adams*

The American colonies were products of imperial
expansion, and they replicated the imperial social structures of plutocracy and theocracy of the European nations that created them. From
the beginning, however, there were also important counterforces at
work that fostered a rebellious spirit, favored religious pluralism, and
prepared the way for a people to walk away from their king, discover
their common identity, and form a new nation bathed in the rhetoric of
liberty and justice for all.

FORCES OF PLURALISM

There were early exceptions to the narrow and brutal Calvinist and
Episcopalian sectarianism. Some settlers, particularly the Quakers, came
to North America with a truly democratic consciousness tolerant of religious diversity, at least within the boundaries of the Protestant faith,
and a concern for the rights of all.

William Penn, who founded Pennsylvania, was a Quaker who had
spent time in prison in England for his religious beliefs. Penn populated
the lands granted to him by royal charter by appealing to religious dissenters from across Europe with the promise of land and religious liberty. He attracted Quakers and Baptists from England, Huguenots from
France, and Pietist and Reformed groups out of favor with Lutheran or
Catholic princes in Germany. Pennsylvania and New Jersey, which were
both predominantly Quaker, welcomed all persons of Protestant faith,
but excluded atheists and non-Christians—a category that by their
reckoning included Catholics.

Roger Williams, a Puritan minister from Salem who was a fierce advocate of the separation of spiritual and civil power, contended that all people are answerable only to God for their religious beliefs, not to the state. Banned from Massachusetts for his defiance of both religious and civil authority, he founded a new colony in Rhode Island that welcomed all Protestants.

Although Anglicanism was the official religion in Georgia and New York, it was much weaker in those states than in Virginia, Maryland, and the Carolinas. Both Georgia and New York guaranteed tolerance for dissenters. Georgia welcomed settlers of all faiths, including Jews.

The struggle between theocrats and religious pluralists also played out in Pennsylvania, however, as factions of Calvinists, Anglicans, and others complained that the Quakers were restricting their religious freedom by prohibiting them from making their religion the official religion to be imposed on all by law. The Quakers who dominated the legislative bodies eventually split into two factions, one of which remained committed to religious pluralism while the other called for making Quakerism the official faith.

As populations grew and exchanges between colonies and between the church parishes within the colonies became inevitable, the diversity of faiths made it increasingly difficult to maintain uniformity. In 1684, the Crown withdrew the original charter of the Massachusetts Bay Colony, in part because of its discrimination against Anglicans, and issued a new charter guaranteeing religious liberty to all Protestants.

The individual parish churches were strong enough to maintain their establishment for a time, but by the 1740s the pressures of a growing immigrant population and an increasing flow of trade began to break down the established religious boundaries. Itinerant evangelical preachers traveled from parish to parish preaching that salvation is a matter of individual conscience, not church doctrine.

Denominations fragmented and churches of diverse faiths began springing up everywhere—Congregational, Baptist, Anabaptist, Quaker, Anglican, Methodist, Presbyterian, Huguenot, and in some places even Catholic and Jewish. Within the space of little more than a generation the nation had moved from a consensus that an imposed uniformity of religious views was essential to the social and moral order to a consensus that the social order and moral order were best served by guaranteeing freedom of conscience to all people.

By the time the founding fathers declared the formation of a new nation independent from England's rule, it was clear that unless the laws of the new nation prohibited the establishment of any of the competing Protestant sects as the official religion, unification would be impossible. Thus, Article VI of the U.S. Constitution established that "no religious Test shall ever be required as a Qualification to any Office or public Trust under the United States," and the First Amendment established that "Congress shall make no law respecting an establishment of religion." In a historic breakthrough of epic importance the pluralism of Earth Community prevailed over the theocratic hegemony of Empire.

A REBELLIOUS AND ITINERANT SPIRIT

In another of history's great ironies, the imperial processes by which the American colonies were settled created a population prone to a rebellious spirit. The slaves and bonded laborers who came by force or desperation had little stake in the prevailing system of authority. Those who came in dissent against established religious authority had a history of walking away from distasteful constraints. Members of the continent's new Cloud Minder class had become accustomed to ruling their fiefdoms largely free from English taxes and oversight and resented the arrogance of European elites who treated them as less worthy country cousins.

The passage of time also brought important changes. The conditions of life became less harsh, and communities grew less dependent on strong leadership and cultural homogeneity to hold them together. Those who had arrived as bonded laborers eventually gained freedom for themselves and their children. Even some slaves won their freedom. The children of those whose parents had come with visions of "a city upon a hill" harshly ruled by biblical law grew weary of the restraints on their own freedom of conscience. These developments fueled resentment of the continuing injustice of the deep divisions between those who enjoyed lives of privilege and pampered luxury and the free farmers, workers, and artisans who struggled in comparative hardship at the margins—to say nothing of the increasing bitterness of the slaves condemned to perpetual bondage.

Those who had come voluntarily to America to seek their fortune or their liberty demonstrated by that act a rebellious and itinerant spirit ready to pull up stakes and move on when things didn't work out, a spirit that sustained a continuous westward push. The frontier promised both opportunity and liberty from the tyranny of class in return for the harsh reality of a life in which each man depended for his survival on his own wits and labor. The hardy frontiersmen were a particularly rowdy lot ill disposed to taxes and to any attempt to curtail their individual liberty. They were also skilled in the use of firearms to hunt game and protect the land they occupied.

Forerunners of contemporary America's militiamen and libertarians, they lived by the aphorism "A fool can put on his own coat better than a wise man can do it for him."[2] The lives of these self-reliant individualists posed a stark contrast to life in the strong but socially stratified communities of the coastal settlements ruled by appointed governors, corporations, landed gentry, and wealthy merchants. The frontiersmen and the coastal settlers, however, shared a deep hostility to the rules and taxes of a distant king and a parliament in which they had no representation. Together these conditions set the stage for an alliance between widely disparate elements in a call for liberty from the Crown.

WALKING AWAY FROM THE KING

In the 1750s and '60s, the British government began to assert greater authority over its American colonies, which by now had developed economies of sufficient consequence to attract attention as a source of taxes and trading profits. Britain began to assert stronger administrative authority and to impose new taxes on an increasingly rebellious and independent-minded people accustomed to the benign neglect of the Crown and disinclined to accept such an intrusion. Their response was, in effect, to walk away from the king. Herein lies a profound lesson in democracy.

Imperial rulers of whatever title depend on the obedience of the ruled. If the people choose en masse to ignore the king's demands to serve in his armies, he is powerless. The power of the king, and by extension the power of Empire, resides ultimately with the people, and it is within the people's means to withhold it.

Initial efforts by the Crown to increase tax collections through import duties largely failed, as a New England merchant class given to slave trading and piracy had no reservations about adding smuggling to their business portfolios and easily evaded the notice of a distant king's tax collectors. The Crown turned to increasingly intrusive measures, and the people responded with growing defiance.

Tax Revolt

The end of the Seven Years' War among the great European powers in 1763 left the British treasury deep in debt. Many in Britain felt that the colonies had been the primary beneficiaries of the war, which had strengthened Britain's position in North America, and that it was only right and proper for the colonies to pay a share. To this end, the British parliament imposed a stamp tax in 1765 on all colonial commercial and legal papers, newspapers, pamphlets, and almanacs.

The colonists felt differently. Under the banner of Sons of Neptune, maritime workers organized a widespread tax revolt that featured demonstrations, a refusal to use the stamps, and attacks on the property of British officials. Some wealthy merchants supported the protests behind the scenes but became increasingly nervous when the anger began to spill over to a general resentment of the rich. The British parliament caved in and repealed the Stamp Act in March 1766, only to replace it with the Revenue Act of 1767, which imposed tariffs on a number of imported goods, including lead, glass, paper, and tea.

The Revenue Act taxes were rescinded in 1770, with the sole exception of the tax on tea. Later, Parliament passed the Tea Act of 1773 to benefit the financially troubled British East India Company, in which the king and prominent members of Parliament held shares. The act gave the company a special exemption from the tea tax and refunded the taxes it had already paid on the large quantities of tea it was holding unsold in inventory, thus allowing it to undercut the prices of its smaller competitors, put them out of business, and establish a tea monopoly.

Outrage over the Tea Act gradually grew and on December 16, 1774, a group of Boston rebels organized the Boston Tea Party. Dressed as Indians, they boarded three British ships anchored in the harbor, broke up chests of tea, and threw them into the sea. Similar tea parties were held in other ports. In Annapolis a tea ship was burned. Some students of the American Revolution consider this a tax revolt. More than that, however, it was a protest against the legally sanctioned abuse of corporate monopoly power.[3]

The British responded to these acts of rebellion by closing Boston Harbor and demanding compensation for the tea, dissolving the Bay

Colony government, prohibiting public meetings without explicit permission of the British governor, building up British military fortifications and troop presence, and ordering colonists to quarter British troops in their homes. This further fanned the flames of rebellion. Colonists throughout Massachusetts responded by forming local militias, stockpiling weapons, and holding town meetings in defiance of British orders.

Participatory Democracy

Opponents of the Crown's effort to tighten colonial administration and tax collection formed local resistance groups, with names such as Sons of Liberty, Regulators, Associators, and Liberty Boys, to engage in acts of noncooperation such as refusing to purchase and use the Crown's tax stamps, boycotting British goods, and subjecting merchants who failed to honor the boycott to public humiliation. Artisans and laborers refused to participate in building military fortifications for the British. When the British Crown decided to assert its authority over the Massachusetts Supreme Court by paying its judges directly from the royal treasury, the people responded by refusing to serve as jurors under the judges.

The colonists also undertook initiatives aimed at getting control of economic life through local production. Women played a particularly crucial role by organizing Daughters of Liberty committees to produce substitutes for imported products.

Others formed Committees of Correspondence, groups of citizens engaged in sharing ideas and information through regularized exchanges of letters carried by ship and horseback. These committees linked elements of diverse citizen movements in common cause—carrying out a function similar to that of the Internet in our own day. The first such committee was formed in Boston in 1764. A similar committee formed the next year in New York and took the lead in convening representatives of nine colonies as the Stamp Act Congress in New York in October 1765 to formulate a unified response to Stamp Act provisions. By 1774, all the colonial legislatures had responded to a proposal of the Virginia legislature that they each appoint a standing committee to engage in intercolonial correspondence, which led to their convening the First Colonial Congress in Philadelphia in September 1774.

The Congress was composed of white male property-owning aristocrats who were educated in the ideas of the Enlightenment and desirous of winning recognition as equals of the English aristocracy and obtaining greater freedom to govern their own affairs and those of the colonies. Thoughts of creating an independent nation were still far from the minds of the delegates who gathered in Philadelphia. Their concern was with securing a guarantee of their rights under a distant British king and a parliament in which they had no representation.

To this end, the Colonial Congress adopted a Declaration of Colonial Rights on October 14, 1774, that claimed for the people of the English colonies the rights to life, liberty, property, assembly, and trial by jury. It denounced taxation without representation and the maintenance of British troops in the American colonies without local consent. It called for a boycott of all British goods and an embargo on the export of American products to Britain in the event that the king failed to accept their demands.[4] These events awakened a new political consciousness throughout the colonies.

We see in these actions two ultimately competing strands of activity that continue to play out in U.S. politics to this day. One was a self-organizing populist uprising that created the social and institutional infrastructure of a coherent, nonviolent, and radically democratic bottom-up resistance movement similar in its underlying dynamic to the global peace and justice movement of our own time. The other involved a top-down alliance of the ruling elites of previously insular colonies to strengthen their position vis-à-vis the king, regularize the competition among themselves, and protect their privilege from the threat of what they viewed as mob rule. These two strands created a new reality and provided experience in two quite different forms of democratic practice — one radically populist and the other fundamentally elitist — that remain in dynamic opposition to this day.

Creating a New Reality

John Adams, one of the defining figures of the founding, set forth in his correspondence near the end of his life the thesis that the history of the founding of the United States should not be confused with the Revolutionary War. By Adams's account, the war was not a war to gain the independence of the thirteen colonies, but rather the military defense of an existing system of independent government already in place against an attempt by a foreign power to force what was effectively an independent nation back into the fold of imperial rule.[5] In this same spirit, historian Roger Wilkins suggests that the decade preceding the Declaration of Independence may have been the most important in U.S. history.

> The stunning achievements of the 1765–1775 period were not only instances of resistance to specific obnoxious acts of the British government but also key stages in the development of a continental revolutionary consciousness and impulse toward self-government, as well as the creation of the rudimentary instruments to carry out those purposes....
>
> All of the practices and arts of politics were deployed in that fruitful decade. The colonists paid careful attention to public affairs. They spent time alone exploring and honing their opinions on important issues by reading history and philosophy as well as the latest correspondence, dispatches, and political tracts. They thought hard about what was occurring and consulted with others in order to inform and sharpen their views. They became involved in local and colonial politics by standing for office and putting forward proposals for action. When necessary—when, for example, colonial legislatures were disbanded, or when new instruments for protest and self-governance were required—they crafted appropriate new mechanisms. But most of all they thought, talked, debated, listened to one another, wrote, and created in ever-widening circles. All the while, their activities were fraught with great personal, political, and financial risk.[6]

A diverse, and in many respects deeply divided, people preoccupied with matters of their own daily survival had found the time to create a new political reality through acts of participatory democracy: engaging in dialogue, forging new alliances, and creating institutions of democratic communities. Once the people had expressed their will through their actions, the British had only Empire's final option, the use of troops to force submission on pain of death.

ELITE TAKEOVER

The colonial resistance had on occasion involved violence against property, but avoided violence against persons. The British changed the rules of engagement by initiating the use of deadly military force and thereby confronted the rebels with Empire's classic fight-or-die logic.

British troops landed in Boston Harbor and armed conflict broke out on April 19, 1775, when they attempted to destroy the military stores of American rebels at Concord. It escalated from there.

Not even the patriots who organized the resistance had fully come to terms with the new reality they had already created. Even as the armed engagement began, scarcely anyone was thinking of total independence. It is especially significant that the armed conflict between local militias and British troops was already under way when the Continental Congress decided in mid-June 1775 to bring order to the rebellion by appointing an army and commissioning George Washington to head it. The colonial elites who controlled the Continental Congress were responding to the leadership exercised by thousands of ordinary people engaged in a living democratic expression. If the delegates to the Congress had not acted to bring the rebellion under their control, they would have been reduced to an irrelevant debating society with no political base or authority and would likely have been swept away by the victor, whether the British or the rebels.

Within a year popular sentiment shifted and talk of independence filled the air. The Continental Congress responded by signing a formal Declaration of Independence on July 4, 1776, giving expression to what had by then become a widespread public sentiment. It was a revolutionary document written by men of property and privilege to stir the passions of the masses to fight for liberty from a king who refused them the respect and rights they felt they were due. The people led and the leaders followed, which is how real democracy is supposed to work.

In the end, General Washington and his army expelled the British with the help of France, Spain, and the Netherlands. The war ended with the Treaty of Paris, signed on September 3, 1783. A rebellious people inspired by a vision of liberty gave birth to new nation. It was a remarkable contribution to humanity's long journey beyond monarchy and theocracy, but it was only a beginning on the road to real democracy.

The diversity of circumstances, interests, races, values, religious beliefs, and national origins of the people who made up the new nation speaks to the magnitude of the ambition of joining together the thirteen colonies into a new nation with a democratic vision.

Overall, precious little beyond their shared antipathy to British taxes and corporate monopolies bound the people of the new nation together. Accustomed to being the subjects of arbitrary rule by those in positions of power, many had no experience beyond the frame of the Imperial Consciousness that equates personal liberty with a license to abuse others, and they had no particular reason to consider the law as anything other than a means by which the few exploit the many.

Aristotle would not be alone in considering these conditions an inauspicious beginning for the formation of a democratic nation. Yet for all their diversity and lack of experience with organized self-rule, the grassroots rebels who initiated and led the revolution in its earliest manifestations demonstrated a remarkable capacity to express the popular will through self-organizing groups and networks—long one of democracy's most meaningful and effective forms of expression.

It is also significant that the American Revolution did not start as an armed rebellion. This was an auspicious sign of a greater maturity of thought than might have been expected under the circumstances. It is axiomatic: democracy cannot be achieved at the point of a gun. The gun itself affirms the imperial principle of domination by superior force, which affirms the relationships of Empire. Violence against life, by its nature, is antithetical to the relationships of Earth Community.

When the British changed the rules of engagement from nonviolence to violence, the rebels felt compelled to respond in kind. As the violence escalated, it created a situation that both allowed and compelled the elites of the Continental Congress to assert their authority by raising an army that assumed control of the rebellion and restored imperial order under a new command. The colonial elites who had long aspired to equal status with their European counterparts went on to form a new nation ruled by a wealthy aristocracy with its own agenda of imperial expansion. The British lost the war, but Empire remained robust, reasserting its dominion in North America as plutocracy cloaked in the guise of democracy.

We are left with a troubling and perhaps unanswerable question: Did the American Revolution, as widely believed, bring democracy to North America and to the modern era? Or, by consolidating the power of America's own ruling aristocracy and giving birth to an imperial nation destined to become far more powerful than any empire that preceded it, did that revolution set back the advance to universal suffrage and democratic citizen rule by many generations?

CHAPTER 11

Empire's Victory

> This is an impressive crowd. The haves and the have-mores.
> Some people call you the elite. I call you my base.[1]
>
> *George W. Bush*

> We can either have democracy in this country, or we can have
> great wealth concentrated in the hands of a few, but we can't
> have both.
>
> *Louis Brandeis, U.S. Supreme Court Justice (1861–1939)*

Extreme inequality is the surest indicator of a society organized by the dominator relationships of Empire. It is no coincidence that the United States has the most unequal wealth distribution of any major industrial nation and is the most imperial of modern nations.

In 1998, the top 1 percent of U.S. households owned 47 percent of all household financial assets, more than the entire bottom 95 percent — and the gap is growing. In the decade between 1989 and 1999, the number of U.S. billionaires increased from 66 to 268. The number of people living below the pitifully inadequate official poverty line (about $13,000 for a family of three in 1999) increased from 31.5 to 34.5 million. The ratio of CEO pay to the pay of an average worker rose from 141 to 1 in 1995 to 301 to 1 in 2003. The legacy of slavery's destruction of families and its denial of opportunities for intergenerational wealth accumulation by black Americans is revealed in the fact that the total wealth of the average European American household is 5.5 times that of the average African American household.[2]

For more than thirty years, political science professor Thomas Dye has been documenting in a series of studies titled *Who's Running America?* just how small the U.S. ruling class is. In the 2001 edition, which documented elite rule under the then newly established administration of George W. Bush (Bush II), Dye identified 7,314 individuals, out of a U.S. population of 288 million, who by their positions of power and authority controlled almost three-quarters of the nation's industrial (nonfinancial) assets, almost two-thirds of all banking assets, and more than three-quarters of all insurance assets, and... directed the nation's largest investment firms. They commanded over half of all assets of private foundations and universities and controlled the television networks, the national press, and the major newspaper chains. They dominated the nation's top law firms and the most prestigious civic and cultural associations, and they occupied key federal government posts in the executive, legislative, and judicial branches and the top military commands.[3]

These are truly America's Cloud Minders, members of a privileged elite that rule from a separate world of luxury and privilege far above the mundane. Traveling in private jets and chauffeured limousines, attending elite schools, living in gated communities and private estates, socializing in exclusive clubs, and getting their news from elite publications and news services that cater to an exclusive audience, these are the have-mores who live in world far removed from the mere haves, let alone the have-nots.

The 2004 U.S. presidential race between George W. Bush and John Kerry, two white males from wealthy families who had each graduated from Yale University and belonged to the Skull and Bones society, underscored the narrowness of the path to the highest positions of political power. Indeed, the two presidents prior to Bush II, Bill Clinton and George H.W. Bush, also held degrees from Yale University, and Bush I had also been a member of Skull and Bones.

As history and a close reading of the original U.S. Constitution make clear, the intention of the architects of what we look to as American democracy was not to create a democracy; it was to create a plutocracy, a nation ruled by a wealthy elite—and they were very successful. Their efforts are worth a brief review, not only to remind ourselves of the realities of our history, but also to comprehend how past misdeeds and slanderous political rhetoric formed a template for our own time.

WHO WILL RULE? A NATION BY, FOR, AND OF WHITE MEN OF PROPERTY

The members of the Continental Congress who had issued the Declaration of Colonial Rights in 1774 and the Declaration of Independence in 1776 were all white male property owners named as representatives to the Congress by colonial legislative bodies, which themselves comprised white male property owners. Many, including Jefferson, included slaves in their property. It was the same for the Constitutional Convention. The free male laborers, who enjoyed minimal rights, and the women, slaves, bonded workers, and Native Americans, who had no legal rights, made up more than 90 percent of the population of the new nation, but had no representative in either body.

To Insure Domestic Tranquility

The decision to establish a strong federal government following the successful conclusion of the Revolution was prompted in consequential measure by Shay's Rebellion of 1786–87. Farmer patriots who had fought on the side of liberty for worthless government IOUs had, in the classic pattern of Empire, returned home to face bankruptcy and foreclosure on their farms at the hands of financiers whose patriotic service in the war had been limited to profiteering.[4]

Their resentment gave rise to an armed rebellion in defiance of court-issued foreclosure orders. Authorities called on the local militia to defend the courts and the law of the land. The citizen militia, however, was composed largely of armed farmers who sided with their neighbors. A group of wealthy Boston merchants eventually financed an army to put down the uprising.

The advocates of popular sovereignty considered Shay's Rebellion an exhilarating example of an active and organized citizenry seeking a redress of grievances against an abusive establishment—much as the minutemen had come forth in opposition to the British Crown. The elite establishment considered Shay's Rebellion to be an unsettling example of the dangers of mob rule and convened a Constitutional Convention in 1787 to create a strong federal government with the power to raise an army to impose domestic order. Article I, Section 8 of the U.S. Constitution gives the Congress the power to "provide for calling forth the Militia to execute the Laws of the Union, suppress Insurrections and repel Invasions." It is telling that executing the law and suppressing insurrection both come before repelling invasions in order of priority.

The bold vision of liberty and justice for all spelled out in the Declaration of Colonial Rights and the subsequent Declaration of Independence and signed earlier by members of the Continental Congress in a moment of revolutionary fervor was nowhere in evidence in the original

Constitution. Those who drafted it were no longer concerned with protecting their rights against a distant king, but rather with securing their power in the new nation. This post-Revolution reality brought forth a division within the ranks of the delegates to the Constitutional Convention, personified by two men: Thomas Jefferson and Alexander Hamilton.

Jefferson's Democracy versus Hamilton's Plutocracy

Jefferson, a leading voice for democracy, had an abiding faith in the wisdom of ordinary people and believed that democracy properly rests on the bedrock of economic democracy and a strong middle class. Much like Aristotle, he championed a nation of land-owning family farmers and independent artisans who would own the land and tools essential to their crafts and livelihoods. Jefferson's greatest fear was that America might come to mirror Europe's deep divisions between a hereditary class of pretentious and unproductive aristocrats and a hereditary class of the desperately poor. In his ideal, all men would be men of property. He once said, "I am not among those who fear the people. They and not the rich are our dependence for continued freedom."[5]

In his reference to those who fear the people, Jefferson no doubt had in mind Alexander Hamilton, the unabashed champion of elite rule, who once asserted:

> All communities divide themselves into the few and the many.
> The first are the rich and well born, the other the mass of the
> people. The voice of the people has been said to be the voice
> of God; and however generally this maxim has been quoted
> and believed, it is not true in fact. The people are turbulent
> and changing; they seldom judge right. Give therefore to the
> first class a distinct permanent share in the government.[6]

Suspicious of the masses, Hamilton equated democracy with mob rule and felt that to become a strong nation America must concentrate power in a class of wealthy aristocrats able to organize and lead the nation to imperial greatness. At the Constitutional Convention Hamilton proposed that a president and a senate be chosen for life.[7]

Underlying the differences between Jefferson and Hamilton is the basic truth that those who do not own property live in subservience to those who do. The U.S. Constitution represented a partial compromise between Jeffersonians and Hamiltonians, but the latter largely prevailed. The United States would be a constitutional plutocracy—more politely, a republic—a democracy of elites in which the propertied classes establish priorities and agendas and from time to time compete among themselves in open elections for the favor of lesser classes. In the end, the Constitution proved an artful exercise in securing the rights and privileges of property while granting enough liberty to the common man to discourage rebellion.

CONSTITUTIONAL PLUTOCRACY

George Mason, a delegate from Virginia, led the demand that the Constitution include a "bill of rights." Mason lost the battle in the Constitutional Convention. Freedom from England had been won, and the majority of the delegates now felt that the constitutional provisions securing slavery, free trade among the states, creditors' rights, and an electoral system that assured them control of the institutions of government provided all the protection they needed. They felt no need for a bill of rights.[8]

Guarantees for Slavery, Free Trade, and Creditors

The Constitutional Convention was strongly influenced by three sets of propertied interests. Northern industrialists wanted a single market with uniform rules established at the federal level, and a common external tariff system free of interference by state regulators, so that they could secure unrestricted access to a unified market. They got the interstate commerce clause of the Constitution, which effectively guarantees an integrated national market beyond the reach of state legislators, much as contemporary trade agreements guarantee global corporations global access to national economies, free from interference from national legislators and regulators.

Northern financiers wanted to secure their right to collect on debts owed to them irrespective of the state in which the obligation was contracted. They won provisions giving the federal government the power to prohibit the individual states from granting relief to indebted farmers, issuing their own currencies, allowing debts to be repaid in anything but gold and silver, or making any laws invalidating contracts such as mortgages and loans.[9] These provisions secured the rights of creditors and assured the classic pattern of wealth transfer from the working classes to the owning classes.

Southern plantation owners sought to secure the institution of slavery. They got provisions barring Congress from prohibiting the importation of slaves before 1808 and prohibiting one state from providing sanctuary to a slave or bonded laborer from another.

Only Cloud Minders Need Apply

The elite bias is also evident in other provisions of the original Constitution. For example, state legislatures, which as noted above comprised white male landowners, would appoint the state's two senators. An Electoral College comprising members similarly appointed by the state legislatures would choose the president.

The ultimate guarantee of elite privilege was the constitutional provision for a powerful high court composed of justices appointed for life by the president, with the power to overturn virtually any act of the legislative and executive branches of government. As a practical matter, appointments to the Supreme Court are available only to graduates of elite law schools, which at the time were open only to sons of the propertied class. As demonstrated by the U.S. Supreme Court's appointment of George W. Bush as president in 2000, the law is whatever a majority of the sitting justices choose to say it is. There is no mechanism for appeal or dissent no matter how arbitrary or contrary to established law or the public interest its decisions may be.

The authority of the Supreme Court has at times served the cause of justice, as when a relatively progressive court advanced the cause of civil rights for African Americans and Native Americans in the late twentieth century. The overall record of the court, however, is one of persistent bias in favor of elite interests over broader public interests.

Concession to Public Outrage

The proposed Constitution as put forward for ratification by the states was widely criticized by patriots who saw it quite correctly as a design for plutocracy rather than for democracy. The Federalists—persons of wealth and authority who stood most to benefit from the Constitution as drafted—organized a well-funded campaign to get it ratified as quickly as possible. In a pattern familiar to this day, they circulated false reports to discredit opponents. Advertisers put pressure on newspapers that opposed ratification.[10]

In the end, most states did ratify, but only with the assurance that a Bill of Rights would be added later. The Constitution was amended accordingly on December 15, 1791, but it took many years and amendments for the Constitution to clearly establish that the protections of the Bill of Rights apply to all persons, not just white men of property.[11]

The Thirteenth Amendment abolished slavery in 1865. In 1868, the Fourteenth Amendment declared that all persons born or naturalized in the United States and subject to its jurisdiction were citizens and thereby entitled to the equal protection of the law. In 1870, the Fifteenth Amendment declared that no citizen could be denied the right to vote because of race, color, or previous condition of servitude. It was not until 1920, nearly 150 years after the founding, that the Nineteenth Amendment recognized women as persons entitled to the full rights of citizenship by prohibiting any denial or abridgement of the right to vote based on sex. From our contemporary perspective these advances seem painfully slow, yet within the context of five thousand years of Empire they came with remarkable speed.

THE FEDERALIST PROGRAM

The contrasting visions of Hamiltonian plutocracy and Jeffersonian democracy played out in the subsequent political division between the Federalist Party of Hamilton, Washington, and Adams and the Democratic-Republican Party of Jefferson, Madison, and Monroe. Merchants and financiers backed the Federalists. Planters, farmers, and artisans favored the Democratic-Republicans.[12]

Profiteers before Patriots

Alexander Hamilton, the champion of plutocracy, served as the first U.S. secretary of the treasury under President George Washington (1789–97). When the administration of George Washington took office, the costs of the Revolutionary War had put the new nation in financial crisis. Hamilton seized the moment.

In the name of securing the government's creditworthiness, he sponsored a program to redeem all wartime debts of both federal and state governments at face value—including notes issued to soldiers in lieu of pay. Providing due compensation to soldiers and others who had borne the burdens of the war would seem to be a noble act, except that by this time the original debt holders had sold most of the debt papers for a pittance to speculators. Indeed, prior to the public announcement of Hamilton's plan, wealthy Federalist supporters and officeholders with insider knowledge scoured the country for federal and state debt instruments, bought them up at deep discounts from the unknowing, and then redeemed them at face value for tidy profits when the plan was implemented.[13]

Adding insult to injury, Hamilton raised the funds to pay for the debt redemption by levying a tax on whiskey production, which placed the burden primarily on small farmers in the backcountry, many of whom had been the original holders of scrip issued for military service. The understandable outrage sparked the armed Whiskey Rebellion of 1794 in western Pennsylvania. No longer dependent on local militia, President Washington ordered 13,000 troops into the area to put it down.

Private Profit from Public Credit

Hamilton also founded the privately owned First Bank of the United States (1791–1811), chartered for twenty years by the Congress to serve as a repository for federal funds, to act as the government's fiscal agent, and to make loans to both governments and private interests. Some say it was a stroke of financial genius that set the stage for the United States to become a world economic power. Others revile it as a major fraud against the public.

The bank's charter, issued in 1790, called for a total capitalization of $10 million, of which $2 million was to come from government and $8 million from private investors. The government put in its contribution. The private shares were quickly bought, but many of the private subscribers made only small down payments and never paid the balance.[14] It appears that the private investors who placed little or none of their own capital at risk reaped significant profits as the beneficial owners of an enterprise financed almost entirely by public money and credit.

When the bank's charter came up for renewal, the renewal application was rejected and the bank expired in 1811.[15] It was followed by the Second Bank of the United States (1816–36), and ultimately by the Federal Reserve System, established in 1913, which is likewise run by private bankers under the guise of being a public institution and which accomplishes much the same outcome of creating private wealth from public assets and credit through a more sophisticated and less transparent process.[16]

Criminalizing Dissent

When the Federalist John Adams succeeded the Federalist George Washington to become the second U.S. president (1797–1801), with the Democratic-Republican Thomas Jefferson as his vice president, the nation was experiencing wrenching political tension. Religious fundamentalists had revived the witch trials and were railing against atheists —who by the reckoning of the fundamentalists included deists such as Tom Paine, Thomas Jefferson, and others who professed a belief in God but rejected the fundamentalists' claims to exclusive truth.

Adams persuaded the Federalist Congress to pass the Alien and Sedition Acts—a forerunner of the Patriot Act of Bush II—to suppress political dissent and undermine support for Jefferson's party. The Sedition Act made it a criminal offense to publish false or malicious writings against the government or to incite opposition to any act of Congress or the president. The Sedition Act was used to arrest twenty-five men, most of them editors of newspapers sympathetic to Jefferson, and force the closure of their newspapers. Adams also packed the federal judiciary with extreme conservatives—foremost among them Chief Justice John Marshall, who throughout his term from 1801 to 1835 stood steadfast for protecting the interests of property.[17]

THE JEFFERSONIAN PROGRAM

Partly in response to public outrage against the Alien and Sedition Acts, Jefferson won the presidency in 1800, in spite of warnings from Federalist opponents that his victory would evoke the "just vengeance of an insulted heaven," with "dwellings in flames, hoary hairs bathed in blood, female chastity violated... children writhing on the pike."[18]

As president, Jefferson brought a halt to the excesses of the Adams regime, nullified the Alien and Sedition Acts, and signed into law the Act of 1808, ending the importation of slaves.[19] The Democratic-Republicans, with wide support from white working men, began to break the Federalist hold on state and local governments, increased the proportion of local officials subject to direct election, began to provide for public education, eliminated imprisonment for debt, and stopped enforcing indenture contracts for craft apprentices. Jefferson's party was successful in all but three states in winning voting rights for every white male citizen irrespective of whether they were property owners. All but two states moved to choosing presidential electors by direct election rather than leaving their selection to state legislators.[20]

In the end, however, Jefferson's program featured Empire with a more friendly and democratic face. For all the acrimonious and sometimes violent tension between the parties, the underlying power structure and bias for elite privilege remained remarkably stable. Federal policies continued to allow slavery, favor big industrialists and financiers, and advance the forceful appropriation of Native lands by the U.S. Army.[21]

The defining act of Jefferson's administration was to negotiate the Louisiana Purchase from France in 1803, thereby doubling the size of the United States, providing a safety valve for the pent-up tensions of America's deep class conflict, and removing potential imperial competitors from the nation's immediate borders. In an early demonstration of the gift of American politicians for Orwellian doublespeak, Jefferson dubbed the expanding U.S. nation "An Empire for Liberty."

WESTWARD EXPANSION

Hardy pioneers were attracted to the newly opened frontier by the promise of freedom from rent collectors, legalized loan sharks, and other institutions of imperial bondage. Yet the predators were quick to follow, and the newly established free farmers all too soon found themselves back in debt, yielding to the local bank its annual pound of flesh — until a bad harvest brought default and the bank claimed everything. The passions that might otherwise have been channeled into open revolt were defused by the continuing promise of yet more virgin territory just beyond the horizon. The United States became a nation of restless, rootless vagabonds, bags always packed and one foot on the wagon.[22]

After the Louisiana Purchase came the War of 1812, which opened the way for expansion into Florida, Canada, and Indian territories further to the west.[23] When Mexico won its independence in a revolutionary war against Spain, its territory included what are now the states of Texas, New Mexico, Utah, Nevada, Arizona, California, and part of Colorado.

Ignoring Mexico's claims, as they ignored the claims of the indigenous peoples, thousands of settlers poured into Mexican territory from the United States with the support of the U.S. government. During the Mexican-American War that followed, the United States annexed by brutal armed force half the total territory of Mexico. The only provocation from the Mexican government was its justified attempt to protect its rightful territory.[24]

The westward expansion followed a common pattern. Missionaries who offered schools, hospitals, and salvation led the way. Traders, land speculators, mineral prospectors, and farmers soon followed. Then came the railroad, banking, and resource-extraction corporations to consolidate control over the land and its resources. When the indigenous people mobilized in resistance, the military stepped in as needed to secure the claims to land and resources established by the missionaries, settlers, and corporations.

IMPERIAL CORPORATIONS

With memories of the abuse of corporate monopoly power fresh in mind, public sentiment in the early days of the new nation demanded strict limitations on corporate charters. Consequently, state legislatures issued such charters only for fixed periods to serve narrowly defined purposes, kept a close watch on corporate operations, and retained the power to revoke charters at will. It was also common practice to place specific limits on corporate borrowing, ownership of land, and even profits. Owners were held personally liable for all debts incurred during the period of their participation, large and small investors had equal voting rights, interlocking corporate directorates were prohibited, and one corporation was not allowed to own shares in another—all bothersome restrictions resented by powerful interests.

The U.S. Civil War (1861–65) marked a turning point for the U.S. corporation. The country was in chaos and divided against itself. The federal government was beholden to the military contractors who provisioned the troops in the field. Political corruption flourished as industrial interests used the outsize profits from military contracts to curry favor with politicians to further inflate their profits and thus their ability to pay for yet more political favors in their campaign to eliminate legal constraints on the freedom of corporate action.

Powerful railroad corporations led the way, through manipulation of public opinion, legislatures, and the courts. In one early victory for corporate interests, the Pennsylvania legislature removed the restriction on one corporation's owning shares in another. This seemingly innocuous change greatly increased the financial leverage of an individual corporation by allowing it to acquire controlling interests in other companies without having to put up sufficient capital to buy them outright.

Step by step through courts and legislatures—rarely with public debate or notice—corporations eliminated the restrictions on their freedom of action. By the beginning of the twentieth century, corporate charters were being issued automatically on demand with no limits on life span, mobility, or purpose. Owners had gained exemptions from liability, and corporations had become virtually immune to charter revocation. Protections for minority shareholders were largely eliminated, allowing a consolidation of the power of the larger shareholders.

Through courtroom victories, corporations successfully claimed the status of legal personhood entitled to the same constitutional protections accorded to real persons under the Bill of Rights. Most of it happened with no public discussion and even without the vote of elected legislators.[25]

GOING GLOBAL

In 1823, even as the westward expansion was still in progress, President James Monroe enunciated the Monroe Doctrine as a cornerstone of U.S. policy. The publicly expressed intent was to protect independent Latin American and Caribbean nations from efforts by European powers to recolonize them; the implicit message was that the United States claimed hegemony over the Western Hemisphere.

Theodore Roosevelt took the Monroe doctrine a step further during his presidency (1901–9), announcing that the United States claimed the right to intervene in the internal affairs of any nation that engaged in "flagrant and chronic wrongdoing." Future U.S. administrations defined this to mean any nation that transgressed against a U.S. trade or investment interest. A 1962 U.S. State Department report to the Congress listed 103 U.S. military interventions in the affairs of other countries between 1798 and 1895, including interventions in Argentina, Japan, Uruguay, China, Angola, Hawaii, and Nicaragua. The reasons were often obscure but usually related to the investments of one or more U.S. corporations.[26]

In the Spanish-American War (1898) the United States expelled Spain from Cuba and took possession of the Philippines, claiming it was fighting on behalf of Philippine independence. In the subsequent peace treaty, Spain ceded Guam, Puerto Rico, and the Philippines to the United States. A long and bloody U.S. war against determined Filipino resistance followed.[27]

Visions of imperial grandeur danced in the heads of politicians, missionaries, and the Daughters of the American Revolution. One exuberant advocate who later became a U.S. senator declared, "We are a conquering race…. American law, American order, American civilization, and the American flag will plant themselves on shores hitherto bloody and benighted, but by those agencies of God henceforth to be made beautiful and bright."[28]

In 1893, U.S. citizens who had settled in Hawaii as the ungrateful guests of the kingdom organized a rebellion to overthrow Queen Liliuokalani. A detachment of U.S. soldiers and marines was dispatched to "protect American property and lives." A provisional government formed under U.S. supervision promptly signed an annexation agreement with the United States.[29]

In the first half of the twentieth century, in addition to World Wars I and II, U.S. Marines invaded and occupied Cuba from 1898 to 1902, Panama from 1903 to 1914, Honduras six times between 1911 and 1925, Nicaragua in 1912 and again from 1926 to 1933, Mexico in 1914 and 1916, and Haiti from 1915 to 1934.[30]

The pattern of U.S. expansion abroad was similar to that of the westward expansion except the goal was to expropriate agricultural lands and resources to produce goods for export back to the United States. Usually, those resources belonged to indigenous peoples, and the terms of the expropriation served to enrich the local elites, and thereby win their support. Missionaries led the way; corporations followed to organize management and extraction. The U.S. military intervened when necessary to put down resistance and depose uncooperative leaders. It was an offer most ruling elites could not refuse.

The role of the missionaries in imperial expansion was closely akin to that of the Trojan horse, the hollow wooden construction presented by the Greeks to Troy as a gift in a ruse that placed Greek warriors inside the city walls with a mission to open its gates to the invading Greek army. The missionaries offered gifts of medicine, clothing, reading, and salvation. Their ministrations opened the gate of trust; corporations poured in to sack the lands and economies. In a world of Empire, there is wisdom in the ancient warning "Beware of strangers bearing gifts."

Following World War II the tainted gifts came, not from missionaries, but from foreign aid agencies, most particularly loans from the World Bank and regional banks that operated in its image. The official aid-dispensing agencies appropriately referred to their local offices and planning teams as missions. Economists steeped in the religion of neo-classical economics took on the missionary role of preaching stories of the salvation that converting to unregulated markets, open borders, and foreign borrowing would bring. The proselytes, however, did not become the saved souls of Christianity but international debtors in the church of global capital.

DRIVE TO IMPERIAL HEGEMONY

The only serious rival to U.S. global imperial hegemony following World War II was the Soviet Union. The aftermath of the war set the stage for a grand confrontation between the two superpowers.

Design for a Grand Area

Even before the Japanese bombed Pearl Harbor in December 1941 and drew the United States into World War II, a U.S. foreign-policy elite was laying the groundwork for postwar U.S. initiatives that would capitalize on the consequences of the war and create an integrated global economy dominated by U.S. interests. Haunted by the specter of the Great Depression, State Department planners believed that to curb capitalism's boom-bust cycles, the United States would have to either move to a form of socialism or secure adequate export markets to absorb goods produced in excess of domestic demand. They chose the latter.

Memorandum E-B34, presented on July 24, 1941, by a joint planning group to the president and the State Department, outlined the concept of a "Grand Area." This was the geographic area the planners estimated the United States would need to dominate economically and militarily to assure materials for its industries while experiencing the fewest possible stresses, "such as unwieldy export surpluses or severe shortages of consumer goods," that might lead to economic "disintegration."[31]

The preferred scope of the Grand Area encompassed the entire Western Hemisphere, the United Kingdom, the remainder of the British Commonwealth and Empire, the Dutch East Indies, China, and Japan. It would be expanded by weaving in other areas as circumstances permitted.

The strategic concept called for the initial economic integration of as much of the core area as possible. The more fully the Grand Area could be opened to unrestricted trade and foreign investment, the more readily the economic interests of the United States, as the strongest economic power, would be able to dominate it.

The public version of the Grand Area strategy, which was intended to rally the support of those who would be the imperial subjects, called for the creation of a free and equal community of nations and gave birth to the United Nations.

The real intention of the United States was articulated in U.S. State Department Policy Planning Study 23, a top-secret document written in 1948 by George Kennan, a leading architect of the post–World War II world.

> We have about 50% of the world's wealth, but only 6.3% of its population.... In this situation we cannot fail to be the object of envy and resentment. Our real task in the coming period is to devise a pattern of relationships which will permit us to maintain this position of disparity.... To do so, we will have to dispense with all sentimentality and day-dreaming; and our intention will have to be concentrated everywhere on our immediate national objectives.... We should cease to talk about vague... unreal objectives such as human rights, the raising of living standards, and democratization. The day is not far off when we are going to have to deal in straight power concepts. The less we are then hampered by idealistic slogans, the better."[32]

This was the real agenda, and the agencies of its implementation would be the Bretton Woods institutions: the World Bank, the International Monetary Fund (IMF), and the General Agreement on Tariffs and Trade (GATT).[33] In 1995, the World Trade Organization (WTO) replaced the less powerful GATT.

The difference between the public and private visions was similar to the difference between the professed ideals of the U.S. Declaration of

Independence, which was a document intended to mobilize popular support, and the reality of the U.S. Constitution, which institutionalized the power and privilege of a ruling plutocracy. The United Nations had mostly a symbolic moral authority. The Bretton Woods institutions had the power to set rules and back them with economic sanctions.

Competing Empires

The very real threat of Soviet military power provided a democratic rationale for a buildup of military power by the United States, the provision of military assistance to trusted allies, and the positioning of military bases around the world. The expressed purpose was to counter the Soviet threat and protect the free nations of the world from assimilation into the Soviet Empire.

However, U.S. military power was rarely, if ever, used in support of democratic governments and movements, which by their nature threatened U.S. imperial interests. To the contrary, when the U.S. military intervened abroad it was usually to put down popular liberation movements that sought the right to democratic self-determination, and to install or protect dictators friendly to U.S. interests. The dictators favored by both Republican and Democratic U.S. administrations following World War II included Pinochet in Chile, Somoza in Nicaragua, Marcos in the Philippines, Suharto in Indonesia, the shah of Iran, the Saudi royal family in Saudi Arabia, and (until the Gulf War in 1991) Saddam Hussein in Iraq.

As U.S. economic and military power grew in the postwar years, the imperial agenda became more expansive. Earlier the focus was on access to land and natural resources. The new agenda included the domination of markets, culture, finance, and technology.

The New Colonialism

The end of World War II began a process of phasing out traditional colonialism based on military occupation. The United States pioneered the use of foreign aid, investment, and trade to dominate the cultures, economies, and governments of client states through less overtly violent means—but with the threat of military intervention always in the background. Initial implementation of the strategy relied on global corporations, the IMF, and the World Bank. Subsequently, regional trade agreements and the WTO became favored instruments. All the while, the United States used its military power to support regimes that were friendly to imperial U.S. interests and to bring down those that were not.[34]

In the post–World War II period the United States provided over $200 billion in military assistance to some eighty countries to train, equip, and subsidize more than 2.3 million troops and internal security forces. Just as President Washington had used federal troops to put down the Whiskey Rebellion, so the primary responsibility of these security forces was to protect elite interests, including those of U.S. corporations, from domestic disturbances.

Recipients of military aid included notoriously repressive military regimes in "Turkey, Zaire, Chad, Pakistan, Morocco, Indonesia, Honduras, Peru, Colombia, El Salvador, Haiti, Cuba (under Batista), Nicaragua (under Somoza), Iran (under the Shah), the Philippines (under Marcos), and Portugal (under Salazar)." In addition, the United States funded and aided the military overthrow of "democratically elected reformist governments in Guatemala, Guyana, the Dominican Republic, Brazil, Chile, Uruguay, Syria, Indonesia (under Sukarno), Greece, Argentina, Bolivia, and Haiti." It "participated in covert actions or proxy mercenary wars against revolutionary governments in Cuba, Angola, Mozambique, Ethiopia, Portugal, Nicaragua, Cambodia, East Timor, and Western Sahara." And it took hostile action "against reformist governments in Egypt, Lebanon, Peru, Iran, Syria, Zaire, Jamaica, South Yemen, and the Fiji Islands."[35] Just since 1961 the United States has been involved in overt military engagements in Vietnam (1961–73), Lebanon (1982–84), Grenada (1983), Libya (1986), Panama (1989), Kuwait/Iraq (1990–91), Somalia (1992–93), Haiti (1994), Bosnia (1995), Kosovo (1999), Afghanistan (2001–), and Iraq (2003–).[36]

Contrary to the assessments of many historically challenged commentators, the 2003 preemptive first-strike U.S. invasion of Iraq was far from the first time the United States had launched a unilateral preemptive first-strike invasion of another country. The United States has a long history of launching unilateral first-strike attacks against small nations of inferior military power for questionable ends. Some of these wars were minor skirmishes. Others, like the occupation of the Philippines and the current war in Iraq, were full-scale invasions costly in lives and treasure. Many were in support of brutal dictators. Rarely did they advance a democratic cause.

The Debt Weapon of Mass Destruction

As noted in previous chapters, debt has long been a favored instrument by which the privileged use their control over access to money to appropriate the resources of the gullible and the desperate. During the period of its post–World War II expansion the United States pioneered the transformation of debt-funded development assistance into a weapon of mass destruction to seduce corrupt rulers, generate profits for U.S. corporations, and leave the "assisted" countries in the iron grip of international creditors. It is an extraordinary tale spelled out in *Confessions of an Economic Hit Man*, by John Perkins, whose job as chief economist for a major international economic consulting firm was to generate and defend grossly inflated economic projections to justify supersized infrastructure projects financed with loans from the World Bank and other foreign creditors that the borrowers could never repay.[37]

Intentionally making uncollectable loans to foreign governments may seem the work of fools, but the money flowed directly to the bottom lines of well-connected U.S. construction and energy companies like Bechtel and Halliburton, which built the infrastructure. The perpetual indebtedness of those nations gave global financial institutions a stranglehold over their economic and political resources. The overpriced infrastructure in turn subsidized the operations of transnational mining corporations, agricultural estates, and offshore production facilities. These loans and contracts created opportunities for lucrative payoffs to corrupt dictators who served U.S. interests, and they aligned the recipient nations with the United States on crucial UN votes. The ruling classes of the debtor nations, who benefited financially and politically, rarely objected; the people who suffered the consequences—including future generations—had no voice. The human and environmental costs have been unconscionable.

Most of those involved believed the ideological rhetoric they used to justify it all as a holy mission. Others, like Perkins, who were trained and rewarded to manufacture and defend the lies that turned these programs into weapons of mass destruction, knew exactly the true nature and purpose of their work, as the Perkins account makes clear.

The U.S. Constitution initiated the first major modern experiment in replacing hereditary monarchs with elected leaders, and it secured freedom of worship and thought through the separation of church and state. These achievements represented a seminal contribution to bending the arc of history in the direction of democracy and Earth Community. The idea that the architects of the U.S. Constitution created a government that secured for ordinary people the democratic ideals of popular sovereignty is, however, little more than a highly successful triumph of public relations image building over reality.

Once independence was won, the colonial elites who inserted themselves to take control of what had been a self-organized rebellion turned their attention to securing their hold on the institutions of government. The human rights that had been carefully delineated in the earlier Declaration of Colonial Rights, and the principle that all men are born equal and enjoy a natural right to life, liberty, and the pursuit of happiness so elegantly articulated in the Declaration of Independence, fell by the wayside. The focus shifted to securing the interests of industrialists, bankers, and slave-owning plantation owners and assuring that the powers of government would remain in the hands of white men of means. Empire morphed once again into a new form but remained true to the essential organizing principle of domination. What the founders brought forth is best described as a constitutional plutocracy with an agenda of imperial expansion.

Most every American will readily acknowledge that the United States is a superpower. To acknowledge that we are an imperial power feels less comfortable, as it contradicts our national self-concept as a democratic nation and a global beacon of freedom. The facts of our history, however, make it painfully clear that imperial expansion to dominate other peoples and appropriate their resources has been integral to our nation's domestic and foreign policy throughout our history. It is the classic imperial solution to the problem of domestic tensions resulting from the injustice of an extreme division of society between people who own and people who work.

Our forebears who settled the narrow bit of land along the east coast of North America took the land by force and deceit from its indigenous inhabitants. They imported slaves forcibly abducted from Africa to work the land. When they found that land insufficient to their needs, they embarked on an imperial westward expansion to appropriate by force all of the Native and Mexican lands between themselves and the far distant Pacific Ocean, displacing or killing the original inhabitants as they went.

Reaching out beyond our own borders, we converted cooperative dictatorships into client states by giving their ruling classes a choice of aligning themselves with our economic and political interests and sharing in the booty or being eliminated by military force. Following World War II, when the classic forms of colonial rule became unacceptable, we turned to international debt as our favored instrument for imperial control and later to trade agreements that opened foreign economies to direct ownership and control by transnational corporations.

As our history makes clear, democracy is not a gift granted by benevolent power holders. Those to whom it has been denied achieve it only through organization and sustained struggle.

CHAPTER 12

Struggle for Justice

> I have a dream that one day this nation will rise up and live out the true meaning of its creed: "We hold these truths to be self-evident, that all men are created equal."[1]
>
> *Martin Luther King Jr.*

Humans commonly confine to the realm of the unconscious those aspects of the self that the conscious mind denies because they challenge a favored self-image. Psychoanalyst Carl Jung referred to these denied aspects of the self as the shadow. Actualizing the full potential of the self requires acknowledging and healing the pain underlying the denial.

It is much the same for nations as for individuals. We Americans have been inclined to confine both the stories of U.S. imperial expansion and the stories of the repression of nonwhites, women, and working-class people within our own borders to a collective unconscious as too painfully contrary to our national self-concept to acknowledge. It is not only a denial of the injustice in which we are complicit but also a denial of the reality of Empire and the troubling truth that our nation is not—and never has been—a democracy. To achieve the democracy that is central to our national self-image we must first acknowledge that we have never had it.

We are slowly making progress as a nation toward achieving liberty and justice for all only through the long and difficult struggles of the excluded. To know these struggles is to appreciate both the progress achieved and the magnitude of the challenge that remains.

WORDS THAT REFUSE TO DIE

The U.S. Constitution fell far short of securing for all the promise of the inalienable rights to life, liberty, and the pursuit of happiness. Yet the bold words of the Declaration of Independence refused to die and continue to this day to inspire those who would make the promise a reality.

The Declaration said, "All men are created equal." There was nothing about only white men or men of property. If all men, why not all women? Such questions inspired a series of struggles, each of which made historic contributions to advancing the United States and the world on the path to the mature democracy of Earth Community—a journey that remains to this day far from complete.

Abolishing Slavery

Frederick Douglass, Sojourner Truth, Harriet Tubman, Nat Turner, and David Walker were among the free blacks who campaigned openly, at the risk of their lives and freedom, to mobilize resistance against the institution of slavery.[2] Brave white allies of a mature democratic consciousness shared their outrage and joined in the struggle. The Quakers at Germantown, Pennsylvania, condemned slavery as early as 1688. Boston Puritan Samuel Sewall published America's first abolitionist tract, *The Selling of Joseph*, in 1700. William Lloyd Garrison founded *The Liberator* in 1831, a newspaper dedicated to rallying public support for abolition. Harriet Beecher Stowe's *Uncle Tom's Cabin*, published in 1851, was one of history's most influential books.[3] In the end, it took the Civil War to bring an end to legally sanctioned slavery in the United States and to grant black men full citizenship and the right to vote—a legal recognition of their humanity that continued to be denied to women of any race.

Blacks were technically free, but whites owned the land and controlled the jobs on which blacks depended for survival. Continuing the imperial pattern, the rights of capital continued to trump the rights of labor as the moneylenders stepped in for the kill. Blatantly unfair sharecropper arrangements forced blacks into debts that became an instrument of bondage only one step removed from an outright return to slavery.[4]

Oppression and terror prevailed until the civil rights movement of the latter half of the twentieth century achieved an important, but still partial, cultural transformation in race relationships and backed it with legal sanctions against those who overtly denied African Americans their basic civil rights.

Securing Civil Rights for People of Color

The modern civil rights movement was born in Montgomery, Alabama, when Rosa Parks, a middle-aged African American seamstress and longtime activist leader with the National Association for the Advancement of Colored People (NAACP), was arrested on December 1, 1955, for refusing to give up her seat to a white patron. The success of the subsequent bus boycott led by the Reverend Martin Luther King Jr. unleashed a sense of pride and possibility in black communities across the country, inspiring wave after wave of protest—and often deadly white reprisals. As awareness of the injustices of segregation spread, thousands of whites were inspired to join blacks in their struggle. The resulting political pressures resulted in the omnibus Civil Rights Act of 1964, which prohibited "discrimination by race, color, sex, religion, or national origin in voter registration, employment, public education, and public accommodations."[5]

White backlash became increasingly deadly, causing many black leaders to question whether peaceful integration into the mainstream of society was possible or even desirable. Black anger found expression in increasingly violent inner-city rebellions, including the August 1965 Watts rebellion, in which thirty-four people were killed, nearly a thousand injured, and more than four thousand arrested. King's valiant calls for nonviolence fell on increasingly deaf ears, and by the time of his assassination on April 4, 1968, the movement was beginning to stall as the FBI became increasingly aggressive in infiltrating, disrupting, and discrediting major civil rights groups.[6]

Within the broad limits permitted by the prevailing institutions and culture of Empire, the civil rights movement transformed the self-concept of African Americans, brought the issue of race relations to the fore of the national consciousness, and removed many of the more overt manifestations of racial discrimination. As with the American Revolution itself, the impetus for change came from an assertion of rights by the oppressed.

Although we remain far from realizing King's dream of a free and equal multiracial society, the accomplishments of the civil rights movement were a major step toward the realization of that democratic ideal. Furthermore, it inspired the many progressive movements that followed—giving impetus to a still ongoing cultural turning toward the partnership relations of Earth Community.

Equality for Women

The movement for equal rights for women has deep roots in the movement to abolish slavery based on race. Early on, a group of visionary women concluded that eliminating race-based slavery was a necessary first step toward eliminating gender-based slavery. Thus when, in February of 1828, Angelina Grimké became the first woman to address a legislative body in the United States, it was to present to the Massachusetts General Court an antislavery petition signed by twenty thousand women.[7]

A critical turning point in feminist activism occurred in 1840, when the male majority at the World Anti-Slavery Convention in London barred women from participating in the proceedings. Feminist antislavery crusaders Lucretia Mott and Elizabeth Cady Stanton were so infuriated that they turned their attention to a direct demand for women's rights. Stanton organized the first American Women's Rights Convention at Seneca Falls, New York, in July 1848, which issued its own Declaration of Independence, beginning with the words, "We hold these truths to be self-evident, that all men and women are created equal."[8]

In 1920, the ratification of the Nineteenth Amendment finally guaranteed female suffrage in the United States. Unfortunately, however, it no more guaranteed full dignity for women than early Constitutional Amendments had guaranteed it for black men.[9]

A second wave of feminism emerged in the 1960s, stirred by Betty Friedan's book, *The Feminine Mystique*, and the experience of activist women in the civil rights and other liberation movements of the time. Friedan awakened a new consciousness of the extent to which women's confining roles were socially constructed by men to secure their dominant position and by advertisers engaged in assuring demand for the often frivolous products of a growing economy. The result of the second wave of feminism was a cultural revolution that continues to transform the relationships between men and women and to challenge the underlying social structures of sexism worldwide.

Citizenship for the Original Citizens

One of the darkest of all the dark chapters of U.S. imperial history concerns the fate of the Native Americans against whom the European American settlers waged a campaign of genocide to expropriate their lands and destroy their cultures. Massive waves of European immigration fueled an explosive population growth in the new nation, which rose from an estimated 4 million people in 1790 to 31 million in 1860. Territorial expansion proceeded apace. The new nation occupied a land area of 865,000 square miles in 1790. When the westward expansion to the Pacific was completed in 1853, the continental United States occupied 3 million square miles.[10] What was for the European immigrants an experience of liberty, expansion, prosperity, and opportunity was for the Native Americans who stood in their path an experience of tyranny, contraction, poverty, and confinement.

Initially the Native Americans—steeped in the values and ways of Community—sought accommodation with those they had at first greeted as their honored guests. Steeped in the values and ways of Empire, the guests responded with ruthless duplicity. It was the endlessly repeated story of the landing of Columbus.

As the United States encroached ever deeper into Native lands in the relentless drive to the West, Native resistance grew, but it was ultimately overwhelmed by the sheer magnitude of the immigration and the superior firepower of the U.S. military. Reduced to a tenth of their number from the days when the intrusions began, those Native peoples who remained were confined to reservations on isolated fragments of land the Europeans considered to be of little or no value. Even then, the press to appropriate what remained of Indian lands and to assimilate the remaining indigenous population into the European culture continued. In the period between 1946 and 1960, Indian tribes lost an additional 3.3 million acres of land.[11]

Many of the Native American cultures those of European descent sought to destroy gave far greater expression to the Enlightenment ideals of liberty, democracy, and human dignity than any European culture before or since. Many Native peoples remain to this day repositories of the ancient wisdom of those who lived in Community, and they retain a memory of human possibilities that Empire denies. Those whose special status rests on the ruthless injustice of Empire have good reason to consider that memory a threat to their privilege.

It was not until 1924 that Native Americans won through their struggles an act of Congress granting them full and automatic citizenship in the land that was once their own. In 1978, the U.S. Congress passed the American Indian Religious Freedom Act, guaranteeing the right of Native Americans to practice their traditional religions.[12] Finally, citizenship was restored to the original citizens of North America who in a more just world would have been the ones to decide who among the visiting Europeans were qualified to become citizens of the continent's preexisting First Nations and on what conditions.

STRUGGLES OF THE MIDDLE AND WORKING CLASSES

Aristotle, Thomas Jefferson, and Adam Smith all shared an appreciation for the importance to a stable and democratic society of a strong middle class composed of independent farmers and artisans who owned the instruments of their production. A strong middle-class ownership society in which the same people who own the productive assets also provide the labor that makes the assets productive is the antithesis of Empire and an essential foundation of Earth Community.

In the immediate pre- and post-Revolution periods, most free white males made their living as independent farmers, merchants, and artisans of modest but adequate means. They prepared the way for the American Revolution, demanded that the Bill of Rights be added to the Constitution, and kept watch on the issuance of corporate charters. They presented a threat to the imperial designs of the domestic ruling class, which rallied to reduce the upstarts to serfdom.

Eroding the Middle Class

As population and markets grew, the merchant capitalists of New England who had built their fleets and fortunes through privateering, slaving, and war profiteering capitalized on growing demand for manufactured goods by importing cheap goods from England to undersell the independent local craftsmen and drive them out of business. Forced into the wage labor force, these artisans had no choice but to sell their labor to the owners of larger aggregations of capital on whatever terms the owners offered.

Growing numbers of white farmers in the Northeast suffered a similar fate as they were driven out of family farming by land shortages, debt, and competition from midwestern agriculture. Westward expansion provided a safety valve for the displaced until the closing of the western land frontier around 1860. As noted in chapter 11, however, the bankers followed and the farmers soon found themselves once again captive to a system that drove them to mortgage their lands to secure debts they had no means to repay.[13] The resulting frustrations brought forth the rapid growth in the 1890s of an agrarian populist movement that took aim at the deeper structural causes of economic injustice and for a time became a potent rural force. Led primarily by land-owning family farmers, it was unable to bridge the divide between whites and blacks or between landowning farmers and landless farm workers. Its briefly successful but short-lived People's Party was absorbed into the Democratic Party, and the movement disappeared.[14]

The displaced who were not attracted to homesteading sought work in mines, factories, and construction, where they were commonly required to work twelve- to fourteen-hour days, six days a week, with Sunday off to attend church. Women who lacked the support of a husband worked as domestics or in textile factories. Domestics had virtually no time to themselves. Workers of either sex had few if any rights, and bosses continually drove them to produce more for less pay.[15] The greater the monopolization of productive assets by the money people, the fewer the options available to working people, and the greater the power advantage of the owners of capital—thus deepening the classic asymmetrical power relationship of Empire.

The recourse was the same as the recourse against British rule: to organize. The first to do so were white craftsmen, those who had the most resources and options and retained a foothold in the middle class.

In 1827 a number of craft unions in Philadelphia formed the Mechanics' Union of Trade Associations. Similar federations formed in thirteen cities from 1833 through 1836, coordinating their efforts through the National Trades Union founded in 1834. They sponsored labor newspapers, supported strikes, organized other workers, and lobbied for reforms that included improving public education, eliminating compulsory militia musters, and repealing legal restrictions on the formation of labor unions. Their defining cause was a demand to reduce the workday to ten hours.[16]

Employers responded by firing and blacklisting labor organizers and taking unions to court on charges of criminal conspiracy to violate the constitutional rights of employers. In 1835, the New York State Supreme Court ruled unions and strikes illegal under conspiracy laws. The court thus affirmed the owners' claim that it was legal for owners to organize to deny workers their basic rights, but that workers who organized in defense of their rights were engaged in an illegal conspiracy to restrain trade and the beneficial forces of the free market.[17]

Workers responded by turning from strikes to petition drives aimed at winning legislators to their cause and to voter mobilization in support of political candidates sympathetic to their demands, which included a ten-hour day and the distribution of public lands to homesteaders to reduce unemployment and the downward pressure on wages. As fast as state legislatures yielded to worker pressures to pass laws on working hours, however, employers found and exploited loopholes to circumvent them, often with the support of judges sympathetic to their interests.[18]

Growing Power of Property

As the country and the railroads expanded, vast tracts of the land expropriated by the government from the Native Americans by deadly force were given to railroad corporations as an incentive to rapidly extend their rail networks into lands newly opened to white settlement. The railroads in turn sold the land to major corporate forestry, agribusiness, or mining interests.

Corporations combined this windfall with the proceeds of profiteering from the Civil War to create large pools of financial capital at a time when new energy technologies were coming online to substitute fossil fuels for the sheer muscle power of labor. The loss of jobs from this conversion combined with rapid population growth to create a significant labor surplus and a corresponding downward pressure on wages that further increased the profits and influence of the leading industrialists.

In 1860, the United States ranked fourth behind the United Kingdom, France, and Germany in the value of its manufacturing production. By 1894, it ranked number one, with an output of manufactured goods more than double that of the United Kingdom, its nearest rival. As industrial corporations became even more powerful, hopes for economic justice for the working class suffered a corresponding decline.[19]

Corporate leverage over workers was further increased by an economic recession that led to widespread joblessness and starvation. Employers imposed deep wage cuts that fanned growing resentment.

In 1877, the resentment culminated in the Great Railroad Strike. All across the country blacks and whites, women and men, joined in solidarity to block rail transport and shut down ports, shipping, and factories in what came close to a national strike. State and federal governments sided unerringly with the corporations. At the behest of the railroads, state militias were called out. When state militia units refused to fire on their neighbors, federal troops stepped in, firing on the crowds and making arrests until the plutocracy was firmly back in control.[20] Once again, the federal troops were used to insure domestic tranquility as defined by the owning class.

True to the original intention, the courts sided with the owning class in case after case. The Supreme Court consistently upheld decisions of state courts that nullified laws limiting an employee's hours of work, establishing a minimum wage, or otherwise restricting the rights of employers.[21] In virtually every sector money power prevailed over people power. The opinion-making forces of the press, schools, and churches all aligned with the interests of money.[22] The barons of wealth and Imperial Consciousness saw themselves as instruments of a great religious mission based on a Darwinian vision of human progress ordained by God. Priscilla Murolo and A.B. Chitty sum it up:

> The steel tycoon Andrew Carnegie wrote in 1889 that, "Individualism, Private Property, the Law of Accumulation of Wealth, and the Law of Competition" were "the highest result of human experience." John D. Rockefeller, Sr., the oil and mining potentate, declared in a lecture to Sunday-school students: "The growth of a large business is merely a survival of the fittest.... This is not an evil tendency in business... merely the working-out of a law of nature and a law of God." William Graham Sumner, Yale professor of political and social science and a favorite lapdog of the rich, opined that, "The millionaires are a product of natural selection, acting on the whole body of men to pick out those who can meet the requirement."[23]

Millionaires built ostentatious mansions and summer homes modeled on European castles, while the less fortunate went homeless and scavenged for crumbs. The disdain of the powerful for the working class was exemplified by the famous boast of Jay Gould, whose empire included several steamship lines, the Western Union Telegraph Company, and a number of railroads: "I can hire one-half of the working class to kill the other half," he proclaimed.[24] Gould may have been right about his half of the labor force, but the half he could not hire continued organizing with an impressive solidarity among men, women, whites, and blacks even in the face of violent repression by courts, private security guards, and federal troops.

As they had done following Bacon's Rebellion, employers used every opportunity to exploit divisions between men and women, and between whites and blacks. Labor proved to be strongest when it succeeded in maintaining solidarity among working people across race, gender, and occupational lines.

Labor Populists versus Labor Plutocrats

The most powerful labor organization of the post–Civil War period was the Knights of Labor, formed in 1869 in Philadelphia as a secret organization of garment workers. Of a deeply inclusive populist persuasion, the Knights welcomed all "producing classes" to its membership, including housewives, farmers, clergymen, shopkeepers, and professionals. It even included employers if they had come from the wage-earning class and treated their workers fairly. Only corporate lawyers, bankers, stockbrokers, professional gamblers, and liquor dealers were excluded summarily. The Knights grew to be a significant force with a comprehensive agenda of reforms intended to transform the system, including a progressive income tax, the abolition of child labor, workers' compensation, an eight-hour day, and public ownership of the railroads. It also embraced a program of economic democratization by organizing mines and factories as worker cooperatives.[25]

As economic conditions for labor deteriorated further, strikes became more frequent and the confrontations more violent. Police fired on strikers and arrested leaders. Four labor leaders were hanged based on what many believed to be trumped-up charges. The military and police firepower of the state ultimately restored domestic tranquility for the corporate robber barons. As the Knights faded into history, the American Federation of Labor (AFL) emerged to take its place.[26]

The AFL, which was less expansive in its membership and more narrowly focused in its aims, was only interested in organizing skilled workers to win them a bigger piece of the pie through the negotiation of favorable contracts. It took no interest in less skilled workers, women, African Americans, and new immigrants or in matters of public policy.[27]

Whereas the Knights had more of the qualities of a self-organizing social movement, the AFL created an institutional superstructure of professional negotiators and organizers with a classic imperial gap between its own management and the rank-and-file workers it professed to serve. Functioning much like a corporation in the business of supplying contract labor to other corporations, AFL leaders were perfectly comfortable with the established system of power, moved easily within the circles of the plutocracy, and negotiated sweetheart deals with employers in return for bribes. With a substantial lock on worker access to jobs, the AFL's membership grew rapidly from the 1890s through the first decade of the twentieth century, even as corporations continued to undermine union power and the Supreme Court continued to side with management.

In 1905, workers of a more radical political bent formed the Industrial Workers of the World (IWW), as a counterforce to the AFL. In contrast to the AFL, which largely aligned itself with the capitalist cause, the declared mission of the IWW was to overthrow the capitalist system. Popularly known as the Wobblies, the IWW was at the center of labor activism in the early twentieth century. It catered to African Americans, unskilled workers, and new immigrants, pursued a broad agenda of social reform, and threatened the establishment. Its members hated the more conservative AFL almost as much as they hated capitalism.[28]

The labor unrest of this period built up to a massive 1913 mineworkers strike against the Colorado Fuel & Iron Company, which ended in a major defeat for the workers when company guards and state militiamen fired on the strikers with machine guns and torched their tent colony. By the time the strikers returned to work, sixty-nine miners and family members had been murdered.[29]

Capitalist Excess and the Great Depression

In the 1920s, the Republican presidencies of Warren Harding, Calvin Coolidge, and Herbert Hoover, backed by a Republican-controlled Congress, carried corporate influence over government to what for that time was a new extreme. The Harding administration was famous for graft and corruption, the fraudulent sale of government property, and the looting of Native American assets. Coolidge cut the income taxes of the rich in half and sharply reduced the inheritance tax. Hoover supported U.S. corporate expansion into foreign markets. These administrations promoted loans to foreign governments to create more markets for U.S. corporations and regularly fielded troops to protect overseas corporate investments in China, Haiti, Honduras, and Nicaragua.[30]

Inequality grew rapidly in the 1920s. Privileged groups, including skilled workers in unionized trades, generally did well. Most working people, however, gained little or nothing from the burst of prosperity, and many workers suffered falling wages. Labor racketeering became well established in the building trades, and the Mafia took over some local unions to raid their treasuries and sell "strike insurance" to employers.[31]

Working people were not earning enough to buy the goods being produced by the overheated economy. Fraud and speculation were rampant in unregulated financial markets. The excesses of materialism, political corruption, speculation, and financial fraud could not be sustained. The illusion evaporated, and the nation was hit by the economic collapse of October 1929, which brought on the Great Depression.

A NEW DEAL

Elected by a landslide on a visionary reform platform, a New York patrician named Franklin D. Roosevelt took office as president on March 4, 1933, at the depth of the Great Depression. His proclaimed commitment was to save capitalism from itself. Immediately on taking office, he began implementing a program of regulatory reform to limit the worst excesses of capitalism and to revitalize the economy by putting more money in the hands of working people. He immediately tightened the public regulation of banks and financial markets, implemented employment-generating public works programs, funded relief programs that extended aid to a fifth of the national population, and pushed through legislation guaranteeing labor's right to organize and bargain collectively.[32] Roosevelt's actions energized labor and appalled his peers, who denounced him as a class traitor.

Leveling the Playing Field

Although the federal government proved unable to enforce its own labor rights guarantees in the face of defiance by the corporate plutocrats, Roosevelt, unlike previous presidents, declined to send out troops to fight on the side of the corporations. That made all the difference. Union membership skyrocketed, and everywhere workers struck for better wages and working conditions.

Corporations responded by mobilizing support from hate groups like the Ku Klux Klan to "save America from labor radicals," hired private goon squads to rough up union members, launched public relations campaigns to denounce labor organizers as Communists, and called on local police and national guard units to put down strikers. The excesses of the industrialists succeeded in swinging public sentiment in the favor of labor and strengthening Roosevelt's political base and resolve.

In 1935, Roosevelt initiated the Second New Deal based on a partnership with workers. It included Social Security, national unemployment insurance, substantial tax increases for corporations and wealthy individuals, and antitrust action to break up corporate monopolies. Reelected with strong union support against a pro-business Republican in 1936, Roosevelt won over 60 percent of the popular vote and carried every state but Maine and Vermont. Aggressive organizing drives increased union membership from 3.6 million in 1935 to 8.7 million in 1940.

Right-wing sentiment surged in the 1938–40 period among corporate leaders, a number of whom expressed overt sympathy for German and Italian fascism. Henry Ford and James Watson (president of IBM) accepted Nazi medals. Major corporations formed the America First Committee to oppose intervention against Hitler. A former president of the National Association of Manufacturers suggested that "American business might be forced to turn to some form of disguised Fascist dictatorship," and the association distributed two million copies of a pamphlet titled "Join the CIO and Help Build a Soviet America."[33]

Middle-Class Ascendance

On December 7, 1941, the Japanese launched a surprise air attack on the U.S. fleet in Pearl Harbor, Hawaii. A suddenly unified nation mobilized to defeat a common enemy. Pumping money into defense industries, it created the most powerful industrial and military force the world had ever known, paid for in part by raising marginal tax rates on the rich. The economy boomed, corporate profits soared on cost-plus government contracts, and widespread unemployment was replaced by critical labor shortages.

Unions generally lived by their pledge not to strike during the war but continued organizing. By 1945, union membership had risen to 14.3 million, which was 35.5 percent of the workforce.[34] Following the war, the defense industries retooled for civilian production as pent-up consumer demand fueled the economy.

Backing their demands with a wave of strikes, labor pressed for and won major wage increases and brought working people more rights and benefits than they had enjoyed at any other time in U.S. history. Unions were strong. Health care and retirement benefits were pretty much a given for working people. The earnings of a typical wage earner were adequate to support a family, and working parents came home to have dinner with their children. Home ownership was growing, and everyone was capturing a portion of the gains from the increasing economic output—narrowing the wealth gap and decreasing the relative power of the plutocracy.[35]

The terms *downsizing* and *outsourcing* had not yet entered the vocabulary. The American Dream of comfortable affluence continued to elude people of color, but for most Americans of European descent, it had become a reality.

The United States became the envy of the world and the model that others sought to emulate at a time when, in the world at large, the great colonial empires of the past were being dismantled. People everywhere were demanding a democratic voice and a fair share of the wealth they helped to create. For a time it seemed the entire world might eventually enjoy a level of affluence comparable to that of the American middle class.

The ideals set forth in the stirring rhetoric of the Declaration of Independence notwithstanding, the founding of the United States and the drafting and ratification of the U.S. Constitution did not bring democracy to North America. Rather, it created a context for a long struggle to overcome an inherited cultural and institutional legacy of five thousand years of Empire—a struggle violently opposed by the elites in power. The historical reality of the genocide against Native Americans, the enslavement of blacks, the denial of the basic rights and humanity of women, and the denial of a just share of profits to those who toil to make capital productive manifests this legacy, underscores the magnitude of the challenge, and reveals how much remains undone.

It is only from a deeper historical perspective that we can appreciate the substantial accomplishments of these struggles. Monarchy is now little more than a historical curiosity. A clear separation of church and state secures freedom of religious conscience and worship. A system of checks and balances has for over two centuries successfully barred one elite faction from establishing permanent control of the institutions of government. Active genocide against Native Americans has ended and genocide against any group is now universally condemned. Slavery is no longer a legally protected institution and is culturally unacceptable.

Native Americans, people of color, people without property, and women now all have the legal right to vote and to participate fully in the political process. Pervasive though it remains in practice, open discrimination to deny the political rights of any group is now culturally unacceptable.

The fact that we now take these accomplishments for granted underscores how significant our progress has been, given that not so long ago they would have been considered unthinkable. Each of these achievements depended on the sustained commitment and sacrifice of millions of extraordinary people committed to a vision of a world that works for all.

Many of us who grew up in the United States in the post–World War II years came to accept democracy and economic justice as something of an automatic birthright. We were raised to believe that we were blessed to live in a classless society of opportunity for all who are willing to apply themselves and play by the rules.

The experience of the middle class in those years seemed to confirm this story, and those of us who were a part of it were inclined to dismiss people who spoke of issues of class as malcontents who would rather promote class warfare than accept responsibility for putting in an honest day's work. Sure, there had been problems in the past, but thanks to our intellectual genius and high ideals, we Americans had resolved them and rendered them irrelevant to our present. Now it was our due and our responsibility to make the rest of the world more like us. I now recognize how wrong we were.

Yet the middle-class ascendance of the post–World War II years was in fact an extraordinary demonstration of the possibilities of democracy grounded in a belief that everyone should share in the benefits of a well-functioning society. Unfortunately, however, it turned out to be only a temporary popular victory in the war of the owning class against the rest that is a defining condition of Empire and that has defined the American experience from the day Columbus first set foot on a Caribbean island. All the disparate popular struggles of our history to achieve justice for workers, women, and people of color, as well as the struggles for peace and the environment, are subtexts of a larger meta-struggle against the cultural mindset and institutions of Empire.

The owning classes have long recognized that their imperial class privilege is placed at risk by a unification of the oppressed. The claims of identity politics based on race, gender, and occupational specialization are tolerable to Empire because they emphasize and perpetuate division. Discussion of class, however, is forbidden, because it exposes common interests and deeper structural issues with a potential to lead to a unified resistance.

The enduring class divide is between owners and workers—between those who live on the returns to capital and those who live on the returns to their own labor. Jefferson sought to close the divide by making every worker an owner. Hamilton sought to secure the position of an elite ruling class by assuring that ownership remained concentrated in its hands.

As I document in the next chapter, in the late twentieth and early twenty-first centuries, the heirs to the Hamiltonian vision reminded us of their presence and their commitment to the dominator relationships of Empire even as the changing human condition renders their vision untenable. I still find it difficult to accept that there are those among the leaders of the most powerful U.S. institutions who pursue Empire as a holy mission and are prepared to use every means—from lies to assassinations to perpetual war—to block progress toward justice for all and to roll back the gains already achieved. I can no longer deny, however, that such people do exist, that they have successfully manipulated the culture to achieve substantial followings, and that a necessary part of the work of the Great Turning is to neutralize their power by exposing their lies, methods, and imperial agendas.

CHAPTER 13

Wake-Up Call

America is lurching to the right.... Until the 1960s, there had been almost no relevant right-wing organizations in America.... By the 1970s, the Right had been transformed into an institutionalized, disciplined, well-organized, and well-funded movement of loosely knit affiliates.... The New Right network supports whoever shares its desire for radical political change and its resentments of the status quo. As such, the New Right is anything but conservative.[1]

Alan Crawford

The evil was very grave: the Republicans, entrenched in power, cynically abused it; they subverted the integrity of the vote, and of the press; they mocked the spirit of the Constitution through partisan legislation, and copying the tactics of tyrants, used overseas wars to deflect attention from their actions.[2]

José Martí, Cuban poet and independence hero on the U.S. election of 1884

Following World War II, the United States developed a broad middle class that made it the envy of the world. Achieving this took a devastating depression, a labor-friendly president who refused to field federal troops to fire on striking workers, a world war, and a strong, well-organized labor movement. Those elements combined to create a dynamic that for a time moderated the excesses of Empire.

The reforms, however, did not challenge Empire's underlying institutions and culture. Ownership remained concentrated and economic power remained vested in a few large corporations. The labor unions were themselves organized as imperial hierarchies headed by labor leaders as jealous of their power as any corporate CEO or incumbent politician. In the manner of an immature democracy, the political culture focused on individual rights, with little sense of the civic responsibility required of a mature democracy. Then a deeper cultural challenge began to emerge.

CULTURAL AND ECONOMIC CHALLENGES TO EMPIRE

The 1960s were a time of cultural ferment. A new generation told the corporate plutocrats, "We don't buy into your consumerism and your wars." It told the theocrats, "We have no use for your narrow interpretations of biblical authority and rigid standards of sexual morality." African Americans and women of all races were telling both plutocrats and theocrats, "We reject your efforts to define us as something less than fully human; we demand recognition of our humanity." Traditional lines of authority, including those of the traditional family, were eroding.

There was also a growing global environmental consciousness that challenged the conventional wisdom of economic growth. The Club of Rome's study, *Limits to Growth*, published in 1972, pointed out that the human burden on the ecosystem was rapidly approaching the limits of what the planet could sustain. Although the study was dismissed by economists as doomsaying, many of the planet's crucial natural systems were already in decline. A sharp rise in oil prices precipitated by actions of the OPEC oil cartel focused attention on the limits of global petroleum reserves and the vulnerability of the U.S. economy's dependence on foreign oil. The environmental movement began to gain strength. The foundational values of a new culture of Earth Community were finding growing acceptance, posing an increasingly serious challenge to the institutions of Empire.

At the same time, the United States faced serious economic challenges from abroad. In addition to the political and military threat of the Soviet Union, several nations of Asia, including Japan, South Korea, Hong Kong, and Singapore, were developing strong export-oriented economies that were challenging U.S. corporations at home and abroad. Other nations were telling U.S. corporate plutocrats: "We can play the game of global competition better than you can, even on your home turf." These developments threatened not only the hegemony of U.S. corporations but also the jobs of American workers.

Elitist plutocrats and theocrats felt the foundations of their power and privilege eroding. Empire was at risk. The movement to choose a more democratic human future was in ascendance. Earth Community was in gestation. Empire mobilized to strike back.

Television was transforming how people used their time and related to the world. Beginning about 1960, passive forms of participation in public life began displacing more active forms. People were patronizing fast-food outlets, professional sporting events, and gambling casinos with greater frequency. There were corresponding declines in voter participation, newspaper readership, Parent Teacher Association membership, union membership, frequency of family meals, philanthropic giving, and perceptions of honesty and morality.[3] Relationships among people were not so much changing as simply eroding. People were feeling increasingly vulnerable and disconnected. There was a troubling sense in the air, particularly among self-identified conservatives, that the moral and social foundations of society were disintegrating. The uncertainty and resentment created fertile ground for the demagogues of Empire.

Renewing the Historic Alliance

Historically, rejection of the democratic ideal in America has coalesced around one or both of two fundamentalisms. Plutocrats, heirs to the vision of Alexander Hamilton, embrace a market fundamentalism that legitimates unaccountable rule by persons of financial means. Theocrats, heirs to the Calvinist vision of John Winthrop, embrace a religious fundamentalism that legitimates unaccountable rule by those of a prescribed faith and celebrates wealth and power as a mark of God's favor. Although plutocrats give priority to material values and theocrats to spiritual values, their shared drive for dominator power and aversion to democracy make them allies of convenience.

In the late 1960s, a small group of plutocrats and theocrats formed an alliance to avert the fall of Empire and drive the U.S. political center sharply to the right. It proved a powerful combination. The plutocrats delivered the money in record amounts for political campaigns, think tanks, and media outreach. The theocrats delivered the votes by mobilizing the resentment of the frightened and alienated who felt themselves being pushed out of the middle class. They called themselves the New Right, although their agenda was scarcely new. United by their antipathy for democracy and their drive for power, they worked together to gain control of the Republican Party and move both the Republican and Democratic parties well to the right of the former political center.

Organizing for Dominion

The elites of the corporate plutocracy have long organized through trade associations and umbrella organizations like chambers of commerce.[4] They also have a long history of supporting conservative think tanks, such as the Hoover Institute, established at Stanford University in 1919. The Council on Foreign Relations, founded in 1921 by a group of prominent businessmen, bankers, and lawyers, played a defining role in shaping State Department planning for U.S. global dominance of world resources and markets following World War II. President Franklin Roosevelt formed the Business Advisory Council in 1933 to strengthen ties between the corporate world and the U.S. Department of Commerce. David Rockefeller founded the Trilateral Commission in 1973 to foster cooperation among the elites of Europe, North America, and Japan in advancing neoliberal economic policies and corporate globalization.

Influential though they were, these institutions generally functioned as polite old-boys' clubs outside the public spotlight. This changed dramatically as leading plutocrats mobilized to reassert control of the nation's political agenda. They launched a sophisticated and well-funded campaign to control the mass media, organize new lobbying alliances, mobilize grassroots support, and finance supportive intellectuals, think tanks, and university departments. They offered special courses and junkets for judges and law students, bankrolled friendly politicians, and brought to bear the most advanced tools of corporate advertising and PR to shape the political culture and agenda.

In 1971, the U.S. Chamber of Commerce sought the advice of Virginia attorney and future Supreme Court justice Lewis Powell about what it perceived to be a growing domestic threat to capitalism. Powell responded with a memo titled "Attack on American Free Enterprise System." In it, he warned of an assault by environmentalists, consumer activists, and others who "propagandize against the system, seeking insidiously and constantly to sabotage it." He called on the chamber to mobilize "the wisdom, ingenuity and resources of American business… against those who would destroy it."[5] On Powell's recommendation, in 1973 the chamber formed the Pacific Legal Foundation to defend corporations against public-interest efforts to enforce environmental regulations, protect workers' rights, and tax corporate profits.

William E. Simon, who served as secretary of the treasury under presidents Nixon and Ford, left the Treasury Department in 1977 to become president of the Olin Foundation. There he mobilized conservative foundations behind a strategic effort to align the judicial system with corporate interests and to build a network of influential right-wing think tanks. He served as a trustee of the John Templeton Foundation, helped shape the program of the Bradley Foundation, and joined the boards of several right-wing think tanks funded by the Olin Foundation, including the Heritage Foundation and the Hoover Institute.

In 1972, the CEOs of a number of America's largest corporations formed the Business Roundtable to lobby the Congress on behalf of U.S. corporations and their top executives. The Roundtable played a major role in the 1980 presidential election of Ronald Reagan, the passage of tax breaks for corporations, and the Republican takeover of the Congress in 1994. The Roundtable also had a leading role in the passage of the North American Free Trade Agreement and other trade agreements written by and for corporate interests.

Before 1970, few Fortune 500 companies had public affairs offices in Washington, D.C. By 1980, more than 80 percent did. The flow of corporate funds to political campaign coffers grew accordingly. Corporate-funded front organizations with misleading names like Keep America Beautiful presented themselves as grassroots citizen initiatives to mobilize political support for corporate-sponsored policy agendas.

New funds flowed to existing right-wing think tanks, including the American Enterprise Institute (founded in 1943), the Center for Strategic and International Studies (founded in 1962), the Hudson Institute (founded in 1961), and the Hoover Institute. New right-wing think tanks included the Heritage Foundation (1973), which shaped much of the Reagan administration agenda, the Cato Institute (1977), and Citizens for a Sound Economy (1984).

Building a Voter Base

Efforts by the theocrats to build a loyal conservative voting base centered on mobilizing conservative white Christians. Early strategists who had been active in Barry Goldwater's failed 1964 presidential campaign formulated a "family values" agenda and framed the idea of a mass-based "Moral Majority" movement of conservative Christians. To this end, they formed Focus on the Family in 1977 and Concerned Women for America in 1979.[6] By the end of the 1990s, Focus on the Family controlled a radio and publishing empire with an annual budget of $110 million, over 1,300 employees, its own zip code in Colorado Springs, Colorado, and a syndicated talk radio show broadcast on some 1,500 stations in North America and 3,400 stations around the world.[7] In 1979, they recruited conservative televangelist Jerry Falwell as point person to recruit conservative white Christian churches to the movement.[8]

Weekly meetings of the Religious Roundtable, founded 1979 in Washington, D.C., facilitated coordination of the political efforts of the New Right. Then in 1981, the Religious Roundtable became the Council on National Policy to provide a more formal body to coordinate a broader coalition of secular and religious groups.[9] Strategy for the 1996 presidential election was coordinated through weekly meetings convened by Grover Norquist, president of Americans for Tax Reform, bringing together such groups as the Christian Coalition, the National Rifle Association, the U.S. Chamber of Commerce, the American Farm Bureau, and the National Right to Life Committee.[10]

Outsiders marvel at the success of the Far Right in unifying its fractious base of conflicting interests and values behind a common political agenda. The key is that in the classic dominator relationships of Empire, the coordination of diverse factions and the settling of differences takes place at the leadership level where shared power goals generally override sometimes sharp ideological differences. The leaders tailor their messages to their individual constituencies to gain support for centrally chosen policies and candidates. Since the organizing is from the top down, there is little need for cross-constituency communication and coordination at the grassroots level. This pattern contrasts with the more complex organizing dynamic of global civil society, which self-organizes through interconstituency communication and cooperation at the popular level—the partnership model of Earth Community.

After the failure of his 1988 bid for the Republican presidential nomination, televangelist Pat Robertson founded the politically sophisticated Christian Coalition and embarked on a strategy crafted by his savvy chief lieutenants, Ralph Reed and Guy Rogers, to take control of the Republican Party. Rogers spelled out the simple arithmetic underlying their electoral strategy at the coalition's first national conference in November 1991.[11]

> In a presidential election, when more voters turn out than in any other election, only 15 percent of eligible voters actually determine the outcome.... Of all the adults 18 and over eligible to vote, only about 60 percent are registered.... Of those registered to vote, in a good turnout, only half go to the polls.

That means 30 percent of those eligible are actually voting.
So 15 percent determines the outcome in a high-turnout election. In low-turnout elections... the percentage that determines who wins can be as low as 6 or 7 percent.... We don't
have to persuade a majority of Americans to agree with us....
Most of them stay home and watch television.[12]

As Robertson was building the Christian Coalition to mobilize the grass
roots, other right-wing strategists and funders were creating two networks of think tanks to replicate at the state level the political infrastructure that had been the foundation of their success at the national
level. One network, comprising think tanks modeled on the Heritage
Foundation, was coordinated through the State Policy Network. The second network, comprising Family Policy Councils developed by Focus
on the Family, was loosely modeled on the Family Research Council in
Washington, D.C. These networks generally functioned as an arm of the
Republican Party. Their primary purpose was to market an ideological
agenda of conservative economic- and social-policy proposals.[13]

STEALTH POLITICS

The alliance faced a difficult barrier in its effort to mobilize a voter base.
The plutocrats' agenda of subverting democracy, shrinking the middle
class, and making a few people fabulously wealthy and powerful at the
expense of the rest does not naturally attract a broad popular constituency. It violates basic moral principles of economic and social justice and runs counter to the self-interest of all but the very rich.

The theocrats faced other challenges distinctive to their faith. First,
a major portion of the Christian Right constituency on which they
pinned their hopes believes that the earthly world is the domain of the
devil and beyond redemption. Many also believe that the Rapture, the
time when Christ will return to lift the faithful bodily to heaven, is imminent. Because these beliefs render political action pointless, most
Christian groups of such persuasion took little interest in political life
and had to be convinced of their Christian duty to engage politically.

The second challenge for those who sought to mobilize the Christian Right as a political base was the deep influence of the ideas of R. J.
Rushdoony, a champion of Christian Reconstructionism, whose articles
were regularly published in Falwell's newspaper. Journalist Frederick

Clarkson, who specializes in reporting on the Christian Right, explains that

> generally, Reconstructionism seeks to replace democracy
> with a theocracy that would govern by imposing their ver-
> sion of "Biblical Law." As incredible as it seems, democratic
> institutions such as labor unions, civil rights laws, and public
> schools would be on the short list for elimination. Women
> would be generally relegated to hearth and home. Men
> deemed insufficiently Christian would be denied citizenship,
> perhaps executed. So severe is this theocracy that capital
> punishment would be extended beyond such crimes as kid-
> napping, rape, and murder to include, among other things,
> blasphemy, heresy, adultery and homosexuality.[14]

In short, the vision calls for creating a theocratic state with legal codes similar to those of the early Calvinist colonies in New England. A program akin to that of Islamic fundamentalists who seek to create Islamic states, it lacks broad popular appeal. To build a loyal voter base, plutocrats and theocrats alike had to become skilled in waging stealth campaigns that played to the resentments of those who were being squeezed out of the middle class while cloaking the real agenda in populist rhetoric and values.

Mobilizing Resentment

The New Right alliance became especially effective in targeting the resentment of small-business owners, farmers, and wage laborers whose middle-class status was threatened by the very system they were being mobilized to promote. It was a diabolically effective strategy. Since the actual intention was to advance a neoliberal economic agenda hostile to the middle class, the greater the New Right's success, the greater the anxiety and resentment it engendered. Through skillful scapegoating, the resentment of the middle class was deflected away from the economic policies that were the real source of its affliction and was turned instead against gays, people of color, feminists, welfare recipients, immigrants, drug addicts, government workers, Jews, and the liberals who support them.[15]

All the while corporate advertisers were cultivating an individualistic culture of greed and materialism and using sex and violence to keep people glued to television sets, thus fueling social alienation and a sense of decline in moral values. As liberal reformers focused their attention on expanding the rights and freedoms of women, people of color, children, and gays and lesbians, the New Right accused the reformers of being responsible for the breakdown of the moral order of traditional American cultural norms—"the work ethic, sexual restraint, self-reliance, patriarchy, Christian worship, and patriotism."[16] The New Right found it particularly easy to generate resentment among struggling working-class taxpayers against welfare recipients.

The New Right found that three story themes worked particularly well to mobilize their constituencies: social ills are the result of permissive liberalism; free market capitalism is more effective than government in delivering prosperity; and the external threat of Communism (later terrorism) requires a strong defense.[17] These themes in turn supported cuts in social welfare programs, the deregulation of markets, and lucrative military contracts for corporate sponsors. As observed by researcher Jean Hardisty,

> In confusing and frightening times, Christian Right groups provide clear rules of conduct and theologically ordained answers to life's problems.... The New Right captured and mobilized widespread social stress caused by rapid social and economic change. It did not create backlash sentiments out of whole cloth. They had already existed, at least latently. New Right leaders listened to them, took them seriously, and then mobilized and manipulated them.[18]

The theocrats respond to attacks on their positions with the charge that opponents are motivated by a hatred of Christians, America, and the moral order. This tactic disguises the fact that promoting hatred and intolerance—particularly against society's most vulnerable people—places them sharply at odds with the foundational values of the Declaration of Independence, the teachings of Jesus, and the beliefs of the substantial majority of Christians. Indeed, most Christians, including many who identify themselves as fundamentalist or evangelical, are compassionate, committed to progressive democratic values, and deeply offended by the un-Christian aims of leaders of the theocratic right and their distortions of Christian teaching. Hardisty and Clarkson each underscore the essential distinction between the *followers* of the New Right, who are struggling with legitimate concerns, and the *leaders* of the New Right, who manipulate those concerns for political advantage.[19]

Exploiting Family Breakdown

The New Right has been brilliantly successful in restoring the imperial status quo in relations between the owning and the working classes. Since 1983, nearly all the gains from economic growth have gone to the very richest Americans as union membership has declined and the real wages of working people have fallen.

As the wages of a typical male worker fell below the level required to support a family, women who earlier had begun to experience a new sense of freedom found that workplace participation was no longer a choice but a necessity. Many were forced into jobs paying less than a living wage. They no longer had the time or energy to prepare home-cooked meals and care for their own children.

With no one to care for the home, demand grew for corporate-produced processed foods and corporate-operated fast-food chains. Declining nutrition generated more business for the health care industry. Children left in the care of television sets were programmed for their consumer roles. Each of these developments opened new marketing opportunities for corporations and advanced economic growth while simultaneously advancing the family and community breakdown, alienation, and stress that provided fertile ground for political demagogues.

Men who played by the rules felt betrayed by the loss of the provider role that was once the foundation of their identity.[20] Women, feminist and antifeminist alike, felt betrayed as the jobs that once promised greater freedom became imperatives that limited their freedom. The family life essential to the well-being of men, women, and children had been replaced by the depersonalized marketplace.

The greater the moral decay and family breakdown, the greater the fear and resentment that gave the New Right its power. Blame feminists. Blame liberals. Blame people of color. Blame welfare moms. Just don't blame the people who are dismantling the institutions of family, community, and democracy.

Those at the bottom of the economic ladder were most commonly people of color—especially African Americans—who were frequently targets of the scapegoating. With few options available, some turned to the drug trade as their best hope for economic success. This led to sharp increases in drug convictions and a swelling prison population, which in turn had a devastating impact on many African American families and drew funds from education and other public needs. It worked out well, however, for the corporate elites who profited from the public contracts to build and operate prisons and the ability to employ prison labor for a pittance.[21]

Struggling to make ends meet and maintain some semblance of the consumer lifestyle, middle- and lower-income households went deeper into debt—thus obligating themselves to turn over an ever growing share of their hard-earned income as interest payments to bankers. Those who had previously enjoyed a comparatively relaxed middle-class life were forced to work harder to support a declining standard of living, even as those at the top enjoyed gourmet restaurants, exotic vacations, private jets, and ever larger and more numerous homes.

PLUTOCRACY AS A BIPARTISAN CAUSE

The New Right's first major political triumph was the election of Ronald Reagan to the presidency in 1980. The Reagan administration (1981–89) took the lead in implementing the neoliberal economic agenda in the United States, as the administration of Margaret Thatcher advanced the cause in the United Kingdom. In addition to the measures noted above, military expenditures were increased, and the abandonment of antitrust enforcement allowed for ever larger corporate mergers. Europe, Canada, and Japan were pressured to similarly "modernize" their economies.

The third-world debt crisis of 1982 created the necessary pretext for the IMF and World Bank—operating under the direction of the U.S. Treasury Department—to impose the neoliberal agenda on indebted low-income countries. Through their structural-adjustment programs, the IMF and World Bank stripped governments, some democratically elected, of their ability to set and enforce social, environmental, and workplace standards or even to give preference to firms that hired locally or employed union workers.

After the Republican Ronald Reagan, the presidency passed to the Republican George H. W. Bush (1989–93) and then to the Democrat Bill Clinton (1993–2001). Each administration differed in style and priorities, but America's plutocracy remained fully in charge and its pro-corporate agenda moved seamlessly forward, irrespective of which party was in power.

Clinton, although a member of the presumably more liberal Democratic Party, made major contributions to the New Right agenda by rolling back social welfare programs, pushing through the North American Free Trade Agreement, and replacing the GATT with the more powerful WTO. His administration also expanded the number of crimes qualifying for the death penalty and rejected efforts to slow executions. It eliminated 10 million of 14 million people from the welfare roles, supported lowering the capital gains tax, presided over an increase in the number of people without health insurance, refused to sign the international Land Mine Treaty, accelerated drilling for gas and oil on federal lands, and became the first administration since Richard Nixon not to raise the standard for automobile fuel efficiency.[22]

By the time George W. Bush assumed the powers of the U.S. presidency in January 2001, the New Right had already made significant progress in rolling back the gains of the earlier challenge to Empire. It is telling that the Republican president Richard Nixon (1969–74), considered in his time an archconservative, was by today's standards a champion of labor and the environment somewhat to the left of the current mainstream of the Democratic Party. In 1970, he created the Environmental Protection Agency and signed into law the Clean Air Act, setting deadlines for reducing automobile emissions. He signed the Endangered Species Acts of 1969 and 1973. In 1971, he signed the law that established the Occupational Safety and Health Administration, which enforces standards for workplace safety.[23] He also opened the way to a peaceful political relationship between the United States and Communist China.

WAKE-UP CALL

For all its populist pretensions, the New Right takeover of the U.S. government was far from a spontaneous expression of the popular will. Rather it was the product of a carefully crafted campaign to manipulate the popular culture to serve the private interests of an imperial elite. It involved a well-organized and well-funded alliance of corporate plutocrats and religious theocrats who brought money and votes to the table in an intentional bid to turn back the clock on democracy, civil liberties, the economic advances of the middle class, and cultural and religious pluralism. The seriousness of the threat to democracy, peace, and U.S. world power and prestige did not hit home for most Americans, however, until the most extremist administration in memory took power after the turn of the century. By the overreach of its extremist agenda, this administration exposed the reality of the New Right's intentions. It also drew attention to the elite bias of the U.S. political system and its vulnerability to a takeover by political extremists with a deep aversion to democracy.

In his 2000 presidential campaign, Bush presented himself as a compassionate conservative who would work for ordinary people, leave no child behind, protect the environment, be fiscally responsible, and pursue a peaceful, cooperative, and nonbelligerent foreign policy respectful of the rights and interests of others.

In his inaugural address on January 20, 2001, Bush reiterated his promises, pledging that his administration would embody "a new commitment to live out our nation's promise through civility, courage, compassion, and character" and challenged Americans to become engaged in the nation's civic life.[24] He further pledged that in foreign affairs the United States would "show purpose without arrogance.... Civility is not a tactic or a sentiment. It is the determined choice of trust over cynicism, of community over chaos."[25]

These were uplifting words true to America's founding ideals. Most of those who voted for Bush took him at his word. As it turned out, Bush and the small circle of former corporate officers and lobbyists, neoconservative military hawks, religious fundamentalists, and Washington insiders he installed in the top ranks of his administration took power with a well-developed agenda sharply at odds with those professed commitments.

Given that Mr. Bush had never previously distinguished himself for his managerial skills, the speed with which the regime he brought to power took control of the entire administrative branch of the U. S. government was truly stunning. Behind him was a well-disciplined political cabal that had been developing its relationships and agenda for years before the Supreme Court handed Mr. Bush the keys to the White House.

The new regime wasted no time in demonstrating that its intentions were less than compassionate and more than conservative. Within days of taking office, the regime had halted action on several thousand pages of progressive executive orders Bill Clinton had issued in his final days.[26] It had denied aid to overseas groups that mention abortion to women as a medical option, developed a $1.6 trillion tax-cut proposal for the super-rich, and introduced an education program centered on vouchers and standardized testing[27] designed to undermine public education.

By March 2001, the regime had announced that the United States was withdrawing from the Kyoto Protocol on global warming[28] and had issued a seemingly endless flow of orders loosening restrictions on oil and gas drilling, mining, logging, and coal-fired power generation. It was soon clear to many that the administration's larger goal was to nullify previous efforts made on behalf of democracy, the middle class, and the environment in favor of global imperial rule by a dynastic U.S. ruling class headed by the House of Bush.[29]

Within a few months of taking office, Bush, who had promised a cooperative, nonbelligerent foreign policy, had expelled fifty Russian diplomats from the United States on unsubstantiated charges of spying, pulled back from engagement in peace and reconciliation processes in Ireland, the Middle East, and the Korean Peninsula, and withdrawn from the Anti-Ballistic Missile Treaty in order to implement a missile defense shield. An increasingly unilateral and belligerent U.S. foreign policy created growing alarm among long-standing U.S. allies in Europe.[30]

VISION OF PAX AMERICANA

The thrust of the new regime's foreign policy, including plans to invade Iraq, had been worked out years before it took office. In 1992, after the disintegration of the Soviet Union, Dick Cheney, then secretary of defense in the Bush I administration, commissioned a group headed by Paul Wolfowitz to prepare a document on a post–cold war defense strategy for the United States. The report, completed in January 1993 just before the presidential inauguration of Bill Clinton, presented a clear message: the United States must maintain sufficient military force to dominate any potential rival and be prepared to use that force unilaterally to maintain its dominant position in the world. Iran and Iraq were named as competitors for power in the Middle East and therefore potential threats to U.S. control of the region's oil resources. Leading Republican neoconservatives Bill Kristol and Robert Kagan followed up with an article in *Foreign Affairs* that called for the United States to establish a "benevolent global hegemony."

In 1997, Kristol and Kagan joined a virtual who's who of top-level defense officials and advisers from the Reagan and Bush I administrations to form the Project for a New American Century (PNAC).

Founding members included Cheney, Wolfowitz, Donald Rumsfeld, and Richard Perle, who formed the Bush II defense-policy team; and Jeb Bush, Bush II's brother. In September 2000, PNAC issued a report titled *Rebuilding America's Defenses: Strategy, Forces and Resources for a New Century.* The report spelled out a plan for global U.S. military domination. It envisioned imposing a Pax Americana on the world in the manner of the Pax Romana of the ancient Roman Empire.[31] The report became the blueprint for the military plans and policies of the Bush II regime.

The PNAC report observed that mobilizing public support for its agenda of global military dominance would be difficult "absent some catastrophic and catalyzing event—like a new Pearl Harbor."[32] Osama bin Laden's September 11, 2001, attack provided the regime just what it needed. Well prepared, it moved quickly to embrace what key members, including Bush, Rumsfeld, and Condoleezza Rice described in National Security Council meetings as a "great opportunity."[33] Playing to the fear and insecurity that followed the attacks, the regime quickly seized the moment to advance an unabashed imperial agenda at home and abroad.

Bin Laden's Gift to Bush

Public support for the Bush II administration, which had been falling steadily in the midst of a moribund economy, suddenly soared following the attack. The nation rallied in support of its commander in chief as the regime invaded Afghanistan in search of Osama bin Laden, the mastermind of the terrorist attack. Global civil society, which had significantly slowed efforts to advance global neoliberal economic policies, was stunned into temporary quiescence. Bush declared perpetual war against terrorism and announced a military doctrine allowing for unilateral preemptive first strikes, including the possible use of nuclear weapons.

Domestically, Bush demanded that the Congress act immediately to pass new tax cuts for the rich, increase corporate subsidies, expand domestic police powers, roll back civil liberties, create a Department of Homeland Security, weaken social and environmental protections, increase military budgets, and weaponize space. The administration pushed this agenda in the name of national unity, security, and patriotism, branding those who opposed it as traitors who sided with the terrorists. Congressional Republicans celebrated, and congressional

Democrats fell into line behind them to give Bush most of what he had asked for. The world was on notice that the historic forces of Empire had regrouped.

Then on December 2, 2001, the Enron Corporation declared bankruptcy in the first of a wave of disclosures of corporate accounting fraud of unprecedented magnitude, to which a number of top officials, including both Bush and Cheney, were closely linked. Investor confidence was shattered and share markets fell sharply.

Public support for a thorough rethinking and transformation of badly broken economic institutions was building. The plutocracy was again on the defensive, and things looked bad for the Republican members of Congress who faced the voters in the 2002 midterm elections. An administration desperately in need of another diversion again began beating the drums of war.

The message went out: Iraq possesses weapons of mass destruction, intends to use them against the United States, and was complicit in the September 11 terrorist attack. The pundits of corporate media and the New Right picked up the cry. Public attention again turned to preparations for war, and in the 2002 elections the Republicans further consolidated their control over Congress.

Ever the master of the stealth campaign, Bush used his January 2003 State of the Union message to buttress his claim to being a compassionate conservative and build support for war against Iraq. He spoke of a job for every man and woman who wanted one; support for small business; tax relief for middle-income workers; affordable health care for all Americans; energy independence; a major investment in nonpolluting hydrogen energy; human services for the homeless, the fatherless, the addicted, battered women, and seniors; and a major AIDS initiative for Africa. Even as he spoke, he was working to cut funds for these and other popular programs.

In this same speech, he charged Iraq with posing a threat to U.S. and global security and asserted that a U.S. invasion of Iraq would remove a ruthless dictator and his weapons of mass destruction while bringing food, medical supplies, and freedom to Iraq's people. It was a masterful piece of theater amplified by the corporate media. Although it fooled no one abroad, it played well at home, and Bush's approval ratings soared. Bin Laden had given Bush the greatest political gift of his career. Bush reciprocated by giving Bin Laden the greatest political gift of his.

Bush's Gift to Bin Laden

In disregard of an unprecedented global expression of public opposition, Bush began the bombing of Baghdad on March 19, 2003. The PNAC plan for U.S. global military domination was now in play. On cue, the nation rallied behind the administration. On March 21, 2003, with public attention focused on the war, a Republican-controlled Congress began debating a new White House tax plan that would further cut taxes for the wealthiest Americans and reduce benefits for veterans.

Far from being the major military threat the administration had claimed it to be, Iraq turned out to be nearly defenseless. Its weak and demoralized military promptly disintegrated in the face of the massive firepower of U.S. forces. On May 1, 2003, Bush landed in a jet fighter aboard the USS *Abraham Lincoln* against the backdrop of a huge banner declaring "Mission Accomplished," to announce victory in a war that had scarcely begun.

In carrying forward the long-planned Iraq invasion, the Bush II administration combined ruthless dishonesty with arrogant incompetence to squander U.S. power in what James Webb, former secretary of the navy under President Reagan, called "the greatest strategic blunder in modern memory"—a costly and bungled invasion of the wrong country for the wrong reasons. A ruthless dictator was removed, but there were no weapons of mass destruction. Iraq had taken no part in the terrorist attack against the United States.

The invasion brought the Iraqi people mainly death, the devastation of their physical infrastructure, and political instability. The blunder fueled worldwide terrorist recruiting, turned world opinion against the United States, isolated it from its former allies, depleted its treasury, and squandered its military resources on a violent quagmire with no exit strategy.[34]

Meanwhile, Al Qaeda's ranks swelled with new recruits, and Bin Laden's reputation soared. Al Qaeda, however, had no need to launch further terrorist attacks on the United States, because the U.S. administration continued flawlessly playing out Bin Laden's script of weakening the United States militarily, economically, and morally.

Delusion and Denial

This brings us to the question of how Mr. Bush won the loyalty, even the love, of so many Americans. Political success with a democratic electorate depends on the ability of the politician to project an image people can connect to psychologically. With the help of Karl Rove, master of the Machiavellian arts, Bush crafted a public image of himself as a strong father protector who cares for those loyal to him, vanquishes those who oppose him, and keeps his children safe from harm.

The September 11, 2001, terrorist attack sent shock waves of fear and insecurity through the nation. Fear is the demagogue's best friend because it causes regression to more primitive levels of emotion and behavior that are more easily manipulated. The ability of nineteen men armed only with box cutters to so easily penetrate the defenses of a nation protected by the world's most powerful military to such dramatic effect dealt a devastating blow to our self-identity and sense of security. Suddenly it was clear that we were hated by people who have the means to do us substantial harm and from whom our expensive military establishment offers no protection.

It was a national moment of great need and opportunity. Americans were ready to unite behind a great cause to demonstrate our solidarity in the face of adversity. A global effort to eliminate the injustice and intolerance that are root causes of terrorism would have been a suitable cause—as would a national effort to dramatically reduce oil consumption in general and dependence on Middle East oil in particular.

Playing the role of national father protector, George W. fulfilled both his own need for a sense of personal omnipotence and his constituency's need for reassurance, promising to keep us safe in return for unquestioning loyalty and obedience. He drew on the self-righteous exceptionalism characteristic of an Imperial Consciousness to assure the nation that the attack was, pure and simple, the work of evildoers who hate America for its freedom and democracy. Rejecting the possibility that we might bear any guilt, he retaliated with the full force of U.S. military power against the closest thing he could find to a visible enemy, ignoring the reality that the use of military force against invisible terrorist networks is both futile and counterproductive.

Most Americans went into denial and rallied around the office of the president. Others were intimidated by the threat of being branded America haters, terrorist lovers, or Bush bashers. It took five years for the majority to acknowledge that the Bush II administration was bankrupting the nation and sending its youth off to be killed and maimed in an unwinnable war based on lies. It took Hurricane Katrina, the near total destruction by flooding of New Orleans, one of the most fabled of

U.S. cities, and the needless deaths of more than a thousand poor blacks to awaken the nation to the gross incompetence and corruption of an administration once embraced as national savior, and to the lingering realities of race and class in America.

Confronting Our National Shadow

In Jungian psychoanalysis, the term "shadow" refers to aspects of the self that have been denied and relegated to the unconscious mind as threats to the conscious mind's preferred self-image. It includes not only negative qualities but also positive potentials the conscious mind finds too unnerving to accept. For example, a man may deny those aspects of himself associated with the feminine; a woman may deny those aspects of herself associated with the masculine.

It is much the same for nations. This is a time of sorrow and denial for the United States. We suffer from the considerable gap between our idealized self-image as a democratic, peace-loving nation and the reality of our history of genocide, slavery, discrimination, exploitation of working people, and imperial expansion. The denial of our national shadow comes at a heavy price, for we cannot correct disabilities we deny. An essential mark of maturity in both individuals and nations is the capacity to acknowledge and address all the dimensions of one's character, both positive and negative. To become the people and the nation of our ideals, we must find the wisdom and the courage to collectively acknowledge and learn from our past transgressions and to engage in a process of national and global healing and reconciliation.

Those who dismiss such critical examination as an act of disloyalty, even treason, reveal that they have yet to develop the emotional maturity to acknowledge the shadow of our national experience and to assume the full responsibilities of democratic citizenship, which requires a capacity for critical self-examination, both individually and nationally.

We the people of the United States have received a wake-up call to the reality, perils, and sorrows of Empire we cannot afford to ignore. The devastating policy failures visited on the United States in the opening years of the twenty-first century speak to more than the sins of a corrupt and incompetent administration intent on rolling back the post–World War II economic and political gains of the U.S. middle class and asserting global imperial rule by military force. They speak to a five-thousand-year imperial legacy, a plutocracy posing as a democracy, and a wounded national psyche in denial of the shadow side of our national story.

The idea that our proud nation could fall under the spell of extremist political forces is itself so alien to our self-image as to be difficult to accept. We have had our wake-up call to the reality that we are far from immune to the susceptibilities of an immature consciousness that have held our species captive to the self-destructive social pathologies of Empire for five thousand years. It is also a wake-up call to the power of stories in shaping our self-image and the course of history.

CHAPTER 14

Prisons of the Mind

> Perhaps the only limits to the human mind are those we believe in.[1]
>
> *Willis W. Harman*

Those who control the stories that define the culture of a society control its politics and its economy. This truth is crucial to explaining how a small cabal of right-wing extremists was able to render the democratic safeguards of the U.S. political system ineffective and gain control of the governing institutions of the nation. It is also crucial to framing a strategy for advancing the Great Turning.

The leaders of the New Right view the world from the perspective of an Imperial Consciousness that holds elite rule to be the only viable option for maintaining social order. To build their political base they set about to frame the larger stories that would legitimate this worldview in the public mind and bind the political debate to their interests.

Thus, the true believers of the New Right gained power not by their numbers, which are relatively small, but by their ability to control the stories that answer three basic questions: How do we prosper? How do we maintain order and keep ourselves secure? How do we find a sense of meaning and purpose in life? We might call these our prosperity, security, and meaning stories. The New Right has carefully honed and incessantly retold imperial versions of these stories to legitimate, even celebrate, the ordering of society by hierarchies of domination.

Given the long history of elite rule in the United States and other Western democracies, many elements of the stories they needed were already familiar within the culture, as they are but variations of the stories imperial rulers have relied upon for millennia to legitimate injustice. The leaders of the New Right only needed to organize them into simple messages and recruit sympathetic scholars, preachers, politicians, media personalities, and think tank pundits to repeat them constantly through the megaphone of the corporate media. Together they created an echo chamber that embedded their stories in the culture and limited the boundaries of public discourse to a choice among policies that favor elite interests.

We hear these stories echoed so often in so many different contexts that we come simply to accept them as statements of reality. Their narratives become prisons of the mind that confine us to the lower orders of consciousness and possibility. To liberate ourselves we must first recognize these narratives for what they are.

IMPERIAL PROSPERITY STORY

By definition, imperial elites inhabit a world of power and privilege based largely on their ownership of the productive assets on which the lives of all depend. They understandably favor stories that affirm the importance and legitimate the privilege of the owning class.

The Story

These are the essential elements of the imperial prosperity story:

> Economic growth, which expands the pie of wealth to create prosperity for all, depends on investment and therefore a wealthy investor class. The greater the financial returns to members of the investor class, the greater their incentive to invest. The more they invest, the faster the economy grows and the faster the lives of all improve. Since the market rewards individual investors in proportion to their contribution, inequality is natural, healthy, and essential to prosperity. Only the simpleminded or mean-spirited would begrudge the rich their due reward, because as the rich get richer, so does everyone else.
>
> Through regulation, taxes, and trade barriers, government limits profits for investors and reduces their incentive to invest, raises prices for consumers, and destroys jobs–thus impoverishing the society. Through welfare programs, government eliminates the incentive for the poor to work–thus eroding the moral fabric.
>
> In a free market capitalist economy, anyone can make it if they really try; individual failure is the mark of a character defect. Eliminating welfare programs to force the poor to work builds their character and brings them into the mainstream of society.

To achieve prosperity and end poverty, we must free the wealthy from taxes, regulations, and trade barriers; sell off public assets and services to private investors, who are by nature more efficient and responsive to consumer interests; and eliminate the disincentive of public welfare programs. The free market will put people to work, eliminate poverty, get money in people's pockets so they can make their own choices, create the wealth necessary to protect the environment, and provide people with better services at a cheaper price.

Global corporations are benevolent, efficient, public-spirited institutions with an unequaled capacity to find and exploit natural resources, drive technological innovation, open new markets, create employment, and maximize the efficient use of productive assets to meet human needs. The greater their freedom, the faster poverty is eliminated, the environment is restored, and the people of the world enjoy universal freedom, democracy, peace, and prosperity.

Global integration, market deregulation, and privatization are inexorable and beneficial historical forces that advance the wealth-creation process. Economic globalization is inevitable, there is no alternative, and resistance is futile. The winners will be those who adapt to the reality and take advantage of its opportunities. It is the beneficent mission of the Bretton Woods institutions – the World Bank, International Monetary Fund, and World Trade Organization – to facilitate the orderly advancement of these processes. Only the misinformed or mean-spirited who would deny the poor their opportunity for a better life oppose these institutions and their sacred mission.

This story is commonly referred to as the Washington consensus, because it is propagated by the U.S. Treasury Department, the World Bank, the IMF, and various related think tanks, lobbyists, and contractors based in Washington, D.C. It is also known as economic liberalism, neoliberalism, and corporate libertarianism. Because advocates of the Washington consensus cling to their story with the blind faith of true believers in denial of all contrary evidence, international financier George Soros calls them "market fundamentalists."

Of the contemporary stories of Empire, the New Right prosperity story is the most often repeated and celebrated in policy papers and scholarly publications, taught in universities, and recited by pundits of the corporate media. Corporate globalists subscribe to it as their cate-chism. They differ among themselves mainly on their views of the extent to which it is appropriate for government to subsidize private corpora-tions or to provide safety nets to cushion the fall of the losers in the market's relentless competition.

Neoliberal Elitism

Economist Milton Friedman, the leader of the Chicago school of mon-etary economics, and technological futurist George Gilder played lead-ing roles in legitimating and popularizing the neoliberal story. They were favorites of President Ronald Reagan (1981–89), who presented both with presidential awards.

Friedman's most influential work, *Capitalism and Freedom*, first published in 1962, argues that individual freedom is the inviolate moral absolute of economic life and that it is best secured through markets that guarantee the freedom of persons of wealth to use their money and property in whatever way they consider most beneficial to their individ-ual interest. He is famous for his extraordinary assertion that it is im-moral for any individual to sacrifice personal gain for a public interest. "It is easy to argue that he [the monopolist] should discharge his power not solely to further his own interests but to further socially desirable ends. Yet the widespread application of such a doctrine would destroy a free society."[2] Friedman argues against any public intervention that would constrain the ability of private monopolies of capital to maximize private financial gain. There is only one form of private monopoly that in Friedman's view constitutes a threat to freedom— a monopoly cre-ated by a labor union to raise the wages of working people.[3]

In his most influential work, *Wealth and Poverty*, originally pub-lished in 1981 at the beginning of Reagan's tenure, Gilder is explicit in his view that the direction of influence in setting political and economic priorities properly flows from the top down. He dismisses any demand that might flow upward from "mass sentiment" as a threat to national progress and the proper social order. In Gilder's words,

> In a democratic system, a reversal of the appropriate direc-tion of influence allows impressionable figments of mass sentiment to dictate to the powerful and permanent mecha-nisms of representative leadership. The result is a restive and alienated electorate, a failure of political authority, a sluggish

and uncreative government, and a tendency toward national decline.[4]

Friedman and Gilder provide useful reminders that the elitist bias of the New Right economic agenda is not accidental or inadvertent. In the tradition of Alexander Hamilton, it is a clear intention of influential individuals possessed of an Imperial Consciousness who abhor democracy and any infringement by ordinary people on the prerogatives of the imperial elite.

The Reality

The elitist prosperity story has a superficial coherence and a logic that on critical examination quickly fall apart. It assumes, for example, that prosperity can be measured solely by goods and services available for purchase in the marketplace. It takes no account of many of the essentials of a healthy life, such as clean air and water, mutual trust, job security, safe neighborhoods, well-maintained streets, loving families, and much else that unregulated markets cannot provide and often actively undermine.

Many things neoliberal economists count as positive contributions to economic growth actually devalue the quality of our lives. Examples include the sales of tobacco, guns, and violent video games to children; the fees of divorce lawyers who specialize in breaking up families; the costs of security guards and devices; the production and use of toxic chemicals; and the costs of treating the illnesses that toxins cause.

The claim that unregulated markets allocate wealth in direct proportion to individual contribution neglects the obvious reality that many personal fortunes began with a large inheritance or were acquired all or in part through fraud and deception, monopoly power, corporate welfare, preferential tax breaks, usury, financial speculation, market manipulation, and the exploitation of workers and the environment. Recall that many of the early American fortunes were the product of privateering, war profiteering, trading in slaves, and the utilization of slave labor. Corporate history is replete with stories of financial fraud and abuses of power; only the scale is unique to our time.

The unregulated market has a persistent bias for financial values over life values, short-term private profits over the long-term public good, inequality over equality, and rich people over poor people. To work efficiently, markets require impartially enforced rules to assure honest dealing, limit monopoly power, place the costs of pollution on the pol-luter, secure the health and safety of workers, and maintain a living wage. As societies all over the world are now experiencing, unregulated markets lead to collapsing environmental systems and an ever more ob-scene division between the super-rich, who enjoy lavishly extravagant lifestyles, and the desperately poor, who lack basic food, clothing, and shelter. As the devastation spreads, institutional legitimacy erodes and the anger and desperation of the disaffected create fertile recruiting grounds for political demagogues and terrorists, increasing the security threat for all.

For all its flaws, the imperial prosperity story carries the day in the political discourse because it is the only prosperity story most people ever hear. Progressive voices are often heard calling for the redistribu-tion of existing wealth to help the poor and save the environment, but we only rarely challenge the imperial definition of prosperity. Our sto-ries of how we would create new wealth in environmentally sustainable ways are ill formed and rarely communicated beyond insider groups of activists.

Imperial demagogues accuse progressives of taxing the productive to reward the lazy and sacrificing people to save exotic species. No mat-ter how truthful our progressive claim that imperial economic policies actually destroy wealth, take from the poor to give to the rich, and ac-celerate environmental destruction, the elitist story will carry the day until it is regularly countered with a more compelling prosperity story. There is a progressive prosperity story, as outlined in chapter 18, but most people rarely hear it.

IMPERIAL SECURITY STORY

One of the primary imperatives of imperial rule is to maintain a mili-tary and police establishment sufficient to secure the system of elite privilege against dissent and rebellion. Recall that the move in the founding days of the United States from a loose confederation of inde-pendent states to the creation of a federal structure was prompted in part by Shay's Rebellion, where farmer patriots faced foreclosure on their property by war profiteers. The imperial elites of the day decided that they needed a strong federal government with the necessary troops to keep the disaffected in line and maintain the established order.

It is awkward for the rulers of a presumptive democracy to tell the working classes they must pay more taxes to support the military and police forces that enforce their bondage to the owning class. The classic answer has been to cultivate fear of domestic criminals—particularly criminal elements among the disaffected classes—and foreign enemies. The "evil empire" of the Soviet Union provided the external enemy from World War II until its collapse. The imperial elites of the United States were desperate to find a suitable replacement. On September 11, 2001, Osama bin Laden handed them a solution.

Because the imperial security story centers on the cultivation of fear, it involves far more than simply justifying an outsize military and police establishment. It resonates at a deep psychological level and plays to the desire of the alienated and insecure for a replacement for the strong father we either had or longed for as children, a protector who provides for the security and needs of the family in return for loyalty and obedience. We need simply substitute the corporation, the religious leader, or the political ruler for the father.

Thus, the imperial *security* story becomes more broadly an imperial *political* story in which elections are reduced to choosing between candidates for the role of surrogate father, each of whom promise that in return for our vote they will keep us safer and more prosperous than their opponent. In so doing, the candidates affirm our status as dependent children and suppress development of our higher orders of consciousness and active civic engagement beyond voting every two years.

Bush II gave the imperial security story new national prominence following September 11, 2001. Taking the attack as his call from God, he gave the classic story a messianic edge and made it the defining framework of U.S. national policy, his presidency, and his public image. With time it became clear that, in fact, boots on the ground was his answer to every security problem, whether it be terrorism, flood, or pandemic—revealing the reality that the real goal was to centralize power.

The Story

The contemporary imperial security story goes something like this:

> We face evil enemies who hate us for our freedoms and our righteousness and who seek to destroy us with weapons of mass destruction. We must have strong leaders who will use the full force of the police and

military power of the state in preemptive action to destroy them before they can do us harm.

The war against evil is perpetual; war is the natural state of humankind. Peace and order prevail only when imposed by the military power of a righteous nation. It is the responsibility of such nations to bring peace, liberty, and prosperity to the world by eliminating evil rulers and bringing democracy and free markets to oppressed peoples. As a righteous and powerful nation, we will act accordingly, in concert with our friends when possible and unilaterally when necessary.

There can be no compromise in the war against evil. Those who do not stand with us stand with evil, and we must deal with them accordingly.

We must be equally firm in dealing with domestic evildoers. To protect the good and the righteous and to deter others who may harbor evil intentions, we must punish criminals who threaten the established order and remove them permanently from society through imprisonment or execution.

Imperial rulers have been telling versions of this story down through the ages, adapting the details to their particular time and the designated enemy.

The Reality

The imperial security story draws attention away from the economic injustice that lies behind most crime and terrorism and justifies the suppression of all forms of dissent to protect the imperial status quo. The emphasis on loyalty and obedience to a strong ruler minimizes the role of responsible citizenship and, most particularly, the essential role of the citizen in holding those in positions of power publicly accountable for their actions.

The imperial security story also draws attention away from threats far larger and more certain than terrorism: for example, climate change; the growing scarcity of freshwater; the chemical contamination of land, air, and water; the rapid spread of deadly viruses; the consequences of peak oil; and skyrocketing trade deficits. It results in misguided decisions to invade and occupy whole nations at the cost of tens of thousands of innocent civilian lives in a largely futile effort to capture a few hundred terrorists scattered in hidden networks. The misplaced priorities create instability, fuel terrorist recruiting, and waste resources needed to address the most serious and immediate threats to human security.

In the case of the United States, terrorists hate us not for the freedom bestowed on us by democratic institutions, but rather for our frequent use of our economic and military power to arbitrarily oppress and humiliate other nations and peoples. Terrorists must be brought to justice, but this can be achieved only through international cooperation among nations working together in the spirit of trust and respect. A counterterrorism strategy based on launching unilateral preemptive wars against weak nation-states is counterproductive, because it weakens the moral authority of the invader, undermines the systems of international cooperation needed to identify and bring actual terrorists to justice, squanders military resources in no-win conflicts, and swells the ranks of terrorist organizations with rage-filled recruits.

With regard to keeping the public safe from more ordinary criminals, the United States has the highest per capita rate of incarceration of any nation in the world—an indicator of significant social breakdown. Instead of dealing with the breakdown, the imperial elites use prisons to treat its symptoms. This is the mark not of a democracy but of a police state. More than two million people are now held in U.S. prisons—the majority for nonviolent drug offenses. A young African American male has a greater prospect of going to prison than to college. The interests of security and public morality would be far better served if most of the immense budget now devoted to maintaining the U.S. military and criminal-justice establishments were devoted to social and economic programs that address the root causes of violence and criminality—for example, improving public education and recreational and employment opportunities for marginalized youth.

Every society has its criminal elements, and there are among them habitual criminals who are beyond redemption and who must be locked up for the good of society once their guilt is established through diligent due process. Such persons are few in number, however, and they are randomly distributed through the population without regard to class, race, education, or religion. When petty nonviolent criminals and minor drug offenders receive long prison sentences and crimes of much greater consequence committed by political and corporate power holders go unpunished, it is evident that the domestic security agenda is more about securing privilege than securing the rule of law.

Yet for all its flaws, the imperial security story carries the day because it is the only security story most people ever hear. Progressives call for peace and justice but we do not offer a compelling story of how we will deal with real threats to those who fear for the safety of themselves and their loved ones. Imperial demagogues portray progressives as traitors who hate America, side with terrorists and criminals, and pose a security threat.

IMPERIAL MEANING STORIES

We humans have long shared our deepest beliefs about the origin and meaning of our being through creation stories that help us make sense of what often seems an arbitrary and hostile world. Because creation stories are foundational to all human belief systems, the legitimacy of the dominator structures of Empire ultimately rests on creation stories that affirm the righteousness of unjust institutions. The imperial elites of the Western Christian tradition offer two somewhat conflicting creation stories, a biblical story for the religious and a scientific story for the secular. As elaborated in previous chapters, both serve to affirm the legitimacy of Empire.

The Imperial Biblical Meaning Story

There are many versions of the biblical meaning story. One commonly promoted by the imperial elite goes something like this:

> God created the world in six days, rested on the seventh, and gave his creation to man in return for strict obedience to his will. God is all-powerful and all-knowing, and all that happens in creation is by his will. In his righteous judgment, God favors the obedient with wealth and power and thus identifies them as the pure and righteous; poverty and suffering are the fate of the impure and the disobedient.
>
> It is both the due and the responsibility of those God has marked as the pure and righteous to judge the less righteous and to make and enforce the rules others must follow in the marketplace, politics, and relations among nations.
>
> Life on Earth is but a way station to the afterlife. Our work here is to prove our faith through our piety. The pious and obedient will be rewarded with eternal salvation in the afterlife; the impious and disobedient will be doomed to eternal torment.

A hierarchy of authority and righteousness defines the natural order of creation: God over human rulers, rulers over their subjects, humans over nature, men over women, white races over other races. We each serve God's plan by finding and accepting our place in the hierarchy and obeying his word as revealed in scripture.

The Imperial Secular Meaning Story

The imperial secular story favored by the New Right is grounded in out-dated Newtonian physics and the pseudoscience of social Darwinism.

Matter is the only reality. The whole of the cosmos is a product of the orderly playing out of physical forces amenable to description and predic-tion by mathematical equations. Life is the accidental outcome of material complexity. Consciousness and free will are illusions, nothing more. Be-cause life has no intrinsic meaning, the only rational course for the intelli-gent individual is to seek material gratification through the accumulation of wealth and power.

The evolution of living species occurs through a competitive struggle in which the fittest survive and the less fit perish. Mammalian species naturally organize themselves into hierarchies of dominance for mutual protection and breeding success.

Human progress likewise depends on competitive struggle in which the most fit triumph and those of second rank serve the most fit. The win-ners prove their superior worth and thereby their contribution to the bet-terment of the whole by virtue of their victory. They have a natural right to the rewards of their victory as their just due. There is no reason for guilt or for concern for those whom the struggle destroys or leaves behind, as their loss is itself proof that they are the less fit. For the betterment of the whole, we must all accept that this is their proper fate.

The Reality

The imperial biblical story claims biblical scripture as its source of au-thority. Yet it presents an interpretation of scripture that dishonors the life and teaching of Jesus, who chose a life of poverty, taught that the poor enjoy God's special blessing, urged compassion for all people, and preached a gospel of peace and justice that challenged the defining premises of Empire. It ignores the Gospels that biblical scholars believe present the most accurate accounts of the words and teachings of Jesus —the ones that speak of love and compassion. Most religious faiths, including Judaism, Islam, and Hinduism, have their equivalent extremists who twist the teachings of their scripture to support programs of domination, exploitation, and violence wholly contrary to the messages of love and compassion that are foundational to every major religion.

The imperial science story is based on physical theories that predate the findings and insights of quantum physics and on ideological interpretations of the theories of Charles Darwin. It also ignores the findings of the new biology—documented in subsequent chapters—that life is at its core a cooperative enterprise and that successful species survive by finding their place of service to the whole.

Although the two imperial meaning stories are grounded in wholly contrary starting premises, both lend credence to a morality of self-righteous elitism in the service of Empire. Both obscure the deep truth that much of the arbitrary violence we humans experience in our daily lives is the work neither of a righteous God nor of some law of nature. Rather, the violence is the self-fulfilling prophecy of cultures based on imperial stories that legitimate injustice.

Most people accept one or the other of these imperial meaning stories because they are pretty much the only two articulated with any coherence and recited with regularity in public discourse. For most Americans who desperately seek a source of sacred meaning, the imperial elitist biblical story is the only creation story with a spiritual foundation to which they have ever been exposed. Except for the civil rights movement, progressive movements have generally been self-consciously secular—carefully avoiding discussion of the sacred. Although most leaders of progressive movements are acting from a deep sense of spiritual connection and responsibility and strenuously reject social Darwinism, we rarely speak publicly of our beliefs one way or another. Imperial demagogues say progressives have no values and hate Christians.

NARROWING THE DEBATE

Once the debate on economic policy is framed in terms of what courses of action will most effectively drive growth as measured by GDP or, more recently, as measured by share markets, from there on it is simply a matter of working out the details. Whatever policies are forthcoming will serve to further the concentration of power in elite hands.

As soon as the security debate is framed in terms of what measures will most effectively protect us from evil criminals and foreigners, the security debate is already defined as a need to strengthen the police and military powers of the state. From there it is simply a matter of debating the details of how best to do it.

The deeper cultural underpinning for these prosperity and security debates is provided by the imperial biblical and secular creation stories. The imperial biblical story affirms the righteousness of the rich and powerful, demands faith in the divine order, renders challenges to its authority a sacrilege, and dismisses efforts to improve the conditions of the poor or protect the environment as irrelevant. Whatever exists manifests God's will, and the imminent Rapture will lift the faithful to heaven and destroy the wicked. The future is preordained, and the faithful need to do nothing but pray and wait. This version of the biblical story also celebrates material displays of power and affluence as symbols of righteousness.

Although it proceeds from a rejection of any divine or supernatural being, the imperial secular story serves virtually identical ends. It sanctifies a hierarchy of domination as the natural order, provides a logical basis for dismissing demands that the rich and powerful accept responsibility for the public consequences of their actions, and celebrates the benefits and legitimacy of material accumulation and public display.

Stories are a key to the New Right's success in gaining control of the U.S. political system. The imperial stories of the New Right are contemporary versions of narratives that can be traced back to the empires of ancient times. The culture-specific variants of these stories shape the public cultures of most all the world's nations and are often told and celebrated by their own imperial elites.

Media pundits, intellectuals, think tank spokespersons, politicians, and religious figures sympathetic to the imperial worldview create a cultural echo chamber by endlessly repeating elements of the factually flawed and morally bankrupt imperial narratives as if speaking from an identical sheet of talking points. A concentration of media ownership in the hands of proponents of the imperial agenda amplifies their voices far out of proportion to their numbers in the population—shaping the political culture and defining right and wrong for the swing voters who view the world through the lens of the Socialized Consciousness.

As these stories become embedded in the culture, they systematically diminish our collective sense of human possibility, undermine our commitment to public-interest politics, and limit political debate to choices that strengthen the dominator relations of Empire. It never occurs to most of us to deconstruct the narratives to examine the validity or the devastating implications of their premises for the societies in which we live.

Empire's prosperity story celebrates the idolatrous worship of money and material acquisition and a concentration of ownership that leads to spiritual impoverishment for all and material impoverishment for the vast majority. Empire's security story focuses on building strong police and military forces to impose order by physical coercion to protect established relationships of domination, thus perpetuating a system of oppression and injustice that leads to environmental destruction, social unrest, and faux democracy. Empire's biblical meaning story focuses on the afterlife. Empire's secular meaning story reduces life to matter and mechanism. Both lead to alienation from life and strip our earthly existence of meaning and purpose.

Individually and collectively these stories legitimate imperial rule, deny our humanity, and lead to the material and spiritual impoverishment of human societies. Yet they are very effective in serving the New Right's intended purpose because they are the only stories most people hear.

Logic suggests that exposing the flawed assumptions of these imperial stories would strip them of their power. That is, however, a false conclusion. We humans live by stories. Once a story has currency in our minds, we inevitably return to it because it provides the only answer we know to our very real questions about things that are important to us.

Stories are the key. To redirect the course of humanity, change the stories by which we live. Stories that deny life's possibilities and sacred purpose have stifled the development of the higher orders of human consciousness and held us captive to the sorrows of Empire. Stories that affirm life's possibilities and sacred purpose liberate our minds from this self-imposed limitation and call us to carry forward the Great Turning.

PART IV

The Great Turning

There can be no respect for our place in the environment and the environment's place in us without a spirituality that teaches us reverence for the cosmos in which we find ourselves.[1]

Matthew Fox

We humans live by stories that embody the shared wisdom of our cultures about our possibilities, values, and the nature of the cosmos. Through these stories, most particularly the stories of our origin, we define ourselves, the meaning of our lives, and our relationship to the sacred. When the stories a society shares are out of tune with its circumstances, they can become self-limiting, even a threat to survival. That is our current situation.

It is now within our means to make an epic choice to put the sorrows of Empire behind us in favor of the joys of Earth Community. We have the knowledge and the technology. The remaining barriers are primarily self-limiting beliefs that have no reality beyond the human mind.

The explosive advance of human knowledge in the past hundred years greatly expands not only our understanding of our nature and possibilities but also the capacity for cooperative self-organization and mutual service inherent in the very nature of life itself. To navigate successfully the turbulent waters of the Great Turning, we must revisit and update the stories by which we communicate our common understanding of our human origin, purpose, and possibility.

CHAPTER 15

Beyond Strict Father versus Aging Clock

> Science without religion is lame; religion without science is blind.
>
> *Albert Einstein*

> For peoples, generally, their story of the universe and the human role in the universe is their primary source of intelligibility and value.... The deepest crises experienced by any society are those moments of change when the story becomes inadequate for meeting the survival demands of a present situation.[1]
>
> *Thomas Berry*

Alienated from life and lacking a story appropriate to our time and understanding, we contemporary humans are condemned to seek meaning where it is not to be found. We pursue money as a measure of our worth, go shopping to distract us from our loneliness, dominate and destroy to affirm our existence, and turn for moral guidance to dogmas that affirm the disabilities of our alienation rather than challenge us to fulfill our potential.

The last century was a time of extraordinary advance in human understanding regarding the origins of the universe, the evolution of life, and the developmental path of the human individual. For the most part both science and religion remain wedded to stories of older origin that incorporate nothing of this new knowledge. These outdated stories impair our vision of the possibilities of our higher nature, our connection to life, and our place in Creation.

GRAND CONFRONTATION

The long-standing conflict in the West between science and religion pits the religion of the strict father against the science of a mechanistic world likened to an aging clock. This contest has raged in the West since the beginning of the scientific revolution.

Religion of the Strict Father

By the time of the early scientific revolution in the sixteenth century, prevailing Christian theology had fallen into a distrust of the human intellect and its ability to perceive truth from observations of the material world. Indeed, excessive concern with material phenomena was considered a sign of a neglected soul. Religious authorities maintained that divine revelation as enshrined in scripture and interpreted by themselves was the only valid source of truth and that the universe is governed by forces beyond human knowing. The prevailing Western worldview of that time, particularly as defined by the Catholic faith,

- viewed the human relation to God as one of a child to a father who demands strict loyalty and obedience;
- ascribed to God both human emotions and the power to create and destroy whole worlds by an arbitrary act of will;
- held humans to be both the purpose and center of God's creation;
- venerated a pantheon of saints with powers to intervene in matters of the heart and flesh;
- attributed physical and mental afflictions to possession by malevolent spirits; and
- claimed for religious authorities the power to guarantee a place in heaven.

A dramatic shift in the dominant cultural perception began to take place around 1660, as the mechanistic worldview of the scientific revolution took hold in Europe. The shift from magic to mechanism was a bold step that opened the way to extraordinary advances in understanding and technology, much as the child's awakening to physical mechanism is an important step on the path to a mature consciousness. Unfortunately, however, the scientific revolution brought not only a rejection of the magical fantasies of the lowest order of consciousness but also a denial of the spiritual foundation of reality and a deep alienation from life.

Science of the Aging Clock

In sharp contrast to the belief systems of most religions, the ideological frame of standard Western science steadfastly maintains that the physical world is the only reality and that the disciplined observation of physical phenomena is the only source of truth. That stance began with the theories of Nicolaus Copernicus (1473–1543) and the proofs of Galileo Galilei (1564–1642) that the sun is the center of the solar system and Earth is but one of its several orbiting planets.

The conventional scientific wisdom of that day held that nature functions with the predictable precision of a mechanical clock and that its mechanisms are fully amenable to human understanding.[2] Unable to explain the origins of the complex machine postulated by their theories, the early philosophers of the scientific revolution conceded that territory to the theologians, suggesting that the universe was created and set in motion by a master clock maker who then left it to wind down as the embodied energy potential of its wound-up spring was depleted.

The contrast between the doctrines of science and the prevailing doctrines of the Christian churches of that day could scarcely have been more stark. Religious doctrine maintained that the material realm is an illusion, even the work of the devil to distract and deceive, and only the spirit realm is real. Scientific doctrine maintained that only the material is real. Religious doctrine proclaimed that humans are the center of God's attention and the purpose of his creation. Scientific doctrine placed humans at the periphery of a vast, godless universe devoid of purpose or meaning.

Rather than recognize material mechanism as but one of reality's dimensions, the science fundamentalism replaced the self-limiting dogma of the religious establishment with a self-limiting dogma of its own—denying the very existence of whatever it could not measure and explain in terms of replicable mathematical relationships. It thus proclaimed life an accidental outcome of material complexity and came to treat it as a mere collection of chemicals and genetic codes subject to physical manipulation for human convenience. Science fundamentalism not only denied the higher orders of human consciousness, it declared all consciousness, spirit, and intention to be mere illusions, essentially stripping away any apparent foundation for personal moral responsibility.

Culture of Alienation

The rigid dogma of science fundamentalism was useful in imposing on science an uncompromising intellectual discipline that has led to enormous advances in human knowledge and technology. Unfortunately, the premise that only what can be observed is real came to be treated as proven fact rather than a useful basis for conducting science. It shaped the worldview of modern culture—thus perpetuating the alienation from life that is a primary driver of the addictions of Empire. Any competing view is dismissed by science fundamentalism as mere unproven religious belief. Such a stance neglects the reality that by its dogmatic rejection of intelligence and consciousness, science fundamentalism itself crosses the line that separates scientific inquiry from the propagation of unverifiable religious dogma.

Thomas Hobbes (1588–1679) set forth perhaps the clearest exposition of the philosophy to which the scientific revolution gave rise. Taking material mechanism to its logical extreme, Hobbes postulated that there is no meaning to existence and therefore no objective standard against which to distinguish between good and evil. According to Hobbes the only rational course is for each individual to pursue that which brings pleasure and avoid that which brings pain—essentially the simple motivational profile of the consciousness of very young children.

From this premise Hobbes concluded that, given the natural right and inclination of each person to pursue immediate impulsive pleasures, order requires a strong state headed by an absolute ruler and law giver who has a free hand to determine what constitutes the public good and to impose order unhindered by any covenant with the people. In a stroke, Hobbes thus turned the scientific denial of that which makes us human into a rationale for an economics of greed and materialism and a politics of totalitarian rule.

The Evolution Wars

The long-standing tension between science and religion has again come to the fore in the United States in a struggle between creationists and evolutionists over what public schools will teach their students regarding the origins of the human species. At one extreme are scientific true believers like British biologist Richard Dawkins, who insist that life has evolved through a purely mechanistic process of chance mutation and natural selection and that this is settled fact not subject to challenge by rational minds. At the other extreme are the religious true believers like evangelical theologian Albert Mohler, who considers it settled fact that God created the cosmos, Earth, and all of Earth's living beings in six days in a series of discrete events that culminated in the creation of man in God's own image. By the reckoning of the Albert Mohlers, belief in

God and belief in evolution are mutually exclusive.[3]

A considerable number of scientists and theologians hold positions all along the continuum between these extremes. One increasingly popular school of thought that draws support from some members of both the scientific and faith communities is the theory of intelligent design, which maintains that life's complexity bears the mark of an intelligent designer. Some among this group believe that the fossil record can be explained by the theory that God intervened periodically to create new species over time. Others believe that God set creation in motion to play out through mutation and natural selection like a computer program.[4]

The public debate on evolution continues to be conducted entirely within the basic frame of pre-twentieth-century stories. The assumption is that, if intelligence was in any way involved in creation, it must reside in an external God who exists apart from his creation and functions in the manner of a magician waving a wand or an engineer constructing a machine from mechanical parts—another variation of the imperial meaning story.

There is no consideration of the possibility that creation may be the manifestation of a creative intelligent consciousness intrinsic to all being, and most particularly to all life. Such an idea is integral to the experience and teachings of religious mystics, but it is alien to conventional science and treated as heresy by many Western religious leaders. The significance of whether we think of God as extrinsic or intrinsic to Creation was brought home to me in 1999, when I had occasion to meet religious scholar Marcus Borg at a conference sponsored by the Washington Association of Churches at which we were both speaking.

TELL ME YOUR IMAGE OF GOD

In his presentation, Borg challenged us with the assertion, "Tell me your image of God and I'll tell you your politics."

Serving Different Masters

Borg elaborates that the Christian Bible describes God in terms of two quite different clusters of metaphors that evoke different images and suggest quite different relationships between humans and the sacred. These metaphors spring from contrasting voices within the biblical tradition and reflect sharply different worldviews.[5] One affirms the dominator relations of Empire and the other the partnership relations of Earth Community.

The first cluster uses the familiar anthropomorphic metaphors of king, lord, and father, which evoke an image of a distant male authority figure with a physical human form to whom humans are presumed to owe unquestioning loyalty and strict obedience akin to that of a child to a traditional father, or a subject to a king. Borg calls it the monarchical model of God.[6]

The most common modern understanding of God, both in the church and in the broader culture, centers on the monarchical model. By this understanding God is a supernatural being who resides in a distant place, created the world a long time ago, and established natural laws to order his creation. The main disputes center on whether God chooses from time to time to intervene in the affairs of his creation. In this conception, humans are not only the centerpiece of creation but also the realization of its purpose.

The second cluster includes both non-anthropomorphic metaphors—such as wind, breath, fire, light, wisdom, and rock—and more anthropomorphic metaphors—such as sage, lover, and mother—that evoke images of an immanent caring, unifying spiritual presence, an image generally consistent with the worldview of the Spiritual Consciousness, the highest order of human consciousness described in chapter 2. Borg calls it the spirit model. The Christian spiritual teacher Matthew Fox documents in *One River, Many Wells* that the religious mystics of virtually all the world's spiritual traditions describe God with images evocative of the spirit model.[7]

In contrast to the monarchical model, the spirit model suggests that our human relationship to God is one of an ungendered belonging and intimacy. Jesus—who taught a message of universal love, compassion, and preference for the poor—was a prophet of the spirit model and used metaphors and parables appropriate to the understanding of his audience—including the metaphor of a loving and compassionate father. The loving and compassionate father of whom he spoke presented, however, a stark contrast to the stern and wrathful imperial God of the Old Testament.[8]

The God of Empire

According to Borg, the earliest layers of the gospel tradition do not suggest that Jesus thought of himself as the Messiah or Son of God in some special sense. "His message was *theocentric,* not christocentric—centered in God, not centered in messianic proclamation about himself."[9]

The idea of Jesus as the messianic Christ and founder of an imperial church was a reconstruction that did not come to fruition until nearly three centuries after his crucifixion, when the emperor Constantine embraced Christianity and made it the official religion of the Roman Empire.[10] Christianity has served Empire ever since, lending moral legitimacy to unconscionable violence and oppression in the name of the man whose life was devoted to teaching love and compassion.

The Roman Church eventually superseded Rome's secular empire to function as an imperial power in its own right, even fielding its own armies in the Holy Crusades against Islam. Christianity subsequently aligned with the imperial conquests of the Spanish, English, French, and Portuguese kings in the lands of Africa, Asia, and the Americas and the claim of the colonizers that their goal was to civilize and Christianize the native peoples.

The monarchical model of God establishes associations with the familiar characteristics of human fathers and kings, who are commonly jealous of their authority, demand obedience to their word, extract harsh punishment from those who displease them, and lavish rewards on their favored children and subjects. Because the monarchical God is presumed to be all-powerful and all-knowing, the idea follows quite naturally that the rich and powerful enjoy God's favor and are therefore entitled to rule earthly affairs as his representatives—the explicit underlying premise of Calvinism. It sets the pattern for what is sometimes referred to as the great chain of being, in which those closest to God rule over those less favored: God over the secular king, the secular king over men, men over women, and humans over nature. It also follows from the perspective of the believer that those who worship a different god are enemies of the true God and must be destroyed or forced to submit to the true God's dominion.

Monarchical/imperial, as contrasted to prophetic/spiritual, Christianity affirms a hierarchy of domination and sends a pointed message: accept your earthly circumstance because whatever it may be, it is the will of God. Redemption for the faithful and obedient comes in the afterlife. Disobey or challenge in the name of justice those who speak for God, and you shall surely burn forever in the torment of hell.

The assertion that salvation is individual and based on faith rather than works keeps society fractured and absolves the individual from responsibility for acting to create a more just and peaceful world. The focus on the hereafter and the premise that God resides in a far place contribute to an alienation from the experience of living in a creative relationship to community and nature. This alienation has become so stressful that many Christian fundamentalists turn to a longing for the Rapture.

Waiting for the Rapture

The *Left Behind* series of novels written by Tim LaHaye and Jerry Jenkins presents a portrayal of the Rapture as understood by many of its believers. By mid-2004 total sales of the books in this twelve-book series exceeded 65 million copies and generated more than $650 million in sales, making it one of the most successful publishing projects of all time.[11] The fictional account of Christ's final return to Earth in the last book of the series, *Glorious Appearing: The End Days*, gives this chilling account of how the Prince of Peace is expected to dispense with nonbelievers in the end time.

> Jesus merely raised one hand a few inches and a yawning chasm opened in the earth, stretching far and wide enough to swallow all of them. They tumbled in, howling and screeching, but their wailing was soon quashed and all was silent when the earth closed itself again.... [The surviving Christians find they must drive their cars with care to avoid] hitting splayed and filleted bodies of men and women and horses.... [T]he riders not thrown leaped from their horses and tried to control them with the reins, but even as they struggled, their own flesh dissolved, their eyes melted and their tongues disintegrated.[12]

More stunning than the book's narrative is the comment by an adoring reader reviewer posted on the Amazon Web site. "Book #12 grabbed my heart like none of the others... LaHaye's and Jenkins'... message of God's love and redemption will speak to any reader who wants to open their heart and mind to him." Another reader called it "a glorious ending."

At a dinner party I attended while writing this book, I chanced to sit next to the host, a man of fundamentalist Christian conviction with a respected and well-paid professional job; a spacious, elegant home in a beautiful countryside setting; and a beautiful, loving family blessed with an abundance of musical talent. In the course of our dinner conversation, he spoke of the Rapture, expressed his belief that it would happen soon, and shared his sense of joy at the prospect of leaving this world to be in an eternal relationship with God. I left the conversation with deep sense of sadness at the tragedy of a thoughtful man so focused on the afterlife that he seemed unable to appreciate the great blessing of the life he had in hand.

Many millions of people, desperate for relief from the alienation of modern life, are attracted to the Rapture's promise of eternal bliss and Christ's retribution against those they believe to be their enemies. Like the science stories of a mechanistic world, the stories of the God of Empire are the creations of prophets possessed of an Imperial Consciousness, who would draw our attention away from the profound reality that we are integrally united with the whole of Creation—not just some small fragment of it—by an unbreakable spiritual bond.

The alienation from which we seek relief is a consequence of the fabricated cultural beliefs of Empire that distract us from our place in Creation and rob us of the birthright of our humanity. Finding the meaning that is inherent in our very existence is a matter of awakening from the collective cultural trance of Empire and embracing life itself as a spiritual practice.

The God of Earth Community

Marcus Borg, Matthew Fox, Jim Wallis, Walter Wink, and other contemporary religious scholars describe the historical Jesus as a person for whom the Spirit is an experiential reality, a teacher of wisdom who used parables and aphorisms to communicate subversive wisdom. They characterize him as a social prophet who challenged the elites' power by disputing the conventional wisdom and as the founder of a Jewish renewal devoted to breaking down the chauvinistic social barriers that supported the imperial structures of his day.[13] He dedicated his life to changing the prevailing stories.

Down through the ages there have been persons in most every culture who have regularly had vivid subjective experiences of ecstasy and deep sacred knowing in which the ego gives way to an experience of the spiritual energy and intelligence integral to all being. In addition to Jesus, some of the most influential mystics within the Christian tradition include Hildegard of Bingen (1098–1179), Francis of Assisi (1181–1226), Thomas Aquinas (1225–74), and Meister Eckhart (ca. 1260–1327).[14]

The spirit model suggests a living cosmos that continues to grow and evolve as the eternal Spirit continuously manifests itself by vibrating Creation into existence in a manner suggestive of the ways in which quantum physics describes material reality.[15] By the understanding of this model, God, the Spirit of Creation, the ground of being, is manifest in every person, creature, rock, particle, and thought—in all that is. Therefore, we are quite literally living in relationship with the Spirit we call God in every aspect of every minute of our lives, for we have no existence apart from this relationship. We have only the choice to be true to the relationship or to betray it.

This spiritual reality is exclusive neither to a particular tribe nor to a place apart. It is here and everywhere, now and forever. Different traditions use different metaphors and know it by different names—Yahweh, Brahma, Atman, Allah, the Tao, Great Spirit, God—but all speak to the same Spirit.[16]

By the reckoning of the spirit model, a sin is committed when in an act of infidelity we metaphorically forsake the Spirit for other lovers—for example, money or violence. Sin is defined not as a transgression of some set of laws, but rather as a betrayal of the Spirit. The Spirit has no need to judge. The punishment for infidelity is the self-inflicted pain of alienation that is a direct and inevitable consequence of the faithless act itself. By this reckoning any institution or doctrine—political, economic, scientific, or religious—that promotes greed and violence or otherwise systematically counsels and rewards our dalliances with other lovers promotes idolatry and manifests evil.

I once heard a woman on a call-in talk show observe that she considered her time on Earth as nothing more than a brief layover in a cheap hotel. What irony that a person who considers herself a believer can proudly dismiss the whole of God's glorious Creation as so much cheap trash unworthy of her tender sensibilities.

The monarchical model affirms and legitimates the dominator relations of Empire. The spirit model subverts them, calling us to walk away from our bondage to Empire and redirect our life energy to cultivating the partnership relations of Earth Community in loving service to the work of Creation. Fox speaks of "Creation Spirituality," which is an engaged spirituality, the spirituality of mature and responsible adulthood essential to the full realization of our humanity.

It is our responsibility to contribute to bringing forth human cultures and institutions that support all of Creation's children in fully realizing their potentials. Those who wait for a distant God to intervene miss the point. We are not here to obey a God jealous of his authority, but to engage with Creation as partners in a grand adventure. We are the ones we have been waiting for.

❧

SCIENCE OF A LIVING COSMOS

Newtonian science postulated a cosmos composed solely of matter that is running down to an entropic heat death. Contemporary science describes a far more complicated cosmos that exploded into being as diffuse energy particles and that has been evolving upward toward ever greater levels of complexity, potential, and possibility.

The solid matter once embraced as the only reality is now understood by physics to be mostly empty space given form by the relationships among minuscule energy particles that appear seemingly from nowhere, exist in a constant state of flux, and then disappear. Yet the consistency of the relationships among passing particles maintain the form of the apparent object through which they traverse. Paired electrons influence each other across vast distances with no evident mechanism of communication. Whole stars and star systems disappear into black holes as others are born. The processes at work appear to go far beyond any simple notion of material mechanism.

The cutting edge of biology describes living organisms as systems of self-directing cells. These cells engage in constant intercommunication and a reconstitution of their material structures yet are able to maintain a seamless continuity of form and function as they grow and reproduce in ways that are at once predestined and exquisitely adaptive and purposeful. The genetic structures presumed to contain the information codes that determine the reproduction and function of living organisms faithfully reproduce down through endless generations, yet are also engaged in a continuing process of self-repair and revision.

Peptides and other biochemical substances that store our memories and regulate our emotions mediate complex bidirectional links between our conscious and unconscious minds and the physical function of our bodies.[17] Here also such processes are not magic, but they involve something far more mysterious than pure physical mechanism—and that something will surely remain beyond the comprehension of science until scientists admit to the possibility that conscious intelligence has a role not only in the human mind but as well in every aspect of Creation.

The science of mechanism had its place in the study of the physical manifestations of matter. The cutting edge of scientific inquiry has now produced evidence of a reality best explained by the presence of a creative intelligence far more magnificent and mysterious than the descriptions offered by ancient sacred texts written in a time of more limited human understanding of Creation's workings. I find the theory of an integral sacred intelligence to be far more consistent than the established scientific theory of pure chance and mechanism with both the data of science and my own experience. But I can no more prove that an integral intelligence is involved than science can prove that it is not. The more thoughtful scientists recognize that some aspects of reality lie beyond the ability of science to prove or disprove, a truth I learned from Willis Harman, a Stanford University electrical engineering professor of impeccable scientific credentials, who was for many years my mentor.

As an institution, however, standard science continues to deny the deeper implications of its own evidence. It clings to the dogma of an earlier day, when it was quite properly seeking to distance itself from the superstitions of a corrupt religious establishment. Now, failing to distinguish between the facts of scientific observation and the assumptions on which its methods rest, standard science continues to falter in its quest for a unifying theory. This failure may well be the consequence of a self-imposed dogma that denies the existence of the underlying spiritual intelligence that religious mystics through the ages have recognized as the unifying essence of Creation. Science and religion each stand to benefit from a collaboration in search of a grand synthesis.

STEP TO MATURITY

The historic battle between science and religion for cultural hegemony has left us with an untenable choice between a scientific story that denies spirit, intention, meaning, and consciousness and a religious story that denies reason and the evidence of our senses. We have paid a terrible price for this self-imposed myopia. A more accurate and holistic vision of Creation is at hand. Religious sages have been describing it for millennia. Scientists on the cutting edge of their disciplines have been staring it in the face for nearly a century, and a few have recognized its deep significance.

Human survival is now in question because our most powerful institutions have elevated assumptions and theories to the status of proven fact, thus turning them into self-limiting dogmas radically out of step with the most advanced human understanding. As we have seen in earlier chapters, the mind of the mature elder is open to all the many ways of knowing—including sacred texts, indigenous knowledge, history, and modern science—and is fully at home with both the material and the spiritual dimensions of reality. It is time to acknowledge that wisdom and set ourselves the goal of cultivating the potentials of the mature human consciousness.

Scientists need only accept—as many do—that there are truths beyond the reach of the conventional instruments and methods of scientific inquiry that may be acknowledged without diminishing the tremendous value of those instruments and methods. Religious scholars need only return to the core of the teachings of Jesus and other Spirit persons of the world's great religious traditions and acknowledge the many ways in which Creation reveals itself to our species—as many individual theologians do. Scientists and religious scholars and mystics can then work cooperatively to deepen human understanding of the relationship between matter and spirit—as growing numbers are.

The liberation of science and religion would open the way to a profound cultural turning from which economic and political turnings will quite naturally follow. As we humans come to embrace the truth that we are all creatures of the one living, immanent Spirit, competition for dominator power of one over another becomes an anachronism. Gratuitous violence becomes sacrilege. The pursuit of money beyond reasonable need becomes idolatry. Chauvinist exceptionalism becomes a mark of emotional immaturity. A turning from an imperial economics of individual greed and excess to a mature economics of sharing and balance becomes nearly inevitable, as does a turning from an imperial politics focused on competing interests to a mature politics of mutual interests.

The living culture of Earth Community will call us to choose fewer toys, less war, less isolation, and less coercion in return for more fulfilling relationships and the realization of that which makes us human. The living economies and politics that follow from a living culture will be more democratic, ethical, and fulfilling; will secure our children's future; and will honor our responsibility to Creation.

Religion and science are two contending sources of the creation stories by which we humans define ourselves, our moral codes, and the meaning of our existence. Since the beginning of the scientific revolution, religion and science have been engaged in a competition to be the exclusive purveyors and interpreters of the reigning creation story of modern life. Each of these establishments has allowed the more dogmatic extremists within its ranks to define its story in terms that emphasize the contrast between its own position and that of the contending party.

In keeping with the win-lose dynamic of Empire, the struggle for power between the two competing establishments has trumped the search for truth. This leaves the rest of us to choose between two partial stories or to live in divided allegiance between them. To guide our steps on the pathway back to life, we need a shared creation story for our time that honors the whole of the accumulated knowledge and wisdom of the species.

Fortunately, there are individuals of significant standing within each of these establishments who are able to look beyond the dogma in search of a deeper convergence. Reaching out across institutional lines, they are joining forces to challenge the partial stories of their respective traditions and to construct and communicate a more complete and factually grounded contemporary story that draws on the accumulated knowledge and experience of the species.

CHAPTER 16

Creation's Epic Journey

> The dynamic dance of nature is ever conscious at every level, from the tiniest particle to whatever its currently largest configuration or holon is. That is my basic assumption about the living universe, no stranger than any of the assumptions of physics. It is shared by all the indigenous cultures I have come in contact with, as well as all esoteric traditions.[1]
>
> *Elisabet Sahtouris*

> Life is planetary exuberance, a solar phenomenon. It is the astronomically local transmutation of Earth's air, water, and sun into cells.... It is matter gone wild, capable of choosing its own direction.[2]
>
> *Lynn Margulis and Dorion Sagan*

Creation reveals itself to humans in many ways. It spoke to the ancients through the inner voices of the mystics. It speaks to our time through scientists who plumb the secrets of matter, living organisms, and the evolving cosmos. Strip away the scientific dogma that denies the existence of spiritual intelligence, and we can see that the cutting edge of scientific knowledge provides a rich source of ever deepening insight into the purpose of Creation, life, and the human species.

A CONTEMPORARY CREATION STORY

The 14-billion-year story of Creation, based on the available scientific evidence, goes something like this:

> Long ago a new universe flared into being in a massive burst of energy that dispersed tiny energy particles across the vastness of space. With the passing of time, these particles organized themselves into atoms that swirled into great clouds that coalesced into galaxies of countless stars

that grew, died, and were reborn as new stars, star systems, and planets. The cataclysmic energies unleashed by the births and deaths of billions of suns converted simple atoms into more complex atoms and melded them into molecules – each stage transcending the stage before in definition and capacity to create ever more wondrous possibilities.

It took 10 billion years to prepare the way for the seed of life to gain a foothold on the planet we now call Earth. To this day science knows not from whence life came.

Microscopic in size, the early ancestors of all Earth life were single-celled bacteria so simple they lacked even a cell nucleus. Yet these modest creatures proved to have a capacity for learning that gave them remarkable creative potential. The planet's first chemists, they learned to build new kinds of proteins, including new enzymes, to invent new molecules, and to exchange genetic material through their cell walls to share their learning with one another.

As the fruits of life's learning multiplied, individual cells evolved to become more complex and diverse. New bacteriological strains emerged as individuals learned to exploit new ecological niches by cultivating different lifestyles and expertise. The arts of fermentation, photosynthesis, and respiration were discovered in turn, with individual strains specializing in one or another in a competition for food and resources. Each advance allowed the whole to gain greater advantage from the available resource base and prepared the way for the emergence of more complex organisms of still greater potential.

Eventually some of these early competitors reached an accommodation with one another by binding together to create supercells that combined the abilities of individual strains. Over a period of roughly a billion years, these tiny single-celled creatures rearranged the materials of Earth's crust and transformed and stabilized the chemical composition of the entire planet's atmosphere to open the way for yet more extraordinary accomplishments.

Up to this point DNA strands floated freely within the walls of individual cells. Then, some 2 billion years after life first appeared on the planet, the partnerships that had created the supercells led to the clustering of DNA into a nucleus, creating a single nucleated cell a hundred to a thousand times the size of the individual bacterium cells of which it was composed. This in turn prepared the way for the emergence, roughly 900 million years later, of the first multicelled plant and animal life in the form of seaweed, jellyfish, and flatworms.

All the varieties of plant and animal life followed in due course – including dinosaurs, birds, apes, and humans. Step by step, life converted the matter of the planet's surface layer into a splendid self-organizing web of complex, choice-making multicelled organisms, each with capacities far beyond those of their individual cells. Continuously experimenting, interrelating, creating, building, the evolving web of life unfolded into a living tapestry of astonishing variety, beauty, and ever growing capacity for intelligent choice.

Then, 4 million years ago, Creation embarked on its most ambitious and daring experiment. It took a first step toward bringing into being a species with the capacity to reflect on its own consciousness, to experience with awe the beauty and mystery of Creation, to articulate, communicate, and share learning, compose symphonies, build cathedrals, reshape the material world to its own ends, and anticipate and intentionally chose its own future.

The hominids came first, followed 1.4 million years later by *Homo habilis*, larger-brained species that developed skills in hunting and in using stone tools. It took another 2.4 million years to arrive at the next step – a species with a capacity for intentional choice far beyond that of any other. That was a mere 100,000 to 200,000 years ago. We call ourselves human.

The science of the past hundred years has made a seminal contribution to our knowledge of the sequence of events that marked the creative unfolding of the universe and all its wonders. The patterns of that unfolding suggest that the cosmos, and all within it, are the manifestation of a great unifying spiritual intelligence engaged in an epic quest to know itself through the discovery and actualization of its unrealized possibilities. If this is so, then all being exists both as a product of this quest and as a co-creator in the continued unfolding. As it is for all being, so is it is for all of life, including humans.

LIFE IS THE POWER TO CHOOSE

As a young student of psychology, I was required to read the work of B.F. Skinner, a well-known behavioral psychologist of that time famous for his theory that free will is an illusion. By Skinner's reckoning, all behavior is the result of what he called operant conditioning. In essence, our response to any given stimulus depends on what consequences followed from our previous responses to similar stimuli, not as a matter of conscious, intelligent choice, but simply as a mechanistic conditioned response. It is a curious thing that a science dedicated to reason would deny the human capacity for reason, which is by extension a denial of human intelligence and free will. It seemed to me at the time a rather limited view of human possibility, but among academic psychologists seeking to gain respectability for their discipline as a legitimate science, it was quite a popular theory—and certainly not one I was in a position as an undergraduate to openly question.

Science still has difficulty with questions of will, consciousness, and intelligence, in part because it continues to operate from a mechanistic premise. Thus, I was struck by the boldness with which Lynn Margulis, one of the world's foremost life scientists, and her son, science writer Dorion Sagan, proclaimed in their extraordinary book *What Is Life?* that life "is matter gone wild, capable of choosing its own direction."[3] It is one of those simple, obvious, and yet deeply profound observations that turn a long-established worldview on its head. Life is matter with the capacity to choose, and among the species known to humans, our capacity for choice exceeds that of all others.

Free will does not mean we are free to do anything we want. The realities of an interdependent world bind our actions. Every choice we make is shaped by our context and in turn revises that context. Yet the range of the choices available to us is substantial.

From the perspective of conventional wisdom, an individual human life begins in a mother's womb some nine months prior to physical birth and ends at the time of physical death. From a deeper evolutionary perspective, however, we are each expressions of an unbroken flow of the choices made by living organisms since intelligent life energy first began to express itself on planet Earth some 4,000 million years ago.[4]

We can only speculate as to what happens to the individual soul after physical death. We do know, however, that each life is immortal in its contribution, no matter how modest, to shaping life's continued unfolding into the infinite future. Each flower we pick, each seed we plant, each thought we communicate, sends its ripples forward in time through the unfolding fabric of Creation, leaving its mark—positive or negative, large or small—on the biosphere and the collective human consciousness that the Catholic priest and mystic Pierre Teilhard de Chardin called the noosphere. Herein lies the great responsibility of our gift of choice. The choices we make determine whether the mark we leave enhances or diminishes the human contribution to Creation's great quest to actualize its possibilities. We matter. Our choices make a difference.

LIFE IS STRUGGLE

For many years, I imagined the ideal life-centered society to be a place of peace, cooperation, and contentment in which the basic needs of all are met and humanity lives happily ever after. It was perhaps an image evoked by dim memories of life in the womb before birth. It is a widely shared image similar to that of the popular image of heaven — a place of effortless eternal bliss.

Thus, I was a bit put off when I read in John and Linda Friel's book on human maturity, *The Soul of Adulthood*, that "we can only experience life through struggle." My initial reaction was that the authors must have a warped view of life. Then my mind connected the Friels' statement to an observation by Margulis and Sagan that the existence of life's extraordinary ability to invest matter with the capacity to choose depends on life's success in a continuing struggle against the incessant entropic forces of the material world.[5] That idea unlocked for me another profound truth: life is, by its nature, a cooperative struggle for the freedom to choose against the life-denying forces of entropy. Struggle is an inherent condition of living. It is not a curse inflicted on us by a spiteful God. It is, if you will, God's own struggle manifest through us.

The second law of thermodynamics — the law of entropy — is a formalized observation that all physical systems run down as their useful energy is dissipated, ultimately decaying into the disorganization referred to as thermodynamic equilibrium. It is the way of all mechanical objects. Leave an automobile unattended, and eventually it will disintegrate into a pile of useless rust. By extension, the second law declares the physical universe to be dying, as the inexorable processes of entropy play themselves out toward disorder and loss of potential. Life, by contrast, appears to defy the second law by creating order out of disorder. Life thereby presents science with a troubling enigma.

Molecular biologist Mae-Wan Ho, who studies the processes by which living organisms resist the force of entropy, notes that living systems do not actually defy the second law. They do, however, have the ability to maintain themselves in a sustained thermodynamic disequilibrium of negative entropy, which in the sometimes perverse terminology of science means that they maintain themselves in a state of active positive energy potential. The processes involved depend on the ability of the organism to engage the continued and highly efficient intake, storage, and throughput of energy and material in continuous exchange with its environment. Living organisms have learned to be "*anti*-entropic" for so long as they are alive.[6]

In other words, life observes the classic laws, but it has learned to use these laws to maintain energy in an active flow state through constant exchange and recycling, thereby achieving a sustained state of potential far from the stasis of thermodynamic equilibrium. The *what* of the process is well documented. The *how*, however, remains largely beyond the limits of scientific understanding—perhaps because standard science rejects out of hand the possibility of will or intent.

Those scientists with the courage and humility to accept the rather obvious fact of life's capacity for intelligent, willful action sometimes find it necessary to turn to poetic expression to describe the wonder of the process they observe, as in the following excerpt from Margulis and Sagan:

> Thermodynamic systems lose heat to the universe as they convert energy from one form to another. Living matter frees itself from ordinary matter only by perpetually basking in the sun. Confronted with dissolution and destruction, life suffers a permanent death threat. Life is not merely matter, but matter energized, matter organized, matter with a glorious and peculiar built-in history. Life as matter with needs inseparable from its history must maintain and perpetuate itself, swim or sink. The most glorious organic being may indeed be nothing but "temporarily identifiable wiggles," but for millions of years as life has been racing away from disorder autopoietic [self-directing] beings have concerned themselves with themselves, becoming ever more sensitive, ever more future oriented, and ever more focused on what might bring harm to the delicate wave of their matter-surfing form. From a thermodynamic, autopoietic perspective, the basest act of reproduction and the most elegant aesthetic appreciation derive from a common source and ultimately serve the same

purpose: to preserve vivified matter in the face of adversity and a universal tendency toward disorder.[7]

Think of each cell as a packet of self-directing energy potential shielded from entropy's downward pull by the thin wall of its outer membrane. The cell is a bounded system with the ability to recycle energy within itself and slow the dissipation of that active energy into the environment beyond. Unable, however, to eliminate the dissipation entirely, its survival depends on a constant balancing act by which it must regularly capture new energy potential from its environment to replace that which is inevitably lost.

The complexity and dynamism of the thermodynamics of life are breathtaking. Each individual cell is itself a complex interacting web of thousands of ongoing chemical reactions among its individual molecules, each itself engaged in a constant process of renewal within a nested multilevel holarchy of cooperative, self-organizing, self-renewing systems. As explained by molecular biologist Stephen Rose:

> The complex macromolecules, the proteins, nucleic acids, polysaccharides and lipids within each cell have life cycles of their own, continually being broken down and replaced by other, more or less identical cells. The average lifetime of a protein molecule in the body of a mammal is around a fortnight. In an adult human, proteins constitute some 10 percent of body weight, so some 24 grams of protein are being broken down and a fresh 24 grams synthesized every hour of every day—half a gram, or more than a billion billion molecules of protein a minute, throughout our adult life. Why this ceaseless flux?... The answer is simple:... living systems need to be dynamic if they are to survive, able to adjust themselves to the fluctuations which, even in the best-buffered internal milieu, their cooperative existence as part of the greater unity of the organism demands.[8]

LIFE IS MUTUAL EMPOWERMENT

The key to the secret of life's success in populating Earth with ever larger, more complex, and more capable organisms is its ability to self-organize into complex subsystems of cyclical processes that link reactions

requiring energy with those that yield energy. Energy flows continuously and simultaneously in a never ending dance of cooperative exchange between the substructures of each individual cell, between the
cells of multicelled organisms, between the multicelled organisms of individual ecosystems, and between the ecosystems of a living planet.
Through these frugal, self-renewing, and interlinked processes, living
systems are able to at once conserve energy and maintain it in an active
and immediately accessible state.

These mutually empowering processes are the foundation of life's
struggle to create and maintain new potential against the constant pull
of entropy. The cooperative imperative of this struggle explains why life
exists only in relationship to other life, that is, in community. The organizing principle of life is partnership, not domination. Indeed, partnership is one of life's imperatives.

The individual cell or multicellular organism can no more exist
without the larger community of life than the community of life can
exist without the individuals it comprises. Life is a process of mutual
empowerment enhanced by balanced growth and diversification, and it
therefore can be understood only in terms of communities of relationships. The more complex, diverse, and coherent the relationships internal to a living system, the greater the potential of the system and each
of its component members.

At its most elemental, we see the principle of interdependence at
work in what biologists call symbiotic relationships, the mutually beneficial interaction of two organisms that live in close association. Every
child is familiar with the example of the flower and the honeybee. The
flower provides the honeybee with sweet, life-giving nectar, and the
honeybee pollinates the flower to facilitate its reproduction. In this simple
example, the relationship is directly reciprocal.

The real wonder of life is found, however, in complex patterns of
mutual service that go far beyond such tit-for-tat market-style reciprocity. Much of this complexity eludes our normal awareness because it
occurs at a microscopic level; we can perceive and understand it only by
using powerful tools of scientific observation to track the multilevel
dynamics of whole ecosystems over long periods of time.

As you read the following stories of life's extraordinary capacity to
self-organize, note that there is no counterpart to the hierarchical command systems we humans have come to believe are essential to maintain coherence and order in human societies. Do the lowliest bacteria

possess some innate sense of responsibility for the well-being of the whole that eludes us humans? As you read these stories, consider these questions: How long would the forest ecosystem survive and prosper if its individual organisms lived by the neoliberal economic principle of unfettered competition for short-term individual advantage? What might we learn about the possibilities of human societies from how living organisms organize themselves into healthy forest ecosystems?

LESSONS FROM A FOREST ECOSYSTEM

Some of our most advanced insights into the dynamics of natural ecosystems come from studies conducted in the Andrews Forest in Oregon. Science writer Jon R. Luoma relates some of this fascinating research in *The Hidden Forest: Biography of an Ecosystem.*

The Nitrogen Cycle

Think of the forest as a self-reliant living economic system engaged in converting available resources into products and services essential to sustaining the life of the forest and each of its individual participants. Start with a simple maple leaf. Each leaf is actually a system of individual living, self-directing cells that capture pulses of energy radiating from the sun and bundle them into a neat biochemical package, a molecule of sugar. Using little more than a combination of water, sunlight, and carbon dioxide, a healthy mature maple tree will silently produce during the course of one growing season about two tons of sugar and a substantial quantity of oxygen. The energy of the sun is thus stored for hours or even years in molecular form to support the growth and maintenance of the tree. The tree also supports a host of other organisms, including "the mite chewing on tiny bits of the stem, the predatory spider that eats the mite, the flycatcher that eats the spider... the fungi pulling sugar out of the tree's roots on the forest floor... [and] the squirrel or vole or deer that eats a bit of fungus."[9]

Each of the organisms served by the tree in turn contributes services to other organisms, including many on which the tree itself depends. To produce sugar, the tree needs nitrogen, an element abundant in the atmosphere. However, trees, like most other organisms, cannot use the free nitrogen of the air directly. They rely on specialized bacteria to "fix" the nitrogen by turning it into nitrite and nitrate compounds. Typically, these nitrogen-fixing bacteria live in nodules formed by particular species of plants—such as lichens, and the root systems of legumes and red alder trees—that protect and nourish the bacteria. The plants that host the bacteria, however, have their own problem: They require abundant sunlight. When the forest canopy shades out these plants, it kills the host that sustains the bacteria that supply the nitrite and nitrate compounds on which the whole system depends.

Life's solution to this problem reveals an extraordinary capacity for mutuality and adaptation—not only in the moment, but with a sense of foresight that may span a century or more. When fire, volcanic eruption, or a violent windstorm creates an open space in the forest, plants that harbor nitrogen-fixing bacteria colonize the area initially to produce nitrogen in sufficient quantities to support the growth of the trees for as long as two hundred years.

After the forest canopy shades out the nitrogen fixers and the stored nitrogen is exhausted, the trees would be doomed to death except for a dynamic found only in old-growth forests. As the trees reach their hundredth year or so, nitrogen-fixing lichens begin to establish themselves in their upper reaches, where sunlight is abundant. Over the second hundred years of the tree's life, these lichens grow in increasing abundance, creating a forest canopy that functions as a powerful nitrogen-fixing factory. By the time the mature forest is in danger of suffering a nitrogen deficiency, the living canopy is producing and shedding nitrogen-rich waste matter to the ground at a sufficient rate to renew the soil and supply most of the nitrogen required by the entire system.[10]

Beneficial Infection

Another example of complex mutuality is found in the relationship between the evergreen trees of the Andrews Forest and a specialized fungus named *Rhabdocline parkeri* that lives inside their needles. When the Andrews Forest researchers first discovered this fungus, they were surprised to find no indication the tree suffered any ill effect from what they would normally consider a fungal infection. Eventually they discovered that the tree provides the fungi with the energy-rich sugars and starches on which they feed in exchange for the fungi's service of protecting the tree from defoliating insects by producing poisonous alkaloid compounds whenever the tree becomes threatened.

The fungus, it turns out, is remarkably frugal and respectful of the host tree's resources. Its spores initially lance their way into a fresh green needle and wait. They grow virtually not at all, and thus place no burden on the tree, until the time comes for the needle itself to die as part of the tree's natural cycle, at which time the fungus draws energy from the dying needle, matures, and releases its own spore to find and "infect" a fresh green needle. In the meantime, if the needle happens to be attacked by insects, the fungus poisons the insect and then prospers by tapping the dead insect rather than the needle for nutrients.[11]

One might reasonably ask why the tree does not develop its own chemical defense against insect pests. The simple answer speaks further to life's complex intelligence. Insects are short lived, with an ability to rapidly evolve defenses against toxic threats. The similarly short-lived fungi are equally agile in their ability to reformulate their toxins to overcome those defenses in a way the long-lived tree species could not. Here we see another striking example of how life flourishes through the power of partnership.[12]

The Living Soil

Insects, which are abundant not only in their numbers but also in their variety, have essential roles in rebuilding forest soils. Each insect species makes its distinctive contribution to chewing up and processing the waste matter of a dead tree or plant, with many insects of different species ingesting, processing, and evacuating the material in turn in a highly complex recycling process. In simple language, the poop of one becomes the food of another. Indeed, the soil of the forest floor is composed almost entirely of the bodies and feces of microbes and insects.

Biologists believe our planet may be host to as many as thirty million insect species, each of which occupies its own ecological niche. Each maintains itself by performing a distinctive service on behalf of the whole. Scientists are only beginning to sort out the essential roles they play in the health of the forest ecosystem—and by extension in the maintenance of the health and fertility of all the soils so essential to planetary life.[13]

These stories demonstrate the complexity of the relationships underlying the coherent function of a major ecosystem. Each organism contributes to the whole through patterns of relationships that involve loops of reciprocity that may cycle through thousands of species and take a century or more to close.

At every turn, we see evidence of life's astonishing ability to organize for mutual self-empowerment without evident central control or direction. The rain forest ecosystem is one example. Our own bodies are another.

LESSONS FROM THE HUMAN BODY

The creation of an individual human person begins with the joining of two microscopic cells—a sperm and an egg. This merging of genetic materials to create a single composite cell begins a profoundly complex self-directing process of cell division and differentiation. Communicating with the other cells, each individual cell makes the appropriate decision at the appropriate moment to divide or to take on the specialized functions of a brain, liver, or blood cell as the body's specialized organs and structures take on form and function.

A generalized map is embedded in the genetic structure shared by all the cells of a given body. Although there is no dominator cell instructing each of the other cells what action to take at any given moment, each cell, through processes still only dimly understood, makes the right decision at the right time in support of the emergence of the whole body. Countless such individual decisions result ultimately in the growth and division of the two initial cells into a complex organism composed of more than thirty trillion self-directing, self-renewing cells—an organism with the capacity for intelligent, self-reflective choice able to contemplate eternity and to join with similar organisms to reshape the planet and reach out to the stars.

Renewal, Sharing, and Adaptation

The processes of self-renewal that continue throughout the human life span compound the wonder of the human organism. Each minute three billion of the body's cells die—each reliably replaced by a living cell of like kind. The stomach lining replaces itself every five days, the liver every two months, and the skin every six weeks. Ninety-eight percent of the atoms in the body are replaced each year.[14] Except for the occasional error, each of the body's cells has the same genetic coding. Yet they differentiate into many specialized functions, sensing and responding to intercommunication among the cells to take whatever action is appropriate to the needs of the emerging organism. The identity and dynamic coherence of each organ, the body as a whole, and the conscious self with all its memories and intellectual abilities are sustained throughout.

Equally extraordinary is the ability of the body's trillions of cells to move energy instantly from wherever it is stored to wherever it is needed in the event of injury, illness, or a physical threat from the environment. As Elisabet Sahtouris points out, the muscle doesn't tell the heart, "Nothing more until you settle your past due account." It sends what is needed. If necessary, it starts breaking down its own tissues to release additional energy. Nor does the heart say to the muscle that needs an extra measure of oxygen to mobilize the body's flight from an attacker, "Hey, business is business. What's it worth to you?"

Decision Makers Every One

It all makes for an organizational challenge of breath-taking complexity and raises the question of who or what is making the decisions. Genetic programming, the brain, and the central nervous system play their roles, but the essential answer is that the decision-making capacity and responsibility are distributed throughout the body's every cell, microbe, and organ—each sensing and responding to complex flows of information from its environment—suggesting that many levels of self-regulating intelligence may be involved.

These many intelligences are parts of an interdependent whole. The failure of any one part has the potential to destroy the whole, but no individual subsystem, not even the neocortical brain that is the seat of consciousness, is able to dominate the others in the sense of an overall hierarchy of command and control.[15]

Given that healthful bodily function requires the making of billions of decisions each second, it is for good reason that the self-aware consciousness we experience in our waking hours is not in direct communication with these many other centers of awareness and decision making. Because the masses of information involved would quickly overwhelm our conscious mind, most of the processing is handled by the unconscious mind or occurs at the cellular level and does not involve the brain at all.

Each human life in turn depends on the support of the infinitely complex and dynamic web of self-directing, self-regulating relationships that make up the life of the planetary biosphere. The performance of these external systems is as essential to our individual survival and well-being as the performance of our internal systems. Each of these systems is engaged in its own pulsating dance of adaptation and renewal, creating constant variations in air and water quality, temperature, and nutrient supply to which the individual human body and all its complex internal processes must continuously adapt.

In the face of such complexity and foresight, the idea that evolution is nothing more than the playing out of a competitive struggle for dominance seems hopelessly simplistic. More credible is the theory that life is intelligent and purposeful and that each living system embodies many levels of conscious intelligence.

Is self-interest involved? Certainly, but it is the mature and inclusive self-interest of the mutually empowering relations of partnership that come naturally to the highest orders of human consciousness and that constitute the foundation of mature democracy.

Although science remains captive to the premise that reality can be explained entirely by a combination of chance and material mechanism, the story of Creation's unfolding to ever higher levels of complexity and consciousness points to the existence of a profound intelligence engaged in an epic journey of self-discovery. By giving matter the capacity to choose, life accelerates the pace of the journey. Engaged in a cooperative struggle to maintain its choice-making potential against the downward pull of entropy, life exists only in living communities of diverse and mutually interdependent species. For life, partnership is more than an organizing principle; it is its very essence.

CHAPTER 17

Joys of Earth Community

> Destructiveness is the outcome of unlived life. Those individ-
> ual and social conditions that make for suppression of life
> produce the passion for destruction.[1]
>
> *Erich Fromm*

> Being human always points, and is directed, to something,
> or someone, other than oneself—be it a meaning to fulfill or
> another human being to encounter. The more one forgets
> himself—by giving himself to a cause to serve or another
> person to love—the more human he is and the more he
> actualizes himself.[2]
>
> *Viktor Frankl*

Two of the great psychoanalysts of the twentieth
century—Erich Fromm and Viktor Frankl—each had personal encounters with the horror of fascism in Nazi Germany. After World War II
each published his reflections on what in the human psyche can drive
humans to such destructiveness. Each came to much the same simple
yet profound conclusion: the human drive to belong, to connect, to express our presence, is so strong that if our efforts to connect and affirm
our existence through positive means are thwarted, that drive will be
redirected to negative means.

Think of it as a drive to live and thereby to do what other successful
living beings do: find our place of service in a cooperative partnership
with the larger web of life. The development of healthy individuals capable of relationships based on mutual caring and service depends on
healthy communities that nurture healthful individual development.
Healthy individuals and healthy communities go hand in hand, each inseparable from the other.

We humans, because of the gift of reflective consciousness, have the
capacity to live more intentionally and creatively than any other species.
We also, however, have the capacity to make terribly bad choices, as the

sorrows of five thousand years of Empire so tragically demonstrate. The cultures and institutions of Empire alienate us from life, thwart the positive expression of our drive to live, turn our life energy to expressions destructive of both self and community, condition us to choose the path of sorrow and deny the very existence of the path to the joys of Earth Community. Yet as both nonimperial human societies and the living communities of the nonhuman world attest, the way of partnership is a very real possibility.

The work of the Great Turning requires us to free ourselves from the self-inflicted alienation and oppression of Empire as we create societies that support every person in connecting to life in ways that enhance the creative potential of both self and community so that all may enjoy the joys of Earth Community. The work begins in our minds with an awakening to the reality that the drive to connect in a mutually affirming relationship with life is hardwired into our nature and that whether we express that drive in ways that bring sorrow or joy is up to us.

HARDWIRED TO CONNECT

An extraordinary cooperative initiative organized by the YMCA of the USA, the Dartmouth Medical School, and the Institute for American Values brought together thirty-three prominent neuroscientists, children's doctors, and social scientists to review the mental and emotional health of America's children and to recommend practical steps to improve their lives. Organized as the Commission on Children at Risk, their report, *Hardwired to Connect: The New Scientific Case for Authoritative Communities*, is a path-breaking synthesis of science, spiritual wisdom, and conservative and liberal values.[3]

The commission's report, based on scientific studies of the human brain, concludes that we humans are physiologically "wired" to form "close attachments to other people, beginning with our mothers, fathers, and extended family, and then moving out to the broader community."[4]

Using magnetic resonance imaging to take portraits of brain activity, scientists have found during laboratory exercises that the experience of forming a cooperative alliance with another person produces a strong positive response in the pleasure center of the brain—rather like eating chocolate or engaging in good sex.[5] Other studies find that relationships of trust and caring are essential to our emotional health and to the healthful function of society.[6]

The Human Brain

The developmental processes involved in achieving the potentials of our human nature are physiological as well as psychological. Like other aspects of our physiology, the brain matures with time, and the development of its higher-level abilities requires practice.

Starting with the basics, what we call the human brain is actually a complex system of three interlinked brains, each with distinctive functions. This basic three-part structure is common to all mammalian brains. At the core is the reptilian brain, which coordinates basic functions essential to survival, such as breathing, regulating the heart, hunting and eating, reproducing, and engaging the fight-or-flight response to danger. The limbic brain, physically layered on top of the reptilian brain, is the center of the emotional intelligence that gives mammals their distinctive capacity to experience emotion, read the emotional state of other mammals, bond socially, care for their children, and form cooperative communities. The third layer is the neocortical brain, the center of cognitive reasoning, symbolic thought, awareness, and self-aware volition.

In the earliest mammals, the neocortical brain is merely a thin skin covering the older subbrains. In humans, the neocortical brain is the largest of the three by substantial measure.[7] Each of the three brains functions with its own integrity, even as it communicates with and influences the other brains as well as the intelligences of the body's other organs and cellular systems that together give the human organism its vast range of capabilities.

Because reptiles have no limbic brain, they lack the capacity for an emotional life. With no emotional life they have no capacity to bond and experience empathy. They come together briefly to court and mate, but they rarely function as a community and may even eat their own young as a convenient nutrient source.[8]

The emotional intelligence of the limbic brain—the ability to accurately communicate one's emotions and to read the emotions of others through verbal and nonverbal clues—is only partially formed in humans by the time of birth. The limbic brain of the newborn represents a potential that must be cultivated into a usable capacity through emotional exchanges with a primary caretaker—most often the mother. Practice in such exchanges activates the neural connections essential to the intuitive reading of emotional states.

Creating a neural connection in the brain is much like creating a connection between two people within a human social network. Each such new connection, once established, creates a potential that is more easily activated in the future.

It is much the same for the intellectual functions of the neocortical brain. It too is only partially formed by the time of birth and matures through use. Achieving the full potential of the higher orders of consciousness depends on the balanced development of both the limbic and the neocortical brains through their use as the child engages the world.

It is not easy learning to be human. Although we think of our intellectual power as the highest manifestation of our humanity, in many ways our greatest developmental challenges involve our emotional and moral intelligence, a process in which our early experience relating to our primary caretakers is especially important.

Nurturing Parenting

The more active and loving the emotional exchange between the child and the adult caretaker, the fuller the early development of the limbic brain, the more fluent the child's emotional intelligence, and the greater the capacity and subsequent predisposition for empathy, bonding, nurturing parenting, and responsible moral function. Of course, the converse is also true. The less satisfying the human connections experienced by the child, the less of these capacities it will have. Put in the starkest terms, the less developed our limbic brain, the more reptilian our nature.

The developed neurological connections of the limbic brain respond to the experience of a positive relationship by stimulating the brain's pleasure centers to reward subsequent encounters with those same persons to create the condition we call bonding. In a physiological sense, pair-bonded couples are "addicted" to each other. Similar physiological processes are involved in the bonding of the mother to her child.

One of the more startling research findings is that "for men, getting married—becoming sexually and intimately bonded with a spouse—seems to lower testosterone levels," which appears to be associated with a reduction in violent behavior and sexual promiscuity and an increase in positive fathering. There is also evidence linking intimate relationships to strong immune systems and more rapid healing of physical wounds.[9] Conversely, humans deprived of intimate relationships are more prone to poor health and early death. A psychologically healthy childhood is a foundation of a physically and psychologically healthy adulthood.

The implications for society are profound. By supporting the development of the limbic brain through loving interactions, nurturing parents increase the subsequent capacity of their children to function as self-regulating adults with the capacity for empathy, bonding, and moral self-direction that is an essential foundation of mature democratic citizenship. Distant, unresponsive, or abusive parents produce emotionally challenged, self-absorbed adults inclined to turn to coercive hierarchies to impose social order and to the violent acting out of unresolved emotional conflicts.

The reinforcing interactions between parenting styles and adult predispositions reveal the truly monumental costs to the human future of the corporate plutocracy's war against the family. By creating economic conditions that make it virtually impossible for millions of parents to provide their young children with the nurturing attention essential to their healthy emotional development, the economic and social policies promoted by the New Right in the United States and beyond perpetuate the reproduction of emotionally crippled adults for generations to come. That the consequences can be devastating not only for the individual but as well for the larger society is graphically demonstrated by a recent case in point that brings to mind the biblical warning of Ecclesiastes 10:16, "Woe to thee, O land, when thy king is a child."

When Things Go Wrong

Justin A. Frank, a respected Washington, D.C., psychoanalyst and a professor of psychiatry at the George Washington University Medical Center, points to George W. Bush as an example of the potentially tragic consequences of nonnurturant parenting. By his reading of the public record of George W.'s early childhood experience, Dr. Frank concludes that young George suffered a serious lack of nurturing parenting, with devastating consequences for the United States and the world as he subsequently acted out his unresolved childhood conflicts on the global stage.[10]

Young George's father, George H.W. Bush, was largely absent from the home and had little role in George W.'s early upbringing. His emotionally distant mother, Barbara Bush, was by her own account a strict disciplinarian who regularly invoked harsh physical punishment. When George was six, his younger sister, Robin, was diagnosed with leukemia, but he did not learn of her illness until after her death. George simply was told not to play with her. In the meantime, his parents frequently flew with her to the East Coast for treatment. On her death, he was left to struggle on his own with unresolved feelings of abandonment, resentment, self-blame, and love associated with the tragedy and his parents' stoic response to it.

Such early experiences profoundly influence whether a child will grow up to perceive the world as largely safe and affirming or threatening and alienating. They also influence whether the child develops a positive self-concept and the ability as an adult to admit error, feel compassion, and see oneself through the eyes of another—in other words, the ability to take the step from an Imperial to a Socialized Consciousness and beyond. (See chapter 2 for more discussion about the levels of human consciousness.) Persistent fears and self-doubt may also translate into learning disabilities, rigid belief systems, claims to moral certainty, and megalomania that bar the passage to the high orders of consciousness. Confined to an Imperial Consciousness, individuals so afflicted are unable to acknowledge even to themselves the evil of the harm they inflict on others or the moral hypocrisy of their positions.

Dr. Frank documents the ways in which all these symptoms of thwarted development have been manifested by the adult George W. during his presidency. This pattern has been common among Empire's ruling elites since the earliest days of Empire, and the species has paid a terrible price.

Pain of an Unlived Life

There is no human pain so great as the feeling of being alone in an existence without meaning. Viktor Frankl called it the "existential vacuum" and observed that the frustrated will to meaning may be "vicariously compensated for by a will to power, including the most primitive form of the will to power, the will to money."[11] Erich Fromm noted that humans will endure all forms of degradation to break from the deadly loneliness of an unlived life.[12] Meaning is a side effect of the transcendence that we experience through selfless acts of creative engagement and contribution.

To the extent that we find our world responsive to our presence in our early years, we develop the physiological and mental abilities to engage life with growing delight. We have the fascination to explore its possibilities and thereby to know ourselves, realize our highest potential, and experience the joy of life in relationship with Creation. If, however, we experience an unresponsive or even hostile world, we may resort to some form of escapism — a kind of despairing withdrawal from experiencing life — or to the pathological dominance-submission forms of relating that are the defining pattern of Empire. The imperial response of dominance-submission brings us into relationship with a larger world, even if only in perverse ways that lead to sorrowful consequences.

The escape response leads in its milder forms to "learned helplessness"[13] or to various forms of escapist addictions, such as our modern afflictions of "shop till you drop" material indulgence, gambling, drugs, overeating, or compulsive television watching. Such practices, however, do nothing to resolve our struggles. They only further numb our awareness and alienate us from life.[14]

Escape is also manifest in political disengagement, chronic cynicism, and the kind of sullen disgruntlement common among those who work in public and private bureaucracies. It may also be manifest in a religious preoccupation with the afterlife — including the longing of Islamic fundamentalists for martyrdom and Christian fundamentalists for the Rapture. In its more extreme forms, the escape response may lead to suicide or psychological catatonia.

The embrace of dominance-submission as a compensating mechanism creates a drive to acquire power, or to connect to a power holder, in order to validate one's own existence by dominating, humiliating, or destroying others. The drive to believe that one's own acts make a positive difference in the world is so strong, however, that even the most brutal and ruthless of evildoers commonly insist that their violence serves a heroic, even sacred, purpose.

For example, Adolf Hitler, notorious for his contributions to the mechanization of genocide and warfare, sanctified his bloodlust with the claim that he was bettering the lives of the peoples of the nations his armies laid waste and was improving the global culture. He saw himself as acting under the command of a higher power to secure peace and freedom, fulfill the eternal laws of nature, and defend the German people from those who meant them harm.[15]

Imperial rulers have been reading from the same script for five thousand years. Some may even claim their acts of sadistic brutality are heroic acts of cleansing intended to purify an evil world.

The stronger the drive for dominance, the more dangerous it becomes. We have previously noted the deranged enthusiasm with which history's more demented rulers rejoiced in their ability to destroy whole cities, peoples, and civilizations, as in the destruction of Babylon by the Assyrians and of Carthage by Rome.

That such acts of destruction reveal the desperate efforts of the emotionally wounded to prove their existence does not excuse them. The criminally deranged belong in prisons or mental institutions, not positions of power. Our longer-term commitment, however, is not to fill the beds in our prisons and mental institutions. It is to eliminate the source of the pathology by redesigning modern human societies to support the healthful development of every individual from birth to passing. We have much to learn in this undertaking from the contrasting ways in which modern and traditional societies organize the basic routines of daily life.

THE INVISIBLE CURRICULUM

The human life cycle is divided into three primary stages: childhood, adulthood, and elderhood. To experience the joy that flows from actualizing the potentials of our humanity we need the support of strong, loving, and stable families and communities in negotiating the invisible curriculum of life through which we develop the fullness of our humanity.

We learn in childhood to obey the word of our parents in return for the care that keeps us safe and healthy. Adulthood, which commonly includes a transition to parenthood, marks a total role transformation from dependence and obedience to full responsibility not only to care for oneself but also to engage in a partnership with one's spouse, to care for one's children, and accept the public responsibilities of citizenship.

The final stage in the human life cycle, mature elderhood, can also be the richest and most fulfilling. With a secure identity, no further need to prove ourselves to the world, a lifetime of experience on which to draw, and our children established in their own families and careers, we are free to explore, embrace, expand, and serve in previously impossible ways.[16]

The ways in which traditional and modern societies deal with the passage through these life stages could scarcely be more different, revealing their strikingly different values and priorities. The way of the traditional society is the outcome of self-organizing processes that flow from an innate sense of the needs of children, families, and the community as a whole, often as mediated by the Spiritual Consciousness of wise elders. The way of the modern society is the outcome of decisions made by the owning classes, commonly mediated by the self-interested sense of personal entitlement of an Imperial Consciousness. At every hand, ordinary people find their choices controlled by the institutional hierarchies of big business, big government, big education, big unions, big media, and big religion and limited to those that favor the interests of some faction of the ruling class.

The Way of Empire

Captive to the addictions of Empire, modern societies characteristically segment the life cycle, sandwiching a frenetically fragmented adulthood between long periods of enforced isolation and dependence during both childhood and elderhood. While the parent or parents try to piece together a living income from multiple jobs, the young child of the modern household is commonly parked in front of the television as a sacrificial offering to corporate advertisers, warehoused in day care centers, or left to fend on the street without adult supervision. The child's primary responsibility in such circumstances is to keep out of the way of busy adults.

After reaching school age, the child is consigned to an educational facility in a state of enforced regimentation for a major portion of the day in the care of seriously overburdened and often undertrained teachers. Although some wonderful schools provide a rich learning environment, in the more typical school the child's main task is to fight off boredom while mastering the mechanics of reading, writing, and arithmetic and memorizing large quantities of information unconnected to any other aspect of his or her life. Where children relate directly with other children, they are pretty much on their own to work things out for themselves, with little adult guidance.

Typically, the experience of the child's parents is similarly fragmented and alienating. Struggling to support themselves and their families with multiple jobs offering less than a family wage and no benefits, they have little time for family, community, spiritual, or leisure life. Lacking other options, most grit their teeth and tough it out.

Negotiating the passage from the dependence of childhood to the responsibilities of parenthood is surely one of the most difficult challenges of the human life cycle, and no work is more important than parenting to the future health of the society. It is, however, much easier to *become* a parent than to *be* a parent. Yet the cultures and institutions of modern Empire not only fail to provide support and preparation for the transition from childhood to parenthood, they make it virtually impossible for parents to fulfill their parental responsibilities.

When and if retirement comes, it too often means enforced isolation and loneliness or confinement in facilities that offer only the company of other elders. Here again, individuals are pretty much on their own, with little or no support from or preparation by the contemporary cultures and institutions of Empire.

It is as if modern imperial societies were intentionally designed to keep life fragmented and disconnected to minimize the possibility that we might experience the enduring, caring relationships that are a foundation of healthful human development. Replication of the sorrows of social pathology is an almost inevitable result. The contrast to the traditional tribal community is stark indeed.

The Way of Earth Community

In many traditional tribal villages, family, work, spiritual, community, and recreational life flow naturally one into the other. Children grow up participating fully in community life, learning by doing under the watchful eye and coaching of parents and of elders revered for their wisdom and service. Older children learn parenting skills by participating in the care of younger children and in the life of hearth, field, and workshop.

The cultural life of the tribe underscores the individual's enduring connection to community, place, and generations past and future. Public celebrations clearly mark graduation from the relationships appropriate to an earlier stage to those appropriate to a later stage, and many role models are always at hand.

When I turned sixty-five, Timothy Iistowanohpataakiiwa, a Native American friend and elder, gave me one of the most important gifts of my life. In a simple Native ceremony attended by a number of friends and colleagues, he initiated me as an elder into the human community and commemorated my graduation with the gift of an eagle feather he had worn during his participation in the sacred Sun Dance ceremony. It totally changed my outlook on aging. Rather than passing into irrelevance on the path to death, I was initiated into elderhood as mentor, teacher, and wisdom keeper.

Although a complete return to traditional ways is neither possible nor appropriate, we have much to learn from those traditional societies, because they embody an innate understanding of the developmental needs of children and of the art of living in relationship to the larger web of life. Contemporary imperial societies organize for money making. Traditional societies organize for living.

More than two thousand years ago, the great Greek philosophers reasoned that the good society is one that supports every person in their journey to the full realization of the highest potentials of their humanity and, in so doing, reproduces the conditions of its own healthful function. Many traditional societies came far closer to actualizing this ideal than do most modern societies, despite the latter's considerable advantages in technology, scientific knowledge, and material resources.

Actualizing the ideal, however, does not require going back to lives of subsistence and isolation. It is entirely possible to create societies that are at once human, rooted in their place, and modern in their global connections, understanding, and use of technology. It begins with applying the organizing principles of partnership to the restructuring of our human institutions. Here we may look to nature as a knowledgeable and inspiring teacher.

NATURE AS TEACHER

Life on Earth has been learning the secrets of organizing by partnership for four billion years. The defining patterns found in virtually every living system on the planet reveal the lessons of that learning. From the descriptions of the workings of these systems authored by biologists Janine Benyus, Mae-Wan Ho, Lynn Margulis, Elisabet Sahtouris, and others we can discern a number of organizing principles for the partnership societies we must now create.[17]

Principle of Cooperative Self-Organization

Life has learned to establish and maintain coherence through an energetic dance of mutual influence, self-regulation, and adaptation that maintains a balance of individual and collective needs at each of life's many levels of organization, from cell to global biosphere. Each level of organization appears to be a choice-making entity in its own right, with its own capacity to choose in the interests of both self and whole.

Conditioned by our imperial cultures, we humans have been so focused on the patterns of competition that contribute to life's dynamism that we have failed to see the deeper narrative of life as a profoundly cooperative enterprise. Life has learned what many of us humans have not —living beings exist only in relationship with other living beings.

According to Lynn Margulis and Dorion Sagan, one of life's most important lessons is that the species that survive and prosper are ultimately those that find a niche in which they meet their own needs in ways that simultaneously serve others.[18] Furthermore, as Sahtouris observes, life has characteristically learned to cooperate through experiencing the negative consequences of unbridled competition. In her words, "One can discern in evolution a repeating pattern in which aggressive competition leads to the threat of extinction, which is then avoided by the formation of cooperative alliances."[19] These observations speak directly to our human time as we learn the extent of the threat that ruthless competition now poses not only to our own species but as well to countless others.

Principle of Place

Life has learned to organize into complex multiorganism ecosystems that adapt to the most intricate details of the microenvironments of their particular physical locale. Each species evolves and learns within the context of the location-specific ecosystem in which it establishes itself, making its individual contributions to a cooperative community effort to capture, share, use, and store the available physical resources to optimize the potentials of the whole. The mutuality of learning and alliance building within any given ecosystem community is underscored by the devastation that sometimes results from the introduction of an alien species, a consequence much like introducing a cancer tumor into a healthy living body, or a Wal-Mart into a previously thriving local economy.

We humans have been relating to the ecosystem of planet Earth as if we were an alien species—the cancer tumor in the body of life—seeking our own unlimited expansion without regard to the consequences for the larger community of life on which our own existence ultimately depends. We must now learn what every successful species has learned before us: to live as members of cooperative living communities exquisitely adapted to the microenvironments of our particular place on Earth.

Principle of Permeable Boundaries

Life has learned that to maintain the coherence of its internal energy flows, it must bound itself at each level of organization with a permeable membrane by which it can manage the intake and dissipation of energy and matter from and into its environment, and exclude predators. For example, if the wall of the cell is breached, the cell's matter and energy instantly mix with the matter and energy of the environment, and it dies. To maintain the coherence of their internal energy and information exchange, multicelled organisms require a skin or other permeable protective covering. Similarly, biological communities or ecosystems need the boundaries provided by oceans, mountains, and climatic zones to exclude invasive species not acculturated to the established community. The planetary biosphere depends on the atmosphere and ozone layer held in place by Earth's gravitational field to control the exchange of radiation with the universe beyond.

Even as it needs boundaries to maintain its integrity, however, life's processes of self-renewal depend on a managed exchange with its environment. Therefore, each organism's boundary membrane must be permeable, and what flows through that membrane in both directions must be subject to management by the organism so that it can maintain itself in a balanced relationship with all around it. Successful living entities protect their borders not out of selfishness but out of a need to maintain their internal integrity and coherence and to assure that exchanges with their neighbors are balanced and mutually beneficial.

The trade agreements that have aroused a powerful global resistance movement seek rules that guarantee the right of corporations to place clear protective boundaries around their interests and to manage these boundaries for their exclusive benefit. These same agreements prohibit individuals, families, communities, and nations from establishing any form of protective boundaries that allow them to maintain the coherence of their internal life-energy flows from assault by predatory corporations intent on extracting the life energy of people and nature to advance the growth of their financial assets. They are akin to a medical practice devoted to protecting the cancer from the body's immune system.

As for any living organism, the healthful function of human communities depends on permeable, managed boundaries. The family, locality, or nation that either leaves itself open to the unregulated intrusion of predatory alien corporations and financial speculators or conversely closes its borders to balanced and beneficial exchange will be quickly drained of its vitality.

Principle of Abundance

Life has learned that frugality and sharing are the keys to abundance for all. Biological communities exquisitely fine-tune the efficient capture and recycling of energy and useful matter. They are living exemplars of the motto "Waste not, want not." The wastes of one become the resources of another through the continuous reuse and recycling of energy and materials within and between cells, organisms, and species cooperating to minimize the dissipation of energy and useful matter beyond their respective individual and collective boundaries.

The abundance of life depends on its ability to both share and conserve energy and matter, and to freely share information in order to grow the potential of the whole. Unrestrained growth based on competitive expropriation is the ideology of cancer cells and alien species. True abundance depends on frugality, mutuality, and sharing.

Principle of Diversity

Life has learned that diversity is an essential foundation of creative potential. Just as life never exists in isolation from other life, neither does it exist in monocultures. Life has learned that the greater the diversity of the bio-community, the greater its resilience in times of crisis and the greater its potential for creative innovation in the pursuit of new possibilities.

Likewise, a diversity of age, gender, culture, religion, and race provides an invaluable contribution to the resilience and creative potential of human communities. We humans have yet to learn to celebrate, cultivate, and harvest the benefits of diversity long denied by our many chauvinisms.

EARTH COMMUNITY

The turning from Empire to Earth Community has two primary elements. First is a turning from money to life as our defining value. Second is a turning from relations of domination to relations of partnership based on organizing principles discerned from the study of healthy living systems.

Partnership in a Contemporary Context

If we were to apply living-system principles to organizing the relations of daily life within our modern context, we would create locally rooted, self-organizing, compact communities that bring work, shopping, and recreation nearer to our residences—thus saving energy and commuting time, reducing CO_2 emissions and dependence on oil, and freeing time for family and community activities. Life would become less dependent on cars, and the needs of automobiles would no longer dominate the landscape. We would convert land now devoted to roads and parking to bike lanes, trails, and parks. Our governance processes would be radically democratic.

We would grow more of our food on local family farms without toxic chemicals, process it nearby, compost organic wastes, and recycle them back into the soil, thus better securing our food supply and improving human and environmental health. We would design environmentally efficient buildings for their specific microenvironments and construct them of local materials to reduce the energy costs of transport. We would produce much of our energy locally from wind and solar sources. Locally generated wastes would be recycled locally to provide materials and energy inputs for local use.

With family life, work life, and community life more geographically proximate and people in more regular and natural contact, our lives would be less fragmented and more coherent, the bonds of community denser, stronger, and more trusting. Children and youth would be naturally engaged in community life, thus acquiring the experience, mentors, and role models they need to prepare for the responsibilities of adulthood. We can provide our youth with courses in developmental psychology, responsible citizenship, and the skills of parenting as part of the school curriculum and encourage them to practice the application of these skills through community service and the care and mentoring of younger children.

With the restoration of community life, elders would become a re-source as caretakers, educators, mentors, and wise advisers to those still negotiating the pathway to a mature consciousness, thus restoring re-spect and meaning to the elder years. The elder who remains engaged in the responsibilities of community life is unlikely to suffer from either a longing for or a fear of death. By their very presence in the fullness of their maturity, they keep alive the flame of the spirit of what can be and serve thereby, often in unassuming ways, as individual and collective guides to the future.

Psychologist Robert Kegan observes that "who comes into a person's life may be the single greatest factor of influence to what that life be-comes."[20] It is particularly important that each child experience a deep and enduring relationship with at least one elder of a mature conscious-ness. I recall the significance of my relationship to my paternal grand-mother, in whom the flame of the spirit of life burned bright and who communicated to me in so many ways her sense of life's wondrous pos-sibilities and the virtue of standing on examined moral principles. It took me many years to fully understand and appreciate the lessons she taught me, but her influence lives on in all that I do.

Empire is expensive. Eliminating wasteful uses of energy and other resources would mean less need to expropriate the resources of other countries through economic and military domination, thus greatly re-ducing the need to divert resources to maintaining a large military force. If foreign interests no longer control the labor and natural re-sources of the world's poorest nations, those resources would be avail-able to the people of those nations for use in improving their own lives. This would reduce the motivation for terrorism and further reduce the need to expend scarce resources on domestic security. Breaking up global corporations into human-scale, locally owned enterprises would free still more resources by eliminating the massive burden of inflated executive compensation packages and by removing bureaucratic barri-ers to innovation.

An economy that responds to the self-defined needs of adults of a mature consciousness would no longer allocate a major portion of its creative talent and communications resources to advertising to make people feel insecure and incomplete in order to create artificial demand. Less advertising would mean less visual pollution, a stronger sense of self-worth for individuals, and a reduction of wasteful consumerism that could be translated into a shorter workweek and more time for family and community.

The savings could finance first-rate education, health care, and community services for all and provide workers with a living family wage. The benefits would ripple out across the social landscape. With ample living wages, educational opportunities, and essential services, crime rates would drop, and prison and other criminal justice costs would fall.

We would be working less and living more. Our lives would be freer and richer. Our environment would be cleaner and healthier. A world no longer divided between the obscenely rich and the desperately poor would know more peace and less violence, more love and less hate, more hope and less fear. There would little need for dominator structures to impose order. Earth could heal itself and provide a home for our children for generations to come. These are all among the abundant joys of Earth Community and all are within our collective means.

Indicators of Success

We might ask by what indicators we will know the Earth Community we seek to create. We will know a society has succeeded when it matches the following description:

- Virtually every adult has achieved at least a Socialized Consciousness and most adults have achieved a Cultural Consciousness by early middle age and a Spiritual Consciousness by late middle age.

- There is a vibrant community life grounded in mutual trust, shared values, and a sense of connection. Risks of physical harm perpetrated by humans against humans through war, terrorism, crime, sexual abuse, and random violence are minimal. Civil liberties are secure even for the most vulnerable.

- All people have a meaningful and dignified vocation that contributes to the well-being of the larger community and fulfills their own basic needs for healthful food, clean water, clothing, shelter, transport, education, entertainment, and health care. Paid employment allows ample time for family, friends, participation in community and political life, healthful physical activity, learning, and spiritual growth.

- Intellectual life and scientific inquiry are vibrant, open, and dedicated to the development and sharing of knowledge and life-serving technologies that address society's priority needs.

- Families are strong and stable. Children are well nourished, receive a quality education, and live in secure and loving homes. Rates of suicide, divorce, abortion, and teenage pregnancy are low.

- Political participation and civic engagement are high, and people feel their political and civic participation makes a positive difference. Persons in formal leadership positions are respected for their wisdom, integrity, and commitment to the public good.

- Forests, fisheries, waterways, the land, and the air are clean, healthy, and vibrant with the diversity of life. Mother's milk is wholesome and toxin free, and endangered species populations are in recovery.

- Physical infrastructure—including public transit, road, bridge, rail, water and sewerage systems, and electric power generation and transmission facilities—is well maintained, accessible to all, and adequate to demand.

The first time through, this list may read like a radical utopian fantasy, but only because it contrasts so starkly with our present experience. In fact, each of these conditions is achievable by all but a very few of the most physically and socially ravaged nations, and each condition aligns with core values shared by both conservatives and liberals. If any of them seem alien, it is only because they all depend absolutely on cooperation and sharing. They are forever beyond the reach of the lone individual and of societies that choose to live by the values and relationships of Empire. They are achievable only by societies that choose to live by the values and relationships of Earth Community.

HAPPINESS IS A CARING COMMUNITY

Becoming more frugal in our use of resources has become a condition of human survival. To the alienated Imperial Consciousness that finds meaning primarily in the addictions of Empire, this seems an almost unthinkable sacrifice. The more mature consciousness recognizes, however, that a turn to Earth Community is neither about self-sacrifice nor about renouncing technology or progress. It is about getting clear on our values, setting new priorities, redefining progress, and consuming less so that we may become more human and in the process experience the abundance of authentic relationships.

During the last half of the twentieth century, most nations came to embrace economic growth as a proxy measure for human progress and happiness. Comparative international studies, however, report that once a nation has achieved a moderate level of per capita income, further increases in wealth bring only slight increases in perceived well-being.[21] This growing body of research on the "economics of happiness" affirms one of the oldest and most universal of spiritual insights. Beyond the minimum level of income essential to meeting basic needs, the authentic relationships of strong communities are a far better predictor of happiness and emotional health than the size of one's paycheck or bank account.

The United States has been the world's most aggressive national proponent of economic growth and consumerism as the tickets to happiness. Over the last half of the twentieth century, inflation-adjusted U.S. gross domestic product per capita tripled, yet surveys indicate that self-reports of satisfaction with life have remained virtually flat.[22] What *did* clearly increase in the United States over this period were measures of depression, anxiety, distrust, and psychological dysfunction. The incidence of depression increased tenfold.[23]

One of the more startling affirmations of the wisdom that relationships are more important to happiness than money and material possessions comes from a study that compared the life-satisfaction scores of groups of people of radically different financial means and physical circumstances. The results showed four groups clustered at the top of the life-satisfaction scale, with almost identical scores.

One group (with a score of 5.8 out of 7) comprised persons on the list of *Forbes* magazine's "richest Americans," the richest of whom own tens of billions of dollars in assets, and the "poorest" hundreds of millions. The other three groups were the Pennsylvania Amish (5.8), the Inuit people in northern Greenland (5.9), and the Maasai (5.7), a traditional herding people in East Africa who have no electricity or running water and who live in huts made of dung.[24] This suggests that in complex modern cultures, it takes a great deal of money, indeed, to equal the happiness that comes in simple societies from a sense of belonging to a place and a strong, caring community.

Perhaps the most revealing comparison was between Calcutta slum dwellers (4.6), whose life-satisfaction score was slightly above a neutral rating (4.0), and Calcutta pavement dwellers (2.9), who were the low-est-scoring of all the groups surveyed. Both the slum dwellers and the pavement dwellers live under appalling conditions of physical depriva-tion. The pavement dwellers, however, have no place or community, while the slum dwellers live in a place they identify as their own located within a bounded, if rudimentary and unstable, community.[25] Rela-tionships of mutual caring and commitment are the variable that most consistently explains these results.

The greater the extent to which our relationships are reduced to im-personal financial exchanges, the greater the sacrifice in happiness, well-being, and emotional health. Money can help to compensate for the loss, but it takes a great deal of money to buy the happiness that com-panionship and community bring for free.[26] Relationships, not money, are the true measure of well-being. What matters most is our connection to and participation in the life of community. If we were to define human progress by the measure of human happiness, we would devote far less of our resources to making money and far more to building community.

My life journey has taken me to the lands of the Maasai in Kenya, and I have walked among the slum dwellers of Calcutta. While I cannot speak with confidence for those Maasai who have retained their tradi-tional ways, I have no doubt that any Calcutta slum dweller would in-stantly choose to trade his life for mine. I am equally clear I would have no interest in such a trade and believe that no one in our modern time should be confined to lives so harsh and limiting. My contact with both groups gives me all the more reason, however, to be respectful of the profound implication of the finding that human happiness depends far more on the relationships of community than on money and material possessions.

Newtonian physics embodied the premise that only matter is real. The more contemporary science of quantum physics teaches the very differ-ent lesson that "solid" matter is mainly empty space given form and substance by a relational fabric of energy particles in constant motion. Relationships are real; matter is an illusion.

The old biology taught that each living being is engaged in an indi-vidualistic competition for survival against every other living being.

The new biology teaches that life exists only in cooperative relation to other life and the species that survive are those that find their place of service. Life is community.

Psychologists are affirming the ancient wisdom that happiness depends not on the quantity of our possessions, but the quality of our relationships. As Empire is the path to sorrow, so Earth Community is the path to joy. Relationships are the foundation of everything.

We humans have a powerful drive to connect with one another and with nature. Perhaps more than any other species we are aware of the vulnerability inherent in the reality that we exist physically and psychologically only in relationship. The pain of separation is so great that we will do most anything to connect, even to the extent of destroying the objects of our love.

Earth Community offers an alternative to the alienation and the sorrows of Empire, a way of living that places life values ahead of financial values and organizes by the principles of partnership rather than the principles of domination. The deeper and more mutually affirming our relationships, the richer and more distinctively human we become. The yawning gap between the integral relationships for which we yearn and the fragmentation and alienation of modern life suggests the epic proportions of the challenge before us.

Yet the key to redirecting our human course is elegant in its simplicity. To change the human course, replace the stories of Empire that presently guide our collective path with stories of Earth Community grounded in the wisdom of the highest orders of human consciousness and informed by the whole of human knowledge and experience.

CHAPTER 18

Stories for a New Era

> The great spiritual-religious wisdom traditions of the world have all taught some variant of this message: The deepest human pleasures come from living in a world based on justice, peace, love, generosity, kindness, and celebration of the universe and service to the ultimate moral law of the universe.[1]
>
> *Rabbi Michael Lerner*

> Gandhi... entered public life as the defender of a small, immigrant minority in a dusty corner of a global empire, but before he was done he had led a movement that, more than any other force, dissolved that empire, and in the process had proposed a way of life in which the constituent activities of existence—the personal, the economic, the social, the political, the spiritual—were brought into a new relationship.[2]
>
> *Jonathan Schell*

It is not enough, as many progressives in the United States are doing, to debate the details of tax and education policies, budgets, war, and trade agreements in search of a positive political agenda. Nor is it enough to craft slogans with broad mass appeal aimed at winning the next elections or policy debate.

Virtually every progressive issue, from peace to environmental protection and the elimination of racism and sexism, traces its roots to the cultures and institutions of Empire. Seeking to resolve them in piecemeal fashion is an exercise in futility. Either we resolve them all by putting Empire behind us, or we accept Empire and resolve none of them. Putting Empire behind us requires putting aside its imperial prosperity, security, and meaning stories and crafting a framing vision communicated through life-affirming stories of the possibilities of Earth Community. Such stories are implicit in the work of millions of people—the organizer cells of the new culture—who are bringing the perspective of the higher orders of human consciousness to bear as they create new cultural spaces that give people the freedom to experiment with cooperative relationships. We must learn to express these stories in clear and coherent narrative.

As the stories of Empire nurture a culture of domination and deny the possibility of partnership, so the stories of Earth Community nurture a culture of partnership, redefine prosperity and security, affirm the possibilities of the higher orders of human consciousness, and call us to find our place of service in Creation's epic quest. As I have attempted to document in previous chapters, caring communities grounded in a love of life are by the very nature of life an essential precondition for achieving human prosperity, security, and meaning. This simple but profound truth is a unifying message of the narrative versions of the Earth Community stories that follow.

Let me say here that I share below versions of the Earth Community stories that work for me at this particular time. They are works in progress that draw on the shared experience and wisdom of many colleagues, but they are only a first cut. The New Right has been honing for many years the imperial stories I related in chapter 14. It will take at least a few years and the contributions of many thousands of people to arrive at comparably honed stories of Earth Community.

EARTH COMMUNITY PROSPERITY STORY

True prosperity depends on life-serving economies that satisfy our basic material needs, maintain a sustainable balance with Earth's natural systems, strengthen the bonds of caring communities, and support all persons in the full realization of their humanity. This requires the localization and distribution of power within a framework of responsible citizenship and international cooperation. It is wholly within our means —and consistent with our human nature—to create such economies. The prosperity story of Earth Community speaks to the possibility.[3]

> Prosperity is measured by the quality of our lives and the realization by each person of the creative potential of their humanity. A high-performing economic system supports the development of this potential, provides every person with an adequate and dignified means of livelihood, maintains the healthy vitality of the planetary ecosystem that is the source of all real wealth, and contributes to building community through strengthening the bonds of affection, trust, and mutual accountability.

Poverty, unemployment, high crime rates, and broken families are all indicators of an economic system that gives higher priority to maintaining and enhancing the power and privilege of a small elite class than to providing the essentials of life to all. Prosperity is best served by the just and equitable distribution of income and ownership among all members of society. As five thousand years of history clearly demonstrate, policies that favor the rich as a privileged class marginalize those who have less and facilitate the expropriation of their labor and resources, thus limiting their creative productive contribution and the prosperity of the whole. Poverty is an inevitable product of an unjust system designed to exploit those who work hard and play by the rules.

Those who make the greatest contributions to the community properly receive a greater material reward, but only within limits consistent with economic justice. Generally, the more equitable a society is, the greater its access to the creative potential of every individual and the greater its potential prosperity. The social costs of inequality increase to the extent that the wealthy use their power advantage to take more rather than to give more. Inequality and sustainability are incompatible as inequality encourages wasteful extravagance among the rich and desperation among the poor.

It is proper that those who have received the most from society pay proportionately higher taxes and contribute a greater portion of their time to community service. Similarly, it is appropriate to continuously restore balance and forestall the creation of family dynasties by a redistribution of assets to the society at the end of each life through an inheritance tax to maintain a balance between individual incentive, equity, and public benefit.

Markets are an essential and beneficial human institution, and as with any other human endeavor their efficient function depends on the participants' exercise of a mature sense of responsibility for the whole. Markets also require impartially enforced rules that assure fair dealing, balance public and private interests, provide public services and infrastructure, maintain the conditions of fair competition, and assure an equitable distribution of ownership and income. There is no beneficial place in a healthy economy for predatory individuals or for enterprises organized for the sole purpose of making money for wealthy absentee owners.

Every person is at risk of becoming unemployed through no fault of their own, or of incurring a serious illness or injury requiring care beyond their means. None of us know how long we will live or what disabilities we may suffer in our elder years. Some will live well beyond the normal life expectancy, and a few among these will need years of expensive care. The quality of life and prosperity of all are enhanced by the sharing of these risks through unemployment benefits, retirement plans, and health insurance programs that guarantee coverage for all, irrespective of means.

In a resource-scarce world, the greater the capacity of the economic system to adapt to specific local conditions, the more efficient the use of resources will be, and thereby the greater the prosperity of the whole. This capacity for adaptation is greatest when each community is living within its own means, decision making is local, and exchanges among communities are fair and balanced. These conditions increase democratic control and accountability; limit the ability of economic predators to bid down labor, health, safety, and environmental standards; and preclude the accumulation of destabilizing external debts.[4]

The Earth Community prosperity story pretty much turns the imperial prosperity story on its head. This is wholly appropriate and scarcely surprising, because the priority of the imperial economy is to maintain the established relations of domination. The priority of the Earth Community economy is to build mutual prosperity through relations of partnership.

EARTH COMMUNITY SECURITY STORY

The primary role of political institutions is to maintain order and set priorities for collective action to advance the common good. Just as their contrasting prosperity stories do, the security stories of Empire and Earth Community reflect their differing priorities. For Empire, security means securing the established hierarchy of privilege, whatever the cost. For Earth Community, it means securing the well-being of present and future generations against avoidable risks and sharing the costs of the risks that are unavoidable. Here is a suggested security story for Earth Community:

Strong families and communities that build relationships of mutual trust and caring and that support all people in realizing the potentials of their humanity are the best guarantee of human security. They also serve as deterrents to criminal activity and as an important resource for apprehending those who engage in criminal acts.

Responsible citizenship, cooperation, and nonviolent conflict resolution come naturally to emotionally and morally mature adults. Long term, our best guarantee of physical security will come from public policies that support a healthy family and community life that strengthens mutual trust and caring and nurtures the growth of every individual to full moral and emotional maturity. The desire to harm, dominate, or demean others is an indicator of the failure of family and community to fulfill their essential roles, which is in turn an indicator of a failure of public policy to provide the necessary support.

The greatest threats to physical security now facing the world, short of nuclear Armageddon, are climate change, toxic contamination, water shortages, rising energy prices, and economic instability created by financial speculation and skyrocketing trade imbalances. These and other consequential security threats — including crime, terrorism, and war — are a direct consequence of the cultures and institutions of Empire that weaken family and community, mismanage natural resources, undermine the legitimacy of official institutions, create extremes of injustice, and suppress development of the higher orders of moral consciousness.

One of the most important indicators of a healthy society is a low crime rate combined with a low rate of incarceration. Imprisonment is a last resort, and for all but the most extreme cases its proper purpose is rehabilitation and eventual reintegration into the community. The goal is to achieve restorative justice that promotes healing and respect for all persons. That said, persons who repeatedly engage in criminal acts must, as a last resort, be subject to imprisonment through due process to prevent them from doing further harm to themselves and others.

Just as strong families and communities are the best guarantee of security against domestic crime, so too a strong community of nations is the best guarantee of security against the threats of international crime, terrorism, and rogue regimes. Militarization begets militarization, which in turn invites the preemptive use of military force to resolve real and imagined threats and grievances.

Military security is best assured through negotiating mutually agreed-upon and verified programs of disarmament, retooling from war economies to peace economies, and working through institutions of international cooperation to eliminate war as an instrument of national policy.

Similarly, violence begets violence, including acts of terrorism. Invading other nations to capture or punish terrorists legitimates violence as the means of settling disputes and fuels terrorist recruitment. Apprehending terrorists and holding them accountable requires the cooperation of national and international law enforcement agencies. The terrorist activities of nonstate political groups are generally acts of desperation by groups that find no other outlet for the expression of their grievances. Democracy to assure every individual a meaningful political voice is the best preventive measure. The United States and other nations can best support democracy by ending their support for dictatorial regimes and their dependence on the foreign resources to which these regimes provide access.

The best response to rogue regimes is cooperative international action to cut off their access to international arms, funds, and the technology required to create offensive weapons. When removal by military force is required as a last resort, it is properly undertaken only with broad international consensus for the use of multilateral military forces dispatched under the authority of the United Nations.

Long supply lines; concentrated supplies of volatile fuels, toxic chemicals, and radioactive materials; disposable workers subject to instant dismissal in a moment of disruption; core industries subject to extreme swings of consumer confidence; and an unstable financial system built on debt and speculation – all these pose security threats in that they can turn even minor local disturbances into major disasters.

We reduce shocks and thereby increase security by favoring local production and procurement to shorten supply lines; reducing reliance on volatile fuels, toxic chemicals, and radioactive materials; giving economic priority to meeting basic needs that generate a stable demand; limiting debt and financial speculation; recycling; and being more frugal in our use of natural resources.

Perhaps the greatest fear any of us can have is that no one will care enough to be with us in our time of need. Again, relationships are the key. Dominator relations create an illusion of security but in fact undermine the security that only caring communities can provide.

EARTH COMMUNITY MEANING STORY

We humans are the only earthly species with the capacity to ask the most basic of questions: "Where did we come from, and what is the purpose of our existence?" We have long sought answers to such questions through creation stories—usually metaphorical and of ancient origin—that embody our collective understanding of our origin and give meaning to our existence.

As discussed in chapter 15, the contemporary culture of Western societies presents us with a cruel choice between two incomplete stories. One, the now seriously outdated story of Newtonian physics, reduces the whole of reality to chance and material causation; denies consciousness, intelligence, and free will; and strips life of meaning. The other, the prevailing Western religious story, affirms the transcendent but denies human experience and observation as sources of valid learning and presents our earthly condition as but a way station in which we are condemned to live out our time in an evil world and to pray for deliverance in the afterlife. To choose either of these stories is to deny the capacities for choice and service that make us distinctively human.

Our creation stories may be based on factual evidence, but the interpretation of what that evidence means and its implications for our lives ultimately come down to questions of belief or faith, which progressives rarely discuss even with one another although they are foundational to our work. I believe it is important that we engage this discussion through sharing our meaning stories. In this spirit, I offer the following as the meaning story that motivates my commitment to the work of the Great Turning.

> The cosmos—and all within it—is an integral interconnected whole that flows forth from a universal spiritual intelligence, the ground of all being. We humans know this intelligence by many names.
>
> This spiritual intelligence is engaged in an epic journey of self-discovery, a quest to know itself by actualizing its possibilities through an eternal process of learning and becoming. Everything that exists is both a product of this sacred quest and an instrument of its continued unfolding. Because Creation is a manifestation of the Spirit some call God, God and Creation are one and the same, which means we live in ever present relationship to God—indeed there is no other possibility, because there is no existence apart from the Spirit.

Life, which instills matter with the capacity to choose, takes Creation's journey of self-discovery to a new level of possibility. By its nature, life exists only in relationship to other life and is at its most vital in cooperative communities rich with diversity and the dynamic interplay of individuals and species engaged in actualizing their individual and collective potential. Competition for territory, food, and sexual partners contributes to the dynamism of the whole, yet is no more than a counterpoint to deeper patterns of cooperation and mutuality.

The well-being of the individual and of the community are inseparable. The health of the whole depends on the health and integrity of the individual, and the health of the individual depends on the health and integrity of the whole; neither can survive and prosper without the other. The species that survive and thrive are those that learn to sustain themselves in ways that simultaneously serve the needs of the whole. The defining challenge for each new species is to find its place of service, a challenge we humans have yet to meet.

As far as we know, we humans are Creation's most daring experiment in reflective consciousness and the capacity for mindful choice. It is our nature to choose and, in our most mature manifestation, to discern the difference between good—that which serves Creation's purpose—and evil—that which is contrary to that purpose. Deepening our understanding of the difference between good and evil so defined, and learning to organize our lives in service to the good, are central to our life's work.

Throughout our history, we humans have demonstrated that hatred and love, greed and generosity, ruthless competition and selfless cooperation, are all within our nature. It is also in our nature to choose among the possibilities of our nature, and it is our responsibility to choose wisely. Because we live in complex and interdependent relationships with one another on a planetary spaceship with a fragile and now overstressed life support system, we humans ultimately share a common destiny. It is ours to choose whether that common destiny will be one of peace, justice, and abundance, or violence, tyranny, and deprivation.

The idea that the human species represents the ultimate accomplishment and end purpose of Creation is an unwarranted conceit of a still immature species—an extension of the ancient conceit that the whole of the cosmos revolves around our earthly planet and thereby around humans. It is an even greater conceit to assume that we humans are the only conscious intelligence manifest in the cosmos. We are manifestations of the Spirit that birthed, and at each instant rebirths, the cosmos, but we should not assume that we are the center of its attention or that it will assure our survival. Many species that once defined the frontiers of evolutionary accomplishment passed into oblivion long before our arrival.

In granting humans the power of reflective consciousness, Creation has given our species a distinctive gift of opportunity. It is left to us to choose how we use that opportunity and to bear the consequences of our choice.

The next step in our own journey is to create societies that support the development of the fullness of our positive human potential as we advance our understanding of how we might best develop that potential and apply it to the service of the whole. Progressive Christians refer to it as creating God's kingdom on Earth – a world of deeply democratic societies in which all people have the opportunity to carry forward the work of Creation through productive and fulfilling lives in dynamic, creative, and balanced relationships with one another and the living Earth.

This story, which draws together the insights of the spiritual wisdom of religious mystics and the data of modern science, sets the deeper frame for Earth Community's prosperity and security stories. The prosperity, security, and meaning stories presented here all converge on Creation's unifying truth that relationships are the foundation of everything. So too, human prosperity, security, and meaning are all found in the life of vibrant, interlinked communities that offer every person—without exception—the opportunity to contribute their creative energy through joyful, creative, engaged relationships with one another and Earth.

Our deepest human desire is to live in caring relationships with one another. This desire is our call to engage the invisible curriculum of our lives through which we learn to become fully human and find our collective place of service both as individuals and as a species. Engaging in the work of the Great Turning is a form of spiritual practice.

DISCOVERING AND SHARING STORIES OF THE POSSIBLE

In the oral traditions of cultural storytelling, stories passed from person to person, generation to generation, as the living, evolving, creative expressions of a people's understanding of themselves and their world. The intention of the storyteller was not the verbatim recitation of some static text. It was to bring alive the underlying truth of a story in a manner appropriate to a particular audience at a particular moment.

I have outlined my own version of three stories based on my current understanding of the truths emerging from the collective inquiry of global civil society. I urge you to approach these stories in the spirit of the ancient oral tradition as contributions to the living, evolving, creative expression of the shared learning of an emerging human era.

If you feel so inclined, I urge you to organize a discussion group with friends and colleagues to reflect on both the stories of Empire presented in chapter 14 and the stories of Earth Community presented above in light of your own experience and understanding. Gather as storytellers of a new era. As you find your own stories, share them with others in your own words and in the manner true to your experience.

We humans devote much of our lives to a search for prosperity, security, and meaning. Whether at this defining moment we choose as our guide the prosperity, security, and meaning stories of Empire or those of Earth Community will in substantial measure determine whether future generations will know our time as the time of the Great Unraveling or the time of the Great Turning.

It is at present far from an equal contest. The New Right echo chamber, greatly amplified through the corporate media megaphone, saturates the information environment with the stories of Empire.

Yet the ultimate advantage lies with those of us who are engaged in the great work of living into being a new era of Earth Community. Empire at its core is the consequence of our alienation from life. Seducing us with fantasies of personal power and glory, Empire entices us to find meaning where it cannot be found—in violence, domination, and material accumulation. Alienated from life, we become blind to the truth that meaning comes from finding our place of service to Creation's continuous unfolding.

The Great Turning begins with relearning how to live, which depends in turn on new life-affirming stories. The life-denying stories of Empire cannot compete with the life-affirming stories of Earth Community, which—in combination with practical demonstrations—give voice to the deep human yearning for healthy children, families, communities, and natural environments.

PART V

Birthing Earth Community

I have set before you life and death, blessing and cursing; therefore choose life, that both thou and thy seed may live.

Deuteronomy 19:30

We must become the change we seek in the world.

Mohandas K. Gandhi

The work of the Great Turning is not to fix Empire. It is to birth a new era that makes the choice for life, gives expression to the higher potential of our nature, and restores to people, families, and communities the power that Empire has usurped. The work is not to claim the dominator power of hierarchy for a better cause. It is to distribute power and eliminate the hierarchy.

Leadership for birthing this new era will not come from those who feel comfortable with the status quo or who are intent on preserving their special privilege. It will come from the people who are feeling out of step with the beliefs and values of the imperial cultures and the institutions of contemporary life. They will live it into being by giving practical expression to the change they seek.

These final chapters offer a framework to help us all see more clearly how our often seemingly small and fragmented individual efforts can add up to a powerful social force to change the course of history as we break the silence, end our isolation, and change the story.

Specifics will vary from country to country, depending on their distinctive histories and circumstances. The examples focus on the United States, where the challenge is particularly daunting. The underlying principles are universal.

CHAPTER 19

Leading from Below

I am done with great things and big things, great institutions and big success, and I am for those tiny invisible molecular moral forces that work from individual to individual, creeping through the crannies of the world like so many rootlets, or like the capillary oozing of water, yet which if you give them time, will rend the hardest monuments of man's pride.

William James

In nature, change doesn't happen from a top-down, strategic approach. There is never a boss in a living system. Change happens from within, from many local actions occurring simultaneously.[1]

Meg Wheatley

Albert Einstein famously observed, "No problem can be solved from the same level of consciousness that created it." Our task is to bring forth the higher levels of human consciousness and recreate our cultures and institutions to align with our possibilities.

Throughout the twentieth century, most revolutionaries used guns to wrest control of dominator institutions from ruling elites in the name of justice. They missed the truth that violence begets violence, domination begets domination; and dominator institutions are unjust no matter the party affiliation of the rulers.

Violent competition for dominator power is the way of Empire, and its practice affirms Empire. Societies based on the organizing principles of community, democracy, and love of life are created only by living them into being through the practice of community, democracy, and love of life.

A few of the twentieth century's greatest leaders, most notably Mohandas K. Gandhi and Martin Luther King Jr., worked with a higher-order vision of how truly transformational change comes about—not from the barrel of a gun, but from living the change that we seek. Their vision and example inspired the great global social movements of the twentieth century that demonstrated the human capacities for radically democratic, nonviolent self-organization and prepared the way for our current work.

The leaders of Empire use the power and resources of the institutions of Empire to motivate followers to submit to their personal authority, values, and definition of purpose. Leadership for Earth Community emerges through processes of mutual empowerment that encourage every person to recognize and express their capacities for leadership on behalf of the whole. Almost inevitably, this leadership comes from outside the institutions of Empire—from the growing millions of people with the mature consciousness that enables them to envision the possibilities of this human moment and to accept responsibility for bringing those possibilities into being. In Earth Community, leadership roles evolve and rotate in response to the needs of the situation and the skills and circumstances of the participants.

Although the leadership styles of Earth Community may seem chaotic and diffuse to those accustomed to the dominator styles of Empire, they fit the pattern by which all healthy living systems self-organize. This pattern of self-organizing, distributed power gives contemporary social movements their distinctive vitality and makes them nearly impossible to suppress.

THE STRATEGY

Global civil society is appropriately engaged on many fronts—a reflection of its diversity and the complexity of its task. Because its leadership is diffuse and self-organizing, it may seem odd to speak of strategy. Yet each act by each of its many leaders—and the convergent expression of those acts—reveal an implicit strategy, with four essential imperatives:[2]

1. ACCELERATE THE AWAKENING OF CULTURAL AND SPIRITUAL CONSCIOUSNESS. Empire's fabricated culture creates a kind of trance. Awakening from that trance occurs one individual at a time, but each occurrence creates a new role model to inspire others. The greater the number of active role models, the more quickly the awakening spreads and the more easily the culturally liberated are able to find one another to break free from the powerlessness induced by isolation. We facilitate the processes of awakening through our individual engagement and

dialogue with others, creating cross-cultural experiences, encouraging deep reflection on meaning and values, exposing the contradictions of Empire, spreading awareness of unrealized human possibilities by changing the prevailing stories.

2. RESIST EMPIRE'S ASSAULT ON CHILDREN, FAMILIES, COMMUNITY, AND NATURE. This means resisting the institutions and agendas of Empire, demanding the repeal of unjust and undemocratic rules, and abolishing programs that serve Empire's interests at the expense of community. The resistance can be assertive and may involve principled civil disobedience, but it must always adhere to the principles of nonviolence as practiced by Gandhi in India's independence movement, Martin Luther King Jr. in the U.S. civil rights movement, and other nonviolent resistance movements—even in the face of violent police and military repression. The discipline of nonviolence underscores Earth Community's moral authority, draws attention to the illegitimacy of Empire, and breaks the cycle of violence.

3. FORM AND CONNECT COMMUNITIES OF CONGRUENCE. The creative potential of the world's hundreds of millions of Cultural and Spiritual Creatives is being expressed through the formation of communities of congruence in which people develop the relationships, institutions, and authentic cultures of living societies. A community of congruence may be as simple as a local study group. It might be a farmers' market, a school to develop inquiring minds, or a course on voluntary simplicity. It might be a socially responsible local business, a church congregation devoted to spiritual inquiry and community service, or a holistic health clinic. No matter how small or isolated such initiatives may originally be, each creates a protected space in which diversity, experimentation, and learning can flourish to create the building blocks of a new mainstream economy, politics, and culture.

As communities of congruence grow and connect, they advance the process of liberation from the cultural trance of Empire and offer visible manifestations of the possibilities of Earth Community. Individually and collectively they become attractors of the life energy that Empire has co-opted—thus weakening Empire and strengthening Earth Community in an emergent process of displacement and eventual succession.

4. BUILD A MAJORITARIAN POLITICAL BASE. As the base strengthens and the stories of Earth Community are refined, the next task is to build a majoritarian political base. This requires taking the culture of Earth Community mainstream through the many formal and informal communications channels beyond corporate control. As communities of congruence begin to tip the balance of the public culture in favor of Earth Community, the radical democratization of the formal institutions of economy, politics, and culture will follow.

These four strategic undertakings are sequential in that each prepares the way for the next. They are also simultaneous in that each is currently in play, developing at its own pace, and contributing to the birthing process. New initiatives are always in gestation as others are reaching maturity. Each expression flows from authentic values, advances the awakening of Cultural and Spiritual Consciousness, expands communities of congruence, and accelerates the redirection of life energy from Empire to Earth Community to add strength and vitality to the emerging whole and thereby to redirect the human future.

Metaphorically, the strategy might be thought of as a process of "walking away from the king," because it centers not on confronting the authority of the king, but on walking away — withdrawing the legitimacy and the life energy on which the king's power depends. Think of it as a conversation with the king along the following lines:

> You have your game. It's called Empire. It may work for you, but it doesn't work for me. So I'm leaving to join with a few million others for whom the game of Empire isn't working either. We are creating a new game with new rules based on the values and principles of Earth Community. You are welcome to join us as a fellow citizen if you are willing to share your power and wealth and to play by the new rules.

This imaginary conversation is acted out through initiatives that turn away from Empire in each of the economic, political, and cultural spheres of public life.

ECONOMIC TURNING

One of the most visible manifestations of global civil society is the popular resistance against corporate globalization and the institutional instruments by which globalization's supporters are imposing their neoliberal policy agenda on the world. Less visible, but ultimately even more important, are the many initiatives aimed at growing corporate-free economies that mimic healthy ecosystems. These initiatives range from "buy local" campaigns and efforts to rebuild local food systems based on independent family farms, to efforts to eliminate corporate subsidies, stop the intrusion of big-box stores, hold corporations accountable for harms committed, and reform corporate chartering. There are groups that encourage humane animal husbandry and sustainable agriculture, seek to abolish factory farms and ban genetically modified seeds, promote green business, introduce sustainable community-based forestry-management practices, and work to roll back the use of toxic chemicals. Other groups are working to strengthen the protection of worker rights, raise the minimum wage, advance worker ownership, increase socially responsible investing, and promote other fiscal and regulatory measures that improve economic justice and encourage environmental responsibility.

In the United States, one national initiative with which I have a close association is the Business Alliance for Local Living Economies (BALLE), an alliance of local groups across the United States and Canada committed to the vision of a planetary system of local living economies free from the pathologies of absentee ownership.[3] BALLE chapters support local businesses in growing webs of economic relationships among themselves, raising consumers' awareness of the implications of their shopping choices, and working with local governments to write rules that favor the locally owned businesses essential to prosperous and vibrant community life. Where local production is not practical, BALLE chapters promote trading relationships between local-economy enterprises in different localities and countries.

Innovative graduate business schools, such as the Bainbridge Graduate Institute, are creating curricula geared to preparing managers for a new economy whose defining goals are social and environmental health. Co-op America supports the marketing efforts of independent green businesses. The American Independent Business Alliance and the New Rules Project of the Institute for Local Self-Reliance help communities develop policy frameworks supportive of local independent businesses.[4] These are only a few of many organizations dedicated to supporting the emergence of locally rooted, life-serving economies in the United States.

Similar initiatives grounded in Earth Community values are taking root most everywhere in the world. As newly liberated economic spaces connect, they may bring forth larger unifying institutional structures, such as cooperative buying and branding groups, but they remain always rooted in and controlled by communities of place. Each such expansion provides people with more choices of where to shop, work, and invest, thereby allowing them to reclaim for their communities more of the life energy that global corporations drain away.

Such efforts might seem futile if not for the fact that community-rooted, human-scale, values-based, independent businesses constitute by far the majority of all businesses, provide most of the jobs, create nearly all new jobs, and serve as the primary source of technological innovation.[5] They include businesses of all sorts, from bookstores to bakeries, land trusts, manufacturing facilities, software developers, organic farms, farmers' markets, community-supported agriculture initiatives, restaurants specializing in locally grown organic produce, worker co-ops, community banks, suppliers of fair-traded coffee, independent media outlets, and many more.

POLITICAL TURNING

Other citizen initiatives are democratizing the structures of government, promoting more active citizen participation in political life, opening the political process to a greater diversity of voices and parties, and shifting public priorities in favor of people, families, communities, and the planet. They are lobbying governments on a host of economic, social, and environmental issues ranging from international trade rules to local building codes that need revising to encourage green construction. Many follow a strategy of building momentum from the bottom up, working with local governments on initiatives in support of living wage rules, corporate accountability, and preferential treatment for local independent enterprises. Even advances on global issues like peace and global warming are beginning with local initiatives, including those begun by local governments and politicians.

In the United States, for example, while the Bush II regime in Washington continued to deny the reality of climate change, some three hundred mayors of major U.S. cities met in June 2005, in Chicago, not to debate whether climate change was an important issue, but rather to share ideas on what they should be doing about it. These discussions led to a unanimous endorsement of the U.S. Mayors Climate Protection Agreement, calling on all cities to take climate change seriously and to commit to reducing global-warming emissions to 93 percent of 1990 levels by 2012. It further called for decisive federal action.

Seattle mayor Greg Nickels, who initiated the Climate Protection Agreement, got climate-change religion during the winter of 2003–4, when an absence of the traditional snow pack on the Cascade Mountains resulted in a cancellation of the ski season and created a serious threat of water and power shortages for the city the following summer. Another signatory, New Orleans mayor Ray Nagin, pointed out that another foot of water in the ocean and New Orleans would be gone.[6] A little more than two months later, on August 29, Hurricane Katrina hit New Orleans and flooded 80 percent of the city in one of the worst disasters in U.S. history.

The climate-change initiative is only one example of what some pundits are noting as an important trend in the United States. Frustrated by the failure of national politicians to deal with impending economic, social, and environmental collapse, the elected officials of U.S. cities are stepping in to lead from below. It is in the cities where the realities of homelessness, poverty, violence, decaying schools, droughts, floods, and industries battered by "free" trade agreements are felt most acutely. This creates the impetus for urban politicians to emerge on the cutting edge of a progressive problem-solving politics.[7] Not only are the imperatives clearer to local political leaders, but they can also break the grip of big money and media spin more easily than national political leaders can. Urban politicians are learning to work with neighborhood networks to counter the smear campaigns organized by big-money interests against innovative programs in child care, affordable housing, recycling, and open-space preservation.[8]

Some of the most interesting and ambitious projects involve alliances among grassroots citizen groups, local governments, and national office holders to put forward visionary Earth Community initiatives even in the face of seemingly overwhelming resistance from the ruling imperial establishment. Two examples from the United States are the Apollo Alliance, which promotes a sustainable and clean energy economy, and the Peace Alliance, which advocates creating a U.S. cabinet-level Department of Peace devoted to advancing peace both domestically and internationally.[9]

CULTURAL TURNING

There is evidence of an emergent global cultural turning associated with the widespread awakening of the Cultural and Spiritual orders of consciousness. As discussed in part I, the awakening is a consequence of increasing cross-cultural experience, the influence of progressive social movements, and exposure to the realities of global interdependence and the fragility of a finite global ecosystem.

It is this awakening that makes the Great Turning possible. It finds popular expression in the many economic and political initiatives mentioned above. It also finds expression in more distinctively cultural initiatives aimed at rebuilding families and communities through such activities as co-housing and eco-village projects, the creation of safe, vibrant public spaces, the voluntary simplicity movement, and programs in intercultural exchange, media awareness, and educational enrichment.

Most particularly, however, the cultural turning is gaining momentum from a number of global turnings that bring new leadership to the fore and accelerate cultural and spiritual awakening. The following are of particular note:

- Indigenous peoples whom Empire and modernity have ruthlessly decimated and marginalized are reclaiming their traditions and identities and reaching out to share their understanding of the human connections to the sacred Earth. Respectful exchange between indigenous peoples and those peoples whom modernity has alienated from the ways of life may prove to be an especially powerful driver of cultural and spiritual awakening.

- Growth in the percentage of elders in the population due to falling fertility rates and increasing life spans contributes to a rise in the percentage of the population that has achieved the maturity of a Cultural or Spiritual Consciousness. There is growing interest in the potential benefits of elders making their experience and wisdom available to the larger society through their continued active engagement, particularly as teachers and mentors.

- Immigration is shifting the racial mix of the northern nations that have been the centers of white power and global domination. The unwillingness of immigrants to remain confined to the role of a racially defined servant class is a source of increasing social tension, but it provides a much needed challenge to white power hegemony and creates a demand for intercultural exchanges that are driving cultural awakening, particularly among the young.

- Perhaps the most significant single contribution to the cultural turning of the past fifty years has been a spreading rejection by women of Empire's definition of their social roles. The reascendance of women may be one of the most significant human social developments of the past five thousand years.

Feminine Leadership

The wave of transition to feminine leadership in the United States bears special mention. The cover story of the May 26, 2003, issue of *Business-Week* calls it "The New Gender Gap" and notes that in America's high schools girls now outnumber boys by substantial margins not only in music and the performing arts but also in the leadership of student government, yearbooks, school newspapers, and academic clubs. Boys maintain their lead only on athletic teams, and girls are rapidly gaining ground there as well. At the college level, women earn nearly 60 percent of U.S. bachelor's and master's degrees, and experts expect the gap to continue growing.

Since the 1960s, more women than men have been voting in U.S. elections. Women still lag far behind men in occupying top positions in corporate management and electoral politics, but this is changing as the emerging patterns of female academic and leadership proficiency work their way through the system.[10] *BusinessWeek* suggests these trends "could make the twenty-first the first female century." It won't actually be the first female century, but if the U.S. trend turns out to also be a global trend, as the evidence suggests, it may be the first in the past five thousand years. Given the needs of our time, it is a decidedly hopeful development.

Recall from the survey research of Paul Ray and Sherry Anderson, described in chapter 4, that two-thirds of Spiritual Creatives (whom they call Core Cultural Creatives) are women. Wherever one turns within contemporary progressive social movements, women are in the lead, quietly organizing around issues of peace, human rights, justice, sustainability, community, and local economies. Although their commonly unassuming networking style of leadership often leaves me—a white male—feeling disoriented and impatient, it usually turns out to be at once highly effective and remarkably efficient. It should not be surprising that women are providing a disproportionate share of the leadership in contemporary progressive movements.

Studies by psychologist Carol Gilligan led her to conclude that men tend to give more weight than women to individual autonomy and freedom, moral reasoning, and the vigilant defense of individual rights. Women give a higher priority to forming strong relationships in which they seek to please or serve others. According to Gilligan, these differences lead men and women to different approaches to resolving conflicts. Men tend to sort out their differences through logical arguments, courts of law, and combat. Women are more inclined to settle differences by talking them through to discover their respective needs and viewpoints. Men are more inclined to structure relationships by hierarchy; women are more inclined toward partnership models of organization.[11]

These differences make women the natural leaders in the work of birthing Earth Community, and they are indeed rising to the challenge. The goal, however, is not to swing to the extreme of domination by females, but rather to achieve a synthesis that brings the feminine and masculine tendencies into a healthy dynamic balance.

Spiritual Inquiry

As examined in part IV, the challenges of our time call us to revisit our deepest defining questions: Where did we come from? What is our purpose? and, What are our values? The public debate in the United States over intelligent design versus mechanism and chance discussed in chapter 15 brings such questions relating to human origin and purpose to the fore and challenges the more extreme and doctrinaire fundamentalism of both the scientific and religious establishments.

Another development in the United States with important implications for the cultural turning is the claim by media pundits that Christian voters decided the outcome of the 2004 U.S. presidential election based on moral values relating to abortion, gay marriage, and stem cell research. This announcement stunned members of the broader faith community—including a great many Evangelicals—who consider war, poverty, and environmental destruction to be far more pressing moral issues. They vowed they would no longer allow a fringe minority with an extremist political agenda at odds with scripture to be the arbiters of Christian morality.

Groups from across the spectrum of Christian denominations reached out to one another and to those of other faiths to engage in a discourse on basic moral questions such as: What did Jesus teach? What is the foundation of moral behavior, and what are valid sources of moral authority? What is the appropriate role of religion in politics? Like the debates on intelligent design, such conversations engage the mind in a critical examination of received wisdom that opens the door to the awakening of Cultural and Spiritual Consciousness.

Because Evangelicals constitute the largest identifiable faith grouping in the United States and because most of the religious Right comes from within their ranks, what is happening within the Evangelical segment of the U.S. faith community is of particular significance. Contrary to the general public perception, Evangelicals are at least as diverse in their political views as other religious groups.[12] Indeed, the number of Evangelicals whose values align easily with those of Earth Community may well be greater than the number who embrace the political agenda of the New Right. The former are coming forward to express a broad and well-examined view of the social mission of Christianity.

At its October 2004, meeting, just before the U.S. presidential election, the board of directors of the National Association of Evangelicals, which represents thirty million Evangelicals in forty-five thousand churches, adopted by a 42-0 vote a carefully nuanced document on political engagement. The document endorses efforts to advance racial justice, religious freedom, economic justice, human rights, environmentalism, peace, and nonviolent conflict resolution.[13] It also calls for humility and cooperation in political discourse and admonishes, "We must take care to employ the language of civility and to avoid denigrating those with whom we disagree."[14] In 2005, Evangelical leaders were calling for strong action on global warming.[15]

Eighty-three percent of Americans consider religion to be important or very important in their lives, which makes the opening of a serious dialogue on political values within the various branches of America's faith community a development of major significance. Rather than simply accepting the received wisdom of religious leaders, people of faith all across the country find themselves challenged to examine critically their personal beliefs and values in relation to their political responsibilities.

Mixing religion and politics can be frightening when undertaken by extremists intent on establishing a theocratic state to impose their particular religious doctrines on others. It is quite another thing when it involves people of faith engaging in a broad and open ecumenical discourse on moral issues and the responsibilities of citizenship. Given the widespread corruption of U.S. political institutions, a spiritually grounded politics devoted to respectful discourse, the peaceful resolution of conflict, justice for all people, and the stewardship of life is a timely idea.

Freed from Empire's cultural trance, Cultural and Spiritual Creatives are walking away from Empire to join with one another in creating liberated cultural spaces within which to experiment with the partnership cultures and institutions of Earth Community.

The outcome of the struggle between Empire and Earth Community ultimately turns on the politics of culture. If a culture of Empire prevails, Empire wins and ours will be the time of the Great Unraveling. If a culture of Earth Community prevails, Earth Community wins and ours will be the time of the Great Turning. The enormous institutional power at the command of Empire notwithstanding, polling data suggest that Earth Community holds a substantial prospective advantage.

CHAPTER 20

Building a Political Majority

> Look and listen for the welfare of the whole people and have always in view not only the present but also the coming generations.
>
> *The Great Law of Peace, Constitution of the Haudenosaunee (Iroquois) Nation*

> The state of the world is most visible in the state of its children.
>
> *Raffi Cavoukian, singer, author, founder of Child Honoring*

Few contemporary nations seem more divided politically than the United States. Beyond the partisan rancor, however, polling data point to a broad consensus on core values and suggest that if the institutions of governmental and corporate power were accountable to the public will, the United States would be pursuing very different policies both domestically and internationally. These institutions have been so at odds for so long with the core values and interests of the nation that most people have given up hope of any change. The residual frustration, however, runs high and represents a powerful latent political force.

There is near universal agreement among adult Americans (83 percent) that as a society the United States focuses on the wrong priorities.[1] Specifically, polling data affirm that the substantial majority of Americans share a desire for strong families and communities, a healthy environment, and high-quality health care and education for all. They are likewise concerned about the unaccountable power of corporations and government, and they prefer to live in a world that puts people ahead of profits, spiritual values ahead of financial values, and international cooperation ahead of international domination.

These are the values of the true political center most everywhere in the world. That center is composed of people who, irrespective of party affiliation, want a politics based on principle, seek real solutions to real problems, and believe government should be accountable and serve the common good. In the United States, as in the world, the defining concerns of the center reveal a deep longing to restore the sense of human connection found in the life of healthy families and communities and reflect a natural desire to support our children in their happy and healthful development.

It is on the foundation of this shared concern for children, family, and community that a majoritarian constituency for Earth Community will be built. It is here that the political extremists of the Far Right are most vulnerable, because their policies constitute nothing less than a war against children, families, and communities.

CULTURAL POLITICS

As I noted in chapter 4, Empire holds the edge in institutional power, but Earth Community holds the winning edge in the moral power of an authentic living culture. In chapter 2, I framed the cultural politics of the Great Turning as a contest between the lower and higher orders of human consciousness for the swing vote of the Socialized Consciousness of the Good Citizen.

Recall that the Magical Consciousness of the Fantasizers and the Imperial Consciousness of the Power Seekers represent the lower orders of human consciousness. The Cultural and Spiritual Consciousness of the Cultural and Spiritual Creatives represent the higher orders. The human future turns on the question of whether the prevailing cultural values and worldview that shape the understanding of the swing majority are those of Empire or those of Earth Community. (See figure 2.1 on page 54.)

What the New Right Knows

In the United States, the competition for the Socialized Consciousness has been a one-sided contest, because few Cultural and Spiritual Creatives recognize the nature and implications of cultural politics. While the New Right focused on a relatively unified effort to frame and communicate cultural stories to win the swing vote of the Good Citizens who play by the rules and values defined by the prevailing culture, progressives fragmented into countless interest groups promoting fragmented policy agendas based on appeals to logic and conscience. As control of the defining cultural stories gave the New Right a growing political edge, progressives found themselves increasingly on the defensive, limited to efforts to stall or moderate the New Right's agenda.

U.S. progressives began to realize they were missing something important only after the 2004 U.S. presidential election, when pundits reported on the basis of exit polls that "moral values" had been the deciding factor that returned to power the most extremist and, by many definitions, least moral and least family-friendly imperial regime in memory. Progressives have since been awakening to the significance of the New Right's mastery of cultural politics and the significance of the swing majority of Good Citizens.

The New Right originally spoke of the "Silent Majority" and claimed to be its voice. Then, realizing that silence does not win elections and legislative battles, the New Right changed the label to the "Moral Majority" and called on Good Citizens to raise their voices in a call for national political morality. Working through churches and the media, the New Right defined morality in terms of issues like abortion and gay marriage, called them family values, and tapped into the near universal concern for the well-being of children and families to mobilize a political majority behind an anti-children, anti-family economic agenda.

Plutocrats and neocons care little about family values, however such values might be defined, but find it useful to emphasize issues like abortion and gay marriage to draw attention away from the economic issues about which they care a great deal. This clever political stroke enabled them to build electoral support for politicians aligned behind the real agenda of monetary concentration and elite imperial rule.

What Progressives Must Learn

If Earth Community is to prevail, progressives must learn to win in the arena of cultural politics. Win that struggle, and electoral and legislative victories will follow naturally. A key to success is to recognize that the different orders of human consciousness operate from different worldviews and differ in their capacities for compassion and understanding. Messages easily understood by a higher order of consciousness may seem illogical or even absurd to a lower order.

Appealing to Power Seekers to recognize the moral hypocrisy of their actions is an exercise in futility, because the Imperial Consciousness lacks the emotional intelligence required to see itself through the eyes of the victims of its actions. It is far less of a stretch, however, for those of a Socialized Consciousness to recognize the hypocrisy, because they already possess the capacity for empathy, even though they may not yet have become practiced in applying that capacity beyond the circle of members of their own identity group.

Each of us, irrespective of the order of consciousness from which we normally function, is subject to competing pulls toward the values and worldview of those orders of consciousness that lie above and below our own. The Socialized Consciousness is pivotal in this regard as it has the ability to swing in the direction of either Empire or Earth Community—depending on the relative strength of the cultural pull. Earth Community enjoys the ultimate advantage, because the natural human drive—if not blocked—is to grow in capacity and understanding and to connect with ever expanding circles of life. Political extremists must engage in manipulation and deception to thwart this natural impulse. Cultural and Spiritual Creatives need only encourage and support it.

The Cultural and Spiritual orders of consciousness are the natural state of the mature adult consciousness, unless systematically suppressed by Empire. As noted in chapter 4, the circumstances of our time are producing a steady increase in the numbers of Cultural and Spiritual Creatives. It is within our means, should we choose to do so, to make the Cultural Consciousness the adult norm, with a majority achieving a Spiritual Consciousness by late middle age.

Compelling, unifying stories that speak to the potentials of the mature human consciousness are essential to the work of birthing Earth Community. Progressive movements should give substantial priority to the development and sharing of those stories, which provide a unifying rationale for our work and the narrative tools needed to turn the prevailing culture to Earth Community. Such stories become all the more compelling when supported by living demonstrations of the generative power of cooperative partnerships.

Bear in mind that cultural change does not take place simultaneously everywhere. It begins with people joining to create new cultural spaces. These spaces gradually grow and link to create yet larger spaces. As the spaces grow, they express and make more visible the opportunities of partnership and thereby facilitate the cultural and spiritual awakening of others.

FOUNDATIONS OF A POLITICAL CONSENSUS

The New Right's divide-and-conquer imperial politics obscures the reality of what is actually a broad consensus on the importance of strong families and communities, environmental health, international cooperation, and democracy. If our attention as a nation and as a species were focused on the state of our children rather than the growth in our stock portfolios, our children would be healthy, our communities strong, and we would be on the path to the Great Turning rather than to the Great Unraveling.

It is instructive to look at what Americans are telling national pollsters about their concerns and values, as it suggests that a desire to strengthen the human connections of family and community and to secure a positive future for our children may be the most politically potent issue of our time.

Strong Families and Communities

Eighty-three percent of Americans believe that we need to rebuild our neighborhoods and small communities and fear that family life is declining.[2] Ninety-three percent agree that we are too focused on working and making money and not focused enough on family and community. Eighty-six percent agree that we are too focused on getting what we want now and not focused enough on the needs of future generations.[3] Eighty-seven percent of adult Americans think "advertising and marketing aimed at kids today make children and teenagers too materialistic," and 70 percent feel advertising "has a negative effect on their values and world view." Seventy-eight percent believe "marketing and advertising put too much pressure on children to buy things that are too expensive, unhealthy, or unnecessary."[4]

Our children agree. A poll of kids aged nine through fourteen commissioned by the Center for the New American Dream reports that 90 percent said friends and family are "way more important" than the things money can buy. Fifty-seven percent would rather spend time doing something fun with mom or dad than go shopping at the mall. Sixty-three percent would like their mom or dad to have a job that gave them more time to do fun things together. Only 13 percent wished their parents made more money. Seventy-five percent are worried that advertising that tries to get kids to buy things causes trouble between kids and parents.[5]

Strong majorities of Americans also believe that education and health are community as well as individual issues and that they merit a community commitment in support of families and children. More than four out of five Americans consider the state of education (86 percent) and health care (82 percent) to be very important.[6] Sixty-nine percent favor increasing federal spending for education.[7] Seventy-nine percent believe it is more important to assure health care coverage for all than to cut taxes.[8]

Healthy Environment

The health and future of our children depend on a healthy environment. Nearly nine out of ten U.S. adults (87 percent) believe we need to treat the planet as a living system and that we should have more respect and reverence for nature. Nearly three out of four (74 percent) are concerned that pollution may destroy farmlands, forests, and seas.[9] More than four out of five (85 percent) believe that the possibility of global warming should be treated as a serious problem.[10] We strongly agree on the importance of setting higher emissions and pollution standards for business and industry (81 percent), spending more government money on developing solar and wind power (79 percent), and being more vigorous in enforcing federal environmental regulations (77 percent).[11]

Two-thirds majorities are prepared to make lifestyle changes to improve environmental health. More than two in three would like to see a return to a simpler way of life with less emphasis on consumption and wealth (68 percent).[12] Sixty-six percent agree that it is a good idea to work fewer hours and spend less money, and 48 percent of us report already having voluntarily made changes in our lives that result in making less money.[13]

International Cooperation

Children are best served by a world of laws in which disputes are settled peacefully by negotiation and compromise. Seventy-six percent of Americans reject the idea that the United States should play the role of world police officer, and 80 percent feel it is playing that role more than it should be. Ninety-four percent believe that the best way to fight terrorism is to work through the United Nations to strengthen international laws against terrorism and to make sure UN members enforce them.[14] Substantial majorities of Americans agree that the United States should participate in the Nuclear Test Ban Treaty (87 percent), the Ottawa Treaty to ban land mines (80 percent), the International Criminal Court (76 percent), and the Kyoto Protocol on climate change (71 percent).[15]

More than two out of three (71 percent) believe that our dependence on oil leads to conflicts and wars with other countries and believe it is better to deal with our dependence on oil by conserving energy (83 percent). Only a small minority (8 percent) prefers using military power to maintain access to oil in the Middle East and other strategic regions.[16]

Real Democracy

One might well wonder why there is such an enormous gap between what people want and what a presumably democratic political system is delivering. Substantial majorities of adults correctly recognize that this reflects the lack of accountability of power.

Nearly three out of four Americans (72 percent) believe corporations have too much power over too many aspects of American life.[17] Clearly distinguishing between big and small businesses, 74 percent say big companies have too much influence over government policy and politicians; 82 percent say small business has too little.[18] Eighty-eight percent distrust corporate executives, and 90 percent want new corporate regulations and tougher enforcement of existing laws.[19] Only 4 percent believe that America is best served when corporations pursue only one goal—making the most profit for their shareholders.[20] Ninety-five percent believe corporations should sacrifice some profit for the sake of making things better for their workers and communities.[21]

Because of the excessive influence over government by corporations and other powerful special interests, only 27 percent of Americans trust the government to do what is right most of the time.[22] Only 37 percent believe that government has a positive impact on their lives. Only 35 percent feel that ordinary people like themselves have any influence on what government does.[23] Nearly two-thirds (64 percent) believe that government is pretty much run by a few big interests.[24]

The large number of respondents (83 percent) who believe that government can have a positive impact[25] on their lives suggests that most people recognize that the issue is accountability and that they are not rejecting government per se. People generally feel more connected to their local governments (51 percent) than to the federal government (33 percent).[26] Most Americans have very little confidence in any of the major institutional concentrations of power, whether it be the executive branch of the federal government (23 percent), the press (15 percent), organized labor (15 percent), the Congress (13 percent), or major companies (12 percent).[27]

The underlying pattern is quite clear. People share a healthy distrust of all forms of unaccountable power, feel powerless to do anything about it, and would rejoice in a transfer of power from the mega-institutions of global Empire to smaller, more local, and more accountable institutions responsive to family and community needs. In short, there is a strong constituency for real democracy in the United States.

FOR THE CHILDREN

Raffi Cavoukian, the troubadour whose music has nurtured a sense of love and wonder in millions of children for three decades, is an impassioned advocate for a humane and sustainable world. In 2004, he issued a call to humanity to create a world of "child-honoring societies" that embrace the principles of the Earth Charter.[28] It is a simple yet elegant idea that speaks to universal moral values and to the imperative and opportunity of our time.

Lead Indicator

The state of our children will be the clearest indicator of when we have successfully navigated the turn to Earth Community. When every human child is receiving the physical and emotional support needed from family and community to actualize the full potential of his or her humanity, we will know we are on course to a new human future. A child-honoring society must also honor family and community. The current state of our children tells us just how far we have yet to travel.

In the United States, 12 million children, 16.7 percent of the total, live in families that fall below the official poverty line, which means the family income is too low to provide even for the most basic needs of their children.[29] An estimated 4 million children in the United States experience prolonged periodic food insufficiency and hunger each year.[30]

Deficiencies affect mental as well as physical well-being. In the United States, the average child in the 1980s reported more anxiety than did the average child *who was receiving psychiatric treatment* in the 1950s.[31] Even as overall death rates for persons one to twenty-four years of age fell by 53 percent from 1950 to 1999, homicide death rates for this age group rose by 134 percent, and suicide rates, the third-leading cause of death, rose by 137 percent.[32] A 2002 National Research Council study reports that "at least one of every four adolescents in the U.S. is currently at serious risk of not achieving productive adulthood."[33] The Commission on Children at Risk calls the increasing incidence of mental illness, emotional distress, and behavioral problems among U.S. children and adolescents an epidemiological crisis.[34]

Numerous studies link the increases in anxiety, depression, and social dysfunction among young people in the United States to a decline in the social connectedness of families and communities[35]—Frankl's existential vacuum. According to U.S. Census Bureau surveys, married-couple households as a portion of all U.S. households have fallen from 80 percent in the 1950s to just 50.7 percent at the turn of the century.[36] Only 73 percent of U.S. children now reside with two biological parents.[37]

Globally, UNICEF reports that of the world's 2.2 billion children, 1 billion, nearly every second child, are living in poverty. Six hundred forty million children live without adequate shelter. Four hundred million have no access to safe water. Two hundred seventy million have no access to health services. More than thirty thousand die each day, eleven million a year before the age of five, mostly from preventable causes.[38]

These are not the young of some alien species; they are our human children, and they represent our future. Failure to provide them with proper care reproduces the physical and psychological disabilities that are driving a descent into the barbarism of the Great Unraveling that, if not reversed, will define the human future for generations to come. The increasing struggle to provide for their needs is a tragedy being experienced by people in virtually every country that has come under the sway of corporate globalization.

Assault on Family Viability

The New Right's propagandists would have us believe that family stress and breakdown are the fault of gay marriage, abortion, feminists, immigrants, and the liberals who support them. They are prepared to blame most anyone or anything except their own economic and social policies. In the pursuit of their personal power and profits, New Right leaders work tirelessly to

- roll back health and safety standards for the environment, consumers, and workers, including workplace safety standards, a meaningful minimum wage, and the right to form unions to bargain collectively for improved wages and working conditions;
- drive down wages and benefits for working people through international job outsourcing;
- shift the tax burden from the investor class to the working class;
- eliminate public services and safety nets, including public education and Social Security;
- generate military contracts for crony corporations;
- secure intellectual property to facilitate monopoly control and pricing of access to information and technology, including essential seeds and medicines; and
- increase tax breaks and subsidies for large corporations to give them a competitive advantage over local businesses.

Each of these policies transfers wealth and power from ordinary people to the ruling elite and leaves families and communities without the means to provide their children with the essentials for healthful physical and mental development.

The following are but a few of the consequences. The details of this list are specific to the United States, but similar consequences are being experienced nearly everywhere as a direct consequence of neoliberal policies.[39]

- High unemployment undermines family formation, and punitive welfare policies force single mothers into jobs paying less than a living wage without affordable, regulated, high-quality child care options. Even two-parent households are forced to piece together multiple jobs, allowing no time or energy for child care or for a normal family and community life. Parents are thus forced to abandon their children to television and an unregulated entertainment and gaming industry that finds it profitable to fill their minds with images of sex and violence and to actively undermine parental authority and values.

- Corporations spend billions on direct marketing to children to create lifetime addictions to junk food, alcohol, and cigarettes, and a childhood obesity epidemic is poised to become the leading cause of premature death.
- Declining health care coverage and skyrocketing health care costs place essential health care beyond the reach of most families.
- A deteriorating public education system is unable to deal with the special needs of children physically and mentally handicapped by the consequences of growing up in physically and socially toxic environments, let alone deal with normal individual differences in learning styles and talents.
- Lax environmental regulations allow corporations to discharge into the air, soil, and water massive quantities of tens of thousands of toxins destructive of children's physical, neurological, and endocrinological development.

Intended or not, these conditions are all a direct result of the neoliberal economic policies that are the real priority of the corporate plutocracy. They leave families with few or no good options, and they lead to mental stress, family breakdown, divorce, the destruction of community life, and a coarsening of moral values. The New Right argues that it is the responsibility of parents, not the state, to provide proper care for their children. Ideally, that would be the case; but the policies the New Right advances virtually guarantee that the substantial majority of parents are unable to fulfill this responsibility.

Assault on Family Values

Advertising aimed explicitly at children in the unregulated marketplace is one of the more pernicious, intentional, and well-funded assaults by corporate plutocrats on family values. Corporate advertising executives long ago became aware that it is highly lucrative to begin conditioning very young children to value individualistic materialism over family and community. Their efforts became truly sinister a few years ago when they learned that "brand loyalty" begins to take shape as early as age two and that at age three, even before they are able to read, children are already making requests for specific brand-name products. Experts estimate that this early identification may be worth $100,000 per child in lifetime sales.[40]

Corporate marketing executives responded to this revelation by targeting advertising to ever younger children and using ever more sophisticated techniques to reach and claim their hearts and minds. Child-oriented marketing exploded in the 1990s, from an estimated $100 million in TV advertising targeted to children in 1983, to $15 billion in total advertising and marketing expenditures directed to children in 2004.[41]

Kid-oriented advertising defines cool as having money and attitude, indulging in material excess and expensive products, outwitting teachers, and tricking parents. Advertisers pride themselves on their ability to make kids feel that they are losers if they lack an advertised product and get them to nag their parents to buy it. The British side of the industry calls it pester power. Boston College sociology professor Juliet Schor documents from her research inside a leading advertising corporation that this effort is conscious and intentional, and that it employs highly sophisticated research and techniques of psychological engineering.[42]

In their efforts to bypass parental filters, corporations have been increasingly successful in bringing their products into schools, inserting product placements into curriculum materials and entertainment programming, and turning school sporting events into corporate billboards. They even hire kids to talk up products with their friends and host slumber parties that become intimate focus groups for testing reactions to new products.[43]

The average child is exposed to more than forty thousand television commercials each year. Approximately 80 percent of the advertisements targeted to children fall into four product categories: toys, cereals, candies, and fast-food restaurants. The task force concluded that child-oriented advertising contributes to child obesity, parent-child conflict, materialistic attitudes, and tobacco and alcohol consumption and that exposure to media violence, including marketed video games, movies, and other media featuring violent content, contributes to fear, anxiety, sleep disturbance, and violent behavior.[44]

A CONSERVATIVE-LIBERAL ALLIANCE

The New Right presents itself as conservative, but that is part of its deception. Its actual policy agenda is far from conservative, at least so far as the term *conservative* is understood by most Americans. There is a culture war in America, but it is not between liberals and conservatives, who in fact share a great many core values — including a commitment to children, family, community, personal responsibility, and democracy. It is between the culture of Empire and the culture of Earth Community. It is between the lower and higher orders of our human nature. It is between an imperial politics of individual greed and power and a democratic politics based on principle and the common good. It is between Power Seekers at the extreme political fringes who remain imprisoned in an Imperial Consciousness and the realists of the political mainstream who truly want to solve the problems that beset us all.

Call those of us on the side of Earth Community progressives—progressive conservatives and progressive liberals. Although we have our differences, we share a commitment to creating a society governed by ordinary people and dedicated to the ideals of liberty, justice, and opportunity for all. We are driven by principle rather than ideology, and we deal in reality rather than delusion. We have no more in common with the ideological extremists of the Far Left who seek violent revolution and state control of every aspect of life than we do with the ideological extremists of the Far Right who pursue imperial wars abroad, a theocratic state at home, and freedom for themselves to oppress the rest.

A politics of mature citizenship properly honors both the conservative values of freedom and individual responsibility and the liberal values of equity and justice for all. It brings together a conservative concern for community and heritage with a liberal concern for inclusiveness and the creation of a world that works for the whole of life and children yet to come. It recognizes the importance of local roots combined with a global consciousness. In the mature human mind, these are complementary values that call us to a path of spiritual health and maturity.

Progressives of all stripes act from deeply shared values that resonate with the most basic of Christian values—do not kill, do not steal, love thy neighbor as thyself, and do unto others as you would have them do unto you. Yet just as these are not exclusively liberal or conservative values, neither are they exclusively Christian values. They are universal human values shared by believers in Christianity, Islam, Judaism, Hinduism, Buddhism, and Native spirituality, among others. From this foundation, we can pull back from the extremes to find common ground even on those issues that presently are the focus of intense political acrimony, including abortion, gay rights, gun control, and the teaching of evolution. For too long we have allowed extremists on both sides to define these debates in all-or-nothing terms that drive out the search for common ground based on shared moral principles.

Beneath the political stresses in the United States that at times threaten to tear our nation apart, we can see the emergent outlines of a largely unrecognized consensus that the world most of us want to bequeath to our children is very different from the world in which we live. Conservatives and liberals share a sense that the dominant culture and institutions of the contemporary world are morally and spiritually bankrupt, unresponsive to human needs and values, and destructive of the strong families and communities we crave and our children desperately need. Deceived by the divide-and-conquer tactics of imperial politics, each places the blame on the other rather than forming a united front to reject Empire's lies and unite in a stand against the New Right's war against children, families, and communities.

Most people are stretched far too thin to spend the time it takes to sort out the competing arguments on whether global warming is taking place, why gas prices are so high, or why the Iraq war turned out to be such a terrible mess. What they know very well, however, is that their lives are stretched to the breaking point; their children suffer from asthma, obesity, and a continuous bombardment of sex and violence on TV and of ads promoting junk food; and they are unable both to keep bread on the table and to supervise their children. To raise healthy children we must have healthy, family-supportive economies, and to have healthy, family-supportive economies we must have healthy, democratically accountable political systems responsive to the needs and values of people, families, and communities. The struggle for the health and well-being of our children is potentially the unifying political issue of our time and an obvious rallying point for building an Earth Community political majority.

It is within our human means to create a world in which families and communities are strong, parents have the time to love and care for their children, high-quality health care and education are available to all, schools and homes are commercial free, the natural environment is healthy and toxin free, and nations cooperate for the common good. It is about renewing the democratic experiment, liberating the creative potential of the species, and coming home to life. It is an idea whose time has come and the foundation of a true political majority.

CHAPTER 21

Liberating Creative Potential

> Let ours be a time remembered for the awakening of a new
> reverence for life, the firm resolve to achieve sustainability,
> the quickening of the struggle for justice and peace, and the
> joyful celebration of life.
>
> *The Earth Charter*

Imperial societies maintain their dominator structures by consolidating control over all three spheres of public life—economic, political, and cultural—thus limiting people, families, and communities to whatever options the institutions of Empire find it in their interest to offer. Having little control over their lives and struggling to make ends meet, people withdraw from active engagement in civic life, causing the creative problem-solving capacity intrinsic to a vital community life to atrophy from neglect.

The basic framework for the work of birthing Earth Community is simple: make the life-affirming values of Earth Community the values of the prevailing culture; renew the democratic experiment to restore to people, families, and communities the power to give expression to those values; and do it all on a global scale. An immodest agenda, this requires, in the words of Frances Moore Lappé, that we take democracy where it has never been before.

Empire has conditioned us to believe that the constitutional plutocracy we have is the democracy to which we feel entitled. As noted in chapter 11, a constitutional plutocracy pits the factions of a ruling aristocracy against one another in a competition for the favor of the electorate. It creates an illusion of popular control without the reality. True democracy is a living practice centered on active community engagement through which we both discover and give direct expression to our vision of the world we want. Such engagement might involve participating in a community play or church choir, operating a local business, testifying at a public hearing, teaching in a local school, serving on a local commission, running for local office, establishing a local elder care facility, volunteering at the library, organizing the cleanup of a park, or promoting a local-first campaign in support of local independent businesses.

None of this eliminates the need either for government or for elections. To the contrary: government is essential to deal with public needs, and elections are an essential feature of democracy. Democracy, however, is more about a way of community life than it is about elections. A living democracy finds expression in living economies, living politics, and living cultures.

The economic sphere is where we come together to transform the gifts of nature into our means of living. The political sphere is where we come together to find agreement on the rules by which we will live and hopefully to solve problems facing us as a community in the best interests of all. The cultural sphere is where we come together to discover and express our shared values, sense of identity, meaning, and relationship to the transcendent.

LIVING ECONOMIES

The local living economies we must create are on every dimension virtual opposites of the suicidal global imperial economy we have. Table 21-1 summarizes the critical features that distinguish the two.

One of the important lessons of history is that those who own, rule. Even in titular democracies, the powers of ownership readily trump the power of the ballot and play an often decisive role in shaping cultural values. For these reasons, growing living economies that democratize economic relationships in the deepest sense is a leading edge of the work of birthing Earth Community. The following are design principles to guide this work.

ECONOMIC DEMOCRACY. Democracy is strongest when people own the homes in which they live and have a direct ownership stake in the assets on which their livelihood depends. When workers are owners, the conflict between workers and owners disappears. When income and ownership are equitably distributed, the market allocates efficiently and responds to the needs of the many rather than the wants of the few. Local owners who have a long-term stake in the enterprises they own are patient investors who stay the course rather than seek quick profits from short-term market swings.

Global imperial economy	Local living economies
The defining purpose is to make money for owners to increase their power and their claims to the resources of the many.	The defining purpose is to secure fulfilling livelihoods for all and increase the generative power of the whole.
The guiding mantra is create global monopolies to eliminate local choice, take all you can get and pass costs to others.	The guiding mantra is create beneficial local options, take only what you need, and accept responsibility for the whole.
The rules favor absentee owners, monopoly-scale enterprises, financial speculators, rights of property, and central planning by global corporations.	The rules favor participating owners, human-scale enterprises, wealth creators, rights of people, and self-organization by people and communities.
Denying any responsibility for public interests, proponents seek to secure impermeable boundaries around the exclusive private interests of corporations and their wealthiest owners, while demanding that communities eliminate any borders protective of public interests.	Recognizing the need of all living entities to protect and balance individual and community interests, proponents support both firms and communities in establishing managed protective borders that support, fair, balanced and mutually beneficial exchange.

TABLE 21-1: Critical distinguishing features

LOCAL PREFERENCE. Communities are most economically secure and most in control of their own economic priorities when most of their basic needs are met by local businesses that employ local labor and use local resources to meet the needs of local residents for employment, goods, and services. Such communities are most likely to manage their environmental resources responsibly and sustainably when they depend on the yield of those resources for their continued well-being. Business decisions are most likely to take into account the health of the community and its natural environment when those who make the decisions live in the community and share in any social and environmental burdens those decisions create.

HUMAN SCALE. Human-scale enterprises and markets foster face-to-face economic relationships of mutual trust and accountability, which are an essential foundation of strong communities. Markets are more efficient and responsive when served by several small local firms rather than one or a few very large firms with absentee owners.

LIVING INDICATORS. Communities that evaluate their economic performance against indicators of social and environmental health are likely to manage their resources in ways consistent with the long-term well-being of children, families, and communities.

FAIR-SHARE TAXATION. It is just and proper that those who enjoy the greatest economic gains from public services and facilities pay the greatest share of the costs of providing and maintaining these public services.

RESPONSIVE MARKETS. The economy functions most efficiently and democratically when businesses respond to the self-defined needs of people rather than spending large sums on advertising to generate demand for unneeded products. Advertising aimed at creating artificial desires distorts the market, wastes resources, serves no public purpose, and is properly discouraged by treating advertising as an after-tax expense.

RESPONSIBILITY FOR HARMS CAUSED. Markets allocate fairly and efficiently only when the full cost of each good and service is internalized in its price. Because unregulated markets lead to the extensive practice of shifting the costs of private decisions onto the public, public intervention through regulation and the assessment of compensatory fees is essential to assure that market prices reflect the full costs—including social and environmental costs—of a good or service. Similarly, it is proper for those who make private decisions and reap the benefits therefrom to bear liability for harms to others resulting from intention or neglect. Limiting the liability of the owners and managers of corporations violates this principle and invites reckless and irresponsible behavior.

PATIENT CAPITAL. Public policy properly favors patient investment over speculative trading that distorts and destabilizes markets and creates perverse incentives for managers to focus on short-term results and engage in fraudulent accounting practices.

GENERATIONAL JUBILEE. In the spirit of the biblical jubilee, it is proper to restore a condition of equity at the end of each lifetime by equitably distributing the assets of large estates on the death of their owners.

INFORMATION AND TECHNOLOGY SHARING. Inventors and artists have a right to fair compensation for their original contributions. There is, however, an overriding public interest in the free sharing of essential information and beneficial technology, and no individual or enterprise has a right to monopolize such information and technology or unduly restrict its use by others.

ECONOMIC SELF-DETERMINATION. It is the right and responsibility of the citizens of every nation to control their own economic resources and to determine their own economic and social priorities, terms of trade, and rules for foreign investors consistent with their needs and values so long as they internalize the costs of their decisions and do not shift costs onto others.

FAIR AND BALANCED TRADE. Trade relationships should be fair and balanced. Fairness means that the price of exports must reflect full production costs—including the cost of providing workers with living wages and benefits and practicing sound environmental stewardship. Balance means each nation's exports and imports must be maintained in balance so there is no buildup of long-term international debt.

These are all basic principles of sound market economies. Market fundamentalists will denounce them as violating market freedom, a code word for the freedom of those members of a society with the most money to do whatever they like without regard to the consequences for others. It is the difference between the democracy of the many championed by Jefferson and the democracy of the very rich championed by Hamilton. The economic principles of Empire create a powerful bias in favor of valuing and concentrating wealth. The economic principles of Earth Community have a bias in favor of life and an equitable distribution of wealth and ownership.

The work of the economic turning centers on developing local living economies that embody these characteristics while resisting the encroachment of global corporations on the rights and well-being of people and communities. The work includes promoting community investment and policy reforms that strengthen local ownership and create a persistent bias in favor of enterprises that are human-scale and owned by those whose livelihoods depend on them.

LIVING POLITICS

Most discussions of democracy focus on the institutions of political democracy and electoral politics. Without economic and cultural democracy, however, political democracy is more illusion than reality, because those who control the processes of economic and cultural choice ultimately control political choice.

The politics of Empire play out as a win-lose competition between elite power brokers who seek personal gain by controlling strategic resources through the control of information, dissent, and rule making. The politics of Earth Community play out as a cooperative effort to solve problems and grow the potential of the whole through open deliberation and consensus building in community forums, the free flow of information through independent media, and the decision making of an open political process.

Citizen Deliberation

Democracy is a hollow exercise when reduced to citizens voting every few years for a preselected slate of candidates known primarily through carefully crafted TV advertisements. The practice of real democracy involves a continuing and vibrant citizen engagement in meaningful deliberations in a wide variety of public forums. These can range from a modest neighborhood gathering in someone's living room; to events organized by local churches, colleges, and community services organizations; and to complex networks organized by national citizen groups using electronic communications media and polling technology to involve thousands, even millions, of people.

America Speaks, a U.S. organization created and led by Carolyn Lukensmeyer, is pioneering approaches that use state-of-the-art communications technologies to engage thousands of citizens in dialogues on local and national issues such as Social Security, to develop a consensus on priorities, to encourage civic engagement, and to communicate community views to policy makers.[1] Since 1982 the Kettering Foundation has been supporting public forums dealing with a range of national issues including health care, campaign finance reform, and national security. In a time of public disengagement, sound-bite journalism, and PR spin, such initiatives are crucial to the process of democracy in order to open the public mind to a wide range of perspectives and possibilities and engage the public in a deep assessment of values and priorities.

Independent Media

As discussed in chapter 4, the human species is in the midst of a communications revolution that is linking the world into a seamless web of communications that can be used either to strengthen elite control or to create an open-access commons with direct communication among people, families, and communities. The profit-driven communications model of the corporate media leads to a further concentration of elite power and control and reproduces the social pathologies of Empire. The service-driven communications model of independent media de-concentrates and democratizes media control, creating a vast potential to accelerate human learning, advance the awakening of Cultural and Spiritual Consciousness, and hasten a global embrace of the life-affirming cultural values of Earth Community.

Advancing a turning from the autocratic corporate media model to the democratic independent media model is an essential priority for citizen initiatives and policy advocacy. There are endless creative possibilities, as many Cultural and Spiritual Creatives are already demon-strating. They are blogging and podcasting; creating magazines, com-munity newspapers, independent radio networks, and low-power community radio stations; and establishing independent media centers. All these are elements of a growing, self-organizing system of independ-ent media.

Others are engaged in resisting corporate media concentration by claiming the communications frequency spectrum and the copper and fiber-optic conduits that deliver electronic media and the Internet as community resources managed as regulated, open-access public utili-ties. Each such initiative contributes to weakening the hold of corporate media monopolies, breaking through censorship barriers, exposing the bias and banality of corporate media programming, and opening polit-ical deliberation to diverse voices and lively debate.

Open Political Process

In the end, elected representatives must translate favored solutions into the decisions that govern public rules and priorities. This requires an open, fair, and honest electoral system responsive to the full spectrum of pop-ular views and interests. The 2000 and 2004 U.S. presidential elections provided a troubling reminder of how far short of this ideal the electoral system in the United States falls. Many of the failings are the result of intentional efforts to subvert the democratic process in the grab for polit-ical power. Following are some of the reforms advocated by U.S. citizen groups to open and democratize U.S. politics and the electoral system.

RIGHT TO VOTE. All adult citizens must be guaranteed the right to vote in a convenient, adequately equipped, and secure polling place and to have their votes duly counted according to voter intentions.

PUBLIC FINANCING. Public elections must be publicly financed under clear and open standards to reduce opportunities for corruption and to focus the attention of elected officials and aspirants on issues and their accountability to the electorate.

VOTING INTEGRITY. Voting machines must use open-source software subject to independent citizen audit, and they must produce a verified record of every vote to support manual recounts in the event of machine malfunction or suspected rigging.

NONPARTISAN ELECTION ADMINISTRATION. Election administration should be the responsibility of nonpartisan officials required to avoid any appearance of partiality. This seems so obvious as to not require mention, yet in the United States elections are administered by partisan state-level officials who are elected by party affiliation and sometimes even serve as campaign managers for contesting candidates, creating a blatant but currently wholly legal conflict of interest that undermines the credibility of the system.

DIRECT ELECTION BASED ON ONE PERSON, ONE VOTE. Replace the Electoral College system, which gives some votes several times the weight of others in presidential races and which can produce a president who receives significantly fewer votes than his opponent, with a system of direct election based on the fundamental principle of one person, one vote.

MEDIA ACCESS. Require radio and television stations licensed to use the public airwaves to provide free airtime for ballot-qualified candidates and the discussion of public issues by persons of diverse views. Allowing the corporations that are granted control of this limited and extremely valuable public resource to grant access only to those politicians who are able to pay whatever advertising fees the stations choose to charge is a major contributor to political corruption.

OPEN DEBATES. Place the administration of political debates in the hands of scrupulously nonpartisan organizations and open them to participation by all credible candidates to give voice to a wider range of points of view.

EQUAL REPRESENTATION. Open the political process to more voices and create an opening for minority representation by instituting instant runoff voting and proportional representation.[2]

POLITICAL RIGHTS FOR PEOPLE. Limit political rights and participation to natural persons and to organizations composed of natural-person members and formed for the specific and exclusive purpose of political action. Corporations organized for the purpose of making money for their owners are artificial legal entities granted a public charter to fulfill a public purpose. It is their responsibility to obey the law, not to write it, and they are properly barred from any effort to influence elections or legislation.

LIVING CULTURES

Living cultures flow from life in family and community and nurture the development of our higher orders of consciousness. As the institutions of Empire have co-opted and centralized the processes of culture formation, they have not only propagated false cultural values but have also weakened the bonds of family and community.

One of the Great Turning's most important challenges is to convert, through an incremental bottom-up process, four primary institutions of imperial culture—family, education, media, and religion—into institutions of living culture supportive of authentic cultural expression and the development of the higher orders of consciousness. The goal is to make cultural formation a participatory and intentional process through which we each discover our own distinctive cultural identity and simultaneously expand our awareness of the creative value of the cultural diversity of the species, thus building mutual trust and facilitating cooperative sharing and exchange.

Family

In modern times Empire has decimated family relationships, first of the extended family and then of the nuclear family. Like any other human institution, extended and nuclear families can be violent centers of oppression, loving centers of creative expression, or anything in between. The basic institution, however, is crucial as a source of the enduring relationships essential to our healthful individual development—and particularly to the healthful development of our children. The challenge is to make those relationships caring and nurturing. The changes come one family at a time but are far easier to achieve when supported by family-friendly living economies and public policies—both arenas for constructive citizen action, as discussed previously. Fractured though it has become, the nuclear family is still common. The extended family has become less common, and we easily forget its benefits.

The extended families of more traditional societies served as the basic unit of social organization and provided an intergenerational support system. Children had multiple stable caretakers to whom they could turn for help and with whom they could bond. Parents could count on sharing resources and the burdens of child care with those who shared the bonds of kinship. Elders remained active and valued and knew they would have caring help near at hand in the event of infirmity. Family celebrations also commonly featured singing, dancing, and other forms of artistic expression.

In modern societies in which even the standard two-parent nuclear family is at risk, it may be neither possible nor appropriate to return to the often insular and oppressive model of the extended biological family. It is possible, however, to create virtual families within the context of intentional communities—such as co-housing compounds and eco-villages—that offer many of the benefits of the extended biological family, with fewer of the disabilities. Such communities readily accommodate a variety of nuclear-family arrangements within virtual extended-family groupings that offer the benefits of age and gender diversity and multiple providers of child and elder care, while being relatively more open and less confining than the biological extended family.

It is essential to social health that families and extended family communities are supported by economic and social policies that encourage the creation of family-wage jobs and the flexible integration of family, work, and community life; multifamily cooperative housing arrangements; and the legalization of stable, caring civil unions and domestic partnerships.

Education

The capacity and desire to learn are inherent in our human nature. We are born to learn from the day of our birth to the day of our death. Empire, however, has given us schools that too often serve as institutions for the confinement and test-driven regimentation of children isolated from the life of community. Such schools are well suited to preparing children for obedient service to the institutions of Empire, but not for life and leadership in vibrant human communities nor for roles as social architects of a new human era. It is little wonder that so many youth rebel, drop out, and turn to sex, drugs, and violence in a desperate effort—as elaborated in chapter 17—to establish any kind of relationship that affirms their existence, even if in fleeting and ultimately self-destructive ways.

It will fall to today's children to reinvent practically everything. Supporting them in developing both the basic skills and the qualities of mind required is an essential responsibility of the current adult generation.

With heroic effort, the best schools and teachers are organizing their classrooms as learning communities that reach beyond the physical walls of the school. Through their involvement in collaborative research and community-service activities, students develop basic skills in reading, writing, and mathematics along with skills in learning, teamwork, citizenship, and artistic expression as they discover the interlinking patterns of their community's history, ecology, and function.[3]

At its best, a school may become a true community learning center that facilitates the lifelong learning of both children and adults through active engagement in community life. Professional and volunteer coaches can help both children and adults draw on all the learning tools their community offers—including opportunities for voluntary community service and internships. Teenagers may receive instruction in the arts of supportive parenting by acting as tutors and caretakers for younger children under the mentoring eye of elders who in turn receive coaching from their peers in the arts of the elder's mentoring role.

Local artists may share their skills in drama, music, the visual arts, poetry, and literature with both children and adults through programs of community beautification and cultural enrichment. Local, national, and international cross-cultural dialogue and exchange programs may actively facilitate the awakening of Cultural Consciousness. Political and religious inquiry may be encouraged and supported by inviting those of differing political and religious traditions to explicate and reflect on their views within settings of respectful dialogue and debate.

There is also a movement among creative dissidents in colleges and university within the United States and around the world to make the university a resource for democratic citizenship and community service. In the United States, 950 college and university presidents have joined

Campus Compact, pledging support for students, faculty, and staff who collaborate with their communities in projects that deal with major public issues.[4] The U.S.-based Democracy Collaborative is a consortium of more than twenty major university research centers cooperating in research, teaching, and community action intended to strengthen democracy and civil society locally, nationally, and globally.[5]

Religion

Many people look to religious institutions as a source of moral guidance. Religion in the service of Empire has often seriously distorted moral teaching and actively suppressed serious moral inquiry. Individual churches, however, generally have considerable freedom to take a different course, to become centers of community building and ethical inquiry and expression—if their members and leadership are so inclined. People of faith who argue that schools should engage students in the examination of alternative theories of creation might well start by demonstrating within their own churches how such instruction might work. In the course of doing so, they would introduce their own members to a process of moral and ethical inquiry rarely seen within the faith community outside of special cloisters and theological seminaries.

Through interfaith councils, they can reach out to explore moral questions with persons of different faiths, thereby learning from others while building cultural awareness and a respect for the diversity of religious traditions. Through community service, church members can develop a consciousness of class and explore the conflicting interpretations of what sacred teaching counsels with regard to proper human relationships. Our churches also have a natural role in facilitating interracial exchanges and dialogue, an essential aspect of awakening and deepening Cultural Consciousness.

Again, such reforms come one church, synagogue, temple, and mosque at a time. Each such initiative becomes additive to a larger process of democratizing the institutions of religion and, more broadly, the institutions of culture and of the larger society.

Empire flourishes when we are content to sleepwalk through life, accepting and playing by the rules presented to us. That is not what being human is supposed to be about. We are an intelligent, self-aware, choice-making species participating in an epic creative journey. When Creation bestowed on us humans a capacity for wise and creative choice, it was presumably with the intention that we use this capacity to beneficial ends.

The birthing of Earth Community begins with liberating the mind from the tyranny of the belief that there is no alternative to Empire. It moves forward as millions of people who glimpse possibilities long denied translate their deepening awareness into new practice.

The ancient Greeks glimpsed the possibility of a democratic alternative and undertook a bold but partial and ultimately abortive experiment to translate their vision of the possible into practice. The patriots of the American Revolution glimpsed a similar possibility and, against seemingly impossible odds, revived the experiment. Partial though the early American experiment proved to be, its vision of possibility ultimately spread throughout the world to create the opportunity now before us to bring the vision to full fruition.

Whether our time will be known as the time of the Great Turning or the time of the Great Unraveling is a question of choice, not destiny. The leadership must come from the growing number of those among us who have awakened from the cultural trance, said no to the addictions of Empire, and acquired the perspective and wisdom of a mature human consciousness.

As growing millions of Cultural and Spiritual Creatives reach out to one another to form communities of congruence, they create liberated spaces in which to experiment with cultural and institutional innovations based on partnership, shared learning, and ever expanding alliances. This is democratic participation in its fullest and most authentic expression.

True democracy is more than a particular set of institutions. It is a living practice expressed through living economies, politics, and cultures. Because life is a never ending process of self-renewal in pursuit of unrealized potential, this living practice leads to the continuous evolution of society's underlying institutional forms in response to changing imperatives and opportunities. This is the lesson to which we now stand poised to give expression. Democracy was an audacious experiment in the eighteenth century. This is the twenty-first century. It is time to bring democracy to full fruition.

CHAPTER 22

Change the Story, Change the Future

> History is governed by those overarching movements that give shape and meaning to life by relating the human venture to the larger destinies of the universe. Creating such a movement might be called the Great Work of a people…. The historical mission of our times is to reinvent the human—at the species level, with critical reflection, within the community of life-systems.[1]
>
> *Thomas Berry*

> To embrace a turning point is to see someone or something differently and then to take action on what you have seen…. These moments, where insight and action intersect, are the training ground for living a life of personal courage.[2]
>
> *Puanani Burgess*

If you feel out of step with the way things are going in your community, nation, and the world, take heart. Your distress indicates that you are among the sane in an insane world and in very good company. Recall the observation of Elisabet Sahtouris in chapter 17 that life has characteristically learned to cooperate through experiencing the negative consequences of unbridled competition. This is the present situation of our species. For some five thousand years, we have experienced the consequences of unbridled competition. Those consequences have now become so severe, and the overhead costs of maintaining Empire's dominator hierarchy so high, that either we learn to cooperate or we suffer the fate of other unviable species that failed to learn life's most essential lesson.

TO CHANGE THE FUTURE

It is impossible to exaggerate the creative challenge before us. Six and a half billion humans must make a choice to change course, to turn to life as our defining value and to partnership as the model for our relations with one another and the planet. Then we must reinvent our cultures, our institutions, and ourselves accordingly. It seems a hopelessly ambitious agenda, yet the key to success is elegantly simple: free ourselves from Empire's cultural trance by changing the stories by which we define our possibilities and responsibilities.

Many of us have serious doubts about the validity and values of the prevailing imperial stories. Yet because we rarely hear them challenged by credible voices, we fear ridicule if we give voice to our doubts. Truth silenced becomes truth denied.

The process of change begins as those who experience an awakening of the higher orders of human consciousness find the courage to break the silence by speaking openly of the truth in their hearts. The more openly we each speak our truth, the more readily others find the courage to speak theirs. We can then more easily find one another and end our isolation as we form communities of congruence in which we share our insights, bolster our courage, and give expression to stories that demonstrate and celebrate the possibilities of Earth Community. As we learn to communicate these stories to an ever growing audience, we begin to tip the cultural balance in favor of Earth Community, thereby changing the course of the human future. We break the silence, end our isolation, and change the story in a continuous cycle that gains momentum with each iteration. (Figure 22.1 is a graphic representation of this dynamic.) Call these expanding conversations Earth Community Dialogues. You can find helpful resources at http://www.greatturning .org/.

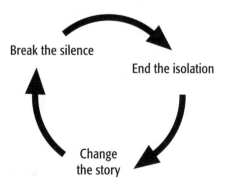

Break the silence

End the isolation

Change
the story

FIGURE 22.1: To change the future

It is hard to admit that we have been living a lie, as to do so seems to call into question our intelligence and integrity. Yet we are in good company, for living a lie has been a chronic affliction of most members of our species for thousands of years. Let us celebrate the awakening that is the key to breaking free from Empire's play-or-die dynamic.

Walk away from the king and join in solidarity to create a different game. It is the basic principle articulated in the question that drove the resistance to the draft in the United States during the Vietnam War: What if they called a war and no one came?

The momentum is building. Around the world people are organizing from the grass roots up to take back their lives, reject calls to war and violence, rebuild their local economies and communities, democratize their political institutions, and create authentic cultures.[3]

Most Earth Community initiatives are small and tentative. Many disappear without a trace. But hope lies in the geometric growth of their numbers, scale, and the linkages among them. Some—like the Landless Workers' Movement in Brazil and the Green Belt Movement in Kenya —have already achieved sufficient scale to inspire people throughout the world. Millions of such initiatives give substance to a shared vision of the world that can be. The faster they grow and link, the faster the human story changes and the faster the life energy of the human species turns away from Empire and aligns with Earth Community.

We are beginning to see whole national stories shifting, particularly in the South American countries of Argentina, Bolivia, Brazil, Chile, Ecuador, Uruguay, and Venezuela. By March 2005, when Uruguayan president Tabare Vazquez was inaugurated, three-quarters of South America's 355 million people were living under governments that were rejecting the doctrinaire economic ideology of neoliberalism for political visions reflecting a tilt in the direction of Earth Community.[4] Elsewhere smaller countries such as Denmark and New Zealand show potential to serve as national laboratories that demonstrate the possibilities of a new era.

FINDING OUR PLACE

To avoid being overwhelmed by the magnitude of the work before us, we need to keep three things in mind. Although the work may at times seem lonely, tens of millions, perhaps hundreds of millions, of people are already engaged in it. Second, every contribution, no matter how seemingly insignificant, helps shift the balance. Third, we each can do no more than our individual best.

When I'm feeling discouraged by the seeming inadequacy of my efforts, I find comfort in the wisdom of Vandana Shiva, whom I mentioned earlier as a partner in the initial framing of this book. Shiva travels constantly, electrifying audiences the world over with her penetrating critique of corporate globalization and her call to create the world that can be. She honors her Indian identity and nationality and is at the same time a true global citizen. Equally comfortable leading street protests, meeting with peasant farmers to revive the traditional practices of saving and exchanging seeds, negotiating with powerful political leaders, or lecturing to packed auditoriums in prestigious universities, she exemplifies the life, philosophy, and humility of the highly evolved Spiritual Consciousness. She is totally engaged in the world, yet maintains the deep sense of inner calm and graciousness of a religious mystic as she pursues her activism as a spiritual practice.

YES! magazine executive editor Sarah van Gelder asked Shiva in an interview how she does it. Shiva replied:

> Well, it's always a mystery, because you don't know why you get depleted or recharged. But, this much I know. I do not allow myself to be overcome by hopelessness, no matter how tough the situation. I believe that if you just do your little bit without thinking of the bigness of what you stand against, if you turn to the enlargement of your own capacities, just that in itself creates new potential.
>
> And I've learned from the Bhagavad Gita and other teachings of our culture to detach myself from the results of what I do, because those are not in my hands. The context is not in your control, but your commitment is yours to make, and you can make the deepest commitment with a total detachment about where it will take you. You want it to lead to a better world, and you shape your actions and take full responsibility for them, but then you have detachment. And that combination of deep passion and deep detachment allows me always to take on the next challenge because I don't cripple myself, I don't tie myself in knots. I function

like a free being. I think getting that freedom is a social duty because I think we owe it to each other not to burden each other with prescription and demands. I think what we owe each other is a celebration of life and to replace fear and hopelessness with fearlessness and joy.[5]

RESPONDING TO THE CALL

Life is a journey, not a destination. We have no idea of the limits of its possibilities. Just as our forebears of even a hundred years ago could not have imagined the possibilities that we now enjoy, we cannot imagine today the possibilities of those who will live a hundred, two hundred, or a thousand years hence.

By the standards of cosmic time, we humans have proved to be remarkably fast learners. During a mere two and a half million years we have developed the capacity for speech, mastered the use of fire, and learned to produce and use sophisticated tools, engage in artistic expression, cultivate our own food, communicate in written form, and establish highly organized societies and systems of knowledge. We are now reaching out to the stars and plumbing the secrets of matter and genetics.

This has occurred in a flash of evolutionary time, providing proof of the evolutionary potential of the gift of reflective consciousness that Creation chose to bestow on our species. Yet five thousand years ago, faced with the organizational challenge of dealing with growing population densities, our forebears made a choice for the dominator relations of Empire. A self-destructive era of warfare, greed, racism, sexism, and suppression of the higher orders of human consciousness followed. We now face the imperative and the opportunity to embark on a path to a new era grounded in the partnership relations of Earth Community.

The time of reckoning with the consequences of Empire's excess is no longer a future event. It is now upon us. Increasing oil prices are but one indicator of the unraveling of an economy based on the depletion of nonrenewable natural resources. An increase in the frequency and severity of extreme weather events is only the most dramatic indicator of the unraveling of the established human relationship with the living systems of the planet. Growth in the frequency and destructiveness of terrorist attacks signal an unraveling in the capacity of Empire to impose its will on subject peoples. Each of these unravelings creates an imperative for a turning from the relationships of Empire to the relationships of Earth Community.

We are getting a wake-up call we cannot ignore. How we respond will determine whether Creation's gift of reflective consciousness was well conceived or overly reckless. To pass the test before us, we humans must demonstrate the intelligence and the moral maturity to liberate ourselves from the addictions of Empire and to use our gifts wisely in the service of the whole.

Rather than give in to despair in this often frightening time, let us rejoice in the privilege of being alive at a moment of creative opportunity unprecedented in the human experience. Peace and justice for all and a sustainable relationship to the planet are within our reach. If we fail to embrace the opportunity, Empire's pessimistic assumption that we are an inherently destructive species becomes a self-fulfilling prophecy and we continue on the path of the Great Unraveling. If we pass the test, we move on to the exploration and realization of untold new possibilities.

Our time has come to trade the sorrows of Empire for the joys of Earth Community. Let our descendants look back on this time as the time of the Great Turning, when humanity made a bold choice to birth a new era devoted to actualizing the higher potentials of our human nature.

The work begins with embracing the truth that it is within our means to choose our future and to place our capacity for reflective choice at the service of Creation's continued unfolding. We are the ones we have been waiting for.

Notes

THE GREAT TURNING

1. Joanna Macy, "The Shift to a Life-Sustaining Civilization," para. 3 on the Web page "The Great Turning," n.d., http://www.joannamacy.net/html/great.html.

Prologue: In Search of the Possible

1. Giovanni Pico della Mirandola, *De hominis dignitate*, as translated by the revered Anglican theologian Richard Hooker (1554–1600).

2. Further details of my life journey can be found in the prologues to *When Corporations Rule the World* and *The Post-Corporate World: Life after Capitalism* and on my Web site (http://www.davidkorten.org/).

3. Deirdre Strachan and David C. Korten, "The Overcrowded Clinic," in Frances F. Korten and David C. Korten, *Casebook for Family Planning Management* (Boston: Pathfinder Fund, 1977), 49–62.

4. The details are extensively documented in Frances F. Korten and Robert Y. Siy Jr., *Transforming a Bureaucracy: The Experience of the Philippine National Irrigation Administration* (West Hartford, CT: Kumarian, 1988); Benjamin U. Bagadion and Frances F. Korten, "Developing Irrigators' Organizations: A Learning Process Approach," in *Putting People First: Sociological Variables in Rural Development,* ed. Michael M. Cernea (New York: Oxford University Press, 1985), 52–90; and David C. Korten, "Community Organization and Rural Development: A Learning Process Approach," *Public Administration Review*, September/October 1980, 480–511.

5. Key works include Mae-Wan Ho, *The Rainbow and the Worm: The Physics of Organisms*, 2nd ed. (Singapore: World Scientific, 1998); Elisabet Sahtouris, *EarthDance: Living Systems in Evolution* (San Jose, CA: iUniversity Press, 2000), also at http://www.ratical.org/LifeWeb/Erthdnce/erthdnce.html; Sidney Liebes, Elisabet Sahtouris, and Brian Swimme, *A Walk through Time: From Stardust to Us: The Evolution of Life on Earth* (New York: John Wiley & Sons, 1998). For an extensive Sahtouris bibliography see http://www.ratical.org/LifeWeb/. For a guide to the ideas and publications of Ho see http://www.ratical.org/co-globalize/MaeWanHo/.

6. A detailed history of the Earth Charter Initiative is available at http://www.earthcharterusa.org/earth_charter.html.

7. Frances Korten and Roberto Vargas, *Movement-Building for Transformation: Bringing Together Diverse Leaders for Connection and Vision* (Bainbridge Island, WA: Positive Futures Network, 2006).

8. We published our joint paper on the Web site of the People-Centered Development Forum in December 2002. David C. Korten, Nicanor Perlas, and Vandana Shiva, "Global Civil Society: The Path Ahead," a discussion paper, http://www.pcdf.org/civilsociety/.

PART I: Choosing Our Future
Chapter 1: The Choice

1. Michael Lerner, "Surviving the Bush and Sharon Years," editorial, *Tikkun*, March/April 2001.

2. Riane Eisler, *The Chalice and the Blade*, rev. ed. (San Francisco: HarperSanFrancisco, 1995), xix–xxiii.

3. This story is abstracted from a teaching case I wrote with John C. Ickis while on the faculty of the Central American Management Institute in Nicaragua.

4. Eisler, *Chalice and Blade*.

5. See http://www.earthcharter.org/ for more details.

6. This discussion of the defining narratives draws from Korten, Perlas, and Shiva, "Global Civil Society."

7. Eisler, *Chalice and Blade*.

8. Jonathan Schell, *The Unconquerable World: Power, Nonviolence, and the Will of the People* (New York: Metropolitan Books, 2003), 28–31.

9. Andrew B. Schmookler, *The Parable of the Tribes: The Problem of Power in Social Evolution*, 2nd ed. (Albany, NY: State University of New York Press, 1994).

10. Viktor E. Frankl, *Man's Search for Meaning*, rev. ed. (New York: Pocket Books, 1984).

11. Ibid., 86–87, 157.

12. Ibid., 86–87.

Chapter 2: The Possibility

1. The description of these five stages is based primarily on Robert Kegan's framing, but it also draws from the work of other developmental psychologists, including Jean Piaget, Erik Erikson, Lawrence Kohlberg, Carol Gilligan, and Stanley Greenspan, to bring in a stronger focus on the moral and emotional dimensions. I am particularly indebted to Larry Daloz and Sharon Parks, who worked with Kegan at Harvard for some years, for their assistance in interpreting and elaborating the Kegan categories. In addition to Kegan's work, the descriptions of the third and fourth orders draw on Eleanor Drago-Severson, *Becoming Adult Learners: Principles and Practices for Effective Development* (New York: Teachers College Press, 2004), 23–32. Discussion of the fifth order draws in part on Laurent A. Parks Daloz, "Transformative Learning for Bioregional Citizenship," in *Learning toward an Ecological Consciousness: Selected Transformative Practices*, ed. Edmund O'Sullivan and Marilyn M. Taylor (New York: Palgrave Macmillan, 2004).

2. Robert Kegan, *In over Our Heads: The Mental Demands of Modern Life* (Cambridge, MA: Harvard University Press, 1994), 39.

3. Robert Kegan, *The Evolving Self: Problem and Process in Human Development* (Cambridge, MA: Harvard University Press, 1982), 56.

4. Paul H. Ray and Sherry Ruth Anderson, *The Cultural Creatives: How 50 Million People Are Changing the World* (New York: Harmony Books, 2000).

5. John C. Friel and Linda Friel, *The Soul of Adulthood: Opening the Doors...* (Deerfield Beach, FL: Health Communications, 1995), 120.

6. Kegan, *In over Our Heads*, 40–41.

7. See Daniel Maguire, *A Moral Creed for All Christians*, forthcoming from Fortress Press.

Chapter 3: The Imperative

1. Frankl, *Man's Search for Meaning*, 179 (see chap. 1, n. 10).

2. Episode 74 first aired on February 28, 1969.

3. Worldwatch Institute, *Vital Signs 2003: Trends That Are Shaping Our Future* (New York: W.W. Norton, 2003), 29.

4. Janet L. Sawin, "Making Better Energy Choices," in Worldwatch Institute, *State of the World 2004*, ed. Linda Starke (New York: W.W. Norton, 2004), 29.

5. Christopher Flavin in Worldwatch Institute, *State of the World 2004*, xviii.

6. Worldwatch Institute, *Vital Signs 2003*, 35, 41, 49.

7. World Wildlife Fund for Nature, *Living Planet Report 2002* (Cambridge, UK: WWF, 2002). Available at http:// www.panda.org/ downloads/general/LPR_2002.pdf.

8. Ibid.

9. Chris Bright, "A History of Our Future," in Worldwatch Institute, *State of the World 2004*, 5.

10. Intergovernmental Panel on Climate Change, World Meteorological Association and United Nations Environment Programme, *Third Assessment Report: Climate Change 2001* (Geneva: 2001), available at http://www.ipcc.ch/pub/online.htm.

11. Jonathan Leake, "Britain Faces Big Chill as Ocean Current Slows," *Sunday Times*, May 8, 2005, http://www.timesonline.co.uk/ article/0,,2087-1602579,00.html.

12. Intergovernmental Panel on Climate Change, *Third Assessment Report*.

13. Peter Schwartz and Doug Randall, *An Abrupt Climate Change Scenario and Its Implications for United States National Security*, October 2003, 1–2, 22, available at http://www.gbn.com/ ArticleDisplayServlet.srv?aid= 26231.

14. Sawin, "Making Better Energy Choices," 27.

15. James Howard Kunstler, *The Long Emergency: Surviving the Long Catastrophes of the Twenty-first Century* (New York: Atlantic Monthly Press, 2005).

16. Nicholas Varchaver, "How to Kick the Oil Habit," *Fortune*, August 23, 2004, 102.

17. The implications for humanity of system overshoot and collapse on a finite planet was a defining theme of Donella H. Meadows et al., *The Limits to Growth* (New York: New American Library, 1972).

18. Worldwatch Institute, *Vital Signs 2003*, 34–35.

19. Kunstler, *The Long Emergency*.

20. James Howard Kunstler, "The Long Emergency," *Rolling Stone*, March 24, 2005, http://www.rollingstone .com/politics/story/_/id/7203633.

21. Ibid.

22. See compilations by Matthew White, available at http://users .erols.com/ mwhite28/warstat8 .htm; and Piero Scaruffi, http://www.scaruffi.com/politics/ massacre.html.

23. World Health Organization, *Injuries and Violence Prevention*, n.d., http://www.who.int/violence_ injury_prevention/violence/ collective/ collective/en/ index2.html.

24. United Nations, "Land Mine Facts" press kit for International Conference on Mine Clearance Technology, 2N, July 4, 1996, Copenhagen, http://www.un.org/Depts/dha/ mct/facts.htm.

25. Doug Rokke, interview by Sunny Miller, "The War against Ourselves," *YES! A Journal of Positive Futures*, Spring 2003, http://www

.yesmagazine.org/article.asp?ID=
594.

26. Chalmers Johnson, *The Sorrows of Empire: Militarism, Secrecy, and the End of the Republic* (New York: Henry Holt, 2004), 100.

27. Public Broadcasting Service, *Now* report on posttraumatic stress disorder, http://www.pbs.org/now/ society/ptsd.html.

28. Immanuel Wallerstein, "The Eagle Has Crash Landed," *Foreign Policy*, July 1, 2002, 60–68.

29. This argument is set forth in elegant detail in Schell, *Unconquerable World* (see chap. 1, n. 8).

30. United Nations Development Programme, *2003 Human Development Report* (New York: Oxford University Press, 2003), 2–8.

31. Luisa Kroll and Lea Goldman, "The World's Billionaires," *Forbes*, March 10, 2005, http://www.forbes .com/billionaires/2005/03/10/cz_lk _lg_0310billintro_billo5.html.

32. Matthew Bentley, "Sustainable Consumption: Ethics, National Indices and International Relations" (PhD dissertation, American Graduate School of International Relations and Diplomacy, Paris, 2003), as reported by Flavin in World-Watch, *State of the World 2004*, xvii.

33. United Nations, "World Population Prospects: The 2002 Revision," February 26, 2003, vi.

34. Market capitalization figures available by subscription from Datastream, a division of Thomson Financial.

35. Edward N. Wolff, *Top Heavy: The Increasing Inequality of Wealth in America and What Can Be Done about It* (New York: New Press, 2002), 29–30.

36. Nelson D. Schwartz, "The Dollar in the Dumps," *Fortune*, December 13, 2004, 113–14.

37. Ibid.

38. Emmanuel Todd, *After the Empire: The Breakdown of the American Order* (New York: Columbia University Press, 2003), 123.

39. Pete Engario and Dexter Roberts, "The China Price," *Business Week*, December 6, 2004, 102–12.

40. Barney Gimbel, "Yule Log Jam," *Fortune*, December 13, 2004, 162–70.

41. Engario and Roberts, "China Price."

42. Stephen Baker and Manjeet Kripalani, "Sofware: Will Outsourcing Hurt America's Supremacy?" *Business Week*, March 1, 2004, 84–94.

43. "Inside the New China," *Fortune*, October 4, 2004, 92.

44. Engario and Roberts, "China Price."

45. *Argentina: Hope in Hard Times* was produced by Mark Dworkin and Melissa Young. For information see http://www.movingimages.org/ page22.html. *The Take* was produced by Avi Lewis and Naomi Klein. See http:// www.nfb.ca/ webextension/thetake/.

Chapter 4: The Opportunity

1. As quoted by Philip H. Duran, "Eight Indigenous Prophecies," http://home.earthlink.net/ ~phil-duran/prophecies.htm.

2. Thomas Berry, *The Great Work* (New York: Bell Tower, 1999), 201.

3. This characterization of the organizer cells is from John Feltwell, *The Natural History of Butterflies* (New York: Facts on File, 1986), 23.

4. Elisabet Sahtouris, *EarthDance: Living Systems in Evolution* (San Jose, CA: iUniversity Press, 2000), 206–7.

5. Paul Ray and Sherry Anderson, interview by Sarah Ruth van Gelder, "A Culture Gets Creative," *YES! A Journal of Positive Futures*, Winter 2001. Ray and Anderson make the link between the civil rights movement and a widespread cultural awakening. Their insight triggered the realization for me that something far more profound is at work than simply a shift in values. In subsequent personal discussions Ray has affirmed his support for the thesis that what his research has uncovered is in fact evidence of a step to a new level of human consciousness that has profound implications.

6. Ray and Anderson, *Cultural Creatives* (see chap. 2, n. 4).

7. As reported by Duane Elgin and Coleen LeDrew, "Global Paradigm Report: Tracking the Shift Underway," *YES! A Journal of Positive Futures*, Winter 1997, 19; Duane Elgin with Coleen LeDrew, *Global Consciousness Change: Indicators of an Emerging Paradigm* (San Anselmo, CA: Millennium Project, 1997). For further information visit http://www.awakeningearth.org/.

8. Ronald Inglehart, *Modernization and Postmodernization: Cultural, Economic, and Political Change in 43 Societies* (Princeton, NJ: Princeton University Press, 1997).

9. Parker J. Palmer, interview by Sarah van Gelder, "Integral Life, Integral Teacher," *YES! A Journal of Positive Futures*, Winter 1999, http://www.yesmagazine.org/article.asp?ID=796.

10. The People's Earth Declaration is included as an annex to David C. Korten, *When Corporations Rule the World* (West Hartford, CT: Kumarian, and San Francisco: Berrett-Koehler, 1995). See also: *NGO Documents for the Earth Summit, 1992*, http://www.earthsummit2002.org/toolkits/Women/ngo-doku/ngo-conf/ngoearth5.htm.

11. For a text and further information on the Earth Charter see http://www.earthcharter.org/.

12. Frances F. Korten, "Report from the World Social Forum," *YES! A Journal of Positive Futures*, Spring 2004, http://www.yesmagazine.org/article.asp?ID=710.

13. Patrick E. Tyler, "A New Power in the Streets," *New York Times*, February 17, 2002.

14. Eisler, *Chalice and Blade*.

PART II: Sorrows of Empire

Introduction

1. Cornel West, "Finding Hope in Dark Times," *Tikkun*, July/August 2004, 18.

Chapter 5: When God Was a Woman

1. Eisler, *Chalice and Blade*, 20.

2. I use *gatherer-hunter* rather than the more familiar hunter-gatherer at the suggestion of Riane Eisler, who points out that in most of these societies the basic subsistence depended more on gathering than hunting. The conventional emphasis on hunting reflects a bias toward presenting men, who generally led the hunt, as the primary providers and downplaying the role of women, who more often had the responsibility for gathering.

3. Eisler, *Chalice and Blade*, 66.

4. Ibid., 66–69.

5. Edward McNall Burns, *Western Civilizations: Their History and Their Culture*, 5th ed. (New York: W.W. Norton, 1958), 11.

6. *Encyclopaedia Britannica 2003,* deluxe ed. CD, s.v. "Human Evolution"; Philip Lee Ralph et al., *Western Civilizations: Their History and Their Culture,* vol. 1, 9th ed. (New York: W.W. Norton, 1997), 6–8.

7. Jared Diamond, *Guns, Germs, and Steel: The Fates of Human Societies* (New York: W. W. Norton, 1999), 267–68.

8. Burns, *Western Civilizations,* 124.

9. Diamond, *Guns, Germs, and Steel,* 16.

10. Eisler, *Chalice and Blade,* 16–21.

11. Merlin Stone, *When God Was a Woman* (San Diego: Harcourt Brace, 1976), 2–4.

12. Eisler, *Chalice and Blade,* 28.

13. Brian Swimme and Thomas Berry, *The Universe Story* (San Francisco: HarperSanFrancisco, 1992), 168–84.

14. Eisler, *Chalice and Blade,* 28.

15. Sydney Smith, in *Myth, Ritual, and Kingship,* ed. S.H. Hooke (London: Oxford University Press, 1958), quoted in Stone, *When God Was a Woman,* 130.

16. Stone, *When God Was a Woman,* 41–42.

17. Ibid., 11–12.

18. A. Moortgat, *The Art of Ancient Mesopotamia* (London: Macmillan, 1970), quoted in Stone, *When God Was a Woman,* 130.

19. Quoted in Stone, *When God Was a Woman,* 34–35.

20. Stone, *When God Was a Woman,* 63–64.

21. Eisler, *Chalice and Blade,* 45.

22. Swimme and Berry, *Universe Story,* 184.

23. Eisler, *Chalice and Blade,* xxiii, 42–48, 51–53.

24. Ibid., 48–53.

25. Ibid., 91–92.

26. The global history of slavery is documented by Milton Meltzer in *Slavery: A World History* (New York: Da Capo, 1993), 1–3.

Chapter 6: Ancient Empire

1. Ilarion (Larry) Merculief, "The Gifts from the Four Directions," *YES! A Journal of Positive Futures,* Spring 2004, 44–45. Based on his studies of oral prophecy.

2. These sources include Ralph et al., *Western Civilizations;* Burns, *Western Civilizations;* Diamond, *Guns, Germs, and Steel;* Will Durant, *Heroes of History: A Brief History of Civilization from Ancient Times to the Dawn of the Modern Age* (New York: Simon & Schuster, 2001); *Encyclopaedia Britannica 2003,* deluxe ed. CD; and a variety of Web resources, including the BBC Internet service history collection, http://www.bbc.co.uk/history/ (accessed September 10, 2005); and http://www.historyguide.org/.

3. Ralph et al., *Western Civilizations,* 32–33.

4. Burns, *Western Civilizations,* 77.

5. Ralph et al., *Western Civilizations,* 36.

6. Ibid., 44.

7. Burns, *Western Civilizations,* 76.

8. Ralph et al., *Western Civilizations,* 44.

9. Diamond, *Guns, Germs, and Steel,* 411.

10. Burns, *Western Civilizations,* 40.

11. Ibid., 46.

12. Ralph et al., *Western Civilizations,* 118–20.

13. Andrew Wallace-Hadrill, *Roman Empire: The Paradox of Power.* From the BBC Internet service

history collection, http://www.bbc
.co.uk/history/ancient/romans/.

14. Ralph et al., *Western Civilizations*,
229.

15. Ibid., 229–30.

16. Durant, *Heroes of History*, 143.

17. This brief survey of emperors who
ruled for more than a hundred
years of the roughly two-hundred-
year Pax Romana is compiled from
Encyclopaedia Britannica 2003,
deluxe ed. CD.

18. Ralph et al., *Western Civilizations*,
249.

19. Walter Wink, *Engaging the Powers:
Discernment and Resistance in a
World of Domination* (Minneapo-
lis: Fortress Press, 1992), 150.

20. Ralph et al., *Western Civilizations*,
711–14.

Chapter 7: Modern Empire

1. William Greider, *The Soul of Capi-
talism: Opening Paths to a Moral
Economy* (New York: Simon and
Schuster, 2003), 35.

2. *Encyclopaedia Britannica 2003*,
deluxe ed. CD, s.v. "Colonialism."
This includes the territories in the
Americas that by 1878 had won
their independence from England,
Spain, and Portugal.

3. Ibid., s.v. "Hernando de Soto."

4. *The Reader's Companion to American History*, s.v. "America in the
British Empire" (by Richard S.
Dunn), Houghton Mifflin College
Division, online edition, http://
college.hmco.com/history/
readerscomp/rcah/html/
ah_003000_americainthe.htm
(accessed October 22, 2005).

5. *Encyclopaedia Britannica 2003*,
deluxe ed. CD, s.v. "Privateer."

6. Kevin Phillips, *Wealth and Democracy* (New York: Broadway Books,
2002), 11, 14.

7. *Encyclopaedia Britannica 2003*,
deluxe ed. CD, s.v. "Morgan, Sir
Henry."

8. Ibid., s.v. "Privateer."

9. Ron Harris, *Industrializing English
Law: Entrepreneurship and Business
Organization, 1720–1844* (Cam-
bridge: Cambridge University
Press, 2000), 41–42, 46–47.

10. Ibid.

11. Burns, *Western Civilizations*, 467;
and *Encyclopaedia Britannica 1998*,
CD, s.v. "British East India Company."

12. *Encyclopaedia Britannica 1998*, CD,
s.v. "Opium Wars."

13. Mark Curtis, "The Ambiguities of
Power: British Foreign Policy since
1945," *The Ecologist* 26, no. 1 (Janu-
ary/February 1996): 5–12.

14. Marjorie Kelly, *The Divine Right of
Capital: Dethroning the Corporate
Aristocracy* (San Francisco: Berrett-
Koehler, 2001).

15. Frances Moore Lappé, *Democracy's
Edge* (Jossey-Bass, 2005), 109–11.

16. Curtis, "Ambiguities of Power."

17. See John Perkins, *Confessions of an
Economic Hit Man* (San Francisco:
Berrett-Koehler, 2004), for an insider account of exactly how it
worked.

18. For detailed documentation on the
real purpose and consequence of
contemporary trade agreements,
see Korten, *When Corporations
Rule the World*; International Forum
on Globalization, ed. John
Cavanagh and Jerry Mander, *Alternatives to Economic Globalization:
A Better World Is Possible* (San
Francisco: Berrett-Koehler, 2002);
Lori Wallach and Patrick Woodall,

Whose Trade Organization? Comprehensive Guide to the WTO (New York: New Press, 2003); and Jerry Mander and Edward Goldsmith eds., *The Case against the Global Economy and for a Turn to the Local* (San Francisco: Sierra Club Books, 1996).

19. See Korten, *When Corporations Rule the World*, 181–85, for further discussion of how money is created and manipulated.

20. "Creative Finance," *Forbes*, May 9, 2005, 46.

Chapter 8: Athenian Experiment

1. Lappé, *Democracy's Edge*.

2. Durant, *Heroes of History*, 80; and Ralph et al., *Western Civilizations*, 164.

3. Durant, *Heroes of History*, 76.

4. Burns, *Western Civilizations*, 152.

5. Those persons of foreign birth who were granted citizenship under the administration of Cleisthenes were an exception. Aristotle, arguably the greatest of all the Greek philosophers, was ineligible to become a citizen of Athens and was for this reason denied appointment as the head of the Academy of Plato in Athens following Plato's death.

6. Eva Keuls, *The Reign of the Phallus: Sexual Politics in Ancient Athens* (Berkeley and Los Angeles: University of California Press, 1993). See also Riane Eisler, *Sacred Pleasure: Sex, Myth, and the Politics of the Body* (New York: HarperCollins, 1995), 104–7.

7. Durant, *Heroes of History*, 80.

8. Jean L. Cohen and Andrew Arato, *Civil Society and Political Theory* (Cambridge, MA: MIT Press, 1992), 85.

9. *Aristotle: The Politics and the Constitution of Athens*, ed. Stephen Everson (Cambridge University Press, 1996), 16–17.

10. Cohen and Arato, *Civil Society*, 7.

11. Burns, *Western Civilizations*, 569.

PART III: America, the Unfinished Project

Chapter 9: Inauspicious Beginning

1. *The Reader's Companion to American History*, s.v. "Southern Colonies" (by Peter H. Wood), Houghton Mifflin College Division, online edition, http://college.hmco.com/history/readerscomp/rcah/html/ah_080500_southerncolo.htm (accessed October 22, 2005).

2. Donald S. Lutz, ed., *Colonial Origins of the American Constitution: A Documentary History* (Indianapolis: Liberty Fund, 1998), includes copies of the official documents spelling out the punishments designated for these and other crimes.

3. Harvey Wasserman, *America Born and Reborn* (New York: Collier Books, 1983), 19.

4. *The Reader's Companion to American History*, s.v, "America in the British Empire" (see chap. 7, n. 4); and Paul Boyer, "Apocalypticism Explained: The Puritans," *Frontline*, Public Broadcasting Service, http://www.pbs.org/wgbh/pages/frontline/shows/apocalypse/explanation/puritans.html.

5. Ibid.

6. Frank Lambert, *The Founding Fathers and the Place of Religion in America* (Princeton, NJ: Princeton University Press, 2003), presents a detailed study of these early dynamics.

7. John Cotton in "Letter to Lord Say and Sele," 1636, http://www .skidmore.edu/~tkuroda/hi321/ LordSay&Sele.htm.

8. Lambert, *Founding Fathers and Religion*, 92.

9. As quoted by Howard Zinn, *A People's History of the United States 1492–Present* (New York: Harper-Perennial, 1995), 1, 3.

10. Numerous such accounts are cited by Zinn, *People's History;* Thom Hartmann, *What Would Jefferson Do? A Return to Democracy* (New York: Harmony Books, 2004); and Wasserman, *America Born and Reborn.*

11. Zinn, *People's History*, 21.

12. Jack Weatherford, "The Untold Story of America's Democracy," *YES! A Journal of Positive Futures,* Spring 2002, 14–17; and Hartmann, *What Would Jefferson Do?*

13. Zinn, *People's History*, 11.

14. Ralph et al., *Western Civilizations*, 676–77.

15. Zinn, *People's History*, 13–16.

16. Priscilla Murolo and A.G. Chitty, *From the Folks Who Brought You the Weekend* (New York: New Press, 2001), 6.

17. Peter Kellman, "The Working Class History Test," in *Defying Corporations, Defining Democracy: A Book of History and Strategies*, ed. Dean Ritz (New York: Apex, 2001), 46–48.

18. Murolo and Chitty, *Folks Who Brought the Weekend*, 21.

19. Murolo and Chitty, *Folks Who Brought the Weekend*, 19; Roger Wilkins, *Jefferson's Pillow: The Founding Fathers and the Dilemma of Black Patriotism* (Boston: Beacon, 2001), 18–19; Zinn, *People's History*, 39–42.

20. Wilkins, *Jefferson's Pillow*, 19–20.

21. Wasserman, *America Born and Reborn*, 76.

Chapter 10: People Power Rebellion

1. In a letter to his friend Richard Rush, as quoted in Schell, *Unconquerable World*, 163 (see chap. 1, n. 8).

2. Leo Huberman, *We, the People: The Drama of America*, rev. ed. (New York: Monthly Review Press, 1947; Modern Reader, 1970), 43–44. Citations are to the Modern Reader edition.

3. Thom Hartmann, *Unequal Protection: The Rise of Corporate Dominance and the Theft of Human Rights* (Emmaus, PA: Rodale, 2002), 52–63; and Ted Nace, *Gangs of America: The Rise of Corporate Power and the Disabling of Democracy* (San Francisco: Berrett-Koehler, 2003), 41–45; Huberman, *We, the People*, 70.

4. *Encyclopaedia Britannica 2003*, deluxe ed. CD, s.v. "Continental Congress." For a copy of the declaration see http://www.constitution .org/bcp/colright.htm.

5. Schell, *Unconquerable World*, 160–63.

6. Wilkins, *Jefferson's Pillow*, 35–36.

Chapter 11: Empire's Victory

1. As reported by CBS News, "Bush and Gore Do New York," October 20, 2000, http://www.cbsnews .com/stories/2000/10/18/politics/ main242210.shtml. President Bush was speaking at the Al Smith fundraising dinner in New York City during the presidential campaign.

2. Wolff, *Top Heavy*, 3, 8 (see chap. 3, n. 35).

3. Thomas R. Dye, *Who's Running America? The Bush Restoration*, 7th

ed. (Upper Saddle River, NY: Prentice Hall, 2002), 204.

4. Huberman, *We, the People*, 75–78.

5. Thomas Jefferson to Samuel Kercheval, 1816, in *The Writings of Thomas Jefferson,* ed. A.A. Lipscomb and Albert E. Bergh, 20 vols. (Thomas Jefferson Memorial Association: Washington, DC, 1903-04), 15:39, http://etext.lib.virginia .edu/jefferson/quotations/ jeffo600.htm.

6. As quoted in Zinn, *People's History*, 95.

7. Zinn, *People's History*, 95.

8. Wilkins, *Jefferson's Pillow.*

9. Murolo and Chitty, *Folks Who Brought the Weekend*, 42.

10. Wasserman, *America Born and Reborn*, 53.

11. Wilkins, *Jefferson's Pillow.*

12. Murolo and Chitty, *Folks Who Brought the Weekend*, 43.

13. Phillips, *Wealth and Democracy*, 16–17 (see chap. 7, n. 6).

14. John Kenneth Galbraith, *Money: Whence It Came, Where It Went* (Boston: Houghton Mifflin, 1975), 73.

15. Phillips, *Wealth and Democracy*, 17; and William Greider, *Secrets of the Temple: How the Federal Reserve Runs the Country* (New York: Touchstone, 1989), 255.

16. See Greider, *Secrets of the Temple,* for a detailed authoritative account of the Federal Reserve.

17. Wasserman, *America Born and Reborn*, 56.

18. Ibid., 57.

19. Hartmann, *What Would Jefferson Do?*

20. Murolo and Chitty, *Folks Who Brought the Weekend*, 44–45.

21. Ibid., 43.

22. I am indebted to Professor Holly Youngbear-Tibbetts of the College of the Menomonee Nation for this characterization.

23. Zinn, *People's History*, 125–26.

24. Stephen F. Knott, *Secret and Sanctioned: Covert Operations and the American Presidency* (New York: Oxford University Press, 1996), 116–20; Zinn, *People's History*, 147–66; and *Encyclopaedia Britannica 2003*, deluxe ed. CD, s.v. "Alamo" and "History of Mexico."

25. See Nace, *Gangs of America*; and Hartmann, *Unequal Protection.*

26. Zinn, *People's History*, 290–91.

27. Ibid.

28. Albert Jeremiah Beveridge, a young scholar and lawyer later elected senator from Indiana, quoted in Stanley Karnow, *In Our Image: America's Empire in the Philippines* (New York: Random House, 1989), 109.

29. Knott, *Secret and Sanctioned*, 150–52.

30. Michael Parenti, *Against Empire* (San Francisco: City Lights Books, 1995), 38–39.

31. Laurence H. Shoup and William Minter, "Shaping a New World Order: The Council on Foreign Relations' Blueprint for World Hegemony," in *Trilateralism: The Trilateral Commission and Elite Planning for World Management*, ed. Holly Sklar (Boston: South End, 1980), 140–49.

32. As quoted in Noam Chomsky, *What Uncle Sam Really Wants* (Tucson, AZ: Odonian, 1992), 9–10.

33. Shoup and Minter, "Shaping a New World Order," 140–49.

34. As compiled by Parenti, *Against Empire*, 37–38.

35. Ibid.

36. "A Chronology of U.S. Military Interventions from Vietnam to the Balkans," *Frontline*, PBS Online and WGBH/Frontline, 1999, http://www.pbs.org/wgbh/pages/frontline/shows/military/etc/cron.html.

37. Perkins, *Economic Hit Man* (see chap. 7, n. 17).

Chapter 12: Struggle for Justice

1. From the "I Had a Dream" speech at the Lincoln Memorial, August 28, 1963.

2. See Zinn, *People's History*, 167–205, for extended documentation of black resistance.

3. Wasserman, *America Born and Reborn*, 78–80.

4. Murolo and Chitty, *Folks Who Brought the Weekend*, 94–95.

5. Ibid., 247–49.

6. Ibid., 250–52.

7. Wasserman, *America Born and Reborn*, 74.

8. Ibid., 75.

9. Sheila Tobias, *Faces of Feminism: An Activist's Reflections on the Women's Movement* (Boulder, CO: Westview, 1997), 22–25.

10. Figures based on information in *The World Almanac and Book of Facts 1997* (New York: St. Martin's); and Geoffrey Barraclough, "The Making of the United States: Westward Expansion 1783 to 1890," in *The Times Atlas of World History*, ed. Geoffrey Barraclough (London: Times Books, 1978), 220–21, http://www.globalpolicy.org/empire/history/1979/79westwardexp.htm.

11. Murolo and Chitty, *Folks Who Brought the Weekend*, 256.

12. *Houghton Mifflin Encyclopedia of North American Indians*, s.v. "Religious Rights" (by Irene S. Vernon) online edition, http://college.hmco.com/history/readerscomp/naind/html/na_032700_religiousrig.htm (accessed November 17, 2005).

13. The rise and fall of the populist movement is documented in detail by Lawrence Goodwyn, *The Populist Moment: A Short History of the Agrarian Revolt in America* (Oxford: Oxford University Press, 1978).

14. Zinn, *People's History*, 279–89; and Goodwyn, *Populist Moment*.

15. Murolo and Chitty, *Folks Who Brought the Weekend*, 59–60.

16. Ibid., 61–62.

17. Ibid., 61–63.

18. Ibid., 64–66.

19. Huberman, *We, the People*, 207.

20. Murolo and Chitty, *Folks Who Brought the Weekend*, 104–8. A gallery of photos of damage to rail facilities in Pittsburgh from the Great Railroad Strike of 1877 is maintained by the University of Pittsburgh at http://www.library.pitt.edu/labor_legacy/rrstrike1877.html.

21. Ibid., 110–12.

22. Huberman, *We, the People*, 235.

23. Murolo and Chitty, *Folks Who Brought the Weekend*, 111–12.

24. Ibid., 110–12.

25. Huberman, *We, the People*, 228.

26. Murolo and Chitty, *Folks Who Brought the Weekend*, 121–27.

27. Huberman, *We, the People*, 231–32.

28. Ibid., 233.

29. Murolo and Chitty, *Folks Who Brought the Weekend*, 150–51.

30. Zinn, *People's History*, 375–76; and Murolo and Chitty, *Folks Who Brought the Weekend*, 177–78.

31. Murolo and Chitty, *Folks Who Brought the Weekend*, 181–84.

32. Ibid., 186–93.

33. Ibid., 216.

34. *The World Almanac 1997*, 175.

35. Wolff, *Top Heavy*, 8–16.

Chapter 13: Wake-Up Call

1. Alan Crawford, *Thunder on the Right: The "New Right" and the Politics of Resentment* (New York: Pantheon Books, 1980), 4–5.

2. As quoted in Francisco Goldman, "'The Evil Was Very Grave...' José Martí's Description of Our 1884 Election Sounds Eerily Contemporary," *The American Prospect*, August 2004, 18.

3. Robert D. Putnam, "The Prosperous Community: Social Capital and Public Affairs," *The American Prospect*, Spring 1993, 2; and Robert D. Putnam et al., *Making Democracy Work: Civic Traditions in Modern Italy* (Princeton, NJ: Princeton University Press, 1993).

4. For an authoritative guide to the institutions of elite consensus building and collective lobbying, see George Draffan, *The Elite Consensus: When Corporations Wield the Constitution* (New York: Apex, 2003).

5. As quoted in *Justice for Sale: Shortchanging the Public Interest for Private Gain* (Washington, DC: Alliance for Justice, 1993), 10–11.

6. Jean Hardisty, *Mobilizing Resentment: Conservative Resurgence* (Boston: Beacon Press, 1999), 47.

7. Frederick Clarkson "Takin' It to the States: The Rise of Conservative State-Level Think Thanks," *The Public Eye* 13, no. 2/3 (Summer/Fall 1999), http:// www.publiceye.org/.

8. Hardisty, *Mobilizing Resentment*, 17; and Chip Berlet and Jean Hardisty, *An Overview of the U.S. Political Right: Drifting Right and Going Wrong*, on the Web site of Political Research Associates, http://www.publiceye.org/frontpage/overview.html.

9. Hardisty, *Mobilizing Resentment*, 47.

10. Ibid., 48.

11. Frederick Clarkson, *Eternal Hostility: The Struggle between Theocracy and Democracy* (Monroe, ME: Common Courage, 1997), 20–22.

12. As quoted in Joe Conason, "Taking On the Untouchables," *Salon*, February 29, 2000, http://archive.salon.com/news/col/cona/2000/02/29/right/index1.html.

13. Clarkson, "Takin' It to States."

14. Clarkson, *Eternal Hostility*, 77. This assertion regarding the deeper intent of the Christian Right is echoed as well by Hardisty, *Mobilizing Resentment*.

15. The early history of what was self-described as the New Right is documented in detail by Crawford (*Thunder on the Right*), a participant who became alarmed by what he considered to be its anticonservative agenda.

16. Hardisty, *Mobilizing Resentment*, 32.

17. Ibid., 39.

18. Ibid., 19, 42.

19. Ibid., 42.

20. This is eloquently documented by Pulitzer Prize–winning author Susan Faludi in *Stiffed: The Betrayal of the American Man* (New York: HarperCollins, 2000).

21. Korten, *When Corporations Rule the World*, 305 (see chap. 4, n. 10).

22. Michael Moore, *Stupid White Men* (New York: Regan Books, 2001), 209–11.

23. Tom Curry, "Nixon: 30 Years," MSNBC Interactive, August 9, 2004, available at http://www.other-net.info/index.php?p=250#more-250.

24. Ian Christopher McCaleb and Matt Smith, "Bush, in First Address as President, Urges Citizenship over Spectatorship," CNN.com, January 20, 2001, http://archives.cnn.com/2001/ALLPOLITICS/stories/01/20/bush.speech/.

25. George W. Bush, Inaugural Address, January 20, 2001, http://www.whitehouse.gov/news/inaugural-address.html.

26. Richard W. Stevenson, "The Inauguration: The Agenda," *New York Times*, January 21, 2001.

27. David E. Sanger, "The New Administration: The Plan," *New York Times*, January 24, 2001.

28. Douglas Jehl with Andrew C. Revkin, "Bush, in Reversal, Won't Seek Cut in Emissions of Carbon Dioxide," *New York Times*, March 14, 2001.

29. The reality is spelled out by former Republican political strategist Kevin Phillips in *American Dynasty: Aristocracy, Fortune, and the Politics of Deceit in the House of Bush* (New York: Viking, 2004).

30. Roger Cohen, "Europe and Bush: Early Storm Clouds to Watch," *New York Times*, March 26, 2001.

31. The report *Rebuilding America's Defenses* is publicly available on the PNAC Web site, http://www.newamericancentury.org/defensenationalsecurity.htm. The call for a Pax Americana is spelled out on page iv.

32. Ibid., 51.

33. These and other references by administration officials and others to the "opportunity" created by September 11 are documented by David Ray Griffin, *The New Pearl Harbor: Disturbing Questions about the Bush Administration and 9/11* (Northampton, MA: Olive Branch, 2004), 129–131.

34. Dave Zweifel, "Republican Stingingly Rebukes Bush," *Progressive Populist*, April 1, 2004, 9.

Chapter 14: Prisons of the Mind

1. Willis W. Harman, *Global Mind Change: The Promise of the 21st Century*, 2nd ed. (Sausalito, CA: Institute of Noetic Sciences, and San Francisco: Berrett-Koehler, 1998), viii.

2. Milton Friedman, *Capitalism and Freedom* (Chicago: University of Chicago Press, 2002), 120.

3. Ibid., 115–17.

4. George Gilder, *Wealth and Poverty*, new ed. (San Francisco: ICS Press, 1993), 40.

PART IV: The Great Turning
Introduction

1. Matthew Fox, *Wrestling with the Prophets: Essays on Creation Spirituality and Everyday Life* (New York: Penguin Group), 76.

Chapter 15: Beyond Strict Father versus Aging Clock

1. Thomas Berry, *Dream of the Earth* (San Francisco: Sierra Club Books, 1988), xi.

2. Ralph et al., *Western Civilizations*, 390 (see chap. 5, n. 6).

3. Claudia Wallis, "The Evolution Wars," *Time*, August 15, 2005, 27–35.

4. Ibid.

5. See Marcus J. Borg, *Meeting Jesus Again for the First Time* (San Francisco: HarperSanFrancisco, 1994) and *The God We Never Knew: Beyond Dogmatic Religion to a More Authentic Contemporary Faith* (San Francisco: HarperSan-Francisco, 1998), especially chapter 3, "Imaging God: Why and How It Matters."

6. See Borg, *Meeting Jesus Again*, 38.

7. Matthew Fox, *One River, Many Wells: Wisdom Springing from Global Faiths* (New York: Penguin Group, 2000), 101–188.

8. Matthew Fox, *The Coming of the Cosmic Christ* (New York: Harper-Collins, 1988); and Borg, *Meeting Jesus Again*.

9. Borg, *Meeting Jesus Again*, 29.

10. Ibid.

11. Biblical Discernment Ministries, *Book Review: The "Left Series*, January 2005, http://www.rapidnet.com/~jbeard/bdm/BookReviews/left.htm.

12. As quoted in Nicholas D. Kristof, "Jesus and Jihad," *New York Times*, July 17, 2004, 25.

13. Borg, *Meeting Jesus Again*, 30.

14. Fox, *Wrestling with Prophets; Sheer Joy: Conversations with Thomas Aquinas on Creation Spirituality* (New York: Penguin Group, 1992); and *Passion for Creation: The Earth-Honoring Spirituality of Meister Eckhart* (Rochester, VT: Inner Traditions, 2000).

15. Two classic works of the 1970s explored the convergence of the ancient wisdom of the Spirit people and the findings of contemporary science: Fritjof Capra, *The Tao of Physics* (New York: Bantam, 1977); and Gary Zukav, *The Dancing Wu Li Masters: An Overview of the New Physics* (New York: Bantam, 1979).

16. Borg, *Meeting Jesus Again*, 33–34.

17. Candace Pert, "Molecules and Choice," *Shift: At the Frontiers of Consciousness*, September–November 2004, 21–24.

Chapter 16: Creation's Epic Journey

1. Willis W. Harman and Elisabet Sahtouris, *Biology Revisioned* (Berkeley, CA: North Atlantic Books, 1998), 166.

2. Lynn Margulis and Dorion Sagan, *What Is Life?* (New York: Simon & Schuster, 1995), 49.

3. Ibid.

4. Ibid.

5. Ibid.

6. Mae-Wan Ho, "Towards a Thermodynamics of Organized Complexity," chapter 6 in *Rainbow and Worm*, 79–94 (see prologue, n. 5).

7. Margulis and Sagan, *What Is Life?* 41.

8. Steven Rose, *Lifelines: Biology beyond Determinism* (New York: Oxford University Press, 1998), 158.

9. Jon R. Luoma, *The Hidden Forest: The Biography of an Ecosystem* (New York: Henry Holt, 1999), 73.

10. Ibid., 51–57.

11. Ibid., 57–62.

12. Ibid., 58–60.

13. Ibid., 92–101.

14. Margulis and Sagan, *What Is Life?*, 23.

15. The functions and interactions of the components of the human brain are described in accessible language by Thomas Lewis, Fari Amini, and Richard Lannon, *A General Theory of Love* (New York: Vintage Books, 2001), 19–34.

Chapter 17: Joys of Earth Community

1. Erich Fromm, *Escape from Freedom* (New York: Rinehart, 1941), 183–84.

2. Frankl, *Man's Search for Meaning*, 131 (see chap. 1, n. 10).

3. *Hardwired to Connect* is available from the Institute for American Values, http://www.americanvalues.org/.

4. Commission on Children at Risk, *Hardwired to Connect: The New Scientific Case for Authoritative Communities*, a commission report prepared jointly by the Institute for American Values, Dartmouth Medical School, and the YMCA of the USA (New York: Institute for American Values, 2003), 14, 33.

5. Natalie Angier, "Why We're So Nice: We're Wired to Cooperate," *New York Times*, July 23, 2002, D1, D8.

6. See, for example, the work of Robert Putnam on social capital.

7. Lewis, Amini, and Lannon, *General Theory of Love*, 20–31.

8. Ibid., 22–24.

9. Commission on Children at Risk, *Hardwired to Connect*, 16–17.

10. This section is based on Justin A. Frank, *Bush on the Couch: Inside the Mind of the President* (New York: Regan Books, 2004).

11. Frankl, *Man's Search for Meaning*, 120–30.

12. Fromm, *Escape from Freedom*, 19–20.

13. The learned-helplessness syndrome was described to me by Charlie Kouns, a professor of marketing and advertising at Virginia Commonwealth University.

14. Friel and Friel, *Soul of Adulthood*, 32 (see chap. 2, n. 5).

15. Fromm, *Escape from Freedom*, 226.

16. William H. Thomas, "What Is Old Age For?" *YES! A Journal of Positive Futures*, Fall 2005, 12–16.

17. The definition of these principles draws from presentations by Janine Benyus and Elisabet Sahtouris, among other sources. See also chapter 7, "How Will We Conduct Business," in Janine M. Benyus, *Biomimicry: Innovation Inspired by Nature* (New York: William Morrow, 1997).

18. Lynn Margulis and Dorion Sagan, *Microcosmos: Four Billion Years of Evolution from Our Microbial Ancestors* (New York: Summit Books, 1986), 248.

19. Elisabet Sahtouris, "The Biology of Globalization" (1998), available on the LifeWeb site, http://www.ratical.org/ LifeWeb/Articles/globalize.html; adapted from first publication in *Perspectives in Business and Social Change*, September 1997.

20. Kegan, *Evolving Self* (see chap. 2, n. 3), 19.

21. Ed Diener and Martin E. P. Seligman, "Beyond Money: Toward an Economy of Well-Being," *Psychological Science in the Public Interest* 5, no. 1 (July 2004), 10, http://www.psychologicalscience.org/pdf/pspi/pspi5_1.pdf.

22. Ibid., 3.

23. Ibid.

24. Ibid., 10.

25. Ibid.

26. Alan Durning, head of Northwest Environment Watch, tracks the research on what he calls the "Economics of Happiness" on his weblog, http://www.northwestwatch.org/scorecard/.

Chapter 18: Stories for a New Era

1. Michael Lerner, "Closed Hearts, Closed Minds," *Tikkun* 18, no. 5 (September/October 2003), 10.

2. Schell, *Unconquerable World*, 106 (see chap. 1, n. 8).

3. The most comprehensive and definitive presentation of the new prosperity story is provided by the report of the International Forum on Globalization edited by John Cavanagh and Jerry Mander, *Alternatives to Economic Globalization: A Better World Is Possible* (San Francisco: Berrett-Koehler, 2004).

4. For further elaboration of the underlying principles as applied to economic relations among nations, see International Forum on Globalization, *Alternatives to Economic Globalization*; and David C. Korten, *Post-Corporate World*.

PART V: Birthing Earth Community
Chapter 19: Leading from Below

1. Margaret J. Wheatley, "Restoring Hope to the Future through Critical Education of Leaders," *Vimukt Shiksha* (a bulletin of Shikshantar, the People's Institute for Rethinking Education and Development, Udaipur, Rajasthan, India), March 2001, available at http://www.margaretwheatley.com/articles/restoringhope.html.

2. Adapted from Korten, Perlas, and Shiva, "Global Civil Society" (see prologue, n. 8).

3. For information on the Business Alliance for Local Living Economies, see http://www.livingeconomies.org/. See also the special Living Economies issue of *YES! A Journal of Positive Futures*, Fall 2002, http://www.yesmagazine.org/default.asp?ID=48. For further discussion of economic alternatives

for the United States, see Gar Alperovitz, *America beyond Capitalism: Reclaiming Our Weatlh, Our Liberty, and Our Democracy* (New York: John Wiley & Sons, 2004); Greider, *Soul of Capitalism* (see chap. 7, n. 1); and Michael Shuman, *Going Local: Creating Self-Reliant Communities in a Global Age* (New York: Free Press, 1998).

4. For information, see the Bainbridge Graduate Institute, http://www.bgiedu.org/; Co-op America, http://www.coopamerica.org/; American Independent Business Alliance, http://www.amiba.net/; and New Rules Project, http://www.newrules.org/.

5. Jaime S. Walters, *Big Vision, Small Business: Four Keys to Success without Growing Big* (San Francisco: Berrett-Koehler, 2002).

6. Amanda Griscom Little, "Mayor Leads Crusade against Global Warming," *Grist Magazine/MSNBC News*, June 20, 2005, http://msnbc.msn.com/id/8291649.

7. John Nichols, "Urban Archipelago," *The Nation,* June 20, 2005, http://www.thenation.com/doc/20050620/nichols.

8. Ibid.

9. See Web sites of the Apollo Alliance, http://www.apolloalliance.org/; the Peace Alliance, http://www.thepeacealliance.org/; and the Peace Alliance Foundation, http://www.peacealliancefound.org/.

10. Michelle Conlin, "The New Gender Gap," *Business Week*, May 26, 2003, 75–84.

11. Clayton E. Tucker-Ladd, "Values and Morals: Guidelines for Living," chapter 3 in *Psychological Self-Help*, the Web publication of the Mental Health Net, http://www.mentalhelp.net/psyhelp/chap3/.

12. Paul Nussbaum, "The Surprising Spectrum of Evangelicals," *Philadelphia Inquirer*, January 19, 2005, http://www.philly.com/mld/philly/news/breaking_news/11929261.htm.

13. "Evangelical Leaders Adopt Landmark Document Urging Greater Civic Engagement," October 8, 2004, press release of the National Association of Evangelicals; and Laurie Goodstein, "Evangelicals Open Debate on Widening Policy Questions," *New York Times*, March 11, 2005.

14. National Association of Evangelicals, "For the Health of the Nation: An Evangelical Call to Civic Responsibility," unanimously adopted by the NAE board of directors on October 7, 2004, http://www.nae.net/images/civic_responsibility2.pdf.

15. Laurie Goodstein, "Evangelical Leaders Swing Influence behind Effort to Combat Global Warming," *New York Times*, March 10, 2005, A14.

Chapter 20: Building a Political Majority

1. Center for a New American Dream, "Public Opinion Poll," conducted July 2004 by Widmeyer Research and Polling (Takoma Park, MD: Center for a New American Dream, 2004), available at http://www.newdream.org/about/PollResults.pdf.

2. Paul H. Ray, "The New Political Compass: The New Political Progressives Are In-Front, Deep Green, against Big Business and Globalization, and beyond Left and Right" (discussion draft, April 2002), 30, http://www.culturalcreatives.org/Library/docs/NewPoliticalCompassV73.pdf.

3. Center for a New American Dream, "Public Opinion Poll."

4. Center for a New American Dream, 1999 poll, cited by Juliet B. Schor, *Born to Buy: The Commercialized Child and the New Consumer Culture* (New York: Scribner, 2004), 185.

5. Betsy Taylor, *What Kids Really Want That Money Can't Buy* (New York: Warner Books, 2003). See http://www.newdream.org/publications/ bookrelease.php.

6. Gallup Poll, February Wave 1, February 6–8, 2004. See http://brain.gallup.com/documents/questionnaire.aspx?STUDY=P0402008 for the poll instrument. Results can be found in the database at http://www.pollingreport.com/prioriti.htm.

7. Chicago Council on Foreign Relations, *Global Views 2004: American Public Opinion and Foreign Policy* (Chicago Council on Foreign Relations, 2004), 15, http://www.ccfr.org/globalviews2004/sub/usa.htm.

8. ABC News/Washington Post poll, October 9–13, 2003, http://abcnews.go.com/sections/living/US/healthcare031020_poll.html.

9. Ray, "New Political Compass," 30.

10. Harris Poll No. 48, August 10–14, 2000, http://www.harrisinteractive.com/harris_poll/index.asp?PID=108.

11. Gallup Poll, March 5–7, 2001. Results can be found in the database at PollingReport.com, http://www.pollingreport.com/enviro.htm.

12 Ray, "New Political Compass," 30.

13. New American Dream, "Public Opinion Poll."

14. Chicago Council on Foreign Relations, *Global Views 2004*, 19.

15. Ibid., 36.

16. New American Dream, "Public Opinion Poll."

17. Aaron Bernstein, "Too Much Corporate Power?" *Business Week*, September 1, 2000, 145–158.

18. Ibid.

19. 2002 Washington Post poll cited by David Sirota, "Debunking 'Centrism,'" *The Nation*, January 3, 2005, 18.

20. Bernstein, "Too Much Corporate Power?"

21. Ibid.

22. Newsweek poll by Princeton Survey Research Associates, Oct 9–10, 2003. Results can be found in the database at PollingReport.com, http://www.pollingreport.com/ politics.htm.

23. CBS News/New York Times poll, May 10–13, 2000. Results can be found in the database at PollingReport.com, http://www .pollingreport.com/politics.htm.

24. CBS News/New York Times poll, July 11–15, 2004. Results can be found in the database at PollingReport.com, http://www .pollingreport.com/institut2.htm.

25. CBS News/New York Times poll, May 10–13, 2000.

26. Council for Excellence in Government, "America Unplugged: Citizens and Their Government," results of a poll conducted May 21– June 1, 1999 (published July 12, 1999), http://www.excelgov.org/ index.php?keyword= a432c11b19d490.

27. Harris Poll No. 18, March 10, 2004, http://www.harrisinteractive.com/ harris_poll/index.asp?PID=447.

28. Information on child honoring and the Covenant for Honouring Children is available at http://www. troubadourfoundation.org/. The song "Where We All Belong," available through the Troubadour Foundation, was written and recorded by Raffi Cavoukian to promote the Earth Charter.

29. Bernadette D. Proctor and Joseph Dalaker, *Poverty in the United States: 2002* (Washington, DC: U.S. Census Bureau, September 2003), http://www.census.gov/prod/ 2003pubs/p60-222.pdf.

30. Ronald E. Kleinman et al., "Hunger in Children in the United States: Potential Behavioral and Emotional Correlates," *Pediatrics* 101, no. 1 (January 1998): e3, http://pediatrics .aappublications.org/cgi/content/ full/101/1/e3.

31. J.M. Twenge, "The Age of Anxiety? The Birth Cohort Change in Anxiety and Neuroticism, 1952–1993," *Journal of Personality and Social Psychology* 79 (2000): 1007–1021.

32. Commission on Children at Risk, *Hardwired to Connect*, 68 (see chap. 17, n. 4).

33. Committee for Community-Level Programs for Youth, National Research Council and Institute of Medicine, Jacquelynne Eccles and Jennifer Appleton Gootman, eds., *Community Programs to Promote Youth Development* (Washington, DC: National Academies, 2002), http://www.nap. edu/catalog/ 10022.html.

34. Commission on Children at Risk, *Hardwired to Connect*, 8.

35. Ibid., 42–43, 68.

36. Michelle Conlin, "UnMarried America," *BusinessWeek*, October 20, 2003, 106.

37. Commission on Children at Risk, *Hardwired to Connect*, 41.

38. UNICEF, *State of the World's Children 2005* (New York: UNICEF,

2004), inside front cover, http://www.unicef.org/sowc05/english/sowc05.pdf.

39. Based on Sharna Olfman, "Introduction," in *Childhood Lost: How American Culture Is Failing Our Kids*, ed. Sharna Olfman, xi–xii (New York: Praeger, 2005).

40. Center for a New American Dream, "Facts about Marketing to Children," n.d., http://www.newdream.org/kids/ facts.php.

41. Schor, *Born to Buy*, 21.

42. Ibid., 48. Schor provides numerous examples of these and other low-road advertising themes on pages 39–68.

43. Ibid., 69–97.

44. American Psychological Association, "Report of the APA Task Force on Advertising and Children: Psychological Issues in the Increasing Commercialization of Childhood," February 20, 2004, http://www.apa.org/releases/childrenads.pdf.

Chapter 21: Liberating Creative Potential

1. See the organization's Web site at http://www.americaspeaks.org/.

2. See the Web site of the Center for Voting and Democracy, http://fairvote.org/, for information on instant runoff voting, proportional representation, and other electoral reforms.

3. Sally Goerner, "Creativity, Consciousness, and the Building of an Integral World," in *The Great Adventure: Toward a Fully Human Theory of Evolution*, ed. David Loye, 153–80 (Albany, NY: State University of New York Press, 2004). See especially 175–79.

4. For more information on Campus Compact, see http://www.compact.org/.

5. For more information on the Democracy Collaborative, see http://www.democracycollaborative.org/.

Chapter 22: Change the Story, Change the Future

1. Berry, *Great Work* (see chap. 4, n. 2), 1, 159.

2. Puanani Burgess in Jack Canfield et al., *Chicken Soup from the Soul of Hawai'i: Stories of Aloha to Create Paradise Wherever You Are* (Deerfield Beach, FL: Health Communications, 2003), 215.

3. It is a primary mission of *YES!* magazine to share the stories of such groups (see http://www.yesmagazine.org/). For other excellent sources dealing with these and other important international experiences, see David Suzuki and Holly Dressel, *Good News for a Change: How Everyday People Are Helping the Planet* (Vancouver, BC: Greystone Books, 2003); Frances Moore Lappé and Anna Lappé, *Hope's Edge: The Next Diet for a Small Planet* (New York: Jeremy P. Tarcher/Putnam, 2002); and International Forum on Globalization, *Alternatives to Economic Globalization*, 253–67 (see chap. 18, n. 3).

4. Larry Rohter, "With New Chief, Uruguay Veers Left, in a Latin Pattern," *New York Times*, March 1, 2005, A3.

5. Vandana Shiva, interview by Sarah van Gelder, "Earth Democracy," *YES! A Journal of Positive Futures*, Winter 2003, http://www.yesmagazine.org/article.asp?ID=570.

Index

About the Author

Dr. David C. Korten worked for more than thirty-five years in preeminent business, academic, and international development institutions before he turned away from the establishment to work exclusively with public interest citizen action groups. He is co-founder and board chair of the Positive Futures Network and *YES! A Journal of Positive Futures*, founder and president of The People-Centered Development Forum, an associate of the International Forum on Globalization, and a member of the Club of Rome. He serves on the boards of the Business Alliance for Local Living Economies and the Bainbridge Graduate Institute.

Korten earned his M.B.A. and Ph.D. degrees at the Stanford University Graduate School of Business. Trained in organization theory, business strategy, and economics, he devoted his early career to setting up business schools in low-income countries—starting with Ethiopia—in the hope that creating a new class of professional business entrepreneurs would be the key to ending global poverty. He completed his military service during the Vietnam War as a captain in the U.S. Air Force, with duty at the Special Air Warfare School, Air Force headquarters command, the Office of the Secretary of Defense, and the Advanced Research Projects Agency.

Korten then served for five and a half years as a faculty member of the Harvard University Graduate School of Business where he taught in Harvard's middle management, M.B.A., and doctoral programs, and served as Harvard's advisor to the Central American Management Institute in Nicaragua. He subsequently joined the staff of the Harvard Institute for International Development, where he headed a Ford Foundation–funded project to strengthen the organization and management of national family planning programs.

In late 1970, Korten left U.S. academia and moved to Southeast Asia, where he lived for nearly fifteen years, serving first as a Ford Foundation project specialist, and later as Asia regional advisor on development management to the U.S. Agency for International Development (USAID). His work there won him international recognition for his contributions to pioneering the development of intervention strategies for transforming public bureaucracies into responsive support systems dedicated to strengthening community control and management of land, water, and forestry resources.

Increasingly concerned that the economic models embraced by official aid agencies were increasing poverty and environmental destruction and that these agencies were impervious to change from within, Korten broke with the official aid system. His last five years in Asia were devoted to working with leaders of Asian nongovernmental organizations on identifying the root causes of development failure in the region and building the capacity of civil society organizations to function as strategic catalysts of positive national- and global-level change.

Korten came to realize that the crisis of deepening poverty, inequality, environmental devastation, and social disintegration he observed in Asia was playing out in nearly every country in the world—including the United States and other "developed" countries. Furthermore, he concluded that the United States was actively promoting—both at home and abroad—the very policies that were deepening the crisis. If there were to be a positive human future, the United States must change. He returned to the United States in 1992 to share with his fellow Americans the lessons he had learned abroad.

Dr. Korten's publications are required reading in university courses around the world. He has authored numerous books, including the international best seller *When Corporations Rule the World* and *The Post-Corporate World: Life After Capitalism*. He contributes regularly to edited books and professional journals, and to a wide variety of periodical publications. He is also a popular international speaker and a regular guest on talk radio and television.

What people are saying about *YES!*

YES! is a superb go-to place for readers of *The Great Turning* who want to engage the great work of changing the human story.

> David Korten, author of *The Great Turning: From Empire to Earth Community*

YES! is not about what's wrong with the world—we have plenty of media willing to cover that—but what's right, and what's possible. Check out *YES!* magazine...

> Anita Roddick, founder of The Body Shop

YES! is a joy to read—it does a beautiful job of telling the new story of what people are doing to create hope in a difficult world.

> Peter Block, author of *Stewardship*

I find *YES!* utterly compelling, inspiring, and very smart.

> Terry Tempest Williams, author and naturalist

...the bible of the sustainability movement.

> *The Seattle Weekly*

Award-winning *YES!* magazine illuminates and encourages the deep shifts in culture and institutions that lead to a more just, sustainable, and compassionate world. *YES!* is published quarterly by the Positive Futures Network, an independent, non-profit organization founded in 1996 by David Korten, *YES!* Editor Sarah van Gelder, and other practical visionaries concerned about the social, economic, ecological, and spiritual crises of our time.

YES! Magazine
www.yesmagazine.org

Connect with the people, ideas, and actions that are advancing The Great Turning.

Subscribe to *YES!*

Connect through *YES!* online. www.yesmagazine.org. Visit the Great Turning area of *YES!* magazine's website for information about Great Turning-related events, podcasts of David Korten's talks, and other articles by Korten. You'll find over 1,000 *YES!* stories, resources for further action, and an opportunity to sign up for the *YES!* newsletter.

Connect through *YES!* in print. Each issue of *YES!* tells of the visionary ideas and practical actions that move us from Empire to Earth Community. You'll find:

- Writers and visionaries such as David Korten, Joanna Macy, Van Jones, Riane Eisler, Matthew Fox, Winona LaDuke, Bill Moyers, Amy Goodman, Frances Moore Lappe, Thich Nhat Hanh, Thom Hartmann, and Vandana Shiva.

- Dynamic social movements that are preparing the ground for big shifts in society — such as the global justice movement, the rise of indigenous power, the emergence of active non-violence, and community initiatives for local living economies.

- Practical ideas you can use to help move to renewable energy sources, advance clean elections, support sustainable agriculture, nurture your inner wisdom, and much more.

- Resource guides featuring publications, videos, web sites, and organizations that can help you learn more and get involved.

Summer 2005

7 Great ideas for movement builders

yes!
a journal of positive futures

From **Abandoned**
to **Beautiful**
Lily Yeh brings her art to the
vacant lots of north Philadelphia

Give Your Neighborhood
a Makeover

Speaking Up for Cities
Just, Green, & Beautiful

Appalachian Ecovillage

**what makes
a great
place?**

Subscribe to *YES!*

Online at: www.yesmagazine.org
By phone: 800/937-4451

YES!
P. O. Box 10818
Bainbridge Island, WA 98110 USA

ALSO FROM KUMARIAN PRESS...

CIVIL SOCIETY AND GLOBAL DEVELOPMENT

A Civil Republic: Beyond Capitalism and Nationalism
Severyn T. Bruyn

Sustainable Capitalism: A Matter of Common Sense
John E. Ikerd

Capitalism and Justice
John Isbister

Creating a Better World: Interpreting Global Civil Society
Edited by Rupert Taylor

Working for Change: Making a Career in International Public Service
Derick W. Brinkerhoff and Jennifer M. Binkerhoff

NEW AND FORTHCOMING KUMARIAN PRESS TITLES

Coming of Age in a Globalized World: The Next Generation
J. Michael Adams and Angelo Carfagna

Transnational Civil Society: An Introduction
Edited by Srilatha Batliwala and L. David Brown

Non-State Actors in the Human Rights Universe
Edited by George Andreopoulos, Zehra Arat, and Peter Juviler

Visit Kumarian Press at www.kpbooks.com or
call toll-free 800.289.2664 for a complete catalog.

ABOUT BERRETT-KOEHLER PUBLISHERS

Berrett-Koehler is an independent publisher dedicated to an ambitious mission: Creating a World that Works for All.

We believe that to truly create a better world, action is needed at all levels —individual, organizational, and societal. At the individual level, our publications help people align their lives and work with their deepest values. At the organizational level, our publications promote progressive leadership and management practices, socially responsible approaches to business, and humane and effective organizations. At the societal level, our publications advance social and economic justice, shared prosperity, sustainable development, and new solutions to national and global issues.

A major theme of our publications is "Opening Up New Space." They challenge conventional thinking, introduce new points of view, and offer new alternatives for change. Their common quest is changing the underlying beliefs, mindsets, institutions, and structures that keep generating the same cycles of problems, no matter who our leaders are or what improvement programs we adopt.

We strive to practice what we preach—to operate our publishing company in line with the ideas in our books. At the core of our approach is stewardship, which we define as a deep sense of responsibility to administer the company for the benefit of all of our "stakeholder" groups: authors, customers, employees, investors, service providers, and the communities and environment around us. We seek to establish a partnering relationship with each stakeholder that is open, equitable, and collaborative.

We are gratified that thousands of readers, authors, and other friends of the company consider themselves to be part of the "BK Community." We hope that you, too, will join our community and connect with us through the ways described on our website at www.bkconnection.com.

A BK CURRENTS TITLE

This book is part of our BK Currents series. BK Currents titles advance social and economic justice by exploring the critical intersections between business and society. Offering a unique combination of thoughtful analysis and progressive alternatives, BK Currents titles promote positive change at the national and global levels.

To find out more, visit www.bkconnection.com.